Bingham

P9-EME-420

Juvenile Justice
in America

Juvenile Justice in America

Problems and Prospects

Randall G. Shelden
University of Nevada–Las Vegas

Daniel Macallair
Center on Juvenile and Criminal Justice

WAVELAND

PRESS, INC.

Long Grove, Illinois

For information about this book, contact:
Waveland Press, Inc.
4180 IL Route 83, Suite 101
Long Grove, IL 60047-9580
(847) 634-0081
info@waveland.com
www.waveland.com

Copyright © 2008 by Waveland Press, Inc.

10-digit ISBN 1-57766-523-6
13-digit ISBN 978-1-57766-523-6

All rights reserved. No part of this book may be reproduced, stored in a retrieval system, or transmitted in any form or by any means without permission in writing from the publisher.

Printed in the United States of America

7   6   5   4   3   2   1

About the Editors

Randall G. Shelden is a Senior Research Fellow with the Center on Juvenile and Criminal Justice (San Francisco) and Professor of Criminal Justice, University of Nevada-Las Vegas, where he has been a faculty member since 1977. He received his Masters Degree in Sociology at Memphis State University and Ph.D. in Sociology at Southern Illinois University. He is the author or coauthor of six books including: *Delinquency and Juvenile Justice in American Society*; *Criminal Justice in America: A Sociological Approach*; *Girls, Delinquency and Juvenile Justice*, with Meda Chesney-Lind (which received the *Hindelang Award* for outstanding contribution to Criminology in 1992); *Youth Gangs in American Society*, with Sharon Tracy and William B. Brown (both of these are third editions); and *Controlling the Dangerous Classes: A Critical Introduction to the History of Criminal Justice*. His most recent book is *Crime and Criminal Justice in American Society*, with William B. Brown, Karen S. Miller, and Randal B. Fritzler. He is also the author of more than 60 journal articles and book chapters on the subject of crime and justice. He is the author of an evaluation of the Detention Diversion Advocacy Project (DDAP), published by the Office of Juvenile Justice and Delinquency. His Web site is: www.sheldensays.com.

Daniel Macallair is the Executive Director and a co-founder of the Center on Juvenile and Criminal Justice. His expertise is in the development and analysis of correctional policy for youth and adult offenders. He has implemented model programs throughout the country. In the past ten years his programs have received national recognition and were cited as exemplary models by the United States Department of Justice and Harvard University's Innovations in American Government program. In 1994, he received a leadership award from the State of Hawaii for his efforts in reforming that state's juvenile correctional system. He is presently a consultant to criminal justice systems around the country and frequently provides expert testimony on correctional practices. His research and publications have appeared in such journals as the *Stanford Law and Policy Review, Crime and Delinquency, Youth and Society, Journal of Juvenile Law*, and the *Western Criminology Review*. His studies and commentary are often cited in national news outlets. He is currently writing a history of California's juvenile justice system. He teaches in the Criminal Justice Department at San Francisco State University and is an invited speaker and trainer at conferences and seminars throughout the country.

About the Contributors

James Austin is a nationally recognized expert in the area of juvenile and criminal justice. Currently he is the President of JFA Associates, LLC, in Washington, DC. He is the coauthor (with John Irwin) of *It's About Time: America's Incarceration Binge*, plus numerous journal articles and technical reports.

Michelle Byrnes is a graduate student in Public Policy at the Goldman School of Public Policy at the University of California–Berkeley.

Meda Chesney-Lind is a Professor in the Women's Studies Department, University of Hawaii at Manoa. Nationally recognized for her work on women and crime, her books include *Girls, Delinquency and Juvenile Justice* (with Randall G. Shelden); *The Female Offender: Girls, Women and Crime* (2nd edition, with Lisa Pasko); *Female Gangs in America*; and *Invisible Punishment: The Collateral Consequences of Mass Incarceration* (with Marc Mauer). She has written dozens of journal articles, book chapters, and reviews.

Megan D. Corcoran is the Director of Communications and Policy for the Center on Juvenile and Criminal Justice in San Francisco. She has a law degree from the University of California–Davis and has worked at the Federal Defenders in the Eastern District of California, the Sacramento County Public Defenders, and the Public Defenders' Office of San Diego. She was a staff attorney with the Neighborhood Legal Services in Los Angeles and has worked as a Facilitator with the Restorative Justice Trust Services in Wellington, New Zealand.

Kelly Dedel Johnson is the Director of One in 37 Research, Inc., in Portland, OR, a criminal justice consultant organization. She has coauthored several reports for the Urban Institute on the subject of prisoner reentry. On behalf of the Bureau of Justice Assistance, she has provided evaluation-related technical assistance to over 60 jurisdictions nationwide, three of which have implemented successful elder abuse programs. She is also on the faculty of the National Judicial College.

Katherine Irwin is a Professor in the Department of Sociology at the University of Hawaii at Manoa. She is the author or coauthor of several articles and book chapters on the subject of crime and delinquency, including "Blueprints for Violence Prevention: From Research to Real-World Settings—Factors Influencing the Successful Replication of Model Programs" and "The Violence of Adolescent Life: Experiencing and Managing Everyday Threats." Her latest work is a forthcoming book about women and crime with Meda Chesney-Lind.

Mike A. Males is a Senior Research Fellow at the Center on Juvenile and Criminal Justice and is on the faculty in the Department of Sociology at the University of California, Santa Cruz. With over 12 years of experience working in youth programs, his research interests are focused on youth issues like crime, drug abuse, pregnancy, and economics. He is the author of dozens of articles and four books, the latest of which is *Kids and Guns: How Politicians, Experts, and the Press Fabricate Fear of Youth*.

Sele Nadel-Hayes is a graduate student at the Goldman School of Public Policy, University of California-Berkeley.

Andrea Shorter is currently President of the San Francisco Commission on the Status of Women. She is the coauthor of their report *Out of Sight, Out of Mind: Girls in the San Francisco Juvenile System* (1996). Formerly she served as the Director of the Detention Diversion Advocacy Project in San Francisco.

Ronald Weitzer is a professor of sociology at The George Washington University in Washington, DC. Among his many publications are *Race and Policing in America: Conflict and Reform* (with Steven Tuch) and *Sex for Sale: Prostitution, Pornography, and the Sex Industry*.

Contents

Preface

The editors of this book have between us more than 60 years of experience researching and writing about juvenile delinquency and juvenile justice and developing and evaluating programs for juvenile offenders. Our experience has led us to the conclusion that there is currently a major crisis within the juvenile justice system. A large part of this stems from the "get tough" attitudes coming from politicians who have convinced a largely uninformed public that juvenile delinquency is out of control and that juveniles are more violent than ever. Various kinds of "zero tolerance" policies have emerged. As a result, more and more minor offenses are being referred to juvenile court. Many of the "crimes" committed are part of normal adolescent behaviors—fighting, sexual experimentation, and general rebelliousness against parental authority. Traditionally, such behaviors have been ignored or handled informally.

Many current problems surrounding juvenile justice are discussed in this book, and some specific solutions are offered. Many of these come from the Center on Juvenile and Criminal Justice, a nonprofit organization in San Francisco established in the 1980s specifically to address problems confronting both the juvenile and adult justice system and to offer specific programs directed to both juveniles and adults. Several articles included here have been previously posted on their Web site (www.cjcj.org).

The lead article by Randall Shelden offers an historical review of these issues. It traces current problems facing detention and "correctional" facilities back to the houses of refuge. It also summarizes some recent scandals, including the former California Youth Authority (the name was changed in 2005, but the CYA represented one of the prime examples of the failure of similar institutions around the country). The next article, also by Shelden, focuses on the continuing issue of the disproportionate jailing of minority offenders, both in detention and in "correctional institutions."

The third article is a recent study by Mike Males, Daniel Macallair, and Megan Corcoran of the Center on Juvenile and Criminal Justice. They debunk the argument that incarceration reduces crime, showing that during the past two decades the incarceration rate for juveniles has declined, along with the juvenile crime rate. They also examined the incarceration/crime rate comparison for adults and found that both went up during this period of time. The results have obvious social policy implications, calling for alternatives for incarceration for both juveniles and adults in order to lower the crime rate.

This is followed by a close examination of one of the most critical areas within the juvenile justice system and one filled with serious problems, namely what is known as "aftercare" in juvenile justice language. Michelle Byrnes, Daniel Macallair, and Andrea Shorter from the Center on Juvenile and Criminal Justice outline some of the critical problems facing this system and its connection to the infamous California Youth Authority.

Finally, Meda Chesney-Lind and Katherine Irwin provide an overview of the continuing issue of the "double standard" within the juvenile justice system. All of the articles underscore the issues of class and racial bias that, along with gender bias, continue to be of paramount importance within the juvenile justice system.

The second part provides some specific recommendations for reform. Randall Shelden begins by noting the need to "think out of the box." He illustrates this by a re-examination of many different ideas, including one proposed more than 30 years ago by Edwin Schur, called "radical non-intervention." He also discusses a little-known view that sees the problem from a Native-American perspective. Both of these approaches challenge us to view the problem of delinquency much differently. The next article is by Sele Nadel-Hayes and Daniel Macallair, who provide some specific suggestions on reforming California's juvenile correctional system.[1] Shelden then reviews one example of a successful program, the Detention Diversion Advocacy Project (DDAP), started in San Francisco in the late 1980s. DDAP has since spread to other cities.

In the next article, James Austin, Kelly Dedel Johnson, and Ronald Weitzer provide an excellent overview of many different alternatives to secure confinement across the country. Finally, Meda Chesney-Lind provides an update on a number of programs specifically designed for girl offenders.

Note

[1] California is the focus of several of the articles in this book largely because of the fact that it has consistently been seen by many as a "bellweather state" leading the way for other states, for better or for worse. Also, few other states have been studied so extensively and hence have so much excellent data. State-level data are often better than national statistics. The recent controversies concerning the former California Youth Authority and the California Department of Corrections have made national news on more than one occasion.

PART I

Problems

From Houses of Refuge to "Youth Corrections"
Same Story, Different Day*

Randall G. Shelden

Many Americans were horrified when the news of the abuses at the Abu Ghraib prison in Iraq broke out. People familiar with the nature of prisons were not nearly as surprised as the public was. Those of us who have studied the problem were well aware of the history of abuses within the walls of "total institutions," well documented, for instance, in the Stanford Prison Experiment conducted more than 30 years ago.[1]

The experiment consisted of setting up a mock prison in the basement of a psychology department building at Stanford University. Two groups of university students were selected. One group was assigned the role of guards, while the other group played the roles of prisoners. The experiment was originally designed to last two weeks, but it was halted after just six days. Ordinary people role-playing prison guards became extremely abusive. Some of the prisoners rebelled, and one escape was barely averted. As the lead author of the study, Philip Zimbardo, stated:

> We had created an overwhelmingly powerful situation—a situation in which prisoners were withdrawing and behaving in pathological ways, and in which some of the guards were behaving sadistically. Even the "good" guards felt helpless to intervene, and none of the guards quit while the study was in progress.

They had an encounter session after the experiment ended. All of the "prisoners" were happy it was over, but most of the "guards" were disappointed it had ended.[2]

Imprisonment has been a dominant form of punishment in the United States for about 200 years. The effects, on both the guarded and

*Portions of this chapter are from my book, *Delinquency and Juvenile Justice in America*. Long Grove, IL: Waveland Press, 2006, reprinted with permission of the publisher.

the guards, have continued to be the same, while failing to put a significant dent in crime. For young offenders it began in the 1820s in New York, with the founding of the New York House of Refuge.

Houses of Refuge: The Start of an Era

Although entirely separate systems to monitor and control the behavior of young people began to appear during the early part of the nineteenth century, differential treatment based on age did not come about overnight. The roots of the juvenile justice system can be traced to much earlier legal and social perspectives on childhood and youth. One of the most important of these was a legal doctrine known as *parens patriae*.

Parens patriae has its origins in medieval England's chancery courts. At that point it had more to do with property law than concern for children; it was, essentially, a means for the crown to administer landed orphans' estates.[3] *Parens patriae* established that the king, in his presumed role as the "father" of his country, had the legal authority to take care of his people, especially those who were unable (for various reasons including age) to take care of themselves. By the nineteenth century this legal doctrine had evolved into the practice of the state's assuming wardship over a minor child and, in effect, playing the role of parent if the child had no parents or their parents had been declared unfit.

In the American colonies, for example, officials could "bind out" as apprentices "children of parents who were poor, not providing good breeding, neglecting their formal education, not teaching a trade, or were idle, dissolute, unchristian or incapable."[4] Later, during the nineteenth century, *parens patriae* supplied (as it still does to some extent), the legal basis for court intervention into the relationship between children and their families.[5] Another legal legacy of the colonial era that relates to the state's involvement in the lives of youth is the *stubborn child law*. Passed in Massachusetts in 1646, it established a clear legal relationship between children and parents and made it a capital offense for a child to disobey his or her parents.

In the United States, interest in the state regulation of youth was directly tied to explosive immigration and population growth. Between 1750 and 1850 the population of the United States went from 1.25 million to 23 million. The population of some states, like Massachusetts, doubled in numbers. New York's population increased fivefold between 1790 and 1830.[6] Many of those coming into the United States during the middle of the nineteenth century were of Irish or German background; the fourfold increase in immigrants between 1830 and 1840 was in large part a product of the economic hardships faced by the Irish during the potato famine.[7] The social controls in small communities were simply overwhelmed by the influx of newcomers, many of whom were either foreign born or of foreign parentage.

The transition to capitalism (specifically the factory system in the New England area) during the late eighteenth and early nineteenth centuries brought more changes. Poor, homeless young people flocked to the cities of the Northeast, particularly New York, looking for work. With this increase came a growing concern among prominent citizens about the "perishing and dangerous classes," as they would be called throughout the nineteenth century.

Prominent citizens in the cities of the East began to notice the poor, especially the children of the poor. The parents were declared unfit because their children wandered the streets unsupervised, committing various assortments of crime to survive. Many believed uncontrolled youths were the source of social problems that, unchecked, would result in even greater problems in the future. Poor and immigrant (in this era the Irish) children, their life styles, and social position would soon be associated with crime and juvenile delinquency.

A number of philanthropic associations emerged in eastern cities to deal with these problems. One of the most notable was the *Society for the Reformation of Juvenile Delinquents* (SRJD), founded in the 1820s.[8] The SRJD, composed primarily of wealthy businessmen and professional people, convinced the New York legislature to pass a bill in 1824 that established the *New York House of Refuge,* the first correctional institution for young offenders in the United States. The bill created the first statutory definition of juvenile delinquency and authorized the managers of the refuge "to receive and take into the house of refuge . . . all children as shall be convicted of criminal offenses . . . or committed as vagrants if the court deems that they are 'proper' objects."[9]

The general aims of the house of refuge, including a definition of "delinquents," are reflected in the following extract from the SRJD:

> The design of the proposed institution is, to furnish, in the first place, an asylum, in which boys under a certain age, who become subject to the notice of our police, either as vagrants, or homeless, or charged with petty crimes, may be received, judiciously classed according to their degree of depravity or innocence, put to work at such employments as will tend to encourage industry and ingenuity, taught reading, writing, and arithmetic, and most carefully instructed in the nature of their moral and religious obligations, while at the same time, they are subjected to a course of treatment, that will afford a prompt and energetic corrective of their vicious propensities, and hold out every possible inducement to reformation and good conduct.[10]

The statute contained vague descriptions of behaviors and life styles which were synonymous with the characteristics of the urban poor. Being homeless, begging, vagrancy, and coming from an "unfit" home (as defined from a middle-class viewpoint) are examples. The legislation that was passed also established specific procedures for identifying the type of youths requiring intervention and the means for the legal handling of cases. According to law, the state, or a representative agency or individual, could intervene in the life of a child if it was determined that he or she needed "care and treatment," the definition of which was left entirely in the hands of the agency or individual who intervened.

Immigrants received the brunt of enforcement of these laws, especially children of Irish parents. Pickett notes that one superintendent accounted for a boy's delinquency because "the lad's parents are Irish and intemperate and that tells the whole story."[11] The results of such beliefs are reflected in the fact that between 1825 and 1855 the percentage of commitments to the refuge of Irish heritage climbed as high as 63%.[12]

The results of the actions by these reformers suggest that the best interests of the child were usually not served. Children confined in the houses of refuge were subjected to strict discipline and control. A former army colonel working in the New York House of Refuge said: "He [the delinquent] is taught that prompt unquestioning obedience is a fundamental military principle."[13] It was strongly believed that rigid discipline would add to a youth's training in self-control (specifically to avoid the temptations of evil surroundings) and respect for authority (which was a basic requirement of a disciplined labor force). Corporal punishments (including hanging children from their thumbs, the use of the "ducking stool" for girls, and severe beatings), solitary confinement, handcuffs, the "ball and chain," uniform dress, the "silent system," and other practices were commonly used in houses of refuge.[14]

Following the lead of New York, other cities soon constructed houses of refuge. Within a few years, there were refuges in Boston, Philadelphia, and Baltimore. It soon became evident, however, that the original plans of the founders were not being fulfilled, for crime and delinquency remained a problem in the cities. In the refuges, protests, riots, escape attempts, and other disturbances were almost daily occurrences.[15] While at first limited to housing first-time youthful offenders and pre-delinquents, the refuges eventually confined more hardened offenders (most of whom had been hardened by the experiences of confinement); overcrowding became a problem. The cycle would repeat itself in institutions of confinement throughout the nineteenth and twentieth centuries and continues today.

The rhetoric of the founders and managers of houses of refuge fell far short of the reality experienced by the youths held in these facilities. The origins of the juvenile justice system were rooted in court challenges to the refuge movement.

Court Decisions and Effects

Ex Parte Crouse

Argued in 1838, *Ex Parte Crouse* arose from a petition of *habeas corpus* filed by the father of Mary Ann Crouse. Without her father's knowledge,

Crouse had been committed to the Philadelphia House of Refuge by her mother on the grounds that she was "incorrigible." Her father argued that the incarceration was illegal because she had not been given a jury trial. The court noted that Mary had been committed on the following complaint:

> said infant by reason of vicious conduct, has rendered her control beyond the power of the said complainant [her mother], and made it manifestly requisite that from regard to the moral and future welfare of the said infant she should be placed under the guardianship of the managers of the House of Refuge.[16]

The Court rejected the appeal, saying that the Bill of Rights did not apply to juveniles. Based on the *parens patriae* doctrine, the court asked, "May not the natural parents, when unequal to the task of education, or unworthy of it, be superseded by the *parens patriae* or common guardian of the community?" Note that the court ignored the fact that Crouse's father had filed the suit, clearly an indication that he felt "equal to the task." Further, the Court observed that: "The infant has been snatched from a course which must have ended in confirmed depravity."[17] Note that the court here predicts future behavior based on vague criteria—a practice that became quite common and continues today.

The ruling assumed that the Philadelphia House of Refuge (and presumably all other houses of refuge) had a beneficial effect on its residents. It "is not a prison, but a school," the Court said, and because of this, not subject to procedural constraints. Further, the aims of such an institution were to reform youngsters by training them "to industry; by imbuing their minds with the principles of morality and religion; by furnishing them with means to earn a living; and above all, by separating them from the corrupting influences of improper associates."[18]

What evidence did the justices consult to support their conclusion that the Philadelphia House of Refuge was not a prison but a school? They solicited testimony only from those who managed the institution. The justices of the Supreme Court came from the same general class background as those who supported the houses of refuge and believed the rhetoric of these supporters. In short, they believed the promises rather than the actions of the reformers. A more objective review of the treatment of youths housed in these places, however, might have led the justices to a very different conclusion. For instance, subsequent investigations found that there was an enormous amount of abuse within these institutions. They were run according to a strict military regimen during which corporal punishment (girls in one institution were "ducked" under water and boys were hung by their thumbs), solitary confinement, and a silent system were part of the routine.[19] Work training was practically nonexistent, and outside companies contracted for cheap inmate labor. Religious instruction was often little more than Protestant indoctrination (many of the youngsters were Catholic). Education, in the conventional meaning of the word, was almost nonexistent.

The O'Connell Case

A most intriguing addendum to the history of the houses of refuge (and to the *Crouse* case) came in 1870 with a Chicago case concerning a boy named Daniel O'Connell in the case of *People v. Turner* (1870). Daniel was incarcerated in the Chicago House of Refuge—not because he had committed a criminal offense but because he was "in danger of growing up to become a pauper." His parents, like Mary Crouse's father, filed a writ of *habeas corpus*, charging that his incarceration was illegal. Although the facts were almost identical to the *Crouse* case, the outcome was the exact opposite.

The case went to the Illinois Supreme Court, which reached three conclusions. First, Daniel was being *punished*—not treated or helped by incarceration in the house of refuge. (Recall that the court had concluded that Mary Crouse was being *helped;* gender could have contributed to the disparate findings.[20]) Second, the Illinois court based its ruling on the *realities* or *actual practices* of the institution, rather than merely on "good intentions" as in the *Crouse* case. Third, the Illinois court rejected the *parens patriae* doctrine. They based their reasoning in concluding that Daniel was imprisoned on traditional legal doctrines of the criminal law, emphasizing the importance of *due process* safeguards. In short, while the court in the Crouse case viewed the houses of refuge in a very rosy light, praising it uncritically, the court in the O'Connell case viewed the refuge in a much more negative light, addressing its cruelty and harshness of treatment.[21] After the O'Connell case, only children who had committed felonies could be sent to reform schools.

The O'Connell decision was to have far-reaching effects in the development of the movement to establish the juvenile court in Chicago in 1899. The founders of the juvenile court, in part, were attempting to get around the argument in the O'Connell case. In the 1905 case of Frank Fisher (ironically another Pennsylvania case), the court returned to the logic used in the Crouse case. In this case, the Pennsylvania Supreme Court ruled:

> To save a child from becoming a criminal, or continuing in a career of crime, to end in maturer [sic] years in public punishment and disgrace, the legislatures surely may provide for the salvation of such a child, if its parents or guardians be unwilling or unable to do so, by bringing it into one of the courts of the state without any process at all, for the purpose of subjecting it to the state's guardianship and protection.[22]

This case would not be overturned until 1967.

Gault and *Kent:* Challenges to the Punitive Nature of Juvenile Justice

Despite the obvious failures of the houses of refuge, reformers continued to respond to juvenile offenders by building institutions. The "edifice complex" endorses building large edifices like "reform schools," "training schools" and most recently "youth correctional centers." The problems found within the houses of refuge continued unabated throughout the twentieth century and into the twenty-first. While there were occasional "voices in the wilderness" calling attention to abuses within institutions, they mostly fell on deaf ears until the 1960s. At that time, the U.S. Supreme Court began to hear cases challenging the underlying foundation of the juvenile justice system, the *parens patriae* doctrine.

The two most significant cases were *Kent v. United States* (383 U.S. 541, 1966) and *In re Gault* (387 U.S. 1, 1967). In the *Kent* case, the Court dealt with the manner of *certification* of a juvenile offender as an adult. The Court ruled that when a case is transferred from the juvenile court to an adult court, the court must provide a written statement giving the reasons for the waiver, the juvenile must be given a hearing, is entitled to counsel, and the defense counsel must be given access to all records and reports used in reaching the decision to waive. Justice Abe Fortas issued one of the strongest indictments of the juvenile court ever in this case. "There is evidence, in fact, that there may be grounds for concern that the child receives the worst of both worlds; that he gets neither the protection accorded to adults nor the solicitous care and regenerative treatment postulated for children."

The circumstances of the *Gault* case involved an overly punitive response to a crank call to a neighbor; a 15-year-old was sentenced to a six-year term in a state training school in Arizona. The Court ruled that at the adjudicatory hearing stage, juvenile court procedures must include (1) adequate written notice of charges, (2) the right to counsel, (3) privilege against self-incrimination, (4) the right to cross-examine accusers, (5) a transcript of the proceedings, and (6) the right to appellate review. Fortas once again provided the concise critique, stating that "the condition of being a boy does not justify a kangaroo court."[23]

Most observers thought that such a critique was long overdue and anticipated significant improvements within the juvenile justice system. Although some of the most glaring injustices were eliminated (access to lawyers helped safeguard the legal rights of juveniles and led to the deinstitutionalization of status offenders), the system continued to rely on incarceration in local detention centers and state and county custodial institutions. More critically, reform-minded people discovered the equivalent of nineteenth-century punishments within these institutions.[24]

Same Story, Different Day:
Abuse and Scandals Continue

Americans avoid discussing how young offenders are punished. In Orwellian fashion, we obfuscate the reality through the use of euphemistic terminology.[25] The plain and simple truth is that juvenile "correctional institutions" are prisons.

A commitment to a juvenile prison often represents the "end of the line" for some youthful offenders; they may never recover from the pains of their imprisonment. Conditions in many of these institutions have improved very little since the houses of refuge. Any treatment programs are the exception rather than the rule; punishment is the hallmark of these institutions.

As most standard textbooks will note, there are several different prisons to which a youth can be committed. Some of these institutions are public (i.e., run by state or local governments) and others are privately funded. Prisons for young offenders can be further subdivided into short-term (usually ranging from a few days to a couple of months) and long-term confinement (ranging from three or four months to one or two years). Each of these examples has had its share of scandals associated with abuse.

Detention Centers

Detention is primarily a temporary holding facility that functions like an adult jail. Youths are placed in detention pending a court hearing to determine whether or not they should be released. In California in 2006, for example, 64% of the youths were detained prior to a court disposition; 13% were detained for violation of a condition of probation; and 20% were detained post-disposition, waiting for court-ordered assignment to a camp or state-run facility.[26] Despite the reforms of the past half century, the conditions within many of the nation's detention centers remain horrible. This is especially true for the growing numbers of youth with serious mental health problems.

An investigation by the *Pittsburgh Post-Gazette* found that "children with mental health problems stay in detention longer than others because placements can't be found for them."[27] The problem is compounded when states close facilities that previously treated youths with problems. As a result, more children wind up in the juvenile justice system. One director noted that most juveniles stay an average of 11 days before placement, but for those with mental problems the average is between 35 and 40 days.

A report by the U.S. Senate's Governmental Affairs Committee concluded that "thousands of children with mental illnesses await needed community mental health services in juvenile detention centers across the country."[28] One expert testified that: "Juvenile detention facilities lack the resources and staff to confront this problem; yet, corrections is being forced to shoulder the burden of the nation's failure to properly diagnose and care for children with mental or emotional disorders."

- Thousands of children are incarcerated in juvenile detention centers awaiting mental health services in the community. Over a six-month period, nearly 15,000 incarcerated youth waited for community mental health services. Each night, nearly 2,000 youth wait in detention for community mental health services, representing 7% of all youth held in juvenile detention. Yet a quarter of the facilities surveyed reported that they provide no or poor mental health services.

- Children are at increased risk of self-harm and violence. Youth waiting in detention for community mental health services attempted suicide in over 160 facilities. According to previously released research, the rate of suicide among juveniles while incarcerated is four times that of youth overall. Children with mental disorders may also be at particular risk of victimization by others due to their illness.

- Detention centers are overwhelmed. A Pennsylvania administrator interviewed for the report noted that "mentally ill youth placed in juvenile detention facilities stress our centers more than any other problem."

- Warehousing children awaiting mental health services is expensive. The report estimates that juvenile detention facilities spend an estimated $100 million each year to house youth who are waiting for mental health services. [29]

Overcrowding invariably leads to abuses, as indicated in the following example about Colorado's juvenile prisons, including detention centers.

> Virtually every institution is overcrowded and unsafe—the exceptions result from a court order and caps on numbers at small, specialized units like boot camps. Holding cells for youngsters waiting for court appearances in the City and County building are so overcrowded that handcuffed children have been detained for several hours on the buses the sheriff uses to transport them. A Denver newspaper photo showed several juveniles handcuffed to their seats when the outside temperature was more than eighty degrees. The buses are not air-conditioned.
>
> Fights are frequent, and many assaults go unreported. Children sleep on floors, crammed two, three and even four at a time into rooms designed for one. There is not enough staff for adequate supervision. In one facility Human Rights Watch visited, Mount View Youth Services Center, a single staff member was sometimes responsible for as many as forty children.
>
> The committed children repeatedly described the staff as indifferent, verbally abusive and sometimes physically abusive. The Colorado Director of Youth Corrections Programs, Betty Marler, said that the staff is frustrated by the overcrowded conditions. "The system brutalizes everyone," she told us. "It leads to burnout and negative attitudes."[30]

The ghosts of houses of refuge remain today in the nation's juvenile detention centers.

Reception and Diagnostic Centers

Offenders, prior to starting their long-term sentence, are evaluated by a psychologist or social worker to determine what sort of treatment will be required. The stay in the reception center, usually attached to a juvenile prison, is no more than a month. Various tests are given to assess the youth's level of intelligence, attitudes, degree of maturity, emotional problems, academic problems and the like. Those in charge of the dormitories or cottages where the youth will live are also involved in this assessment to determine what problems, if any, the youth will have.

Some of these facilities do not in any way fit the image of a reception and diagnostic center. On the contrary, some resemble large institutions. The state of Oklahoma, for instance, has a "Reception and Orientation Center" (ROC). On their Web site this center is described as a place where "residents" (as they are called, rather than "prisoners" or "inmates") are first admitted to the Southwest Oklahoma Juvenile Center. Here the initial response by the staff "is to gain control of the resident's behavior."

> While residents are on the ROC unit, they first learn to memorize eighteen rules of appropriate behavior and how they apply to the crimes they've committed on the "outside." While on the ROC unit, their behavior is strictly and closely monitored. These residents learn compliance. For instance, a resident is only allowed to speak by raising his/her hand, being acknowledged by staff and given permission. All new residents begin their stay at the Southwest Oklahoma juvenile Center on the ROC unit. This allows staff to gain control of the residents' behavior at the beginning of his/her treatment, which results in a smoother cognitive behavioral pattern after he/she leaves this unit. On ROC, residents not only ask permission to speak, but also to enter and exit certain areas. They have no television or radios on this unit, have school on the unit, eat on the unit, and get off the unit only one hour a day for outside recreation.[31]

The military model of discipline is readily apparent. Given the high rates of recidivism among graduates of such institutions, there is no evidence that the military model is effective.

Youth "Correctional Facilities"

In 2003 there were 69,007 youths committed to custody and 26,269 detained.[32] While the most (95%) had been adjudicated delinquent, almost 5% were committed for a status offense. Of those committed, 86.6% were male and 13.4% female; 40% were white, 37% black, and 18% Hispanic. For more details on racial differences, see article 2.

Some Effects of Incarceration:
The Inmate Social System and Victimization

What's wrong with incarcerating young offenders in large institutions?

> Large, congregate-care juvenile facilities, such as training schools, camps, and ranches, have not been effective at rehabilitating juvenile offenders. . . . Small, community-based facilities providing intensive treatment services and special programming in a secure environment offer the best hope for successful treatment of juveniles who require a structured setting. These services include individual and group counseling, educational and training programs, medical services, and intensive staff supervision. Proximity to the community permits direct, regular family involvement with the treatment process, independent living, and a phased reentry into the community.
>
> Since closing its traditional training schools in 1972, Massachusetts has relied on a sophisticated network of small, secure programs for violent youth coupled with a broad range of highly structured, community-based programs for most committed youth. Secure facilities are reserved for the most serious offenders. A study of the State's community-based juvenile system revealed recidivism rates equal to or lower than those of other jurisdictions. In addition, Massachusetts has saved an estimated $11 million a year by relying on community-based sanctions.[33]

There are a number of reasons why large custodial institutions fail. We can begin by taking a look at what life in custody is like for confined youths. Sadly, there has not been much improvement over the years.[34] The pattern established with the New York House of Refuge continues.

Let's begin with a survey of 42 juvenile prisons conducted in the 1970s by the National Assessment of Juvenile Corrections. The study focused on the effects on youths of being institutionalized. It distinguished between newcomers (those who had been at the facility two months or less) and veterans (those who had been incarcerated nine months or more). The survey found significant differences between programs having large proportions of veterans and those having relatively few veterans.[35] Veterans were significantly more likely than newcomers to: (1) commit more offenses and have friends who had committed offenses while incarcerated; (2) have learned more ways to break the law while incarcerated (46% of the veterans, compared to 20% of the newcomers); and (3) become more hardened over time ("hardened" was measured in several ways, such as being critical of the staff, previous encounters with institutions, number and seriousness of offenses while incarcerated).

It was also found that the longer a youth remained in the institution, the more the youth would: (1) fight with other youths, (2) use drugs, (3) steal something, (4) run away, and (5) hit a staff member. These problems become the most acute when, as the authors put it, there is a "critical mass" of veterans within a program. John Irwin's study of adult felons found that a significant number were what he termed *state-raised youth*.[36] These offenders more or less grew up in various institutions (juvenile detention centers or other institutions such as foster care or group homes), rarely spending any significant amounts of time in free society. Irwin describes the worldview of state-raised youths as distorted, stunted, and incoherent. Living in custody has become their only meaningful world.

Numerous studies, some dating back to the 1950s, have found that the strong prey on the weak in institutions. In addition, a potent inmate subculture, similar to the one in adult prisons, has existed since the first of these institutions was established in the nineteenth century.[37] In most of the larger institutions, the peer subculture includes a strongly defined hierarchy.

Youths entering the institution quickly earn reputations, either as strong boys or weak ones.

> Once boys were in the intake cottage, the other boys immediately subjected them to tests designed to ascertain whether they could be exploited for food, clothes, cigarettes, and sex. . . . If the new boy looked and acted tough, exploitation was minimized; if any weaknesses were shown, he was immediately misused by the others.[38]

Three criminologists studied an institution in Columbus, Ohio, in the 1970s. They focused on the extent of victimization within these institutions and described a brutal social system. Within the "jungle" (the term the inmates themselves used), the powerful prey on the weak. The overwhelming majority engaged in some form of exploitation.[39] The researchers observed a number of social roles in the institution. Some youths were classified as "aggressive," while others were "manipulative" and still others were "passive."

Those who pursued the more aggressive roles were "cottage leaders," "lieutenants," and "sexual exploiters." The cottage leader was often referred to variously as "wheel," "bruiser," "duke," and "heavy." The lieutenants who worked for the leaders were called "vice-president," "tough boy," "thug," "bad dude," and even "wise guy" (borrowing organized crime terminology). Sexual exploiters were called such names as "daddy" and "booty bandits."[40]

Manipulators were youths who did what was necessary to survive and to make their stay easier. They would "do their own time." Others called these youths "slick," "cool," and "con man." Those who engaged in various businesses were known as "peddlers" or "merchants."

Passive youth were not deeply involved in the inmate social system and generally were "pro-staff." They were referred to as "straight kid," "quiet type," and "bushboy." Some youths were put down as "messups," "weak-minded," and "lame." Those who were victimized sexually were called "punks," "sweet boy," "girl" and "fag."[41]

The authors of the study returned 15 years later for a follow-up. What they found was not encouraging. They discovered that the youth culture still existed and continued to victimize the weak, although less for sex than for food, clothing, and toiletries. Violent offenders were in the minority; the majority were minor drug dealers, addicts, and users of drugs. Gangs did not dominate the institution, as was popularly believed. While some of those factors were mildly encouraging, the most discouraging fact was that treatment had "all but disappeared," with the lone exception of a drug abuse program. The authors quoted one social worker: "We don't do anything in here for kids." Another member of the staff added: "This place is a warehouse for children."[42]

The state of Mississippi has been the subject of state and federal investigations for abuses. The Civil Rights of Institutionalized Persons Act (CRIPA) passed in 1997 authorizes the attorney general of the United States to conduct investigations and litigation relating to conditions of confinement in state or locally operated institutions (the statute does not cover private facilities). The Special Litigation Section of the Civil Rights Division of the U.S. Department of Justice investigates facilities to determine whether there is a pattern or practice of violations of federal rights.

In June 2004, a CRIPA investigation of the Oakley Training School (also known as the Mississippi Youth Correctional Complex) in Raymond, Mississippi and the Columbia Training School in Columbia, Mississippi found:[43]

- Girls were punished by being forced to run in a field with automobile tires around their bodies or carrying logs.
- Girls reported being forced to eat their own vomit if they threw up while exercising in the hot sun.
- Disciplinary practices included hog-tying, pole-shackling, isolation, staff assaults, and OC/pepper spray abuse.
- Youths who were recommitted were taken to one of the isolation rooms in the intake area and punched and slapped by staff for the recidivism.

Robert Boyd, Jr., an assistant attorney general for the United States, submitted the report to the governor of Mississippi and summarized the findings.

> We find that conditions at Oakley and Columbia violate the constitutional and statutory rights of juveniles. Youth confined at Oakley and Columbia suffer harm or the risk of harm from deficiencies in the facilities' provision of mental health and medical care, protection of juveniles from harm, and juvenile justice management. There are also sanitation deficiencies at Oakley. In addition, both facilities fail to provide required general education services as well as education to eligible youth as required by the Individuals with Disabilities Education Act.[44]

In the section on findings, the report stated:

> Oakley and Columbia do not have any system of positive incentives to manage youth, but instead rely on discipline and force. This leads to unconstitutionally abusive disciplinary practices such as hogtying, pole-shackling, improper use and overuse of restraints and isolation, staff assaulting youth, and OC spray abuse. . . .
>
> Girls in the SIU [Special Intervention Unit] at Columbia are punished for acting out or for being suicidal by being placed in a cell called the "dark room." The "dark room" is a locked, windowless isolation cell with lighting controlled by staff. When the lights are turned out, as the girls reported they are when the room is in use, the room is completely dark. The room is stripped of everything but a drain in the floor which serves as a toilet.[45]

These abuses are reminiscent of those at the New York House of Refuge more than a century ago. The executive director of Parents and Teachers against Violence in Education found another stark similarity.

> [The report] evokes images of prisoner-of-war camps at their worst, but with this distinction: sadistic POW camp guards don't misrepresent themselves as agents of rehabilitation. In that setting, the rules of the game are clear to all parties: the torturers and the tortured know exactly where they stand.[46]

Failed Programs

A Notorious Example

Not since the scandals within the houses of refuge have we witnessed the total failure of prison-like "training schools," as was the case with what was formerly known as the California Youth Authority (CYA). In 2005, the CYA became the Division of Juvenile Justice (DJJ) under the Department of Corrections and Rehabilitation. The system currently consists of 8 youth "correctional institutions," 1 forestry camp, 59 detention facilities, and several dozen "probation camps" scattered all over the state.[47]

The CYA was the result of the passage of The Youth Corrections Authority Act of 1941. The act created a three-person committee to develop a better classification system and to improve parole practices and develop the capacity of local probation departments. The management of the three state training schools remained with the Department of Institutions. The Youth Authority Act of 1944 amended the earlier law and created the California Youth Authority. It transferred managerial responsibility of the training schools to the new agency. The change resulted from two highly publicized and suspicious suicides at the Whittier State Reform School in 1943. The public outcry led the governor to determine that the old administrative structure had to go.

The three-person commission mandated the acceptance of all youths under the age of 23 who had been committed to various prisons and already existing youth facilities (Preston School of Industry and Ventura School for Girls, which still exist, and Fred C. Nelles School for Boys, which closed in 2004 after more than 100 years of operation). A three-person commission was appointed and granted $100,000 to run the Authority for two years.[48] The youths sent to the CYA were referred to as "wards"—a name that has remained ever since. A year later they established "camps" and a unit called "Delinquency Prevention Services." In 1945, the Division of Parole was created.

The official mission statement reads:

> The mission of the California Department of the Youth Authority is to protect the public from criminal activity by providing education, training, and treatment services for youthful offenders committed by the courts; assisting local justice agencies with their efforts to control crime and delinquency; and encouraging the development of state and local programs to prevent crime and delinquency.
>
> In addition to providing education, training, and treatment services for youthful offenders, the Department is broadening its focus to include the needs of victims and communities. It is the Department's intention to address the needs of victims and communities through the provision of direct services as well as programs targeting youthful offenders.[49]

The department also asserts that its values include treating "all people with dignity, respect, and consideration" and that it demonstrates "behavior which is fair, honest, and ethical both on and off the job."[50]

The reality, however, is far different, as revealed by recurring scandals within the CYA (we will use CYA for discussions prior to 2005 and DJJ for more recent years). Three reports condemning practices within the CYA were published in the 1980s.[51] All three reports documented extreme brutality and the lack of meaningful treatment within the California institutions. The final report noted that CYA institutions were "seriously overcrowded, offer minimal treatment value despite their high expense, and are ineffective in long-term protection of public safety."[52] At the time the CYA was 150% over capacity with 9,000 wards packed into institutions designed for 5,840. The report further noted that the Youthful Offender Parole Board (YOPB) played a key role in the overcrowding, resulting in the legislature cutting its budget by one-third because of the board's failure to follow its own guidelines. The report called the board a "structural anomaly" and recommended it be abolished.

A more recent report found that the "wards" of the CYA often lived in constant fear. One youth admitted: "I cried at 3 o'clock in the morning. Quietly. Everyone did. . . . I was living in fear 22 hours a day in that place." Another youth stated: "It was too dangerous to sleep at night." Many youths belonged to gangs before they were taken into custody;

those ties were strengthened once inside. Many youths join gangs for protection. One youth, who was Cuban but looked white, said that he refused to join a gang when he was in but just before his release he was given a warning by a gang leader that if he did not join a gang then "I wouldn't make it."[53]

Apparently the findings of the report fell on deaf ears, for the CYA continued unchanged, although it did begin dealing with the problem of overcrowding and reduced its population from a high of around 10,000 in the mid-1990s (note that the population had increased since the Lerner reports were issued) to a current population 2,500—the lowest in the agency's history.[54] The CYA did adopt a policy in 1998 that required each ward to obtain a high school diploma as a condition of parole—without any commensurate increase in resources. Critics charged that it was mainly for publicity purposes and created another justification to extend ward confinement time. The YOPB would deny youths their parole pending completion of their GED, even if they had no realistic way of completing it due the absence of educational resources.

In 1999 the state legislature enacted a law requiring the department to provide a course of study for all wards not having a high school diploma. While the goal of wards receiving high school diplomas was a positive step forward, to be useful the legislation must be accompanied by funding and a workable plan for implementing the requirements, which

> created a substantial need for additional and upgraded education facilities. A significant amount of the educational program at various institutions is delivered in temporary buildings. These temporary buildings inherently have a rather limited useful life, and have functional deficiencies such as inadequate security and ineffective air conditioning at institutions located in warm climates. The location of some of these temporary buildings is also an issue because they are often located a distance from housing units, requiring intensive staff supervision of ward movements.[55]

Indeed, the education requirements prompted an almost unimaginable solution for disciplinary problems. In 1998 about 70 cages (ranging from 4 feet by 4 feet and tall enough to stand in to 12 feet by 15 feet and 10 feet high) were introduced in four prisons. They were called special protective areas (SPAs) and were used for teaching wards who had been assigned to special detention for assault or other infractions. Before the cages were introduced, wards in special detention had been taught through the food slots in their room doors. While some staff members felt safer, others recognized the dehumanizing nature of using cages.[56]

A coalition of law firms and the nonprofit Prison Law Office filed a federal class-action lawsuit in 2002 alleging unconstitutional treatment of wards. The suit was refiled in state court as a taxpayer action in 2003 alleging that the CYA spent state funds on unlawful practices. The mentally ill nephew of plaintiff Margaret Farrell was locked in a filthy isolation cell for 23 hours a day for seven months. Edward Jermaine Brown received only "blender meals" (pureed food groups) in his cell, and the toilet often did not function. After the lawsuit was filed, the CYA closed the housing unit where Brown had been locked up.

The year 2004 was marked by revelations of extreme brutality, suicides, horrible physical conditions, and almost total failure of the CYA to live up to its mission statement. At a special hearing in February 2004, Gloria Romero (a state senator) called conditions at the CYA "chilling." Some inmates were kept in "steel-mesh cages not much bigger than phone booths." Romero said the CYA was "totally failing in its mission to rehabilitate youths." She called it a system "that is in chaos, ruled by fear and neglect."[57]

The Heman G. Stark Youth Correctional Facility is located in Chino, California. In 2004, there were almost 300 personal attacks—twice the number that occurred in 2003. Wards are housed in programs assigned a letter of the alphabet. K/L is a "special management program" for wards who exhibit ongoing violent and disruptive behavior. K/L houses 10% of the total population. Wards in the special management program spend the majority of time in their rooms except for showers and exercise.

> Dim corridors are lined with the steel doors of a dozen concrete cells.
> The air is dank, and the drip-drip of water echoes quietly, thanks to
> the perpetually leaking showers. On the mental health unit, shouts
> and curses bounce off the walls. In a cell, a young man with his head
> down paces silently, back and forth, back and forth.[58]

Responding to newspaper accounts of brutal and inhumane conditions inside the juvenile prison system, Judge Marta Diaz of San Mateo County ordered that no more youth be sent to the CYA.

> The action makes San Mateo the second Bay Area county planning to
> keep youths in their home counties, rather than subjecting them to
> conditions of confinement inside the state's 10 lock-up facilities. . . .
> Probation officials are also taking action, responding to recently
> released state-commissioned reports that detail a climate of ward-
> on-ward brutality and harsh institutional treatment, including con-
> fining youths in cells 23 hours per day. . . . Substance-abuse treat-
> ment was below national standards, and . . . mental-health services
> were failing the majority of inmates, ages 12 to 25, who suffer from
> psychiatric disorders.[59]

In May 2004 a CYA officer at N.A. Chaderjian Youth Correctional Facility in Stockton was caught on video letting his German shepherd bite a 20-year-old prisoner on the leg, even though the inmate was following orders and lying on the floor. Earlier two correctional counselors at the same institution were videotaped kicking two wards who were lying facedown on the floor.[60] An investigation into the suicide deaths of two CYA inmates held in isolation revealed excessive rates of violence; inadequate mental health care and educational services; overuse of isolation cells; and deplorable conditions, including feces spread all over some of the cells. Some boys were being forced to sit or stand in cages while attending classes, a "normal" situation in the state's Kafkaesque system. . . .

Just as shocking as the litany of CYA abuses is the fact that institutions such as Preston Training School simply don't work. A growing body of research shows that young people incarcerated in large institutions get rearrested more frequently, and for more serious crimes than their counterparts with similar delinquency histories who are not incarcerated. For example, a study that compared matched samples of offenders in Arkansas found that the incarceration experience was the single greatest predictor of future criminal conduct, dwarfing the effects of gang membership or family dysfunction. It's not surprising then, that more than nine out of 10 CYA "graduates" are back in trouble with the law within three years of their release. On top of that, the CYA system costs taxpayers a whopping $85,000 a year per youth. It seems likely that if the majority of CYA youths came from white, middle-class neighborhoods, the public would never stand for its failures and abuses.[61]

Experts testified before a special California Senate committee on corrections in September 2004. They noted that tinkering with the details of current CYA policies was woefully inadequate. Instead, California needed to follow the lead of Massachusetts and Missouri and close lockups that housed as many as 900 inmates and start over with a new model that would better prepare youths to live crime-free once released. Dan Macallair, a 20-year veteran of juvenile justice work, commented: "The California Youth Authority is a dinosaur . . . based on a nineteenth-century model," he said. "The institutions need to be torn down." Despite spending $130,000 annually on each female ward and $80,000 for male wards, more than 50% of released wards were reimprisoned within two years.[62]

On November 16, 2004, Governor Arnold Schwarzenegger announced plans for an overhaul of the CYA. "The lawsuit said that California should have done a better job with its young offenders, and it was right. . . . We are on the right track now."[63] A special master was appointed to oversee the improvements to which the CYA agreed, including reducing time spent in isolation cells, improvements in monitoring wards on suicide watch, and development of a system to separate vulnerable inmates from dangerous ones. Schwarzenegger said that the agreement will "put the focus back on rehabilitation" and give the CYA's 3,700 young inmates "a better chance to succeed in life," noting that this settlement was a step forward in reducing crime and saving the state several million dollars (that would have been spent fighting the lawsuit).

David Steinhart, a veteran juvenile justice expert critic noted:

> This agreement does not transform the CYA, it merely brings it up to
> a tolerable level. The danger is that the governor will tie a ribbon

around this and call it a day, when there's a lot more that needs to be done to re-engineer the system.[64]

Other critics have pointed out that the most essential reform—housing inmates in smaller living units, as opposed to the massive prison-like facilities that typify the CYA—is missing. Most researchers believe, and the experiences of several states have proved, that small groups are much more likely to foster the human connections needed by troubled youths.[65]

An audit by the Office of the Inspector General released in January 2005 accused the CYA of "failing to give offenders the education and training that could save them from a life of crime."[66] In addition, CYA youth prisons continued to confine too many wards for 23 hours a day, a practice the audit called "ineffective and dehumanizing." Inspector General Matthew Cate stated that the most troubling aspect of the CYA was that "many of the deficiencies that have not been corrected are central to the Youth Authority's core mission of rehabilitating the young people entrusted to its care."

On January 31, 2005, the State of California signed an agreement with the juvenile justice advocates who had filed the previous lawsuit. The agreement puts "therapy and positive reinforcement at the heart of California's youth prison system, rejecting today's more punitive approaches in favor of models that have been successful in other states." The court order resulting from the lawsuit says that the CYA must:

- Shift to an "open programming" model, as opposed to one that confines inmates in their cells for long stretches at a time, at all prisons by May 2. Under the change, inmates must be released for education, meals, treatment, and recreation on a daily basis, and dangerous youths would be separated from those considered vulnerable.

- House youths in the facility closest to their homes. This addresses a chief complaint of families, who often live hundreds of miles from their incarcerated children, making visits difficult.

- Involve families in the therapy provided to youths, unless it would be considered detrimental to the inmate.

- Emphasize "positive reinforcement rather than punitive disciplinary methods" to encourage good behavior.

- Require all staff who work with youths to be trained in rehabilitative and treatment services.[67]

Again, however, the size of living units in each youth prison is not specified.

A comment by a retired corrections officer who was stabbed by a ward at Chaderjian reflects the resistance encountered by efforts to reform. "Who wrote this plan, Walt Disney? . . . We're not talking about bicycle thieves and runaways. These are murderers, carjackers, hard-core criminals. Therapy and coloring crayons aren't going to help."[68] His views illustrate a common stereotype about treatment among conservatives, especially those who work within the prison system.

Building a system that works for troubled youths and for the public requires informed participants. Often what is offered is a political solution to pacify a public that is largely uninformed about the realities of youth prisons. "Band-aids" cannot fix a ruptured system that should be abandoned and replaced. Unfortunately the history of reforms generally reveals cosmetic changes. The promises of treatment and rehabilitation so often offered with great fanfare are all too frequently hollow promises. There are simply too many with a vested interest in keeping the system the way it is.

The juvenile justice system in California is one of the most expensive in the United States—approximately $180,000 per ward in 2007, five times the cost of an inmate in an adult prison. Costs are projected to increase to $216,000 in 2008. Since agreeing to the consent decree in 2004 and settling the class action lawsuit, the DJJ has been ordered to introduce fundamental reforms but violence continues to rise. A panel of experts concluded that the California system lags behind other states in almost every category except cost. One legislator remarked that the system was "doomed to failure. There is a tremendous lack of concern for getting results. Nothing has happened."[69]

The increased violence has occurred while the population in the juvenile prisons plummeted from a peak of 10,000 wards in 1996 to 2,551 in April 2007. The declining population should provide an opportunity to implement better policies. At the county level, there has been progress in evidence-based rehabilitative methods to reduce recidivism. A chief probation officer in one of the counties remarked: "Those state facilities are the absolute last place you want to send a kid. The state is the last resort. We do a much better job treating them in the counties, and we use far more successful approaches."[70]

> For the past decade, a system once marked by little but despair has experienced a series of positive changes, and one reason, many experts say, is that the counties have been sending fewer juvenile offenders every year to the state-run juvenile prison system and instead placing them in rehabilitation programs in their home counties. The offenders are generally arrested and adjudicated by county law enforcement authorities, and prosecutors and judges have wide discretion in how and where to handle them.[71]

When crime rates increased, some criminologists had argued that the only way to protect the public was to incarcerate offenders. In fact, California had been a national leader in juvenile rehabilitation until it adopted a punitive approach. Barry Krisberg remarked:

> This is the huge, untold story of the corrections system. What we're seeing is the exact reverse of the old argument that said the only thing that works is incapacitating these juveniles. The crime rates are falling as we got less tough, not tougher.[72]

Dan Macallair agrees: "This is one of the biggest developments in the history of the system. This goes against everything we thought was needed, essentially. This refutes 30 years of social policy."

County probation departments are much more willing to place offenders, even repeat offenders, in day-treatment programs. The fewer youths they incarcerate—while providing treatment—the more they enhance public safety. A juvenile court judge remarked: "We have realized we were locking up kids we didn't need to lock up, especially girls. You don't want to separate them from their families if you can help it."

The California legislature passed Reform Bill SB 81 on August 21, 2007. "If signed by the governor and implemented, it is expected to ultimately shrink the bleak state juvenile prison system nearly out of existence."[73] The bill provides that all but the most violent youths convicted of murder and certain types of sexual assault would be sanctioned only in their home counties. Within three years of implementation, the ward population would be one-tenth of the number of wards held in 1996. The sponsor of the bill, Mike Machado, remarked: "This is a very, very significant step toward major reform in the way we deal with juveniles, and it finally puts us in line with other states."[74] Machado had originally opposed the measure, fearing that it would allow the state to abandon youths who desperately need help and dump them on the counties. The bill includes measures for improving county programs and raises the funds paid to counties from $94,000 per youth to about $130,000 annually.

> Another key to winning support was that the state will allow flexibility in how the counties can spend the money and treat the offenders, which could help spur innovation. The bill also provides $100 million to help the counties build new facilities or set up new rehabilitation programs to manage the increased number of youths.[75]

A Treatment Program that Failed

Most programs fail for one of two reasons: either the theory behind the program is flawed (i.e., a theory of why people commit crime) or the program is not implemented correctly. Sometimes both reasons contribute to the failure, which happened with a program that began in Arizona in the early 1990s. A class action lawsuit, *Johnson v. Upchurch*, in 1986 charged that the policies, practices, and conditions of confinement at a juvenile prison near Tucson amounted to "cruel, unconscionable, and illegal conditions of confinement."[76] A new program was designed to replace inflexible rules that usually dominate prisons and to embrace collective problem solving in an atmosphere of respect. M. A. Bortner and Linda Williams explain that the failure of the program to live up to its promises is not a new story.[77] It has happened over and over again throughout the history of juvenile prisons.

The decline began a mere three months into the program. Only the youths themselves and a small number of dedicated staff seemed to want the program to succeed. Those in charge wanted first and foremost to satisfy the demands of the lawsuit and to demonstrate success quickly. There was constant resistance from staff and administrators (with administrators described as "authoritarian" in their management style) plus political opposition from conservatives. While the model program had admirable goals of encouraging youths to take control over their lives, it ignored the changes necessary to help that happen. For example, most staff members continued to receive "low salaries, demanding working conditions, menial tasks, and perceptions of lack of support and respect from superiors."[78]

There was, however, a more fundamental problem. Good intentions notwithstanding, even the best programs within the juvenile and adult prison system are doomed to failure for the simple reason that the various social and personal contexts that contribute to problems with drugs, gangs, and violence remain unaddressed. As Bortner and Williams note, "For most youths, going home meant a return to poverty and unemployment, troubled homes, the allure of alcohol and drugs, the dominance of gangs, and daily hardships."[79] Indeed, it would be like sending an alcoholic to a 30-day treatment center and then sending him back to a bar and telling him he must "just say no" to alcohol.

> Their support system had been nurtured in a closed environment, but unresolved problems awaited the youths when they were released from prison. Outside the prison, fundamental social conditions remained unchanged. When they were paroled, within a few days or a few hours youths confronted the same old pressures and many reverted to familiar responses and solutions.[80]

Bortner and Williams also perceptively comment that the youths "are placed in an untenable position when they are encouraged to change their behavior and to develop high aspirations, only to return to their virtually unchanged communities."[81]

Some youths did not want to leave the prison; inside they were safe, and they were able to adjust to the surroundings. This phenomenon has been called "institutionalization" or "prisonization" by researchers going back more than 50 years.[82]

Staff members suggested finding new friends who were not into gangs and drugs to avoid old patterns.

> Some youths planned to live with relatives outside their old neighborhoods so peer pressures to return to drugs would not be as intense. Jacob had been incarcerated on three previous occasions, twice for using and selling drugs. Although he had not seen his father for five years, arrangements were made for him to move out of state to live with him. Jacob hoped that because he would not be

going back to the same friends, he might have a chance to stay off drugs. He said the other times he was released he felt like he was "being sucked into a swirling pool."[83]

Many youths spoke of the inevitability of returning to their old ways of behaving. For some, that was probably an accurate assessment. Many would have few alternatives for housing. Many underestimated the magnitude of support they would need to confront the realities of life on the outside.

One additional problem emerged within this program and points to the common failure of implementation: the failure to establish a substance abuse program, which was the last of three specialized, intensive programs developed. This was despite the fact that around 90% of the youths had used drugs. The first specialized unit was for "sexually aggressive behaviors," in spite of the fact that less than 10% were charged with such crimes. Another priority was to address violent behavior, although less than 40% had committed violent offenses. Those priorities might well have been a reflection of the personal priorities of key political figures in the state. Bortner and Williams remark that the program's "failure to confront the youths' extensive drug and alcohol problems mirrored society's failure."[84]

The influence of politics leads to the question of whether deficiencies are simply *planned failures* rather than good intentions gone awry. If those in power really cared, they would address the social conditions that lead youth to crime and drugs. But if readily accepted solutions appeal to the public and award contracts to people who profit from them, there is little incentive for change. The CYA and the prison in Tucson are not unique examples. Juvenile prisons all over the country (and in some other countries) have experienced similar failures. The ghosts of houses of refuge continue to the present day.

High Recidivism Rates Plague Juvenile Prisons

A standard measure of the success of any program dealing with offenders is *recidivism*. Recidivism can be operationally defined in several ways. In juvenile cases, it can be measured as an arrest, a referral to juvenile court, a petition filed, or a re-commitment to an institution.[85] Whatever method is used, it is one of the best methods of measuring the effectiveness of a policy.

Juvenile prisons have a dismal record in terms of recidivism. In fact, some states appear to be reluctant to conduct studies tracking recidivism rates. For example, the Department of Juvenile Justice in South Carolina has not studied the recidivism of incarcerated juveniles since 1995. In 1994, 71% of juveniles released from juvenile institutions committed new crimes after their release. The following year a district court judge used those figures in his finding that the conditions at these institutions violated the constitutional rights of the confined juveniles.

Although exact figures are difficult to obtain, the evidence indicates that between 56 and 82% of DJJ juveniles later commit crimes as adults. In some cases, South Carolina juvenile correctional facilities produce graduates who later swell the populations of adult correctional facilities and figure prominently in the ranks of those who later commit violent offenses as adults.[86]

A study in Minnesota found that between 50 and 75% of males were either petitioned to juvenile court or arrested for crimes as an adult within two years following their release from juvenile correctional facilities. For females the rates were lower but nevertheless ranged from 41 to 58%. In two particular institutions (called Red Wing and Sauk Centre), more than 90% of those released in 1985 were arrested as an adult before the age of 23 and 69% had been sent to adult prison.[87]

A very comprehensive study found that among a cohort of more than 3,000 juvenile offenders, about half of those released from Oregon youth prisons at age 17 or 18 ended up in the adult prison system; about 40% of those released at age 16 ended up in adult prison.[88] The total recidivism rate was 42%. The study also found that females had a significantly lower rate of recidivism (21%) than males (45%). Note here that the definition of "recidivism" was an arrest as an adult. Consistent with other longitudinal studies, the earlier the age of first contact with the juvenile court, the higher the proportion of those who ended up in the adult system (e.g., 57% of those age 12 ended up in the adult system versus 43% of those whose first referral was at age 17).[89] Another interesting finding, also consistent with prior research, was that the longer a youth spent at a juvenile institution, the higher was the recidivism rate.[90]

A research project examined 805 cases of youths released from the Hawaii Youth Correctional Facility (HYCF) between 1995 and 1999. The study found that 82% of those released were re-arrested within two years; 57% were re-convicted; 32% were re-confined at either HYCF or an adult facility. Recidivism rates were significantly higher for those with the greatest number of commitments, the greatest number of parole returns, the most escapes, and the highest number of misconduct reports. The number of runaways, the age of first use of drugs, and the number of suicide risk indicators were also related to recidivism. The report also noted that the recidivism rates for the period studied were greater than a prior study completed in 1984.[91]

The recidivism rates of the CYA were among the highest anywhere; one report noted a recidivism rate of 91%.[92] The *San Jose Mercury News* used a computerized review of police records of more than 28,000 youths who were released between 1988 and 2000 and found that 74% were arrested within three years of their release. Property offenders had a higher recidivism rate than violent offenders (80% versus 70%). The recidivism rate was lower for females (52%); males had a rate of 75%. Recidivism also was lower for the youngest and oldest youths released;

those under 17 had a rate of 60%, which was the same as those over 21. These were in the minority, as most were between 17 and 21 years of age, and their recidivism rate was 76%.[93]

Recidivism rates are significantly lower among youths who receive dispositions other than youth prisons. Holding constant other variables, those who are given probation and provided with a variety of intensive services (e.g., drug treatment, tutoring, mental health counseling, family counseling, etc.) have much lower recidivism rates.[94] The need for such services is demonstrated by the many barriers facing youths who are released from an institution. The study by the Center on Juvenile and Criminal Justice found the following barriers to successful re-entry: [95]

- Lack of educational options: the average age of those released from the CYA is 21, which excludes them from the state's responsibility to provide an education;

- Lack of housing options: many have no families to speak of and there is a short supply of residential housing, especially transitional housing;

- Limited skills and education: in 2001 only 11.5% of those in the CYA passed the California High School Exit Exam;

- Gang affiliations and related racial tensions: just being locked up in the CYA solidifies whatever gang ties a youth had at entry;

- Institutional identity: this relates to the concept of "state-raised youth," which means, among other things, that most CYA youths are never prepared for an independent life upon release;[96]

- Drug problems: more than 65% have drug problems;

- Mental health problems: the CYA estimates that 45% of males and 65% of females have serious mental health issues;

- Lack of community support and role models: most of those released will return to the same impoverished conditions they came from, along with family dysfunctions, drug problems, violence and gangs;

- Legislative barriers: these limit access to education, cash assistance, housing, employment, etc. that are automatically closed to ex-cons.

The authors of this report conclude that: "The multiple service needs and histories of violent behavior among CYA wards necessitate a system of care that addresses the root causes of criminal activity."[97]

A Concluding Thought

Although it has been quoted hundreds of times, the statement by the philosopher George Santayana (1863–1952) is appropriate here: "Those who cannot remember the past are condemned to repeat it."[98] Also, a common definition of "insanity" is repeating the same behavior after repeated failures and thinking that the outcome will be different. This is the legacy of almost 200 years of juvenile imprisonment.

Notes

[1] See the following Web site for details about this famous experiment: http://www.prisonexp.org/

[2] Ibid.

[3] Sutton, J. R. (1988). *Stubborn Children: Controlling Delinquency in the United States.* Berkeley: University of California Press.

[4] Rendleman, D. (1979). "Parens Patriae: From Chancery to Juvenile Court." In F. Faust and P. Brantingham (eds.), *Juvenile Justice Philosophy* (2nd ed.). St. Paul, MN: West, p. 63.

[5] Teitelbaum, L. E. and L. J. Harris. (1977). "Some Historical Perspectives on Governmental Regulation of Children and Parents." In L. E. Teitelbaum and A. R. Gough (eds.), *Beyond Control: Status Offenders in the Juvenile Court.* Cambridge, MA: Ballinger.

[6] Empey, L. T. (ed.). (1979). *The Future of Childhood and Juvenile Justice.* Charlottesville: University Press of Virginia, p. 59.

[7] Brenzel, B. (1983). *Daughters of the State.* Cambridge: MIT Press, p. 11.

[8] This group was formerly called the Society for the Prevention of *Pauperism* (another word for poverty). For a discussion of this group and a detailed description of its upper-class backgrounds see: Pickett, R. (1969). *House of Refuge.* Syracuse: Syracuse University Press, pp. 21–49.

[9] Ibid., p. 33.

[10] Abbott, G. (1938). *The Child and the State.* Chicago: University of Chicago Press, p. 348.

[11] Pickett, *House of Refuge*, p. 15.

[12] Ibid., p. 6.

[13] Mennel, R. (1973). *Thorns and Thistles: Juvenile Delinquents in the U.S., 1820–1940.* Hanover, NH: University Press of New England, p. 103.

[14] Pisciotta, A. (1982). "Saving the Children: The Promise and Practice of *Parens Patriae*, 1838–98." *Crime and Delinquency* 28: 410–425.

[15] Ibid.; Hawes, J. (1971). *Children in Urban Society.* New York: Oxford University Press, pp. 47–48; Bremner, R. H. (ed.). (1970). *Children and Youth in America.* Cambridge: Harvard University Press, pp. 689–691.

[16] The wording is taken *verbatim* from the law passed in Pennsylvania in 1826, which authorized the House of Refuge, "at their discretion, to receive into their care and guardianship, infants, *males under the age of twenty-one years, and females under the age of eighteen years,* committed to their custody" (emphasis added). Note the obvious distinction based on gender. This exact same statute was reproduced in numerous state laws throughout the nineteenth century. I found an example in my own study of Memphis, Tennessee (Shelden, R. G. [1976]. "Rescued from Evil; Origins of the Juvenile Justice System in Memphis, Tennessee, 1900–1917." Ph.D. dissertation, Southern Illinois University, Carbondale; Shelden, R. G. and L. T. Osborne. [1989]. "'For Their Own Good': Class Interests and the Child Saving Movement in Memphis, Tennessee, 1900–1917." *Criminology* 27: 801–821).

[17] *Ex Parte Crouse*, 4 Wharton (Pa.) 9 (1938); for the significance for girls see Shelden, R. G. (1998). "Confronting the Ghost of Mary Ann Crouse: Gender Bias in the Juvenile Justice System." *Juvenile and Family Court Journal* 49: 11–26.

[18] *Ex Parte Crouse.*

[19] All of these charges are well documented in the following works: Mennel, *Thorns and Thistles*; Hawes, *Children in Urban Society*; Bremner, *Children and Youth in America*; Pisciotta, "Saving the Children." Abuses within the juvenile justice system have continued to the present, with one scandal after another.

[20] For further discussion of this issue see Chesney-Lind, M. and R. G. Shelden. (2004). *Girls, Delinquency and Juvenile Justice* (3rd ed.). Belmont, CA: Wadsworth.

[21] Bernard, T. J. (1992). *The Cycle of Juvenile Justice*. Oxford: Oxford University Press, pp. 70–72; "People v. Turner." (1974), in Faust and Brantingham, *Juvenile Justice Philosophy*.

[22] *Commonwealth v. Fisher*, 213 Pa. 48 (1905).

[23] Faust, F. and P. Brantingham (eds.), *Juvenile Justice Philosophy* (2nd ed.). St. Paul, MN: West, p. 299.

[24] Miller, J. (1998). *Last One Over the Wall* (2nd ed.). Columbus: Ohio State University Press.

[25] In the Vietnam War we did the same thing, such as calling the unnecessary killing of innocent civilians "collateral damage."

[26] Juvenile Justice Data Project. (2007). Phase 1: Survey of Interventions and Programs: A Continuum of Graduated Responses for Juvenile Justice in California, p. 11. (http://www.cpoc.org/JJDPSurveyFinalReport.pdf)

[27] Twedt, S. (2001). "U.S. Detention Centers Becoming Warehouses for Mentally Ill Youth." *Pittsburgh Post-Gazette* (July 15). (http://www.post-gazette.com/headlines/20010715surveyJP3.asp)

[28] Bazelon Center for Mental Health Law (2004). "Thousands of Children with Mental Illness Warehoused in Juvenile Detention Centers Awaiting Mental Health Services." July 7. (http://www.bazelon.org/newsroom/7-7-04jjhearing.htm)

[29] Ibid.; the summary points of the report were based on a survey conducted by the Special Investigations Division of the minority staff of the Government Reform Committee of the U.S. House of Representatives; see also "Report: Mentally Ill Teens 'Warehoused' in Jails." *Associated Press*, July 7, 2004. (http://adawatch.org/warehousing.htm)

[30] Human Rights Watch (1997). "High Country Lockup: Children in Confinement in Colorado." (http://www.hrw.org/reports/1997/usacol/)

[31] Oklahoma Department of Corrections. (http://www.state.ok.us/~oja/roc.htm)

[32] Census of Juveniles in Residential Placement Databook. Detailed Offense Profile by Placement Status for United States, 2003. (http://www.ojjdp.ncjrs.org/ojstatbb/cjrp/asp/Offense_Adj.asp)

[33] *Combating Violence: The National Juvenile Justice Action Plan*. (1996). Objective 1. Washington, DC: Office of Juvenile Justice and Delinquency Prevention. (http://ojjdp.ncjrs.org/action/sec1.htm)

[34] For a particularly gruesome account of actions within one of these "correctional" institutions see the movie *Sleepers* (staring Brad Pitt, Robert DeNiro, and Dustin Hoffman).

[35] Vinter, R. D. et al. (eds.). (1976). *Time Out: A National Study of Juvenile Correctional Programs*. Ann Arbor: National Assessment of Juvenile Corrections, The University of Michigan.

[36] Irwin, J. (1970). *The Felon*. Englewood Cliffs, NJ: Prentice-Hall, p. 74. These types still can be found in many prisons today. See Austin, J. and J. Irwin (2001). *It's About Time: America's Incarceration Binge* (3rd ed.). Belmont, CA: Wadsworth.

[37] Barker, G. E. and W. T. Adams. (1959). "The Social Structure of a Correctional Institution." *Journal of Criminal Law, Criminology and Police Science* 49: 417–499; Polsky, H. (1962). *Cottage Six*. New York: Russell Sage Foundation; Jesness, C. F. (1965). *The Fricot Ranch Study*. Sacramento: State of California, Department of the Youth Authority; Street, D., R. D. Vinter, and C. Perrow. (1966). *Organization for Treatment*. New York: Free Press.

[38] Bowker, L. (1977). *Prisoner Subcultures*. Lexington, MA: Heath, p. 100.

[39] Bartollas, C., S. H. Miller, and S. Dinitz. (1976). *Juvenile Victimization: The Institutional Paradox*. Beverly Hills: Sage Publications, Inc.

[40] Bartollas and Miller, *Juvenile Justice in America*, pp. 264–265.

[41] Ibid.

[42] Miller, Bartollas, and Dinitz, *Juvenile Victimization Revisited: A Study of TICO Fifteen Years Later* (unpublished manuscript), cited in Bartollas and Miller, pp. 265–266.

[43] Boyd, R. (June 19, 2003). CRIPA Investigation of Oakley and Columbia Training Schools in Raymond and Columbia, Mississippi. (http://www.usdoj.gov/crt/split/documents/oak_colu_miss_findinglet.pdf)

[44] Ibid., p. 1.

[45] Ibid., pp. 5, 7.

[46] Riak, J. (July 22, 2003). A Mississippi Gulag. (http://nospank.net/msgulag.htm)

[47] California Division of Juvenile Justice. Summary Fact Sheet. (http://www.cdcr.ca.gov/Reports_Research/summarys.html)

[48] Ibid. History. (http://www.cdcr.ca.gov/Divisions_Boards/DJJ/About_DJJ/History.html)

[49] Ibid. Mission Statement. (http://www.cdcr.ca.gov/Divisions_Boards/DJJ/About_DJJ/Mission.html)

[50] Ibid.

[51] Lerner, S. (1982). *The CYA Report, Part I: Conditions of Life at the California Youth Authority.* Bolinas: CA: Commonweal; Lerner, S. (1986). *The CYA Report, Part II: Bodily Harm—The Pattern of Fear and Violence at The California Youth Authority.* Bolinas: CA: Commonweal. The reports were funded by the Commonweal Research Institute.

[52] Lerner, S., P. Demuro, and A. Demuro (1988). *The CYA Report, Part III: Reforming the California Youth Authority—How to End Crowding, Diversify Treatment and Protect the Public without Spending More Money.* Bolinas: CA: Commonweal, p. 11.

[53] Byrnes, M., D. Macallair, and A. D. Shorter (2002). "Aftercare as Afterthought: Reentry and the California Youth Authority." San Francisco: Center on Juvenile and Criminal Justice.

[54] Among the criticisms issued by the Lerner reports (and reports on many other institutions over the years) is that many, if not most, youths did not commit the kinds of offenses that warranted such a strong sentence. There was always the belief among those in charge of sentencing that such offenders were "dangerous" and needed to be "sent up." The fact that the CYA has reduced the number of wards under its control apparently confirms these criticisms.

[55] California Legislative Analyst's Office (2004). "A Review of the California Youth Authority's Infrastructure." (http://www.lao.ca.gov/2004/cya/052504_cya.htm)

[56] Warren, J. (2004). "Disarray in Juvenile Prisons Jolts Capital." *Los Angeles Times* (Feb. 4).

[57] Ibid.

[58] Cannon, A. (2004). "Special Report: Juvenile Injustice." *US News and World Report* (August 3).

[59] de Sá, K. (2004). "Judge Orders Moratorium on Sending Juveniles to CYA Until Review." *San Jose Mercury News* (February 12); see also Bailey, D. and K. de Sá (2004). "Chief Vowing Major Change: Director Takes Big First Steps, But the Deepest Problems Await." *The San Jose Mercury News* (October 17). These and subsequent reports can be found on the Web site for the Center on Juvenile and Criminal Justice (http://cjcj.org/press/archive.php)

[60] Warren, J. (2004). "Attack by Prison Dog Revealed." *Los Angeles Times* (May 7); Warren, J. (2004). "State Youth Prisons on Road to Rehab." *Los Angeles Times* (November 17).

[61] Bell, J. and J. Stauring (2004). "Serious Problems Festering in Juvenile Justice System Require Serious Reforms." *Los Angeles Times* (May 2).

[62] Warren, J. (2004). "Shut Down State Youth Prisons, Experts Say." *Los Angeles Times* (September 22).

[63] Warren, "State Youth Prisons on Road to Rehab."

[64] Ibid.

[65] Ibid.

[66] Reiterman, T. (2005). "Auditors Rebuke Youth Authority." *Los Angeles Times* (January 4).

[67] Warren, J. (2005). "For Young Offenders, a Softer Approach." *Los Angeles Times* (February 1).

[68] Ibid.

[69] Sterngold, J. (2007). "State's Youth Prisons Mired in Hopelessness." *San Francisco Chronicle* (May 7), p. A1. (http://sfgate.com/cgi-bin/article.cgi?f=/c/a/2007/05/07/MNGNEPMD7K1.DTL)

[70] Ibid.

[71] Sterngold, J. (2007). "A New Approach to Help Young Offenders." *San Francisco Chronicle* (May 8), p. A13. (http://sfgate.com/cgi-bin/article.cgi?f=/c/a/2007/05/08/MNG4TPMNBM1.DTL)

[72] Ibid.

[73] Sterngold, J. (2007). "Juvenile Prison Reform Bill Reaches Governor's Desk." *San Franciso Chronicle* (August 22). (http://sfgate.com/cgi-bin/article.cgi?f=/c/a/2007/08/22/BAGADRNBSN5.DTL)

[74] Ibid.

[75] Ibid.

[76] Bortner, M. A. and L. Williams (1997). *Youth in Prison: We the People of Unit Four.* New York: Routledge, p. 2.

[77] Ibid.

[78] Ibid., p. 134.

[79] Ibid., p. 148.

[80] Ibid.

[81] Ibid., p. 152.

[82] Among the research documenting this includes: Clemmer, D. (1958). *The Prison Community.* New York: Holt, Rinehart & Winston; Wheeler, S. (1962). "A Study of Prisonization." In N. Johnston, L. Savitz, and M. E. Wolfgang (eds.), *Sociology of Punishment and Corrections.* New York: John Wiley; Goffman, E. (1961). *Asylums.* New York: Doubleday; Irwin, *The Felon*; Bowker, *Prisoner Subcultures*; Bartollas, Miller, and Dinitz, *Juvenile Victimization.*

[83] Bortner and Williams, *Youth in Prison*, p. 150.

[84] Ibid., p. 151.

[85] See Shelden, R. G. (1999). "Detention Diversion Advocacy: An Evaluation." *OJJDP Juvenile Justice Bulletin* (September). Here I use several different measurements of recidivism.

[86] Smith, T. (2002). "Juvenile Justice Agency Unable to Gauge Progress." *The Greenville News* (April 6). (http://greenvilleonline.com/news/2002/04/06/2002040621705.htm)

[87] Office of the Legislative Auditor, State of Minnesota (1995). "Residential Facilities for Juvenile Offenders." February 15. (www.auditor.leg.state.mn.us/ped/1995/juv.htm)

[88] State of Oregon, Oregon Youth Authority (2003). "Previously Incarcerated Juveniles in Oregon's Adult Corrections System." Salem: State of Oregon, Office of Economic Analysis, May 23. (www.oea.das.state.or.us)

[89] For a good review of "age of onset" see Dryfoos, J. G. (1990). *Adolescents at Risk: Prevalence and Prevention.* New York: Oxford University Press.

[90] Vinter et al., *Time Out*; Beck, J. L. and P. B. Hoffman (1976). "Time Served and Release Performance: A Research Note." *Journal of Research in Crime and Delinquency* 13: 127–132; Orsagh, T. and J. R. Chen (1988). "The Effect of Time Served on Recidivism: An Interdisciplinary Theory." *Journal of Quantitative Criminology* 4: 155–171; Makkai, T., J. Ratcliffe, K. Veraar, and L. Collins (2004). "ACT Recidivist Offenders." Canberra: Australian Institute of Criminology (http://www.aic.gov.au/publications/rpp/54/09_appendix1.html)

[91] Department of the Attorney General, State of Hawaii (February 2001). "Incarcerated Juveniles and Recidivism in Hawaii." Honolulu: State of Hawaii.

[92] Linster, R. (nd). "Frequency of Arrest of the Young, Chronic, Serious Offender Using Two Male Cohorts Parole by the California Youth Authority, 1981–1982 and 1986–1987." Washington, DC: National Institute of Justice Data Resources Program. Cited in Byrnes et al. "Aftercare as Afterthought."

[93] Bailey, B. and G. Palmer (2004). "High Rearrest Rate: Three-Fourths of Wards Released Over 13 Years Held on New Charges." *San Jose Mercury News* (October 17). (http://cjcj.org/press/high_rearrest.html)

[94] See, for example, Dryfoos, *Adolescents at Risk.*

[95] Byrnes, Macallair, and Shorter, "Aftercare as Afterthought."

[96] An interesting concept is what some researchers have called the *Post-Incarceration Syndrome*, which has been defined as "set of symptoms that are present in many currently incarcerated and recently released prisoners caused by prolonged incarceration in environments of punishment with few opportunities for education, job training, or rehabilitation. The severity of symptoms is related to the level of coping skills prior to incarceration, the length of incarceration, the restrictiveness of the incarceration environment, the number and severity of institutional episodes of abuse, the number and

duration of episodes of solitary confinement, and the degree of involvement in educational, vocational, and rehabilitation programs." Mid-Atlantic Technology Transfer Center (March 1, 2001). "Post Incarceration Syndrome." *Addiction Exchange* 3(4). (http://www.mid-attc.org/addex3_4.htm) Terence T. Gorski (www.cenaps.com)

[97] Byrnes, Macallair, and Shorter, "Aftercare as Afterthought," p. iv.

[98] Seldes, G. (1985). *The Great Thoughts*. New York: Ballantine Books, p. 404.

2

Jailing Minority Kids

Randall G. Shelden

"You could abort every black baby in this country, and your crime rate would go down." —William Bennett[1]

"What was false? Well, as a matter of fact, is it not a fact that the per-capita crime rate among blacks is higher than whites? What is false here?" —Brit Hume[2]

As the two quotations above reveal, we live in a racist society. Forty years ago, the Kerner Commission reported on the rioting that took place in several cities during the mid-1960s. It observed that the United States is actually two societies: one white and one black, separate and unequal.[3] In the first decade of the twenty-first century we find that the conditions that created the rioting of the 1960s have become worse. Technological advances, the globalization of the economy, the movement of capital (often to third world countries), and the shift of the economy away from manufacturing to information and services have created hardships for most Americans and particularly for those already situated at the bottom of the social order. The effects have been especially devastating for minority youth.[4]

Structural Conditions

According to the Justice Mapping Center, the majority of people convicted of crimes come from a few, very concentrated neighborhoods. "If you have ever wondered just how hard it is for kids from broken neighborhoods to avoid prison, a glance at data compiled by the Justice Mapping Center gives an easy answer: It's even harder than you think."[5] More than 50% of adult male inmates from New York City come from 14 districts; 6.5% of Arizona inmates come from one community in Phoenix (1% of Arizona's total population). Eric Cadora of the Justice Mapping Center refers to "million-dollar blocks" because of the expense to keep people from those areas behind bars. He points out that programs to target the

Written especially for *Juvenile Justice in America: Problems and Prospects*.

problems of the people who live in those communities would save the state millions of dollars. "Criminal justice isn't what makes people behave. You strengthen the institutions so people have a stake in things."[6]

The distribution of wealth and income remains concentrated at the top, with 1% of the population having about 48% of all financial wealth. The *Gini coefficient* measures income disparity, with 1.0 representing one person having all the income and 0.00 meaning everyone has the same income. The coefficient for the United States is .464, up from .353 in 1970.[7] The racial differences in both income and wealth remain wide, with whites far surpassing blacks and Hispanics. For instance, as of 2002 the median net worth (assets minus debts) for white households stood at $88,651; for black households it was $5,988; for Hispanic households it was $7,932.[8]

Poverty

In 1960, manufacturing industries employed 31% of the labor force; by 1994, the percentage decreased to 15.9, and in 2006 it was 10.8.[9] Manufacturing jobs had provided an opportunity for those without a college degree or advanced skills to earn decent wages and benefits. In 2006, the U.S. Census Bureau listed the poverty threshold for a family of four as $20,614.[10] The percentage of white families living in poverty was 9.3, compared to 25.3 of black families and 21.5 of Hispanic families.[11] The median income of all black families was $31,969, compared to $50,673 for whites and $37,781 for Hispanics.[12]

While location affects the amount of income necessary to meet basic needs, families generally need an income twice the poverty level to make ends meet. For a family of four, the average minimum income would need to be $41,300. Families above the poverty threshold but below this number are referred to as low income.[13] There are 8.8 million children aged 12 through 17 who live in low-income families. Younger children are even more likely to live in low-income families; 43% of children under age six (more than 10 million) live in low-income families. The percentages increase for black and Hispanic children under age 6: 64% (2.2 million) of black children and 63% of Hispanic children (3.6 million).

Increasing numbers of households consist of a woman and her children, contributing to what is sometimes called the *feminization of poverty* (a somewhat misleading term in that it might be interpreted as suggesting that the problem is racially neutral). In 1960 only 6% of all families with one or more children were headed by a woman; by 2005 the percentage was 23.4 (versus 4.7% of households headed by the father). The mother was the head of the household in half of the African-American families compared to 16% for white families and 25% for Hispanic families.[14] In 2004, 29% of families with a black female head of household had incomes below the poverty level compared to 8.1% of families with a white female head of household, and 20.5% of families with a Hispanic female head of household.[15]

Children in single-parent families are more likely to live in poverty. Children living with their mothers in 2005 were more than twice as likely to live in poverty as those living with their fathers (41% versus 18%).[16] While the number of juveniles living in poverty were at the lowest levels since the mid-1970s, black and Hispanic juveniles were three times more likely to live in poverty as white juveniles in 2005.[17] The percentage of persons under the age of 18 living in poverty was 18 versus 13% for all people in the United States.[18]

Education

Young African Americans and other minorities have suffered the most from recent *structural economic* changes. The shift away from manufacturing to an information and service economy has displaced those without sufficient education, often leaving only temporary or low-paying jobs as an alternative. In 2004, the percentage of householders below the poverty level without a high school diploma was: 22.2% white; 37.4% black, and 30.8% Hispanic. For those with a college degree, the percentages were: 2.5% white; 6.8% black, and 3.9% Hispanic.[19] In 2005, the median income of people without a high school degree was: $12,686 for whites; $10,617 for blacks; and $15,165 for Hispanics. For those with a college degree, the median income was: $40,537 for whites, $39,947 for blacks, and $35,843 for Hispanics.[20] Young African-American males are in the group that has the least amount of education. Thus, they are the least likely to have the education necessary to compete for the newly created jobs in areas such as finance, computer technology, and other professional and technical careers (e.g., engineering, law, the sciences).

Employment

A commission that studied the riots[21] following the Rodney King beating verdicts noted the declining investments in inner cities on the part of the federal government. For example, between 1981 and 1992 the amount invested in job training fell from $23 billion to $8 billion. The amounts for local economic development fell from $21 billion to $14 billion; "general revenue sharing" went from $6 billion to zero; and federal support for housing was cut by 80%.[22]

While blacks made up 11% of the labor force in 2006, they accounted for 22% of the unemployed and 28% of the long-term unemployed (27 weeks or longer). The Department of Labor Statistics also tracks what they term "marginally attached," defined as "persons who were available for work and had searched for work during the prior 12 months but who were not currently looking for work." Blacks accounted for 25% of the marginally attached.[23] Hispanics made up 14% of the labor force, 15% of the unemployed, and 13% of the marginally attached. They also accounted for 22% of part-time employment.[24] The unemployment rate of blacks with a college degree (2.8%) was 10 percentage points lower than the rate

for blacks with less than a high school diploma (12.8%). The unemployment rate for Hispanic college graduates (2.2%) was about 3 points below
that of Hispanics with less than a high school diploma (5.5%). The unemployment rate for white college graduates (2.0%) was about 4 points
below that of whites with less than a high school diploma (5.9%).[25]

Unemployment and underemployment continue to plague the lives of
black youths, resulting in greater involvement in petty crimes, gang activity, and drug dealing. In California, a state already reeling with huge budget problems and job losses, the unemployment rate for blacks without a
high school diploma was 15.5%; even for those with a high school diploma
the rate was still high at 9.4%.[26] Employment in New York City was
equally grim for minorities and even more disheartening when those not
usually counted as unemployed are included: 51.8% for black men, 57.1%
for black women, 75.7% for white men, and 65.7% for Latino men.[27]

> Official unemployment figures, of course, greatly understate the
> actual number of adults without jobs. The definition doesn't include
> discouraged people who have stopped looking for work, underem-
> ployed part-timers, students, or those in prison or other institutions.
> In New York City, scarcely half of African-American men between 16
> and 65 had jobs in 2003. . . . Manufacturing job losses in particular
> have hit black workers harder than white workers. In 2000, there
> were 2 million African Americans working in factory jobs. Blacks
> comprised 10.1% of all manufacturing workers, about the same as
> the black share of the overall workforce. Then 300,000 of those jobs,
> or 15%, disappeared. White workers lost 1.7 million factory jobs, but
> that was just 10% of the number they held before the recession. By
> the end of 2003, the share of all factory jobs held by African Ameri-
> cans had fallen to 9.6%.[28]

Disenfranchised Communities

The city of Los Angeles is not unlike many others in the country. The
failure of the "American Dream" to satisfy the needs and wants of people
can be clearly seen in LA's skid row, literally a stone's throw away from
symbols of wealth common to many urban areas. (The city of Las Vegas,
where I live, is perhaps the most extreme expression of massive symbols
of wealth right next to impoverishment.) Zelenne Cardenas, the director
of a human services organization called Social Model Recovery Systems
Inc., provides a searing portrait of poverty in a disenfranchised community.[29] She notes that since 1990 the proportion of impoverished has
gone from 1% to 15%, while the proportion of women has grown to one-
third, up from about 18%.

> Some of the children of skid row sleep on the streets with their fami-
> lies. Others live in dilapidated welfare hotels infested with rats and
> cockroaches. Entire families sleep in a small, single room intended for
> one person. Often there's no kitchen, and the bathroom is down the

hall. Getting to school involves a two-hour bus ride, not to mention dealing with teachers and kids who don't understand that your clothes are dirty because there's no laundromat in your neighborhood.

Worst of all, the children of skid row are a captive audience, propositioned by sexual predators and exposed to the most degenerate forms of human behavior. They watch as paramedics extract yet another comatose individual from a portable toilet with a needle still sticking out of his arm. Used condoms and hypodermic needles litter the sidewalks where the children live and play.

The violence that most of us see only on TV is part of these children's daily lives. This summer, several of the children in our community witnessed the murder of a neighbor—a mother stabbed 17 times in broad daylight just outside the hotel where they live.

When disputes flare up, violence is the first resort. The children, who have nowhere else to go—no backyard or park or community center—are right in the line of fire. It is no wonder that so many of them anesthetize themselves with drugs and drown their sorrows with alcohol.[30]

Skid Row in Los Angeles covers 50 square blocks; 12,000 homeless people live there, the largest concentration of homeless in the United States.

Skid Row evolved as the place to bring together those who needed help—alcoholics, addicts, and the mentally ill—and the social service providers who could give it to them. But after more than 100 years, it has become a containment zone for some of society's most desperate and a magnet for those who prey on them.[31]

The primary response of law enforcement has been to arrest youths and take them to the juvenile court, where they will be "held accountable." We create and sustain social conditions that give rise to gangs and violence and then blame those who respond with predictable behavior. The seventeenth-century poet John Milton once commented that we punch people's eyes out and then reproach them for their blindness.

Processing Rejected Minority Youth

What do we do with the youth who become part of the "surplus population" within the inner cities? Those who have not yet entered the juvenile justice system frequently live in segregated communities and attend poor schools (which sometimes resemble prisons). Once they make contact with the system, evidence of racial bias begins early. It frequently determines how far a youth will be processed through the juvenile justice system: from formal arrest by the police, placement in a "detention center" (a juvenile justice term used instead of jail), to commitment in a juvenile "correctional facility" (a term substituted for prison). Attitudes about race and drugs have heavily influenced this process.

Race and Arrests

It is impossible to talk about juvenile court processing without reference to race and drug offenses. Race often plays an indirect role in the police decision to arrest. One factor contributing to the decision may be the *visibility* of the offense. Behavior in urban neighborhoods, where many minority youth reside, is far more likely to take place where it is visible to the police.

Expectations about demeanor also contribute to the decision to arrest.

> The occupational culture constructed by the police consists of long-standing rules of thumb, a somewhat special language and ideology that help edit a member's everyday experiences, shared standards of relevance, matter-of-fact prejudices, [and] models for street-level etiquette and demeanor.[32]

If the youth appears cooperative and respectful, no formal action will be taken. All other things being equal, if the youth is hostile or, in police parlance, "flunks the attitude test," formal action generally follows. Race, class, and gender play a role here; lower class and minority males are far more likely than white males and females to flunk the attitude test.[33]

Another factor could be the belief that minority youth are more likely to use illegal drugs. However, contrary to popular assumption, at all three grade levels African-American students have substantially lower rates of use of most licit and illicit drugs than do whites. These include any illicit drug use, most of the specific illicit drugs, alcohol, and cigarettes.[34]

Race and the War on Drugs

Surveys on drug usage have consistently shown that there are few differences among whites and minorities in the use of illegal drugs. Table 1 shows the results of the Youth Risk Behavior Surveillance Survey of high school students between 1995 and 2005 for marijuana and cocaine. The Monitoring the Future Survey in 2006 found that black students in the twelfth grade reported lower rates of usage (whether lifetime, annual, 30-day, or daily) of almost all drugs (legal and illegal) than white or Hispanic twelfth graders. The rates were also generally lower for black students in the eighth and tenth grades. By the twelfth grade, white students had the highest lifetime and annual use rates for marijuana, hallucinogens, MDMA, other narcotics, amphetamines, sedatives (barbiturates), tranquilizers, alcohol, and tobacco.[35] Given the lower rates of usage, the differential arrest rates of blacks (30.1% in 2006)[36] for drug offenses require explanation. It may be the result of differential police policies (e.g., targeting low-income, mostly minority neighborhoods) or the location of some offenses in more visible places (especially drug use). Regardless of the reasons, studies have shown race to be a very important factor.[37]

Jerome Miller found that young African-American males have received the brunt of law enforcement efforts to "crack down on drugs."

Table 1 Percentage of High School Students Who Used Selected Illicit Drugs by Sex, Race/Ethnicity, and Grade, Youth Risk Behavior Survey, 1995–2003

Drug Use Behavior and Year	Sex		Race/Ethnicity			Grade Level				All Groups
	Male	Female	White, non-Hispanic	Black, non-Hispanic	Hispanic	9th	10th	11th	12th	
Lifetime marijuana[2]										
1995	46.2	39.4	40.5	47.2	49.2	33.8	41.4	45.8	47.0	42.4
1997	50.7	42.9	45.4	52.2	49.5	38.8	45.9	50.3	52.4	47.1
1999	51.0	43.4	45.9	48.6	51.0	34.8	49.1	49.7	58.4	47.2
2001	46.5	38.4	42.8	40.2	44.7	32.7	41.7	47.2	51.5	42.4
2003	42.7	37.6	39.8	43.3	42.7	30.7	40.4	44.5	48.5	40.2
2005	40.9	35.9	38.0	40.7	42.6	29.3	37.4	42.3	47.6	38.4
Current marijuana[1]										
1995	28.4	22.0	24.6	28.6	27.8	20.9	25.6	27.6	26.2	25.3
1997	30.2	21.4	25.0	28.2	28.6	23.6	25.0	29.3	26.6	26.2
1999	30.8	22.6	26.4	26.4	28.2	21.7	27.8	26.7	31.5	26.7
2001	27.9	20.0	24.4	21.8	24.6	19.4	24.8	25.8	26.9	23.9
2003	25.1	19.3	21.7	23.9	23.8	18.5	22.0	24.1	25.8	22.4
2005	22.1	18.2	20.3	20.4	23.0	17.4	20.2	21.0	22.8	20.2
Lifetime cocaine use[2]										
1995	8.8	5.0	6.5	2.0	16.0	5.7	7.5	7.2	7.4	7.0
1997	9.1	7.2	8.0	1.9	14.4	6.7	7.5	9.1	9.2	8.2
1999	10.7	8.4	9.9	2.2	15.3	5.8	9.9	9.9	13.7	9.5
2001	10.3	8.4	9.9	2.1	14.7	7.2	8.6	10.4	12.1	9.4
2003	9.5	7.7	8.7	3.2	12.5	6.8	8.5	9.0	10.5	8.7
2005	8.4	6.8	7.7	2.3	12.2	6.0	7.2	8.7	8.9	7.6

(continued)

Table 1 *(continued)*

Drug Use Behavior and Year	Sex		Race/Ethnicity			Grade Level				All Groups
	Male	Female	White, non-Hispanic	Black, non-Hispanic	Hispanic	9th	10th	11th	12th	
Current cocaine use[1]										
1995	4.3	1.8	2.6	1.3	7.5	3.1	2.5	3.6	3.1	3.1
1997	4.0	2.4	3.1	0.7	6.2	3.9	2.6	3.1	3.5	3.3
1999	5.2	2.9	4.1	1.1	6.7	3.4	3.7	4.5	4.8	4.0
2001	4.7	3.7	4.2	1.3	7.1	3.7	4.2	4.4	4.5	4.2
2003	4.6	3.5	3.8	2.2	5.7	3.6	3.7	4.1	4.7	4.1
2005	4.0	2.8	3.2	1.5	6.1	3.0	3.1	3.6	3.8	3.4

[1] Used one or more times during the past 30 days.
[2] Ever tried any form of cocaine, including powder, crack, or freebase.

Sources: National Drug Control Strategy Update 2003, February 2003 http://www.whitehousedrugpolicy.gov/publications/policy/ndcs04/table11.doc; Centers for Disease Control and Prevention. *Youth Risk Behavior Surveillance—United States 2005.* Surveillance Summaries, June 9, 2006. MMWR 55 (No. SS-5). http://www.cdc.gov/mmwr/PDF/SS/SS5505.pdf

He notes that in Baltimore, for example, African Americans were being arrested at a rate six times that of whites, and more than 90% of the arrests were for possession.[38] By the age of 17, the drug referral rate for black juveniles was twice the rate for whites.[39]

Selection Bias

Regardless of whether race, class, or demeanor is statistically more relevant, one fact remains: growing numbers of African-American youths are finding themselves within the juvenile justice system. They are more likely to be detained, more likely to have their cases petitioned to go before a judge, more likely to be waived to the adult system and more likely to be institutionalized than their white counterparts.[40]

In a meta-analysis of existing research, Carl Pope and William Feyer-herm found effects within at least one of the stages of juvenile justice processing that adversely affected outcomes for minorities in two-thirds of the studies they reviewed.

> In the last three decades, a body of literature has accumulated which focuses on the problem of selection bias in juvenile justice systems. Much of this literature suggests that processing decisions in many state and local juvenile justice systems are not racially neutral: Minority youth are more likely than majority youth to become involved in the system. The effects of race may be felt at various decision points, they may be direct or indirect, and they may accumulate as youth continue through the system.[41]

Carl Pope, Rick Lovell and Heidi Hsia reviewed research from 1989 through 2001 and found continued evidence of racial bias.[42] The Office of Juvenile Justice and Delinquency Prevention reported in 2006 that racial disparities "can be found at any stage of processing within the juvenile justice system." The disparity "is most pronounced at arrest" and "effects accumulate as youth are processed through the justice system."[43]

As noted in figure 1, African-American youth constitute only 16% of the total population; they are 26% of those arrested, 37% of those detained, 35% of those sent to adult court and 58% of those who end up in state prison.[44]

Quite often the discrepancies are even starker when we look at individual cities and states. In Columbia, South Carolina, African Americans make up less than 20% of the total juvenile population, yet they constitute 60% of all juvenile arrests.[45] In fact, between 1995 and 2003 the number of black youths arrested increased, while the number of whites arrested decreased. The 1996 arrest figures were split almost evenly between whites and blacks (50% black, 49% white), but in 2003 it was 60% black and only 39% white. The police concentrated their patrols in increasing numbers in a 12-square block of mostly black residents. Commensurate with the increased arrests was a much greater detention rate of black youths.

Figure I   African American Proportion of Youth

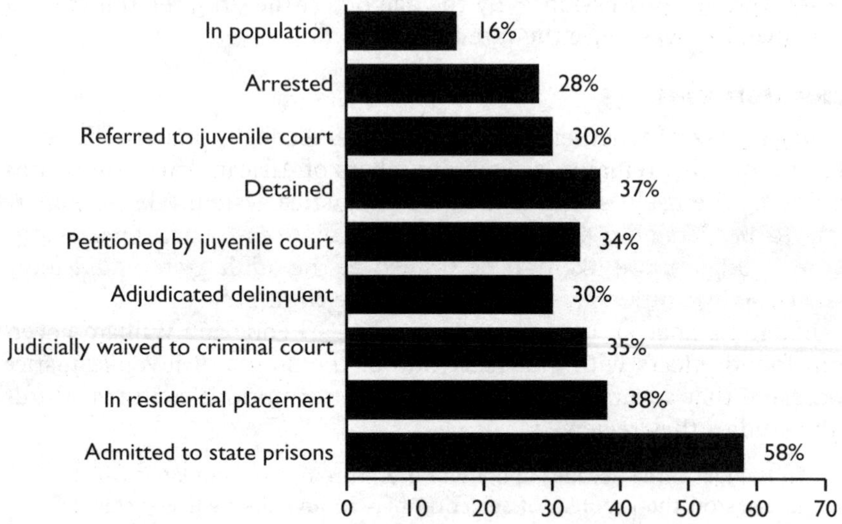

Note: Reflects 2003 population, referrals to juvenile court, detentions, petitions by juvenile court, waivers, residential placement; 2004 arrests; and 2002 admissions to state prisons.

Source: National Council on Crime and Delinquency (2007). *And Justice for Some: Differential Treatment of Youth of Color in the Justice System*, p. 37 (http://www.nccd-crc.org/nccd/pubs/2007jan_justice_for_some.pdf).

A study by the ACLU on juvenile justice processing in Massachusetts found that in 2002 although minority juveniles constituted 23% of the total population and 27% of all arrests, they were 63% of those committed to an institution, up from 57% in 1993.[46] A study in Pennsylvania showed that in 2001 although minority youth constituted 39% of those arrested, they were 62% of those confined in secure facilities.[47]

Jeffrey Butts, a researcher at the Urban Institute, commented on the cumulative effect of disparities.

> At each stage of the process, there's a slight empirical bias. And the problem is that the slight empirical bias at every stage of the decision-making accumulates. By the time you reach the end, you have all minorities in the deep end of the system.[48]

Race and Detention

Race figures prominently in the decision to detain, despite policies designed to curtail minority overrepresentation. A California study, although somewhat dated, found almost half (48.5%) of the African-America youth referred to juvenile court were detained, compared to only 30.6% of white youths. Their overall rate of detention was three times that for whites. In fact, no matter what the offense, African-American youths were more likely to be detained than white youths; this was especially the case for those charged with drug offenses, as 72% of African-American youths charged with felony drug offenses were detained compared to only 43% of white youths. *More dramatically, of those charged with misdemeanor drug offenses, less than 1% of whites were detained, compared to almost 30% of African Americans.* Even when considering probation status, sex, age, and number of offenses, blacks were more likely to be detained.[49]

The most current national figures reveal similar patterns (see table 2). Regardless of offense, African-American youths are far more likely to be detained than their white counterparts. For all delinquent offenses, black youths are about 4 times more likely to be detained (a rate of 214 versus 47), while for personal crimes the ratio is over 5:1. The differences are also very pronounced for drug offenses, with black youth more than 4 times more likely to be detained.

Youth in "Correctional Institutions"

As suggested above, incarceration is a fate that awaits many minority youths. The percentage of incarcerated youth who are racial minorities has risen steadily over the years. The national percentage of minorities in training schools was 23% in 1950, 32% in 1960, 40% in 1970, and 62% in 2003.[50] It is interesting to note that the majority of youths confined in *private* facilities are white. This is no doubt because most of the costs are paid for by family members, usually through their insurance.

Not surprisingly, the overall *rate* of incarceration was considerably higher for minorities. The latest (2003) census of committed juveniles (see table 3 on p. 45) reveals such stark contrasts as: (1) the overall rate for blacks was 528, compared to a rate of 238 for Hispanics and only 140 for whites; (2) even considering the most serious offense charged, commitment rates for minorities far exceeded those of whites; this was especially the case for drug offenses, where the black rate was five times greater than for whites and more than double that for Hispanics; (3) in every other offense category, whites had the lowest rate and blacks had the highest, with Hispanics in the middle. The distribution of these rates, with blacks first, Hispanics second, and whites third, reminds me of a phrase heard repeatedly during the civil rights movement of the 1960s: "If you're white, you're alright, if you're brown, stick around, if you're black, stay back."

California ranked sixth in the United States for its incarceration rate for juveniles in 2003.[51] In 2007, the California Division of Juvenile Justice (DJJ) wards were 51% Hispanic, 31% African American, and 13% white.[52] The national rate of commitment per 100,000 juveniles in 2003 was 754 for blacks, 348 for Hispanics, and 190 for whites.[53] In California, the rates were 1,246 for blacks, 448 for Hispanics, and 217 for whites.

Table 2   Offense Profile of Detained Residents by Sex and Race/Ethnicity for United States, 2003 (Rate per 100,000 juveniles)

Most Serious Offense	Detained Total	Sex		Race/Ethnicity				
		Male	Female	White	Black	Hispanic	American Indian	Asian
Total	83	132	33	47	214	106	124	37
Delinquency	79	127	29	44	205	101	115	35
Person	26	42	9	13	73	31	31	14
Violent Crime Index*	16	28	4	7	49	23	17	11
Other Person	10	14	5	6	24	9	13	3
Property	20	33	6	12	49	23	34	9
Property Crime Index**	16	27	5	9	41	19	28	7
Other Property	4	6	1	2	8	5	5	2
Drug	7	11	2	4	17	8	9	2
Public order	9	14	3	4	23	11	13	3
Technical violation	19	28	9	11	42	27	29	7
Status offense	4	5	3	3	9	5	9	1

* Includes criminal homicide, violent sexual assault, robbery, and aggravated assault.
** Includes burglary, theft, auto theft, and arson.

Source: Sickmund, Melissa, Sladky, T. J., and Kang, Wei. (2005) "Census of Juveniles in Residential Placement Databook." Online. Available: http://www.ojjdp.ncjrs.org/ojstatbb/cjrp/

Table 3   Offense Profile of Committed Residents by Sex and Race/Ethnicity for United States, 2003 (Rate per 100,000 juveniles)

Most Serious Offense	Committed Total	Sex		Race/Ethnicity					
		Male	Female	White	Black	Hispanic	American Indian	Asian
Total	219	370	60	140	528	238	368	76
Delinquency	208	358	52	132	504	232	337	73
Person	78	135	19	47	200	85	127	28
Violent Crime Index*	53	96	8	31	135	61	86	20
Other Person	25	39	12	16	65	24	41	8
Property	65	113	14	44	146	70	101	24
Property Crime Index**	54	95	12	37	124	58	88	21
Other Property	10	18	2	7	22	12	13	3
Drug	19	32	5	10	50	22	27	5
Public order	22	38	4	14	48	27	48	7
Technical violation	25	40	9	16	60	28	34	9
Status offense	11	13	9	9	24	5	30	4

* Includes criminal homicide, violent sexual assault, robbery, and aggravated assault.

** Includes burglary, theft, auto theft, and arson.

Source: Sickmund, Melissa, Sladky, T.J., and Kang, Wei. (2005) "Census of Juveniles in Residential Placement Databook." Online. Available: http://www.ojjdp.ncjrs.org/ojstatbb/cjrp/

Barry Krisberg and James Austin studied the juvenile justice system in California in 1993 and found that the rate of commitment to a private facility was 467 for blacks, compared to only 153 for whites. The rate of commitment to secure county facilities was 1,114 for blacks compared to only 294 for whites. Commitment to secure institutions (juvenile prisons) was 529 for blacks compared to 47 for whites. Regardless of the nature of the offense, current probation status, sex, age, or the number of offenses, African Americans were far more likely than whites to be committed. Like the figures for detention, sentences for drug offenses were dramatic: for felony drug offenses African Americans were *seven times more likely than whites to be committed*.[54] (See the article that follows for more information on commitment in California.)

The disparities are also prevalent in Nevada, where the 2003 rate of juvenile commitment was 958 for blacks, 332 for Hispanics, and 289 for whites.[55] In 1999 Summit View Correctional Center opened in North Las Vegas to house offenders classified as "Level IV"—the highest classification in the state based on the alleged degree of "dangerousness." This new category was based on a point system—the youth's prior record determined the point total. The higher the points, the higher the classification. Careful investigation by the author found no scientific rationale for the point system, and no research was cited to legitimate the system. Not surprisingly, the higher the level of classification, the greater the percentage of minorities. Summit View was built and operated by a private company called Correctional Services Corporation. Within one year of opening, the prison experienced a number of problems, including too many empty beds. The state could not find enough "dangerous" youth to qualify for Level IV (in fact, for a time the prison "borrowed" a few "Level III" youths from the detention center at the juvenile court in Las Vegas). They did, however, find a large number of minority youths to house in this prison; 80% of the youths were minorities.[56]

It is apparent from the available evidence that juvenile detention centers and youth "correctional" institutions have become part of the "new American apartheid." The rate differentials for drug offenses in tables 2 and 3, in particular, demonstrate differential treatment. Part of the explanation lies in who is targeted for arrest in the war on drugs; like their adult counterparts, black juveniles are the most heavily targeted. In 1972 white youths had a *higher* arrest rate for drugs than blacks, but by the early 1980s (at roughly the beginning of the "war on drugs") the difference was reversed. By 1995 the arrest rate for black youths was almost three times greater than for whites—an increase greater than 400% in arrest rates for black youth from 1972 to 1995.[57]

In every state except Vermont, the custody rate for black juvenile offenders exceeded the rate for whites in 2003. The custody rates varied widely by state, with an average ratio of 1 white youth for every 2.6 minority youth. The highest custody rate for blacks was South Dakota

(3,199) and the lowest was Vermont (zero). For Hispanics, the highest rate again was South Dakota (1,449) and the lowest was Alaska (zero).[58] Detention centers and long-term secure facilities held the largest proportions of minority offenders—each holding more than one-third of the minorities in custody. More than 59,000 (61% of the custody population nationwide) minority offenders were in juvenile facilities; black youths accounted for 38% of all offenders in custody.[59] Blacks accounted for 42% of committed drug offenders and Hispanics for 20%. A substantial proportion of all youths were held for technical violations of probation, parole, or court orders (about 15% of all juvenile offenders in custody—higher than any other offense category).[60]

Giving Up on Delinquent Youth: Transfer to Adult Court

Waiver and *certification* are the terms used to designate the transfer of jurisdiction from juvenile to adult court. (In 13 states, all 17-year olds are legally adults and are prosecuted in criminal court.)[61] In general, the transfer is based on the belief that an offender is too dangerous to be treated as a juvenile or judged not amenable to treatment. Legally speaking, the youth's age is waived and he or she is certified as an adult and transferred to the criminal system.[62] Every state has some provisions for transferring offenders to adult courts, but the minimum age varies. Four states allow the certification of 10-year-old juveniles—Indiana, Kansas, Vermont and Wisconsin. The minimum age is 12 in Colorado, Missouri and Montana. The limit is 13 in Georgia, Illinois, Mississippi, New Hampshire, New York, North Carolina, Oklahoma, and Wyoming.[63]

One of the first Supreme Court rulings on judicial waiver was the 1966 case of *Kent v. United States*. In that case, the Court ruled that a juvenile must be given a hearing and is entitled to counsel—who must receive a written statement giving the reasons for the waiver and access to all records and reports used in reaching the decision to waive. While state laws differ, most state laws have a variation or combination of requirements from *Kent v. United States* that meet specific age and serious crime criteria. The crime must be serious, aggressive, violent, premeditated, and done in a willful manner. Further, the crime must be against persons, with a seriousness of personal injury. Juveniles are evaluated on their sophistication or maturity, which is determined by external factors (such as emotional attitude and the juvenile's record). The evaluation must conclude that the public is adequately protected, in that if the juvenile is not treated and punished as an adult, the public is not protected from future victimizations. All of these transfer processes authorize juvenile courts to designate juvenile delinquency cases to adult criminal proceedings. All waivers must meet some aspect in any given case, a minimum age, a specified type or level of offense, serious record of previous delinquency, or a combination of these three criteria. Waivers may be initiated by prosecutors by filing a motion or juvenile court initiation.[64]

There are three main methods of certifying a youth as an adult. One is known as *legislative waiver* or *statutorial exclusion*. State legislatures pass laws that automatically exclude certain offenses from juvenile court jurisdiction. The most common exclusion is homicide, although in some states other crimes against the person and some drug crimes also automatically waive the offender to adult court.

Another method is known as *judicial waiver*. This is the most commonly used method, and it begins at intake and involves input from key staff members, such as probation officers, defense attorneys, and prosecutors. Criteria include: the maturity level of the youth; relationships with parents, school and the community; whether the youth is considered "dangerous"; and whether the youth can be helped by the services available in the court and the community.

The third method is known as *discretionary waiver*. In this case the statutes give juvenile court prosecutors the authority to decide whether or not to certify a youth as an adult. Three states (Nevada, Vermont, and Wyoming) allow charges to be filed in either the juvenile or the adult court. States specify broad standards to be applied for consideration of a waiver. Some state legislation utilizes waivers when public safety or interest requires it or when the juvenile does not seem responsive to rehabilitation. Many states combine these standards. For instance, a waiver in the District of Columbia requires adult prosecution of a juvenile if it is in the interest of the public welfare and security, and there are no prospects for rehabilitation. In contrast, Kansas allows waivers whenever the court finds "good cause," while Missouri and Virginia allow waivers when the juvenile is not a "proper subject" for treatment. In 1997, Hawaii lowered the age limit for discretionary waivers, adding language that allows a waiver of a minor at any age (previous 16) if charged with first- or second-degree murder (or attempts) and there is no evidence that the person is committable to an institution for the mentally defective or mentally ill.[65]

The statutes of fourteen states provide mandatory waivers in cases that meet certain age, offense, or other criteria. In these states, the proceedings are initiated in juvenile court, sending the case to the adult criminal court. All states with mandatory waivers specify age and offense requirements. Ohio requires that a juvenile who commits any criminal offense at the age of 14 or higher and meets certain legislative requirements must be waived to criminal court. West Virginia requires that a juvenile must be 14 and has committed specific felonies before their case is waived to criminal court. Other states (Delaware and Indiana) do not specify an age. In Connecticut, the law stipulates that where the mandatory waiver provision applies, the juvenile's counsel is not permitted to make any argument or file a motion to oppose transfer, arguably a due process violation. The court can make a probable cause finding without notice, a hearing, or any participation on the part of the juvenile or their attorney.

Although these provisions of juvenile transfer to criminal court are generally believed to be responses to a perceived increase in juvenile violence, a large number of laws also include prosecution for nonviolent offenses. Most often arson and burglary (21 states) and drug offenses (19 states) committed by a juvenile may be prosecuted in criminal court. Nine states authorize or mandate prosecution for escape (Arkansas, Illinois, Michigan, and Oregon), soliciting a minor to join a street gang (Arkansas), "aggravated driving under the influence" (Arizona), auto theft (New Jersey), perjury (Texas), and treason (West Virginia). Further, many states allow or require transfers for misdemeanors, ordinance violations, and summary statute violations, such as fish and game violations.[66]

Judicial waivers and prosecutorial discretion are often arbitrary; they fluctuate from judge to judge or jurisdiction to jurisdiction. There are no consistent patterns.[67] One study of judicial waivers in Florida between 1981 and 1984 found that most of the juveniles waived to adult court were predominately low-risk and property offenders.[68] These juveniles were not accused of committing a violent crime. Legislative waivers often reflect perceived public opinion, changing values and norms, and a "get tough" attitude toward juvenile crime.[69] An even more sinister problem is that of racism. The disturbing fact is that African-American youth are proportionately more likely to be transferred.

Targeting Minorities

By 2003, the racial proportions were fairly similar for petitioned and judicially waived cases. African-American youth represented a slightly larger proportion of waived cases than petitioned cases (35% versus 34%). The likelihood of waiver for petitioned delinquency cases was slightly greater for African-American youth (0.8%) than for white youth (0.7%). The pattern varied somewhat with the type of offense. While white youths were 69% of the cases petitioned, they were only 58% of the cases waived. African-American youths were 29% of cases petitioned but 41% of the cases waived. Conversely, white youths were more likely to be waived for property cases (65% of cases petitioned but 73% of those waived). For person offenses, 1.2% of African Americans were waived versus 0.7% of white youths.[70] The historical record in individual states illustrates the roots of differential treatment.

A study of waivers in Los Angeles County over a twenty-year period demonstrated extreme racial bias. While blacks made up only 13% of the juvenile population, they accounted for 95% of the cases waived to the adult court. When expressed as rates per 100,000, it was found that Latinos were 6 times more likely and blacks were 12 times more likely than whites to be transferred. (See the article that follows for additional information on transfer to adult court in California.) Among those sent to adult courts in South Carolina during a 10-year period (1985–1994) 80% were blacks. Studies in Utah and Pennsylvania found that at least half of those transferred were black.[71] The crackdown on juvenile crime affected the number of cases certified dramatically. A study of four Southern states between 1980 and 1988 found that waived cases increased by over 100%.[72] As discussed, the "war on drugs" was a heavy contributor, with an increase of 152% during the period 1987–1991.[73] This suggests that the movement to transfer youth was more of a political issue than a public safety issue. Many local politicians were (and still are) gaining votes for their "get tough" stance on juvenile crime, using mostly anecdotal evidence to support their cause.[74]

Some Negative Consequences of Certification

What is the result of waiving a youth to the adult system? In the mid-1990s, many law enforcement officials began to question this method of responding to youth crime. A full-page ad in the *Washington Times* in 1997 against a proposed juvenile crime bill said the legislation would make their jobs more difficult and bluntly warned: "lock up a 13-year-old with murderers, rapists and robbers, and guess what he'll want to be when he grows up?"[75] Even John DiIulio, head of the conservative Council on Crime in America (a group that originally supported the bill with some very dubious statistics), changed his mind, writing in the *New York Times* that "Most kids who get into serious trouble with the law need adult guidance. And they won't find suitable role models in prison. Jailing youth with adult felons under Spartan conditions will merely produce more street gladiators."[76]

Victimization of young offenders inevitably results in a high likelihood of aggression toward women and children at a later date. Although certifying young offenders as adults may decrease "community risk through lengthy incapacitation of violent youngsters . . . the social costs of imprisoning young offenders in adult facilities may be paid in later crime and violence upon their release."[77] Although the research is sparse, at least one study found that transferring juveniles to adult court *does not result in a reduction of crime and may even contribute to at least a short-term increase in crime.*[78]

While the effects on each individual can be devastating, the numbers of youths sentenced to adult prison are small. The most recent figures reported 9,400 cases waived to criminal court (4,000 person offenses, 3,100 property, 1,400 drug, and 800 public order).[79] The final outcome in criminal court is usually a dismissal of all charges or probation; very few are sentenced to adult prison. However, the few who are transferred are mostly African Americans. The entire process could be described as "cosmetic" to reassure a fearful public that the system will protect them. Of course that ignores the stigma and trauma for offenders being processed.

Specific Examples of Differential Treatment

Many examples of minority youths receiving harsh sentences never come to the attention of the public. A few capture the media's attention and reveal a system that is far from stated ideals of equal justice.

Genarlow Wilson

The 2005 case of a black honor-roll student in Georgia drew national attention. The details of Genarlow Wilson's incarceration were revealed on blogs, national news shows, and editorial pages. Many, including former President Jimmy Carter, said it raised questions about race and the criminal justice system.[80] In a hotel room on New Year's Eve, six male juveniles and two female juveniles engaged in consensual, videotaped sex. Wilson of Douglasville, Georgia, who was 17 years old at the time, engaged in consensual oral sex with a 15-year-old girl. The mother of the girl originally said Wilson should not have been criminally charged but changed her statement after a visit from prosecutors. Wilson would have faced one year in prison had he had sexual intercourse with the girl rather than oral sex and would not have been required to register as a sex offender. (In 2006, lawmakers ended the difference in punishment for oral and vaginal sex but did not make the law retroactive.) The others accepted a plea bargain, but Wilson refused. Most had been in trouble before, but Wilson was a homecoming king with a 3.2 grade point average and no criminal record; colleges were offering football scholarships. Wilson opted for a trial to avoid having a record as a child molester and sex offender. Instead, he was found guilty and received a sentence of 10 years because of mandatory sentencing guidelines. During Wilson's trial, a 27-year-old white teacher was found guilty of having sex with a 17-year-old student— exactly the type of crime for which child molestation statutes were written. She was sentenced to 90 days in jail and 3 years of probation.[81]

After he had served 28 months of his sentence, a judge ordered him released, saying:

> The fact that Genarlow Wilson has spent two years in prison for what is now classified as a misdemeanor, and without assistance from this court, will spend eight more years in prison, is a grave miscarriage of justice. If this court or any court cannot recognize the injustice of what has occurred here, then our court system has lost sight of the goal our judicial system has always strived to accomplish . . . justice being served in a fair and equal manner.[82]

The prosecutor filed a notice of appeal, arguing that Georgia law does not grant a judge the authority to reduce a sentence imposed by the trial court. The governor of Georgia agreed and said it would be unfair to treat Wilson differently from the others who took the plea deals.[83] On June 25, another judge ruled that Wilson's conviction made him inelig ible for bail.[84] On October 26, 2007, the Georgia Supreme Court overturned the conviction, finding that the sentence was "cruel and unusual punishment."[85] Genarlow Wilson left the Al Burruss Correctional Training Center after 32 months behind bars. Charles Steele, president of the Southern Christian Leadership Conference, commented that Wilson was treated unfairly because he is black. "There are many, many more Genarlow Wilson cases throughout this country."

Before the conviction was overturned, one commentator summarized the case:

> After 40 years of "get tough on crime" rhetoric, many prosecutors and politicians have unfortunately come to measure success in our criminal justice system by the number of people they put in jail. Criminal laws—particularly those pertaining to drug and sex crimes—are increasingly written with extraordinary breadth and reach. Police officers typically are rewarded for arrests, not for preventing crimes. Prosecutors tend to be promoted or re-elected based on their ability to win convictions, not their fairness or sense of justice. Appeals courts, meanwhile, generally focus on constitutional and procedural issues. Only in extreme cases will an appellate court review the appropriateness of a verdict. From the writing of laws to their enforcement and prosecution, our system has evolved to the point where justice, mercy and fairness often go overlooked. It's no surprise that the U.S. leads the world in its rate of incarceration, and by a wide margin.[86]

Jena Six

Another case of disproportionate treatment of minority youths was ongoing at the time this collection of articles went to press. Jena High School is located in Jena, Louisiana, a former mill town with a population of about 3,000—12% black and 85% white. There was a large oak tree in the school courtyard where, by convention, whites would gather. During the first week of classes in 2006, a black student asked the vice principal if he could sit under the tree and was told he could sit wherever he liked. He and several black friends went over to the tree to visit some white friends. The next day, three nooses were hanging on the tree's branches. The three white boys who admitted hanging the nooses received three-day, in-school suspensions. The principal had recommended that the three be expelled, but the superintendent overruled, saying "Adolescents play pranks. I don't think it was a threat against anybody."[87]

The school held an assembly in early September and invited the district attorney to speak. Flanked by police officers, he told the students, "I can be your best friend or your worst enemy. With the stroke of my pen, I can make your lives disappear."[88] During the Thanksgiving holiday weekend, one black student was beaten at a party primarily attended by whites; the white student who threw the first punch was charged with simple battery and given probation. A young white man pulled a shotgun on three black students; a black student wrestled the gun away. The white youth was not charged; the black student was charged with theft of a firearm.[89] When school resumed, a black student punched a white student, Justin Barker, who was exiting the gym, knocking him unconscious; a group of five other black students allegedly joined the attack. The white student was treated for injuries at the hospital and released; he attended a class-ring ceremony that evening. The district attorney originally charged six black students with attempted murder. All six were expelled from school.[90]

The district attorney prosecuted sixteen-year-old Mychal Bell as an adult; he was jailed in December because he was unable to post $90,000 bail. He refused the district attorney's plea-bargain offer because he did not want to plead guilty to a felony. After jury selection began, the district attorney reduced the charges to aggravated second-degree battery and conspiracy.[91] On June 28, 2007, an all-white jury convicted Bell after a trial in which his court-appointed attorney (who had tried to convince him to accept a plea bargain) did not challenge the composition of the jury, excluded Bell's parents from the courtroom, and rested his case without calling any witnesses. The aggravated battery charge alleged the use of a dangerous weapon. The district attorney introduced no evidence of a gun, knife, or other weapon; he argued that the tennis shoes Bell was wearing at the time of the attack qualified as a dangerous weapon—and the jury agreed.[92] A number of individuals and institutions protested the conviction. School officials cut down the tree in July, "hoping to eliminate it as a focus of protests."[93] The case continued to attract attention, and about 20,000 demonstrators arrived in Jena on September 20.

Earlier in September, a circuit court of appeal in Louisiana ruled that the district attorney, Reed Walters, had improperly tried Bell as an adult.[94] Walters first vowed to appeal that ruling (which he later decided not to pursue) and immediately initiated juvenile proceedings. He also said he would vigorously pursue his cases against the rest of the teenage defendants, insisting that the white victim had been forgotten amid the controversy. The ruling did not order Bell released, and he remained in jail unable to pay the bond. After more than nine months behind bars, Judge J. P. Mauffray, Jr. (the presiding judge at the criminal trial) agreed to release Bell on $45,000 bond on September 27.[95] The Congressional Black Caucus asked the U.S. Department of Justice to investigate possible civil rights violations and prosecutorial misconduct. "This shocking case has focused national and international attention on what appears to be an unbelievable example of the separate and unequal justice that was once commonplace in the Deep South."[96]

Bell's taste of freedom was short-lived. On October 11, he went to juvenile court for a scheduled hearing. Mauffray revoked a prior probation and sentenced him to 18 months on previous charges of simple battery and criminal destruction of property.[97] The judge ordered all proceedings closed and directed all lawyers in the case not to speak publicly about it. David Utter, founder of the Juvenile Justice Project of Louisiana, commented: "I don't know the motivation for this judge and the district attorney, but what they did goes against the grain of our juvenile code, which holds that home and the community are the best place to treat juveniles."[98] On October 22, a coalition of major media companies filed a First Amendment petition to open the proceedings against Bell, charging that Mauffray's orders are contrary to Louisiana juvenile laws, precedents set by the Louisiana Supreme Court, and the state and U.S. Constitutions.[99]

The Jena 6 case exemplifies the unequal justice that many minority juveniles receive.

> Far harsher criminal charges were brought against the black youths for fighting than the white students for similar infractions. What's true also is that all of the students equally have used poor judgment and all should be held accountable. But considering the circumstances, none of them should have to pay with their lives by possibly facing long prison terms. And that's what the black students are facing. As Richard Cohen from the Southern Poverty Law Center said, the data consistently show that black people are treated more harshly than white people in the criminal justice system. "Blacks aren't often given the benefit of the doubt. If discretion is exercised, it's more often exercised in an adverse way to blacks."[100]

Martin Lee Anderson

In January 2006, 14-year-old Martin Lee Anderson died one day after guards at a juvenile boot camp in Panama City, Florida, forced him to inhale ammonia. They were videotaped kicking, kneeing, and dragging him around for twenty minutes because he had been uncooperative during an exercise program.[101] Martin was black and five of the seven guards were black. An initial autopsy claimed he died of sickle-cell anemia, but national outrage over the death and slow investigation prompted a second autopsy, which concluded the ammonia caused his vocal chords to spasm and block his airway leading to suffocation. Martin, a good student, was sent to boot camp for trespassing at school, a violation of his probation for taking his grandmother's car from a church parking lot. In May 2006 the legislature passed the Martin Lee Anderson Act, which eliminated the five boot camps in Florida. The facilities were renamed Sheriff's Training and Respect programs; stun guns and mechanical restraints are barred unless the child is a threat.[102] Seven former guards and a nurse from the camp were charged with manslaughter in November 2006; they were acquitted in October 2007.

The Government Accountability Office (GAO) investigated boot camps and wilderness programs and released a report in 2007. Gregory Kutz told the House Committee on Education and Labor, "We found thousands of allegations of abuse, some of which involved death, at public and private residential treatment programs across the country between the years 1990 and 2007."[103] In 2005 alone, 33 states reported 1,619 staff members involved in incidents of abuse in residential programs. GAO investigated ten deaths at boot camps from 1990 through 2004. It found significant evidence of ineffective management playing a significant role in the deaths, including the hiring of untrained staff, a lack of adequate nourishment, and reckless or negligent operating practices, including a lack of adequate equipment.[104]

The death of Martin Anderson prompted one commentator to report other appalling treatment of children in detention. He cited a Juvenile Justice Project of Louisiana investigation that had found that more than 100 teenagers were left locked in a flooded prison after Hurricane Katrina. They went five days with no food or water; many had been detained but not convicted of any crime. The majority were black. While New Orleans was 67% black, the prison was more than 95% black—and black people are more than eight times more likely to be imprisoned than whites.

> It is telling how mutely we absorb that fact, which gives tacit approval to this means of controlling a population whose mere existence we have historically found threatening and inconvenient. . . . The means have changed, but the end—repression, control—remains the same.[105]

Shaquanda Cotton

A report by the Texas Rangers about abuse in a prison in Pyote released in February 2007 prompted allegations from other facilities. It was revealed that youths at TYC facilities had filed more than 750 abuse claims since January 2000, but only a handful resulted in convictions.[106] The head of TYC's board and the executive director resigned in March 2007, and the governor appointed Jay Kimbrough a special master to investigate the system.

Kimbrough found that 111 employees of the TYC had felony arrests or convictions, and 437 others had misdemeanor arrests.[107] Kimbrough assembled a panel to review the sentence of each of the 4,700 delinquent youths held in Texas juvenile prisons because of suspicions that their sentences could have been arbitrarily extended by prison authorities in retaliation for filing complaints. Some experts estimated that more than 60% of the inmates could be serving wrongful detentions.[108]

Shaquanda Cotton was the first candidate for early release; her story had been publicized in March 2007 and provoked national attention. The black teenager from Paris, Texas, had been sentenced to seven years for shoving a teacher's aide at her high school. (In comparison, a white offender convicted of arson was sentenced to probation.)[109] Shaquanda was fourteen when convicted and was eligible for early release if she passed specified social, behavioral, and educational phases while in prison. However, officials at the Ron Jackson State Juvenile Correctional Complex repeatedly extended her sentence because she would not admit her guilt and contraband had been found in her cell—an extra pair of socks.[110] She had served one year before the panel ordered her release on March 30, 2007.

Almost ninety percent of juveniles in Texas prisons had been incarcerated on indeterminate sentences. As one member of the sentence review panel noted:

> The system is wide open for abuse and corruption. How difficult would it be for a 12-year-old kid to file a complaint on an assistant superintendent of a facility when that assistant superintendent is actually the one who is sexually abusing her and that same person gets to decide when she gets out? Basically the official gets to say, "Comply and keep quiet or I'll keep you here until you're 21."[111]

In April 2007, the TYC began releasing 550 youths (ages 10 to 21) who had served the minimum sentence and caused no trouble while incarcerated. The costs to repair the system were estimated at $100 million.[112] The acting executive director of the TYC testified to a Texas Senate committee: "We are trying to change the culture, which is a big uphill battle for us, because staff is not used to talking with kids as if they were humans."[113]

Girls and New York Juvenile Prisons

An investigation of the two secure facilities for girls in New York, Tryon and Lansing, found abuses and neglect. Most of the girls were fifteen or sixteen years old, but some were as young as twelve. Almost 73% were African American or Hispanic; many were from poorer neighborhoods in New York City.

> As with incarcerated persons throughout the U.S., a disproportionate number of girls confined in New York are African-Americans from families who have lived in poverty for generations, with parents or other close relatives who themselves have been incarcerated. In many cases, these girls fall into juvenile facilities through vast holes in the social safety net, after child welfare institutions and schools have failed them. In the wake of legal reform in 1996, girls who commit "status offenses" such as disobedience and running away from home are no longer supposed to be placed in custody, but such offenses— and the related issue of involvement with child welfare agencies because of parental abuse and neglect—continue to function as gateways through which particularly vulnerable children are drawn into the juvenile justice system. . . .
>
> All girls sent to Tryon or Lansing are confined in a prison-like physical environment where they may be at risk of abuse and where promised services are often not delivered. One of the most troubling abuses is the use of inappropriate and excessive force by facilities staff against girls.[114]

The report documented three cases in the past five years of staff having intercourse with their wards, instances of inappropriate touching, observing girls as they showered, and humiliating comments about the past sexual history of girls. As the report notes, the lack of public information about what goes on behind bars allows the abuse to continue.

State watchdogs are weak and understaffed, leaving no effective body to demand accountability, and the Office of Children and Family Services itself actively resists public scrutiny. The agency refused to grant researchers access to its facilities and attempted to withhold crucial non-confidential documents from public disclosure. "New York says it locks these girls up for their own good, but then they end up battered and bruised," said Jamie Fellner, director of the U.S. Program at Human Rights Watch. There's no way staff violence against girls can help them get their lives together, particularly when so many of the girls already have personal histories full of violence and abuse.[115]

The problems identified in the report are not limited to New York alone. Nationally more than 95,000 children are in the custody of juvenile justice agencies.[116] After being adjudicated delinquent, youths—frequently from backgrounds of intergenerational poverty—are locked up and often suffer more abuse within the facilities. Even if physical abuse is not present, inadequate educational and mental health services are themselves a form of abuse in a system that purports to provide a space for the rehabilitation of troubled youths. Sometimes violent, often deplorable conditions are more likely to breed recidivism than to offer hope to those who need it most.

Notes

[1] Quoted in Justice Policy Institute (2005). "Crime, Race and Juvenile Justice Policy in Perspective." (http://www.justicepolicy.org/images/upload/05-10_FAC_CrimeRaceJJPolicy_JJ-PS-RD.pdf) Bennett was Secretary of Education 1985 to 1988 and Director of the Office of National Drug Control Policy (drug czar).

[2] Quoted in Justice Policy Institute. Hume is a reporter and commentator; comments made on *Fox News Sunday,* October 02, 2005.

[3] National Advisory Commission on Civil Disorders (1968). *Report of the National Advisory Commission on Civil Disorders.* New York: Bantam Books.

[4] In this article, the term "minority youth" will be defined as black and Hispanic youth only. Several different terms are commonly used to describe persons of Hispanic or Mexican descent. Some prefer to use the more generic term *Hispanic,* while others prefer terms such as *Chicano, Latino,* or *Mexican-American.*

[5] Lee-St. John, J. (March 26, 2007). "A Road Map to Prevention." *Time* 169(13): 56.

[6] Ibid., p. 57.

[7] Webster, B. and A. Bishaw (August, 2006). *Income, Earnings, and Poverty Data from the 2005 American Community Survey.* Washington, DC: U.S. Census Bureau, p. 10. (http://www.census.gov/prod/2006pubs/acs-02.pdf); Miringoff, M., and M. Miringoff (1999). *The Social Health of the Nation.* New York: Oxford University Press, p. 105.

[8] Kochhar, R. (2004). *The Wealth of Hispanic Households: 1996–2002.* Washington, DC: The Pew Hispanic Center.

[9] Sklar, H. (1998). "Let Them Eat Cake." *Z Magazine* (November). The 2006 figures are from the Bureau of Labor Statistics. (http://www.bls.gov/iag/manufacturing.htm)

[10] U.S. Census Bureau. Poverty Thresholds, 2006. (http://www.census.gov/hhes/www/poverty/threshld/thresh06.html)

[11] Webster, B. and A. Bishaw (2007). *Income, Earnings, and Poverty Data from the 2006 American Community Survey*. Washington, DC: U.S. Census Bureau, p. 20. (http://www.census.gov/prod/2007pubs/acs-08.pdf)

[12] DeNavas-Walt, C., B. Proctor, and J. Smith. (2007). *Income, Poverty, and Health Insurance Coverage in the United States: 2006*. Washington, DC: U.S. Census Bureau, p. 5. (http://www.census.gov/prod/2007pubs/p60-233.pdf). For a detailed analysis of wealth and income distribution, see: Gilbert, D. (2003). *The American Class Structure* (6th ed.). Belmont, CA: Thomson/Wadsworth; Perrucci, R. and E. Wysong (2003). *The New Class Society* (2nd ed.). New York: Roman and Littlefield; Phillips, K. (2002). *Wealth and Democracy*. New York: Broadway Books; Collins, C., B. Leondar-Wright, and H. Sklar (1999). *Shifting Fortunes: The Perils of the Growing American Wealth Gap*. Boston: United for a Fair Economy; Heintz, J., N. Folbre, and the Center for Popular Economics (2000). *The Ultimate Field Guide to the U.S. Economy*. New York: The New Press.

[13] National Center for Children in Poverty. *Basic Facts about Low-Income Children*. (http://www.nccp.org/publications/pub_762.html)

[14] U.S. Bureau of the Census. *Statistical Abstract of the United States*. Section 1: Population, table 64. (http://www.census.gov/prod/2006pubs/07statab/pop.pdf)

[15] Ibid., tables 41, 44.

[16] OJJDP Statistical Briefing Book. Juvenile Population Characteristics. (http://ojjdp.ncjrs.org/ojstatbb/population/qa01203.asp?qaDate=2005)

[17] Ibid. (http://ojjdp.ncjrs.org/ojstatbb/population/qa01402.asp?qaDate=2005)

[18] Ibid. (http://ojjdp.ncjrs.org/ojstatbb/population/qa01401.asp?qaDate=2005)

[19] U.S. Census Bureau. *The 2007 Statistical Abstract*. Income, Expenditures, and Wealth: Poverty Table 697. Families Below Poverty Level by Selected Characteristics 2004. (http://www.census.gov/compendia/statab/tables/07s0697.xls)

[20] U.S. Census Bureau (2007). Current Population Survey. 2006 Annual Social and Economic Supplement. Table 8. Income in 2005 by Educational Attainment of the Population 18 Years and Over. (http://www.census.gov/population/socdemo/education/cps2006/tab08-1r.xls)

[21] The rhetoric used to describe events often reveals the ideology of those involved. The white majority most often use the term "riot," while minorities describe the events as "rebellion" or "civil disobedience" or "legitimate protest." For a rare insightful analysis of the Watts riots, see the Robert Conot's *Rivers of Blood, Years of Darkness* (New York: Bantam, 1967). For an exceptional and a brilliant review of the Los Angeles Police Department's response to gangs and riots, see Davis M., (1992), *City of Quartz*. New York: Vintage Books, especially chapter 5. I regularly show a film, *Fire This Time*, contrasting the Rodney King riots with the Watts uprising 25 years earlier. It is disturbing because it implicates the federal and local government, especially law enforcement, in perpetuating the conditions that lead to rebellion and even to create and sustain gangs.

[22] Klein, M. (1995). *The American Street Gang*. New York: Oxford University Press, p. 196.

[23] Bureau of Labor Statistics. *Charting the U.S. Labor Market in 2006*. Chart 4-1. (http://www.bls.gov/cps/labor2006/chart4-1.pdf)

[24] Ibid., Chart 4-2. (http://www.bls.gov/cps/labor2006/chart4-2.pdf)

[25] Ibid., Chart 2-3. (http://www.bls.gov/cps/labor2006/chart2-3.pdf)

[26] Greater Diversity.com (2004). "Blacks in California Leading with the Highest Percentage of Unemployment in 10 Years." (http://www.greaterdiversity.com/career_resources/articles_CR_2003/Black_Unemployment.html#66)

[27] Leondar-Wright, B. (May/June 2004). "Black Job Loss Déjà Vu." *Dollars and Sense*, #253 (http://www.dollarsandsense.org/archives/2004/0504leondar.html)

[28] Ibid.

[29] Cardenas, Z. (December 18, 2004). "Childhood Dies on Skid Row." *Los Angeles Times*.

[30] Ibid.

[31] Streisand, B. (December 18, 2006). "The City of Angels Struggles to Deal with a Devil of a Place." *U.S. News and World Report* 141(23): 50–51.

32 Manning, P. K. and J. Van Maanen (eds.) (1978). *Policing: A View from the Streets.* Santa Monica, CA: Goodyear, p. 267.

33 Piliavin, I. and S. Briar (1964). "Police Encounters with Juveniles." *American Journal of Sociology* 70: 206–214; Werthman, C. and I. Piliavin (1975). "Gang Members and the Police." In J. Skolnick and T. C. Gray (eds.), *Police in America.* Boston: Little, Brown; Klinger, D. A. (1994). "Demeanor or Crime? Why 'Hostile' Citizens Are More Likely to be Arrested." *Criminology* 32: 475–493; Worden, R. E. and R. L. Shepard (1996). "Demeanor, Crime and Police Behavior: A Reexamination of the Police Services Study Data." *Criminology* 34: 61–82.

34 Johnston, L. D., P. M. O'Malley, J. G. Bachman, and J. E. Schulenberg (2007). *Monitoring the Future: National Results on Adolescent Dug Use: Overview of Key Findings, 2006.* (NIH Publication No. 07-6202). Bethesda, MD: National Institute on Drug Abuse, p. 46. For a review of self-report studies on drug usage, see Shelden, *Delinquency and Juvenile Justice in America.* Long Grove, IL: Waveland Press, chapter 2.

35 Johnston, L. D., P. M. O'Malley J. G. Bachman, and J. E. Schulenberg (2007). *Monitoring the Future: National Survey Results on Drug Use, 1975–2006: Volume I, Secondary School Students* (NIH Publication No. 07-6205). Bethesda, MD: National Institute on Drug Abuse, p. 99. (http://www.monitoringthefuture.org/pubs/monographs/vol1_2006.pdf)

36 Federal Bureau of Investigation. *Crime in the United States 2006.* Table 43. (http://www.fbi.gov/ucr/cius2006/data/table_43.html)

37 Leonard, K., C. Pope, and W. Feyerherm (eds.) (1995). *Minorities in Juvenile Justice.* Thousand Oaks, CA: Sage.

38 Miller, J. (1996) *Search and Destroy: African-American Males in the Criminal Justice System.* Cambridge: Cambridge University Press, p. 8. In Miller's study of Baltimore, he found that during 1981 only 15 white juveniles were arrested on drug charges, compared to 86 African Americans; in 1991, however, the number of whites arrested dropped to a mere 13, while the number of African Americans skyrocketed to a phenomenal 1,304, or an increase of 1,416%. The ratio of African-American youths to whites went from about 6:1 to 100:1; similar documentation can be found in the following studies: Currie, E. (1994) *Reckoning: Drugs, the Cities, and the American Future.* New York: Farrer Straus and Giroux; Tonry, M. (1995). *Malign Neglect: Race, Crime, and Punishment in America.* New York: Oxford University Press; Lockwood, D., A. E. Pottieger and J. A. Inciardi (1995). "Crack Use, Crime by Crack Users, and Ethnicity." In D. F. Hawkins (ed.), *Ethnicity, Race, and Crime.* Albany: SUNY Press; McGarrell, E. (1993). "Trends in Racial Disproportionality in Juvenile Court Processing: 1985–1989." *Crime and Delinquency* 39: 29–48; Fellner, J. (October 1996). "Stark Racial Disparities Found in Georgia Drug Law Enforcement," *Overcrowded Times* 7, 5.

39 Stahl, A. L., C. Puzzanchera, S. Livsey, A. Sladky, T. A. Finnegan, N. Tierney, and H. N. Snyder (2007). *Juvenile Court Statistics 2003–2004.* Pittsburgh, PA: National Center for Juvenile Justice, p. 21.

40 Walker, S., C. Spohn, and M. DeLone (2007). *The Color of Justice: Race, Ethnicity, and Crime in America* (4th ed). Belmont, CA: Wadsworth, pp. 392–395.

41 Pope, C. E. and W. Feyerherm (1995). *Minorities and the Juvenile Justice System: Research Summary* (second printing). Washington, DC: U.S. Department of Justice, Office of Juvenile Justice and Delinquency Prevention, p. 1. (http://www.ncjrs.gov/pdffiles/minor.pdf)

42 Pope, C. E., R. Lovell, and H. Hsia (2002). *Disproportionate Minority Confinement: A Review of the Research Literature from 1989 through 2001.* Washington, DC: U.S. Department of Justice, Office of Juvenile Justice and Delinquency Prevention.

43 Snyder, H. N. and M. Sickmund (2006). *Juvenile Offenders and Victims: 2006 National Report.* Washington, DC: U.S. Department of Justice, Office of Juvenile Justice and Delinquency Prevention.

44 National Council on Crime and Delinquency (2007). *And Justice for Some: Differential Treatment of Youth of Color in the Justice System,* p. 37. (http://www.nccd-crc.org/nccd/pubs/2007jan_justice_for_some.pdf)

[45] Moore, D. (2004). "As Some U.S. Cities Make Progress in Lowering the Number of Blacks in Juvenile Detention, Columbia's Numbers Rise." *Columbia Tribune*. (http://archive.columbiatribune.com/2004/feb/20040208feat051.asp)

[46] American Civil Liberties Union (2003). *Disproportionate Minority Confinement in Massachusetts*. (http://www.aclu.org/FilesPDFs/dmc_sum_eng.pdf)

[47] Hurst, H. and S. Sawacki (September 2003). "Minorities in Pennsylvania's Juvenile Justice System." Pennsylvania Commission on Crime and Delinquency, Statistical Bulletin. (http://www.pccd.state.pa.us/pccd/lib/pccd/Juvenile/2003_dmc_statistical_bulletin.pdf)

[48] Center on Juvenile and Criminal Justice. 2004. "Race and Juvenile Justice." (http://cjcj.org/jjic/race_jj.php, emphasis in the original)

[49] Krisberg, B. and J. Austin. (1993). *Reinventing Juvenile Justice*. Thousand Oaks, CA: Sage, pp. 126–127.

[50] *Statistical Abstracts of the U.S.* Washington, DC: U.S. Government Printing Office, 1975, p. 419; 2003 figures from Sickmund, M., T. J. Sladky, and W. Kang, "Census of Juveniles in Residential Placement Databook." (http://ojjdp.ncjrs.org/ojstatbb/cjrp/asp/State_Race.asp?state=&topic=State_Race&year=2003&percent=row)

[51] Ibid., (http://ojjdp.ncjrs.org/ojstatbb/cjrp/asp/State_Adj.asp?state=&topic=State_Adj&year=2003&percent=rate). California's rate was 392; the other rates were: 625 for Washington, DC; 606 for Wyoming, 564 for South Dakota, 452 for Florida, and 415 for Indiana.

[52] California Division of Juvenile Justice. Summary Fact Sheet. (http://www.cdcr.ca.gov/Reports_Research/summarys.html)

[53] Sickmund, Sladky, and Kang, "Census of Juveniles."

[54] Krisberg, B. and J. Austin (1993). *Reinventing Juvenile Justice*. Newbury Park, CA: Sage, pp. 126–128.

[55] Sickmund, Sladky, and Kang, "Census of Juveniles."

[56] Shelden, R. G. "If It Looks Like a Prison . . ." *Las Vegas City Life*, August 13, 1999. An update is found on my Web site (http://www.sheldensays.com/i_told_you_so.htm)

[57] Shelden, R. G. (2001). *Controlling the Dangerous Classes: A Critical Introduction to the History of Criminal Justice*. Boston: Allyn & Bacon, p. 223.

[58] Snyder and Sickmund, *Juvenile Offenders and Victims*, 2006, p. 213.

[59] Ibid., p. 211.

[60] Ibid., p. 212.

[61] Stahl et al, *Juvenile Court Statistics 2003–2004*, p. 103.

[62] One obvious problem that immediately arises, but is rarely discussed, is that if, say, a 15-year-old youth is certified as an adult, does that mean he or she can vote, drop out of school, purchase alcohol, leave home, or do anything an adult can do? In actual fact they cannot, *even if they are placed on probation by the adult court and are still under 18.*

[63] Building Blocks for Youth. Charts on Transferring Youth to Criminal Court. (http://www.buildingblocksforyouth.org/issues/transfer/transchart.html)

[64] Griffin, P., P. Torbet, and L. Szymanski (1998). *Trying Juveniles as Adults in Criminal Court: An Analysis of State Transfer Provisions*. Washington, DC: Office of Juvenile Justice and Delinquency Prevention.

[65] Ibid.

[66] Ibid.

[67] Bishop, D., C. E. Frazier, L. Lanza-Kaduce, and L. Winner (1996). "The Transfer of Juveniles to Criminal Court: Does It Make a Difference?" *Crime and Delinquency* 42: 187–202; Podkopacz, M. R. and B. C. Feld (1996). "The End of the Line: An Empirical Study of Judicial Waiver." *Journal of Criminal Law and Criminology* 86: 449–492; Feld, B. C. (1999). "Criminalizing the American Juvenile Court," in B. C. Feld (ed.), *Readings in Juvenile Justice Administration*. New York: Oxford University Press.

[68] Bishop, D., C. E. Frazier, and J. C. Henretta (1989). "Prosecutorial Waiver: Case Study of a Questionable Reform." *Crime and Delinquency* 35: 179–201.

[69] Feld, B. C. (1999). *Bad Kids: Race and the Transformation of the Juvenile Court*. Oxford: Oxford University Press, p. 190.

[70] National Council on Crime and Delinquency, *And Justice for Some*, pp. 16, 19.

[71] Males, M. and D. Macallair (2000). "Dispelling the Myth: An Analysis of Youth and Adult Crime Patterns in California over the Past 20 Years." San Francisco: Center on Juvenile and Criminal Justice (www.cjcj.org/themyth). The author thanks UNLV graduate student Jodi Olson for pointing out this study in her research paper "Waiver of Juveniles to Criminal Court: Questions of Discretion and Racial Disparity."

[72] Champion, D. J. (1989). "Teenage Felons and Waiver Hearings: Some Recent Trends, 1980–1988." *Crime and Delinquency* 35.

[73] Donziger, S. R. (1996). *The Real War on Crime.* New York: HarperCollins, pp. 135–136.

[74] Bortner, M. A. (1986). "Traditional Rhetoric, Organizational Realities: Remand of Juveniles to Adult Court." *Crime and Delinquency* 32: 53–73.

[75] Cited in Schiraldi, V. and J. Ziedenberg (1997). *The Risks Juveniles Face When They Are Incarcerated with Adults.* (http://www.cjcj.org/pubs/risks/risks.html)

[76] Ibid.

[77] Fagan, J., M. Forst, and T. S. Vivona (1989). "Youth in Prisons and Training Schools: Perceptions and Consequences of the Treatment-Custody Dichotomy." *Juvenile and Family Court Journal* 2.

[78] Bishop et al., "The Transfer of Juveniles to Criminal Court."

[79] Stahl et al., *Juvenile Court Statistics 2003–2004,* pp. 38–42; 56–67.

[80] McCaffrey, S. "Judge Tosses Sentence in Consensual Teen Sex Case." *Chicago Tribune,* June 12, 2007, p. 3.

[81] Pitts, Leonard. "Waiting for Georgia to Come to Its Senses." *Chicago Tribune,* April 3, 2007, p. 17.

[82] McCaffrey. "Judge Tosses Sentence in Consensual Teen Sex Case," p. 3.

[83] McCaffrey, S. "Official: Teen Case May Affect Molesters." *Chicago Tribune,* June 15, 2007, p. 11.

[84] Tribune News Services. "Judge Denies Bail During Appeal In Teen Sex Case." *Chicago Tribune,* June 28, 2007, p. 8.

[85] Fausset, R. and J. Jarvie, "Court Overturns Sex Conviction." *Chicago Tribune,* October 27, 2007, p. 3.

[86] Balko, Radley. "Blinded by the Law: Teen Sex Case Shows That Focusing on the Letter of the Law Doesn't Always Spell Justice." *Chicago Tribune,* June 24, 2007, Sec. 2, pp. 1, 4.

[87] Editorial. "Racism in a Small Town." *Chicago Tribune,* September 20, 2007, p. 20.

[88] Kovach, G. C. and A. Campo-Flores. "A Town in Turmoil." *Newsweek,* August 27, 2007, vol. CL #819, p. 36.

[89] "Racism in a Small Town," p. 20.

[90] Witt, H. "Racial Demons Rear Heads." *Chicago Tribune,* May 20, 2007, p. 3.

[91] Witt, H. "Charge Reduced in 'Jena 6' Case" *Chicago Tribune,* June 26, 2007, p. 4.

[92] Witt, H. "Louisiana Teen Guilty in School Beating Case." *Chicago Tribune,* June 29, 2007, p. 7.

[93] Witt, H. "Demonstrators Descend on Jena." *Chicago Tribune,* September 20, 2007, p. 14.

[94] Black, L. "Jackson Takes Jena 6 Case to Top." *Chicago Tribune,* September 24, 2007, sec. 2, p. 3.

[95] Witt, H. "Jena 6 Defendant Out of Jail." *Chicago Tribune,* September 28, 2007, p. 4.

[96] Ibid.

[97] Witt, H. "Jena 6 Teen's Return to Jail Draws Queries." *Chicago Tribune,* October 13, 2007, p. 3.

[98] Ibid.

[99] Witt, H. "Court Asked to End Jena Trial Secrecy." *Chicago Tribune,* October 23, 2007, p. 4.

[100] Trice, D. T. "Jena 6 Case Isn't Perfect, But It's Clear." *Chicago Tribune,* September 24, 2007, sec. 2, p. 1.

[101] Garcia, J. "Eight Indicted in Boot Camp Death." *Chicago Tribune,* November 29, 2006, p. 4.

[102] "Florida Boots Harsh Tactics." *U.S. News and World Report,* May 8, 2006, p. 6.

[103] Government Accountability Office (October 10, 2007). "Residential Treatment Programs: Concerns Regarding Abuse and Death in Certain Programs for Troubled Youth."

Statement of Gregory D. Kutz, Managing Director Forensic Audits and Special Investigations, and Andy O'Connell, Assistant Director Forensic Audits and Special Investigations. (http://www.gao.gov/new.items/d08146t.pdf)

[104] Ibid., p. 1.

[105] Pitts, L. "Using Boot Camps, Prisons to Control Black Children." *Chicago Tribune*, May 16, 2006, p. 15.

[106] Witkins, G. (March 19, 2007). "Juvenile Justice Troubles in Texas." *U.S. News and World Report* 142(10): 18.

[107] Witt, H. "Juvenile Justice on Trial in Texas." *Chicago Tribune*, March 27, 2007, p. 12.

[108] Ibid., p. 1.

[109] Witt, H. "Girl in Prison for Shove to Get Released Early." *Chicago Tribune*, March 31, 2007, p. 22.

[110] Ibid., p. 12.

[111] Ibid., p. 12.

[112] Editor. (April 16, 2007). "A Troubled System Fails Texas Youth." *U.S. News and World Report* 142(11): 23.

[113] Witt, H. "Texas Prison Official to Review Girl's Case." *Chicago Tribune*, October 13, 2007, p. 4.

[114] Human Rights Watch. (September 2006). *Custody and Control Conditions of Confinement in New York's Juvenile Prisons for Girls.* Summary, p. 4. (http://hrw.org/reports/2006/us0906/2.htm#_Toc145322841)

[115] Human Rights News. (September 25, 2006). "U.S.: Girls Abused in New York's Juvenile Prisons."

[116] Ibid.

3

Testing Incapacitation Theory
Youth Crime and Incarceration in California

Mike A. Males, Daniel Macallair, and Megan D. Corcoran

For much of the past three decades, policies emphasizing incapacitation have dominated California criminal and juvenile justice policy. In 1977, the passage of the determinate sentencing act eliminated rehabilitation as a sentencing goal in the adult context.[1] The state government adopted determinate sentencing with the approbation of both political parties who found the previous system either unfair or unreliable and lenient. With determinate sentencing, the public could be assured that offenders would be placed behind bars for a definite period of time, regardless of any treatment or education undertaken during incarceration. Rehabilitation, thus, became an issue of little import in the adult context.

The stated purpose of the California juvenile justice system has long been the protection of the public through the rehabilitation and correction of young offenders.[2] Despite this intention, the prevailing policy trend initiated by the 1977 act resulted in increased incarceration among juveniles and transfers to adult court. The increased reliance on institutionalization after 1977, coupled with the abominable conditions and lack of treatment opportunities in the DJJ institutions, has created a system that seems more interested in retribution than rehabilitation.[3] Juveniles are now more likely to be subjected to the punitive goals as expressed in the adult context, rather than afforded the benefits of rehabilitative programs. Since 1977, juvenile offenders have been exposed to greater potential for institutionalization in response to California's adherence to incapacitation theory.

The California State Government and the California Division of Juvenile Justice are struggling to improve the myriad deficiencies of the Division of Juvenile Justice institutions (formerly California Youth

Written especially for *Juvenile Justice in America: Problems and Prospects*.

Authority). In 2003, the Prison Law Office filed *Farrell v. Harper* (now referred to as *Farrell v. Hickman*), a taxpayer suit against the director of the DJJ, complaining that taxpayer funds should not be used to "further the illegal conditions that exist in the CYA."[4] The complaint alleged the inhumane and illegal conditions present in California's juvenile justice system contravened the system's goals of rehabilitation, training, and treatment as mandated by Welfare and Institutions Code section 1700.[5] By November 19, 2004, the parties agreed to a consent decree to guide remedial action responding to the problems of the juvenile justice institutions. The court-monitored consent decree and subsequent stipulations pursuant to the settlement of the *Farrell* case requires improvements to be made to DJJ facilities in the provision of educational, medical care, disabilities accommodation, and sexual behavior treatment.[6] In addition, institutions must reduce institutional violence, the use of force against wards, and the use of lock-ups.

Since the settlement was reached in November 2004, however, little progress has been made to improve conditions in the institutions. The cost of incarceration per ward, however, has been estimated to be as high $115,129 per juvenile per year of confinement.[7] The continued reliance on institutionalization is not in the best interests of juvenile offenders, and indeed, as this report indicates, incapacitation of these offenders may not serve the purpose of keeping crime rates down.

Incapacitation Theory and Practice in California

Incapacitation theory argues that reductions in crime rates are achieved through higher imprisonment rates since the offender cannot commit new crimes while incarcerated.[8] The theory is premised on the existence of a small but identifiable number of offenders who can be imprisoned and isolated from the rest of society.[9] The success of incapacitation theory remains a question for consideration. While advocates of the theory note decreased crime rates generally follow increased imprisonment rates, the reasons behind fluctuations in crime rates are unknown.

California's youth incarceration trends for the past two decades offer a rare opportunity to examine the impact of incapacitation theory. Like most of the nation in recent years, California has passed a number of statutes designed to promote higher rates of youth imprisonment. In response to youth offending, California has adopted a strategy akin to throwing a net over more juvenile offenders for prolonged periods of time. Juvenile justice policy relies on incapacitation theory to justify this strategy. By adopting laws that lower the minimum age for juvenile transfer to criminal courts, increasing the range of offenses that warrant placement in the adult system, and allowing prosecutors greater power and discretion to charge juveniles in adult courts, more juveniles become exposed to the risk of incarceration.[10]

These efforts began in 1994 when the age of eligible adult court transfer was lowered from age 16 to age 14.[11] With the change in the law, juveniles as young as 14 could be remanded to adult court if, after a fitness hearing, a juvenile court finds them unfit for juvenile court.[12]

Also in 1994, California voters passed Proposition 184, widely known as the Three Strikes and You're Out law.[13] Further diminishing judicial discretion in criminal sentencing, the law requires enhanced sentences for second and third offenses following any serious or violent felony conviction. The Three Strikes statute also qualified certain juvenile offenses as strikes, if the offense was committed by a juvenile age 16 or older.[14] Thus, longer prison sentences and greater punishment would be meted out by the state in response to a popular demand for increased incarceration.

In 2000, the move towards harsher juvenile imprisonment culminated with the passage of Proposition 21.[15] Proposition 21 was designed to facilitate and expedite the transfer of increased numbers of juveniles to the adult court by reducing judicial discretion, giving prosecutors more authority, and increasing the number of offenders eligible for remand. With these new laws, California appeared poised for unprecedented increases in youth incarceration levels. This emphasis on expansive incarceration, combined with continuing reductions in statewide crime rates following its passage, seemed to confirm the assertions of incapacitation proponents.

Increased imprisonment is often heralded by incarceration proponents as the reason for the state's declining crime rates.[16] California's per-capita adult imprisonment rate has increased five-fold since 1980, from 137 per 100,000 residents to 675 per 100,000 residents in 2005.[17] Meanwhile, the state's rate of reported Part I crimes fell from 3,922 per 100,000 residents in 1980 to 2,464 in 2005, and total felony arrest rates, including both juveniles' and adults', fell from 1,977 arrests per 100,000 people ages 10–69 in 1980 to 1,868 per 100,000 in 2005.[18] These declines in reported crime and felony arrests during a period of increased incarceration would appear to validate the incapacitation argument.

However, this overall reduction in crime masks contradictory trends when considered by age. From 1980 through 2005, despite a 500 percent increase in adult imprisonment rates, the adult felony rate actually *increased* by 13 percent, from 1,741.6 arrests per 100,000 adults in 1980 to 1,961.7 arrests per 100,000 adults in 2005.[19] Surprisingly, the age group between 40 and 59 experienced the greatest increase in imprisonment rates, up 1,200 percent since 1980. Concurrently, the same population also posted the greatest increase in felony rates, up 250 percent from the 1980 levels. In 1980, the age 40–59 group experienced a felony arrest rate of 454 per 100,000 population, compared to 1,167 in 2005.[20] Contrary to incapacitation theory, taking vastly larger numbers of adult felons off the streets and putting them behind bars did not reduce serious crime rates among adults. In fact, the opposite has occurred.

Meanwhile, California youth incarceration trends and felony arrest rates during this same period show an opposite pattern that also directly counters incapacitation theory. While the adult imprisonment rate was expanding, youth incarceration rates in California plunged to record lows (see table 1). Between 1980 and 2005, the rate of juvenile incarceration in California fell by nearly 60 percent. In 1980, juveniles were imprisoned at a rate of 170 per 100,000 youths. By 2005, that number had decreased to 71 imprisonments per 100,000 youths. Despite the presence of fewer youth behind bars, the juvenile felony rates dropped in the same period by 57 percent, from 3,195 arrests per 100,000 youths in 1980 to 1,361 arrests per 100,000 youths in 2005. This reduction included a sharp decline in arrests for violent crime.

Prior to 1982, juveniles ages 10 through 17 were 20 to 25 percent *more* likely to be imprisoned than adults were. In 1983, the imprisonment rate of adults suddenly surpassed that of juveniles, and that trend has continued. Today, youth are less than *one-tenth* as likely to be admitted to a facility as compared to adults.

According to incapacitation theory, California's enormous decline in youth imprisonment should have resulted in more criminal youth on the streets, and more juvenile offending and violence. Similarly, the rapid increase in adult incarceration following 1983 should have removed criminal adults from the public domain, resulting in lower rates of adult offending and violence.

In reality, the opposite has transpired. Compared to their respective levels 30 years ago, violent felony arrest rates for California's youth ages 10–17 are 37 percent lower as of the latest report released by the Criminal Justice Statistics Center in 2005.[21] Over the same period, violent felony arrests for adults increased 14 percent[22] (table 1). Teen violence rates, higher than adult violence rates in 1975, are considerably lower than adult rates as of 2005. Overall, youth felony arrests have dropped 58 percent over the last three decades and now stand at their lowest level since 1955. Youth imprisonment rates, after moderate variation since 1970, have also reached an unprecedented low.[23] Adult felony rates, on the other hand, have increased 23 percent since 1976 even while imprisonment rates reached consistent highs.[24]

California's youth incarceration patterns offer an opportunity to analyze the validity of incapacitation theory as it applies to young people. This study examines California's juvenile incarceration and crime trends over the past 47 years. In addition to statewide trends, county-by-county youth incarceration practices and crime patterns are examined to determine differential outcomes between high incarceration and low incarceration counties. Under incapacitation theory, counties with higher youth incarceration rates are expected to experience accelerated reductions in juvenile crime. Failure to demonstrate reduced crime rates through higher levels of juvenile incarceration calls incapacitation theory into serious question as an effective youth crime reduction strategy.

Table 1   California Youth and Adult Rates of Arrest for Violent Crime and Imprisonment Rates, per 100,000 Population by Age, 1970–2004/06

	Youth (ages 10–17)		Adult (ages 18–69)	
	Violent crime arrest rate	Imprisonment rate	Violent crime arrest rate	Imprisonment rate
1970	310.6	194.5	324.4	161.1
	356.1	163.5	345.4	129.4
	429.2	132.3	357.9	124.1
	475.6	131.2	349.0	143.2
	528.4	140.8	382.7	151.8
1975	551.0	142.9	396.5	116.1
	514.2	139.0	378.9	116.9
	511.6	127.1	383.5	110.2
	500.4	142.1	387.0	121.2
	551.4	161.2	421.6	128.8
1980	555.6	169.9	435.8	137.3
	525.1	182.4	433.7	173.8
	453.6	186.8	409.6	204.5
	390.1	188.7	372.9	226.8
	377.1	196.4	377.5	244.5
1985	394.8	213.7	379.9	275.9
	396.7	246.4	493.9	321.6
	391.5	271.2	519.6	352.0
	448.7	284.7	552.8	390.0
	561.6	272.1	597.1	432.9
1990	641.9	251.6	651.6	473.8
	635.4	243.2	624.5	491.8
	624.5	240.8	638.8	521.1
	610.1	240.2	632.0	569.0
	626.1	245.7	645.8	594.5
1995	596.2	263.5	645.1	642.6
	590.3	261.2	629.2	691.5
	548.6	226.1	632.1	727.9
	504.1	205.2	577.4	739.4
	476.2	190.7	532.6	729.3
2000	408.6	179.7	513.3	713.4
	420.9	160.6	516.4	684.7
	370.8	138.5	496.3	683.4
	361.5	114.3	490.8	680.5
	348.6	91.4	466.6	679.1
2005		71.2		674.6
2006		64.6		689.3

Sources: Compiled by authors from Division of Juvenile Justice, Criminal Justice Statistics Center, and Demographic Research Unit. Numbers for 2006 represent rate to June 2006.

Methodology

This study examines crime trends from 1960 to the present, with a special emphasis on the last 25 years. Comparable youth and adult felony trends dating back to the late 1950s are available, as are imprisonment trends by age. However, age detail for adult arrests was not reported until 1975, and the numbers are not comparable due to a law change in 1976 making low-level possession of marijuana a misdemeanor rather than a felony. Thus, felony arrest trends reported here begin in 1980. These data for imprisonments are compared to statewide crime trends over the last 46 years for youth, and over the last 25 years for adults. In addition, county-by-county DJJ commitment rates, both per 100,000 youth and per 1,000 felony arrests, are compared with youth crime trends and levels over the last 12 years.

Data on state and county youth crime arrests were obtained from the California Department of Justice's Criminal Justice Statistics Center (CJSC). Statistics on youths committed to the Division of Juvenile Justice (formerly California Youth Authority) by age, offense, and county were obtained from the California Department of Corrections and Rehabilitation's (CDCR) Division of Juvenile Justice (DJJ). Population information was obtained through the Demographic Research Unit Data Files of the Department of Finance.

Trends detailed in the DJJ's latest "A Comparison of First Admission Characteristics, 1993–2004" and 2005 DJJ population reports are examined and compared to total juvenile felonies and the California population as a whole over the last 12 years.

Statewide Juvenile Crime Trends

California's current juvenile crime rates, including youth arrested for homicide, violent crime, and property crime, are among the lowest recorded since 1960.[25] Beginning in the early 1960s, juvenile felony arrests rates began a 15-year increase that continued into the mid-1970s.[26] This consistent increase was followed by a cyclical pattern that lasted into the early 1990s (see table 2). After 1994, juvenile felony arrests began a steady and inexorable decline, reaching a 40-year low by 2003. In 2004 and 2005, the numbers of juvenile felony arrests fell below the average annual number of juvenile arrests in the early 1960s. Only 1,361 juvenile felony arrests per 100,000 people aged 10–17 were recorded in 2005. The average rate between 1960–1964 was 1,592 per 100,000 people aged 10–17. Thus, in 2005, a California teenager was less likely to be arrested for a felony (including murder, other violent, and property offenses) than a teenager in the 1960s. Over the last decade, the violent felony arrest rate for juveniles has decreased by 42 percent, and total felony arrest rates have fallen by 41 percent.

Table 2   Arrests per 100,000 Population, Ages 10–17, 1960–2004

Years	Homicide	Violent	Property	Felony Arrest Rate
1960–64	4.9	178.3	1,342.8	1,591.7
1965–69	5.7	224.7	1,618.1	2,418.6
1970–74	9.0	420.0	1,925.6	3,550.7
1975–79	10.7	525.7	2,263.2	3,403.4
1980–84	12.9	460.3	1,758.3	2,683.7
1985–89	11.7	438.6	1,538.0	2,533.8
1990–94	18.5	627.6	1,534.3	2,701.7
1995–99	9.2	543.1	1,059.7	2,089.9
2000–04	4.3	382.1	659.5	1,514.4
2005 only	4.1	346.9	539.4	1,361.1

Sources: Compiled by authors from Division of Juvenile Justice, Criminal Justice Statistics Center, and Demographic Research Unit.

Figure 1   Felony Arrest Rate, Ages 10–17

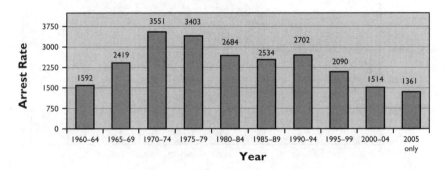

Figure 2   Violent Crime Arrest Rate, Ages 10–17

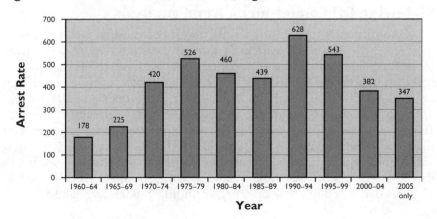

Figure 3   Homicide Arrest Rate, Ages 10–17

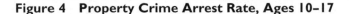

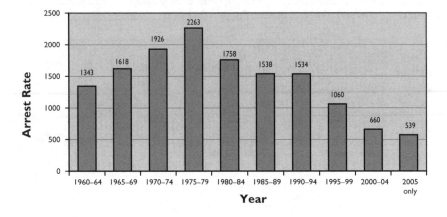

Figure 4   Property Crime Arrest Rate, Ages 10–17

Statewide DJJ Commitment Trend Analysis

Commitments to California state youth correctional facilities are at their lowest levels in 47 years even though the state's youth population more than doubled during this period.[27] As of June 2006, the average daily population in DJJ facilities was 2,910 in a total juvenile population ages 10–17 of 4,506,000.[28] In 1959, the average daily population was 4,279 in a juvenile population of 1,950,000.[29] On a per capita basis, the 1959 population of incarcerated youth was more than three times greater than the same population in 2006. Over the last 11 years, DJJ's new admissions and population dropped by 75 percent, the fastest decline in its six-decade history (see tables 2 and 3). DJJ commitments over the last 12 years decreased in every category, including gender, race, and offense.

Table 3 **DJJ Commitment Rate per 100,000 Population by Sex and Age 10–17, 1959–2006**

	Incarceration Rates			
	Total Rate	Female Rate	Male Rate	Average Daily Population
	213.0	60.0	358.0	4,279
1960	227.5	67.8	380.9	4,811
	251.7	68.2	428.5	5,609
	254.7	76.3	426.6	6,010
	257.4	77.1	430.9	6,478
	250.8	78.3	416.7	6,698
1965	245.9	79.3	406.0	6,778
	228.3	75.5	375.0	6,447
	223.7	72.1	366.0	6,502
	218.1	69.2	356.8	6,490
	208.0	60.8	345.4	6,323
1970	194.5	44.9	340.8	5,915
	163.5	34.7	289.2	5,105
	132.3	24.6	237.5	4,196
	131.2	21.5	238.2	4,208
	140.8	20.3	258.1	4,537
1975	142.9	15.4	266.9	4,602
	139.0	14.4	259.8	4,432
	127.1	12.1	238.4	4,003
	142.1	12.4	267.4	4,405
	161.2	13.8	303.2	4,924
1980	169.9	13.5	319.9	5,179
	182.4	15.3	341.1	5,669
	186.8	18.5	344.9	5,810
	188.7	20.4	345.0	5,869
	196.4	17.6	361.4	6,081
1985	213.7	22.8	389.0	6,638
	246.4	23.7	450.7	7,680
	271.2	25.5	497.5	8,448
	284.7	26.0	524.5	8,812
	272.1	22.6	504.9	8,394
1990	251.6	19.2	469.1	8,096
	243.2	17.1	455.3	8,098
	240.8	15.9	451.7	8,310
	240.2	18.4	447.5	8,499
	245.7	17.3	458.4	8,868
1995	263.5	22.4	487.7	9,674
	261.2	24.4	481.5	9,772
	226.1	23.4	415.1	8,655
	205.2	18.2	380.2	7,991
	190.7	24.1	341.4	7,556

(continued)

Table 3   *(continued)*

| | Incarceration Rates | | | |
	Total Rate	Female Rate	Male Rate	Average Daily Population
2000	179.7	18.1	332.5	7,303
	160.6	18.8	295.2	6,727
	138.5	13.4	257.4	5,954
	114.3	11.3	212.3	5,024
	91.4	9.4	169.3	4,067
2005	71.2	6.9	132.3	3,200
2006	64.6	5.9	120.3	2,910

Sources: Compiled by authors from Division of Juvenile Justice and Demographic Research Unit, California Department of Corrections and Rehabilitation, Division of Juvenile Justice, 2005. Numbers for 2006 represent population to June 2006.

The unprecedented population decline in the state's correctional institutions as of 2006 is further reflected in commitments per 100,000 youth. In 1959, juvenile courts across the state committed youths to correctional institutions at a rate of 213 per 100,000.[30] This rate fell to 131 youths per 100,000 by 1973, then rose to almost 285 youths per 100,000 in 1988. Following this peak, the rate began a decline that accelerated after 1995. As of June 2006, the commitment rate to California youth correctional institutions was 65 per 100,000. This represents the lowest recorded commitment rate in California history. Table 3 details the number and rate of youth incarcerated by DJJ institutions from 1959 through June 2006.

Figure 5   DJJ Average Daily Population, Ages 10–17

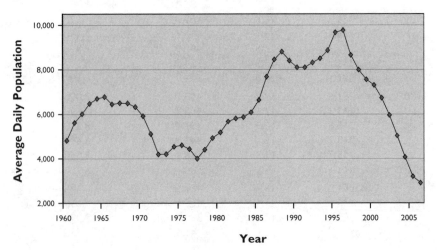

The commitment rates over the past 10 years represent a drastic departure from historical patterns that show relatively stable commitment rates with only minor fluctuations. The previous lowest recorded commitment rate occurred during the period of probation subsidy in the 1970s.[31] During the period of this subsidy, California provided monetary incentives to county probation departments in an effort to reduce commitments to DJJ institutions.[32] The state policy remained in effect until 1978, and the commitment rates subsequently rose upon its termination. No similar subsidy currently exists to explain the low commitment rate among the juvenile population. Although the California budget now includes a $203 million subsidy for county probation departments, this funding replaced federal Temporary Assistance for Needy Families (TANF) funds that became unreliable.[33] These monies enabled probation departments to continue operations, but do not flow as incentives to counties to use alternative placements, as the Probation Subsidy Act did.

County DJJ Commitment Trends and Crime Rates

A county-by-county analysis of DJJ commitment patterns shows a decline in virtually all the major counties. For the past 10 years, 18 of the 21 largest counties, accounting for 75 percent of the total youth population, have reduced their state juvenile commitment rates by over 60 percent. On average, these counties have reduced their juvenile commitment rates by 69 percent per 100,000 juveniles and by 44 percent per 1,000 juvenile felony arrests over the last decade. Table 4 details the number of commitments to DJJ institutions and the percentage change by county.

California counties exercise wide discretion in establishing commitment policies to state correctional institutions.[34] These discretionary policies often reflect practices particular to individual counties. In the juvenile justice context, a county may access a wider variety of options for placement. Certain counties, for instance, prioritize the use of county-funded ranch placements or residential facilities.[35] Although the trend in nearly all counties evidences a sharp decline in DJJ commitment rates, large differences remain with respect to commitment rates based on youth population and arrests. From 2002 through 2004, Monterey County posted the highest DJJ commitment rates, sending its youth to the DJJ at seven times the rate of Orange County, which posted the lowest committing rates. Rates of DJJ commitments per 1,000 juvenile felony arrests ranged from 11 in Orange County to 66 in Madera County.

No identifiable pattern will predict which counties maintain the lowest DJJ commitment rates. Counties as politically divergent as San Francisco and Orange consistently recorded the lowest commitment rates in terms of youth population and felony arrests. Policies supporting the low commitment rates are beyond the scope of this study; however, they may not be dissimilar. The majority of the high committing counties, such as Tulare, Madera, and Fresno, are located in the Central Valley.

**Table 4   DJJ Commitments per 100,000 Population, Ages 10–17
(Ranked by Change, 1993–2004)**

21 Major Counties	1993–95	1996–98	1999–01	2002–04	Change
San Joaquin	355.0	77.9	65.4	28.0	–92%
Kern	196.5	72.7	39.6	24.4	–88%
Santa Barbara	79.5	33.3	24.5	13.8	–83%
Orange	62.1	64.9	28.6	10.8	–83%
Santa Clara	95.9	71.0	34.5	16.8	–82%
San Diego	88.5	61.3	28.0	17.2	–81%
San Mateo	102.3	38.7	44.2	22.3	–78%
Los Angeles	106.3	69.6	45.2	24.3	–77%
Tulare	238.8	127.6	89.1	60.5	–75%
Contra Costa	93.5	51.8	40.9	26.6	–72%
Riverside	89.1	91.2	45.2	25.9	–71%
Sacramento	95.1	57.0	40.6	28.4	–70%
Alameda	112.9	64.3	59.0	34.4	–70%
Stanislaus	109.6	63.5	34.7	33.6	–69%
Madera	207.4	151.8	95.7	66.3	–68%
Fresno	210.6	119.4	84.4	68.9	–67%
San Francisco	78.7	34.3	34.8	28.5	–64%
Ventura	63.8	38.6	38.1	23.2	–64%
Butte	75.7	60.8	25.2	42.8	–43%
San Bernardino	45.9	53.5	91.8	29.3	–36%
Monterey	88.9	132.9	59.9	78.1	–12%

Sources: Compiled by authors from Division of Juvenile Justice and Demographic Research Unit.

Figure 6   DJJ Commitments per 100,000 Population, Ages 10–17

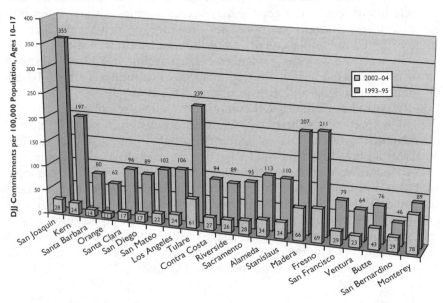

County Juvenile Crime Rates and DJJ Commitments

DJJ county commitment rates are unrelated to juvenile crime patterns. For example, juvenile felony arrest rates declined by 40 percent in both Monterey and San Joaquin counties, but DJJ commitment rates fell by only 12 percent in Monterey County compared to 92 percent in San Joaquin County. Between 2002 and 2004, Monterey County, with a youth population of 51,500, had 764 felony arrests and sent 120 youths to DJJ institutions.[36] By contrast, Orange County has a youth population of 369,000 and recorded 3,293 felony arrests during the same period.[37] Over these two years, Orange County sent 114 youths to DJJ institutions. These numbers translate to a striking disparity between these two counties in the per capita rate of commitment to DJJ institutions. Between 2002 and 2004, Orange County committed 10.8 youth per 100,000 to DJJ institutions while Monterey County committed 78.1 youth per 100,000. (See tables 4 and 5.)

Crime rates fell in all counties regardless of DJJ commitment rates. As table 6 indicates, the five counties with the highest commitment rates imprisoned youth at five times the rate of the five least-committing

Table 5   DJJ Commitments per 1,000 Felony Arrests (Ranked by Change, 1993–2004)

21 Major Counties	1993–95	1996–98	1999–01	2002–04	Change
San Joaquin	98.6	24.4	26.1	12.9	–87%
Kern	64.0	23.8	16.6	12.9	–80%
San Diego	43.0	32.5	17.8	11.5	–73%
Santa Clara	40.1	31.0	21.1	12.7	–68%
Orange	35.2	40.8	24.6	11.2	–68%
Santa Barbara	38.1	18.5	16.0	12.2	–68%
Tulare	109.3	69.7	63.6	38.2	–65%
Riverside	48.4	67.2	32.1	19.6	–59%
San Mateo	43.9	19.8	31.1	19.1	–56%
Los Angeles	40.8	33.3	30.4	18.5	–55%
Stanislaus	33.8	19.6	15.6	17.2	–49%
Sacramento	37.4	28.8	24.2	20.0	–47%
Contra Costa	40.6	24.9	28.1	22.0	–46%
Alameda	34.5	24.7	29.1	20.2	–42%
San Francisco	18.4	8.2	11.4	11.7	–36%
Butte	45.9	33.1	13.9	29.9	–35%
Fresno	54.6	42.7	39.6	40.3	–26%
Ventura	37.2	25.1	35.3	27.9	–25%
Madera	86.0	69.2	63.3	71.0	–17%
San Bernardino	15.8	23.1	60.1	22.1	40%
Monterey	36.7	61.4	36.8	53.7	46%

Sources: Compiled by authors from Division of Juvenile Justice, Criminal Justice Statistics Center, and Demographic Research Unit.

Table 6   Change in Youth Crime Rates, Highest v. Lowest Counties in Youth Imprisonment

	Average commitments per 100,000 pop age 10–17 (2002–2004)	Change in commitment rates (2002–2004 v. 1993–1995)	Change in felony rates (2002–2004 v. 1993–1995)
Most Youth Commitments			
Madera	66.3	–68%	–61%
Monterey	78.1	–12%	–40%
Fresno	68.9	–67%	–56%
Tulare	60.5	–75%	–28%
Butte	42.8	–43%	–13%
Average, highest	63.3	–53%	–40%
Least Youth Commitments			
Santa Clara	12.7	–82%	–45%
Santa Barbara	12.2	–83%	–46%
San Francisco	11.7	–64%	–43%
San Diego	11.5	–81%	–28%
Orange	11.2	–83%	–46%
Average, lowest	11.9	–79%	–42%

Sources: Compiled by authors from Division of Juvenile Justice and Demographic Research Unit.

counties. Further, the lowest imprisoning counties showed much larger declines in youth commitments, averaging a 79 percent reduction; the counties with higher incarceration rates averaged a 53 percent reduction. Yet, there was little difference between counties with regard to youth crime rates. The counties with higher rates of DJJ commitments experienced a 40 percent decrease in their crime rates. Those counties with lower rates of DJJ commitment experienced a similar, but slightly more successful, decrease in crime rates at 42 percent. In fact, the pattern appears random—even large differences in rates of and changes in youth imprisonment by county did not affect rates of or changes in youth felony offending.

As table 6 indicates, the counties with the *highest* commitment rates averaged a 53 percent decrease in juvenile incarceration commitments. This decline in commitment rate accompanies a 40 percent reduction in the felony arrest rate. Those counties that had the lowest commitment rates averaged a 79 percent decrease in juvenile incarceration. Among these counties, the felony arrest rate also decreased by 42 percent. These numbers demonstrate that approximately two-thirds of California's overall decline in youth imprisonment was the result of the large overall decline in juvenile felony arrest rates over the last 12 years. (See tables 1,

2, and 5.) The remaining third may be related to the declining rate of imprisonment per felony over the same period. A comparison of the DJJ commitments per 1,000 juvenile felony arrests in California's 21 major counties demonstrates that all populous counties, except Monterey and San Bernardino, reduced their rates of commitment. Most major counties, like the state as a whole, reported reductions in youth commitments per felony arrests exceeding 50 percent.

Adult Court Transfer Analysis

The declining rates of commitment to DJJ institutions are not the result of greater numbers of youth transfers to adult court. To the contrary, declines in adult court transfers mirror the declines in juvenile court commitments to state institutions.[38] Juveniles transferred to adult courts are typically confined in DJJ facilities until their 18th birthday. Upon reaching the age of majority, they are transferred to the adult corrections system to serve the duration of their sentences.

In the past 15 years, the number of criminal court commitments to DJJ institutions has declined by over 90 percent. In 2004, 80 juveniles, or 2 percent of the 4,067 youth who passed through DJJ facilities in that year, were sentenced by adult criminal courts compared to 31 percent of those in 1990.[39]

The number of DJJ commitments arising from the imposition of sentences delivered in adult court has declined despite the passage of Proposition 21 in March 2000. This initiative, according to the voter handbook,

Figure 7 DJJ Imprisonment Rate, Ages 10–17

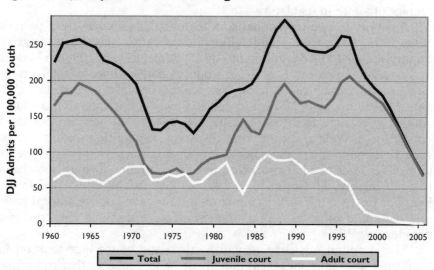

Source: CYA population reports, 1959–2005

explicitly requires "more juvenile offenders to be tried in adult court."[40] Contrary to original predictions, the law has not increased the number of youths transferred and prosecuted in adult court. The current data on criminal court commitments to DJJ suggests that the initiative had little to no impact on adult court transfers.

Conclusion

California correctional policy over the past 25 years has been dominated by incapacitation theory. Thus, correctional policy has been created in the belief that the increase in incarceration rates will produce a decline in crime rates. This argument is often cited as the basis for the decline in crime among adults in California, since overall crime rates fell during the 1990s as adult incarceration levels continued to reach all time highs. While it remains possible for an interest group to cite short-term trends or selected populations to affirm any particular anti-crime theory or strategy, the long-term analysis of major crimes committed by all age groups over the past 25 years shows crime rates rose among those adult age groups whose imprisonment rates rose the fastest, principally ages 40 to 59.[41]

As the above data indicate, the dramatic decline in California's youth imprisonment rate directly contradicts incapacitation theory. As the California youth commitment rate fell to its lowest point in history, youth crime rates also declined to thirty year lows. Indeed, an analysis of juvenile arrests for serious crimes shows that the present generation of youths between the ages of 10 and 17 has the lowest delinquency rates of any recent generation. This unprecedented decline in delinquency rates has occurred at a time when the state was incarcerating the smallest percentage of youth in its history.

A county-by-county comparison demonstrates a concurrent pattern of declining crime rates and falling incarceration rates. Los Angeles County reduced DJJ commitments by 77 percent since 1993 and crime declined by 49 percent. San Diego County decreased commitment rates by 81 percent and juvenile felony arrest rates declined 28 percent. With only 2,910 inmates in 2006, and just 816 new admissions to the state's youth correctional facilities in 2005, DJJ appears to be a least-favored option for juvenile courts around the state. In addition, reductions in statewide commitment have not been offset by increased commitments to local facilities or adult court transfers. The number of youth sentenced to adult prisons fell from 811 in 1995 to just 168 in 2005.[42] California Board of Corrections surveys show the numbers of youths in local juvenile halls and other temporary detention have declined over the last decade as well.[43]

The simultaneous drop in youth crime and youth incarceration in California discredits incapacitation theory and suggests that the crime reduction must be rooted in other societal circumstances. An analysis of long and short-term trends and county-by-county comparisons does not support the premise that reliance on imprisonment as a response to a broad array of offenses beyond serious, violent crimes is an effective public safety strategy.

The study also suggests that youths from primarily rural counties are subject to greater risk of incarceration for less severe offenses than peers from more urban environments. This differential treatment raises serious questions about fairness, given that the different application of sanctions is based solely on the youth's county of origin. The comparison of imprisonment and crime rates between Monterey and Orange County provide a stark example of this disparity.

The findings of this study discredit incapacitation theory and demonstrate the urgent need for California policy makers and legislators to consider alternative theories in response to crime and sentencing. As the Prison Law Office litigation made clear, placing juveniles in DJJ institutions subjects them to potentially inhumane and illegal treatment that has not yet been remedied as ordered in the Consent Decree. Further, the sharp reduction in DJJ commitments illustrates a distinct movement toward new interventions to carry out appropriate treatment and rehabilitation of juvenile offenders. As most major counties are now relying less on state correctional institutions, state policy makers must examine the shifting of state resources to local jurisdictions to improve the capacity of counties to provide a broader range of interventions that will achieve the stated goals of the juvenile justice system.

Notes

[1] In 1977, California adopted the Uniform Determinate Sentencing Act at California Penal Code section 1170. It was hailed as a solution to rampant disparities in sentencing and also removed much discretion from judges by requiring uniform sentences for the same offenses committed under similar circumstances.

[2] Welfare & Institutions Code sec. 1700 describes the purpose of juvenile justice as follows: "to protect society from the consequences of criminal activity and to that purpose community restoration, victim restoration, and offender training and treatment shall be substituted for retributive punishment and shall be directed toward the correction and rehabilitation of young persons who have committed public offenses."

[3] See *Farrell v. Hickman*, Sup. Ct. of Cal., County of Alameda, Case No. RG03079344, Consent Decree (Nov. 19, 2004).

[4] *Farrell v. Hickman*, Amended Complaint for Injunctive and Declaratory Relief (Sept. 23, 2003).

[5] Ibid.

[6] *Farrell v. Hickman*, Consent Decree (Nov. 19, 2004).

[7] Murray, Christopher, Chris Baird, Ned Loughran, Fred Mills, John Platt, "Safety and Welfare Plan: Implementing Reform in California," California Department of Corrections and Rehabilitation, Division of Juvenile Justice (Mar. 31, 2006). The cost per ward reported by DJJ for 2004–05 is $71,700 per year. See Ward Per Capita Cost 2004/05 available at http://www.cdcr.ca.gov/ReportsResearch/wardcost_0405.htm.

[8] Clear, T. and G. Cole, *American Corrections*. Belmont, CA: Wadsworth, 2000. See also Zedlewski, E. "Making Confinement Decisions," National Institute of Justice, Washington, DC (1987), arguing that incarceration is a cost-effective means of controlling crime.

[9] Greenwood, P. W. *Selective Incapacitation.* Santa Monica, CA: RAND Corporation, 1982.

[10] Sheperd, R. E. Jr., "Juvenile Justice," *Journal of Criminal Justice* (Summer 1995).

[11] In 1994, the California legislature passed AB 560, which amended Welfare and Institutions Code 707 to allow the transfer of offenders age 16 and over to adult court.

[12] Welfare & Institutions Code section 707.

[13] On March 7, 1994, the Three Strikes law became effective in California via legislative enactment of AB 971, codified as California Penal Code 667. It was also adopted by the people of California through the initiative process as Proposition 184 in November 1994. As such, it cannot be reformed without the approval of a supermajority of the California legislature.

[14] Cal. Penal Code section 667(d)(3)(A) requires that the offender is age 16 or over. Cal. Penal Code 667(d)(3)(B) describes offenses that may count as strikes when committed by a juvenile, including the offenses listed in Welfare and Institutions Code 707(b).

[15] Proposition 21 passed on March 7, 2000, with 62 percent of the vote. It increased punishment for gang-related felonies, required that more juvenile offenders are tried in adult court, and expanded the list of offenses for which longer prison sentences would be imposed.

[16] Clear and Cole, *American Corrections.* See also Greenwood, *Selective Incapacitation.*

[17] Cal. Dept. of Corrections and Rehabilitation, Population Reports and Statistics (1960–2005, 2006), available at http://www.corr.ca.gov/CDC/rep_stats.asp (*hereinafter Cal. Dept. Corrections Population Reports*). See also California Dept. of Justice, *Crime & Delinquency in California,* Table 16 (2005).

[18] Cal. Dept. of Justice, *Crime & Delinquency in California,* Table 16 (2005). This rate includes all felony arrests for ages 10–69.

[19] Cal. Dept. of Justice, *Crime & Delinquency in California,* Table 16 (2005). This rate includes felony arrests for ages 18–69.

[20] Cal. Dept. of Corrections and Rehabilitation, *California Prisoners & Parolees,* Table 15 (2005). See also Cal. Dept. of Justice, Criminal Justice Statistics Center, *Crime and Delinquency in California,* 1980–2005 and supplement.

[21] Demographic Research Unit, Data Files (1970–1990, 1990–1999, 2000–2006), California Department of Finance, available at http://www.dof.ca.gov/HTML/DEMOGRAP/ DRU_datafiles/DRU_DataFiles.htm. Information obtained in files was used in Tables 1–6. See also Cal. Dept. of Justice, Criminal Justice Statistics Center, *Crime & Delinquency 1970–2005,* and supplement (2005) available at http://ag.ca.gov/cjsc/index.htm.

[22] Ibid.

[23] Ibid. See also First Commitments 1990–2001, data compiled by CYA Research Division, Ward Information and Research Bureau, available at http://www.cdcr.ca.gov/ ReportsResearch/commitments.html. Between 1986 and 2001, first commitments to California Division of Juvenile Justice institutions decreased by 58 percent.

[24] Ibid.

[25] Data compiled from Division of Juvenile Justice, California Department of Corrections and Rehabilitation, "Characteristics of First Admissions: 1959–2001," "A Comparison of First Commitment Characteristics: 1993–2004," "Population Movement Summary: September 2005."

[26] California crime reports were less reliable prior to 1960. Therefore, data recorded prior to 1960 are not considered.

[27] Between 1959 and 2005, California's youth population ages 10–17 increased from 1.95 million to 4.50 million. See supra fn 25, "Characteristics of First Admissions: 1959–2001."

[28] Cal. Dept. of Corrections and Rehabilitation, Division of Juvenile Justice 2005, 2006. Information gathered by phone call to DJJ on June 16, 2006.

[29] Ibid.

[30] Ibid.

[31] See Nieto, M. "Community Correction Punishments: An Alternative to Incarceration for Non-Violent Offenders," California Research Bureau, Cal. State Library (May 1996). In 1965, California enacted the Probation Subsidy Act to provide counties up to $4000 per juvenile or adult not committed to a state-run institution. The subsidy was responsible for the diversion of 45,000 offenders to community-run programs.

[32] Probation Subsidy Act of 1965.

[33] Prevent Violence.org California Budget Bulletin, "Final FY 2004/05 Preserves Most Funding for Youth Crime & Violence Prevention Programs" (Aug. 23, 2004).

[34] Several California counties have established moratoria preventing commitment to DJJ institutions for a variety of reasons. See Burrell, S. and J. Laba, "Violence Prone Youth Authority Still Fails its Children, its Taxpayers," *San Francisco Daily Journal*, Apr. 26, 2006, Forum Column.

[35] In San Francisco, the Board of Supervisors urged judges to refrain from committing youth to DJJ facilities in February 2004, citing the use of cages to "house unruly youth" and failures in mental health, education, health care, and discipline. Herel, S. "Supes Urge Judges Not to Use CYA," *San Francisco Chronicle*, Feb. 25, 2004, at A-16.

[36] Of the 764 felony arrests in Monterey County, 200 were for violent crimes and two were for homicide.

[37] Of the 3,293 felony arrests in Orange County, 636 were for violent crimes and 10 were for homicide.

[38] Division of Juvenile Justice, California Department of Corrections and Rehabilitation, "Characteristics of First Admissions: 1959–2001," "A Comparison of First Commitment Characteristics: 1993–2004."

[39] Prior to 1996 and passage of an administration-sponsored bill, it was common practice for adult courts to sentence offenders over the age of 18, but under 21, to California Youth Authority facilities. After this practice was stopped, only adult court commitments who were under the age 18 could be housed in these facilities. See Governor Pete Wilson's 1996–97 State Proposed Budget, estimating an offset in CYA population due to transfer of inmates over 18 and sentenced in criminal court to California Department of Corrections.

[40] Meaning of Voting Yes, Proposition 21 Juvenile Crime, Initiative Constitutional Amendment and Statute, March 7, 2000 available at http://www.smartvoter.org/2000/03/07/ca/state/prop/21/.

[41] See above, note 20, CJSC 1975–2004.

[42] Juvenile Research Branch, Office of Research (2006). Cal. Dept. of Corrections and Rehabilitation, Court of Commitment by Admission Year, 1988–2005.

[43] California Board of Corrections, Juvenile Detention Profile Surveys (2004, 2005).

4

Aftercare as Afterthought
Reentry and the
California Youth Authority

Michelle Byrnes, Daniel Macallair, and Andrea Shorter

The movement of youthful offenders from correctional institution to community has gained increased attention in recent years from policy makers and legislators. However, this critical point in justice system processing remains significantly under-researched and under-funded, and has not received the level of public attention commensurate with the widespread concern over juvenile crime and arrest rates.[1] Within the youthful offender population in California, the youths released from the California Youth Authority (CYA) represent the most serious juvenile offenders; many were committed to the CYA with histories of repeat criminal behavior, much of it violent.[2] All of these individuals will eventually be released to the community. As over 2,000 CYA youth and young adults are paroled each year to cities and towns throughout the state, their ability to successfully reintegrate into their communities presents one of the largest and most crucial challenges in the juvenile justice field. Many adult offenders start committing offenses at a young age and approximately 40 percent of adult prison populations are graduates of institution-based juvenile justice systems.[3] The return of youthful offenders presents an opportunity to stop the revolving door that places a significant financial, administrative, and public safety burden on the communities of return.

A successful reentry process begins at the point that a youth is committed to the CYA, and continues until he or she is released from parole.[4] The success of reentry depends on the individual's capacity to return to society as a productive, contributing member and the presence of services to prepare for and facilitate this return. Confinement in a secure CYA facility can in theory provide the first phase in preparing for the inevitable transition to the outside world through education and coun-

Written especially for *Juvenile Justice in America: Problems and Prospects*.

seling programs. Unfortunately, despite the CYA's recognition of the importance of structured reentry services, the reality is far different.

According to a study by the Bureau of Justice Statistics, of adult offenders released in 1994, 67 percent were recommitted within three years.[5] A similar study of CYA recidivism showed that *91 percent of youth offenders released from the CYA will reoffend in the same time period.*[6] At a cost of $48,400 per CYA ward per year, this failure to rehabilitate comes at a high price. These startling statistics quantify the ineffectiveness of the current juvenile justice system at rehabilitation and raise serious questions about the efficacy of current state policies.

After release, parolees frequently return to their families in the cities and towns where their trouble arose. A successful reentry process includes, at a minimum, the services and supports necessary to deter the parolee from recommitment. Recent initiatives, such as the Department of Justice's *Going Home: Serious and Violent Offender Reentry Program* and the collaborative *Young Offender Initiative: Reentry Grant Program* reflect an increasing awareness of the need to find creative, community-based alternatives to reduce recidivism among youthful and adult offenders.[7] A recent poll indicates near unanimous public support for rehabilitation and reentry programs: 94 percent of those surveyed support requiring prisoners to work and receive job training to ensure that they leave prison with job skills, and 88 percent favor providing job training and placement to released prisoners.[8]

Defining Recidivism

The California Youth Authority does not directly measure recidivism. Instead, the department measures certain Youthful Offender Parole Board actions concerning individuals under direct parole supervision. The National Institute of Justice compiled comprehensive recidivism data for CYA releases in the 1980s. These two measurements, described below, yield far different results.

The California Youth Authority calculated recidivism based on the number of parolees who were removed from parole for a technical or law violation within 24 months. Local arrests, convictions, and incarcerations were not included if they did not result in revocation or discharge by the Youthful Offender Parole Board. Any arrests, convictions, or incarcerations that occurred after discharge from the Youth Authority, even if they occurred within 24 months of parole release, were not included. This calculation yields a 47.3 percent parole violation rate in 2001.[9]

The National Institute of Justice calculated recidivism based on the number of wards released who were rearrested within a 3 year time period. Ninety-one percent (91 percent) of CYA wards in 1986–87 were arrested or had parole revoked within three years. This data, presented at a meeting of the American Society of Criminologists in 1995, was never published or released.[10]

According to the *Young Offender Initiative*, "Compared with information about reentry adult offenders, little is known in general about reentry issues affecting youth."[11] This article attempts to address this gap and to initiate a dialogue about this pressing concern. The goals of this article are to:

- Highlight the importance of reentry and aftercare programs in reducing recidivism and improving public safety
- Document the current reintegration process and the specific barriers facing CYA parolees
- Identify the challenges to families and communities presented by the reentry process and the collateral effects of recidivism
- Identify successful institutional and community-based aftercare programs that provide effective care at lower costs than incarceration
- Recommend strategies to improve the rate of successful parolee reintegration

An Inadequate Reentry Process

The process of reentry for California Youth Authority parolees fails to adequately prepare them for an independent, self-sufficient lifestyle outside of a correctional institution. The current system is highly fragmented and relies too heavily on CYA parole agents constrained by large caseloads and insufficient resources. Current systems fail to adequately address the 91 percent recidivism rate and perpetuate a costly, ineffective juvenile justice system, in which youthful offenders cycle in and out of institutional facilities. The damaging collateral effects of the current system are felt at the individual, community, and statewide level, as large numbers of violent youthful offenders leave institutions and camps with limited skills and education, fractured social supports, and strong gang affiliations.

Upon release, parolees face unique challenges as they attempt to make the transition from a highly structured locked facility to a life of relative independence. CYA wards live in a highly structured locked facility for over two years on average during a critical developmental period. Studies indicate that living conditions within the CYA, such as dormitory-style sleeping quarters and constant fear of violence, are not conducive to rehabilitation efforts.[12]

Average sentence lengths have increased considerably in the last twenty years, from 11.5 months in 1971 to 28.3 months in 2001.[13] Longer sentences compound wards' isolation, solidify their institutional identity, and reduce their connections to families and communities. In an environment where inmate-on-inmate violence is a daily occurrence, immediate survival and coping are far more germane to wards' lives than preparation and planning for the future. This reality makes the transition to a "mainstream" life on the outside even more difficult.

The following excerpt from a qualitative examination of formerly incarcerated youth highlights the ongoing challenges facing the youthful offender reentry population:

> The current transitional focus on individual accountability and responsibility ignores several important facts about this population:
>
> - Youth ex-offenders are still adolescents, many of whom are experiencing delayed emotional and cognitive development due to [emotional abuse] and early drug use.
> - They have never successfully used problem-solving or coping skills outside of the correctional setting.
> - They still have no adults in their lives to help them learn the skills they need to deal with [normal life challenges].[14]

While the specific elements of an effective reentry program may vary, the ultimate goal is the same: to preserve public safety, reduce recidivism, and assist individuals to achieve success. Reentry experts identify the following minimum components of an individual's "success": an individual not being rearrested since release, not being recommitted for a parole violation, and attending school and/or maintaining employment.[15] Despite the increasing recognition in theory of the role of reentry programs in reducing recidivism, federal and state policies devote insufficient resources to prevention and intervention programs with demonstrable records of effective treatment provision at lower costs than institutionalization. The high costs of crime demonstrate that failing to invest in our youth costs society far more than the direct costs of incarceration (see table 1). *It costs society more than $1.7 million for each youth who drops out of school to become involved in a life of crime and drug abuse.*[16] Therefore, investing in reintegration programs that produce even a moderate reduction in recidivism reflects a sound, cost-effective investment decision. As Gary Melton asks,

> Why wouldn't policy makers, policy administrators, and third-party payers rush to adopt service models that—in contrast to the services that are now widely available—are inexpensive, carefully and positively evaluated, easy to understand, and consistent with long-established values of respect for family integrity and personal liberty and privacy? If innovation is cheaper but more effective than current practices, why wouldn't it be quickly and widely adopted?
>
> The nearly universal failure to adopt innovative service models as standard practice reflects intrinsic but often tractable obstacles to reform.[17]

Scope and Methodology

This article will describe issues with CYA parolee reintegration. As a first step, we reviewed relevant studies and reports, including academic

Table 1 The Costs of Juvenile Crime

Description	Cost
Crime	
Juvenile career (4 years @ 1–4 crimes/year)	
Victim costs	$62,000–$250,000
Juvenile justice costs	$21,000–$84,000
Adult career (6 years @ 10.6 crimes/year)	
Victim costs	$1,000,000
Criminal justice costs	$335,000
Offender productivity costs	$64,000
Total crime cost	**$1.5–$1.8 million**
Present value	**$1.3–$1.5 million**
Drug Abuse	
Resources devoted to drug market	$84,000–$168,000
Reduced productivity loss	$27,600
Drug treatment costs	$10,200
Medical treatment of drug-related illnesses	$11,000
Premature death	$31,800–$223,000
Criminal justice costs associated with drug crimes	$40,500
Total drug abuse cost	**$200,000–$480,000**
Present value 1999	**$150,000–$360,000**
Costs imposed by high school dropout	
Lost wage productivity	$300,000
Fringe benefits	$75,000
Nonmarket losses	$95,000–$375,000
Total dropout costs	**$470,000–$750,000**
Present value*	**$243,000–$388,000**
Total loss	**$2.2–$3 million**
Present value*	**$1.7–$2.3 million**

* Present value is the amount of money that would have to be invested today in order to cover future costs of the youth's behavior.

and criminal justice publications related to juvenile and adult offender reentry; data on institutional, transitional, and aftercare services available for youthful offenders; evaluations of existing violence prevention and intervention programs; and current and previous funding initiatives. Our literature review was not comprehensive, but it provides a foundation for the recommendations in this article.

We gathered official ward and parolee data from the California Department of Corrections and Rehabilitation and recidivism data from the National Institute of Justice.[18] We conducted interviews with CYA staff at various levels of authority, including the director, institutional staff members, and field parole agents. These interviews supplement the quantitative population data and inform the recommendations. References refer simply to "staff" to respect the wishes of many staff members who requested that their names not be used in this article.

To identify model programs in the field of juvenile aftercare, we conducted a national search of model transition and aftercare programs for juvenile offenders. Interviews were conducted in person and by telephone with program directors and staff members at public, private, and nonprofit violence prevention and intervention community organizations and advocacy groups.

Our recommendations are based on the assessment of the current state of reentry after release from the CYA, existing research on the reentry process, identification of model reentry principles and practices, and specific recommendations made by institutional and program staff.

The California Youth Authority

A Shrinking Population

There are currently over 5,700 people in CYA institutions and camps, but first admissions to the CYA have dramatically declined in the past decade, from 3,483 in 1990 to 1,501 in 2001.[19] This significant reduction in commitments presents an ideal opportunity to divert resources from daily custodial functions to quality institutional and transitional programs through higher staff-to-ward ratios and improved training opportunities for institutional staff.

Highlighted below are characteristics of *wards* in the CYA.[20]

- The average ward is 19 years old
- The average age at admission is 17 years
- Wards are institutionalized for 2.4 years on average
- Ninety-five percent of wards are male
- Hispanics comprise 48 percent of the ward population
- Fifty-four percent of wards come from Los Angeles County
- In 2002, 84 percent of admissions were first commitments
- Seventeen percent of first commitments had no prior conviction or sustained petition
- Thirty-eight percent of first commitments had no prior local commitment
- The majority of wards were committed for violent offenses (58.6 percent of the institution population as of June 30, 2002)

The following characteristics pertain to *parolees*.[21]

- The shrinking institutional population translates into a declining parole population, which is expected to continue its decline through 2006

- The average age upon release to parole is 21 years
- Seventy percent of parolees were committed for violent crimes
- The number of parolees committed for narcotic and drug offenses has declined significantly in the past decade, from 13.9 percent in 1992 to 3.3 percent in 2001
- Over 75 percent are on their first parole
- The average amount of time spent on parole was 1.8 years for those leaving parole in 2001
- Parolees are concentrated in specific counties: over 60 percent of parolees were released to seven counties in 2001 (see table 2)

Table 2 shows the seven counties with the highest numbers of CYA parolees, as of June 30, 2002. Percentages are shown in parentheses.

Table 2   CYA Parole Releases and Population by County (Top 7 Counties)

County	CYA Parolees Released 2001	Total CYA Parole Population June 30, 2002
Los Angeles	651 (25.8%)	1,050 (24.8%)
San Bernardino	200 (7.8%)	339 (8.0%)
Fresno	207 (8.0%)	315 (7.4%)
Orange	179 (7.0%)	287 (6.8%)
San Diego	152 (5.9%)	247 (5.8%)
Santa Clara	100 (3.9%)	230 (5.4%)
Riverside	145 (5.7%)	216 (5.1%)
Total, Top 7 Counties	1,634	2,684
Parole Releases/Population (All CA Counties)	2,565	4,237
Percent of Total	63.7%	63.3%

Source: California Youth Authority

Disproportionate Minority Confinement

It is impossible to ignore the high proportion of ethnic minorities within the CYA ward and parolee populations. In 2001, ethnic minorities accounted for 83 percent of first commitments to the Youth Authority, with Hispanics comprising 48 percent (see table 3).[22] Such disproportionate minority confinement reflects a national trend in adult and youth correctional facilities. Although examining these numbers in detail is beyond the scope of this paper, these statistics raise important questions that warrant further research about the relationship between race, access to critical services, and rates of incarceration. As highlighted by Roche et al., examining these demographics "trains our eyes on crime as a quality

Table 3   CYA Population by Race

Race/Ethnicity	Wards	Parolees
Hispanic	48%	51.3%
African American	30%	24.1%
Caucasian	17%	13.6%
Asian	4%	7.6%
Other	1%	3.3%

Source: California Youth Authority

of life issue that cannot be disentangled and dealt with in isolation from the issues of poverty, education, employment, substance abuse, housing and other critical issues that face our communities."[23] These figures also underline the importance of developing culturally sensitive counseling and services for wards and parolees.

Girls in the California Youth Authority

Although the number of girls and young women committed to the CYA is still relatively small (279 as of June 30, 2002), there is a disturbing upward trend in female institutional populations—girls represented 3 percent of the CYA population in 1992, and 4.7 percent in 2002.[24]

Young women and girls in the CYA parole population comprise 6 percent of the total parole population.[25] Twenty-two percent of female wards come from Los Angeles County. Female offenders are committed at higher rates for property and drug offenses than their male counterparts: in 2001, 38.5 percent of girls and 33 percent of boys were committed for property offenses and drug offenses accounted for 7.7 percent of female and 5.1 percent of male first commitments.[26]

The only CYA facility that accepts girls is located in Ventura County in Southern California. With over 50 percent of girls committed from the Northern region, this distant location, inaccessible by public transportation, presents a barrier to an increasing number of families. Accepting long distance collect calls and making visits poses a great challenge for many families with limited financial resources. Without this family contact, female youth within the system become increasingly isolated and alienated.

Special Needs of Wards

Many wards have a range of special needs, due to histories of poor educational outcomes, mental illness, and substance abuse. In 2001, 7.9 percent of new commitments had a documented physical or mental disability.[27] This figure likely underestimates the numbers of youth with disabilities in the CYA; studies indicate that as many as 70 percent of incarcerated youth suffer from disabling conditions, and a comprehensive assessment of the mental health system in the CYA concluded that on average, 50 percent of wards have 3–4 psychiatric diagnoses.[28]

Collectively, these data point to a youthful offender population with a relatively serious criminal history and intense social service needs. This type of population information has been used to justify a highly punitive environment at the CYA. Indeed, policies and practices within the CYA have been subject to legal scrutiny for failure to meet the basic health and educational needs of wards.[29] In contrast, the same data is presented here to demonstrate the need for a continuum of care services to address the root causes of criminal behavior.

Life in the California Youth Authority

> "I lost God while I was at the YA. I thought, 'if there were a God, He would never let this place exist.'"[30]
>
> —former CYA ward

Experience with local juvenile halls and other county facilities do little to prepare wards for the violent, penal environment at the Youth Authority. Youth enter the CYA through one of three reception centers, where they begin an ongoing two-tiered process of evaluation and testing; one tier encompasses the formal evaluative process undertaken by institutional staff, including psychiatric and education batteries. However, evaluations and counseling are significantly hampered by wards' constant fear: "I cried at 3 o'clock in the morning. Quietly. Everyone did. . . . I was living in fear 22 hours a day in that place. There was no way I was going to open up during group therapy."[31]

Fellow wards conduct a second, informal tier of evaluation, a series of ongoing tests that ultimately have the most bearing on a ward's daily quality of life within the institution. New wards are immediately sized up for potential weakness and vulnerability. Race, city of origin, gang affiliation, and physical size all contribute to the wards' social ranking and subsequent treatment. Youths determined to be "weak" are subject to regular victimization by other wards, including physical and sexual abuse. The wards are particularly vulnerable to attacks at night, when "50 or 60 young men are bedded down in a dormitory which is overseen by a single guard."[32]

> It was too dangerous to sleep at night. One night, this guy had the flu, and he was breathin' real loud. Another guy in the unit kept saying, "Hey, knock it off. Stop breathin' so loud," but the guy was on cough medicine or something, and was knocked out, couldn't hear a thing. Finally the guy gets so frustrated with the noise that he goes to the trashcan and grabs a metal dustpan. He raises it over his head and BAM, smacks the [sick] guy, splits his skull open with one hit.[33]

Most wards are affiliated with gangs before their commitment to the Youth Authority, and these ties are strengthened during their tenure. Many others join gangs for self-protection.

> I'm Cuban, but I look white. First they wanted me to join the white car [gang], but I wouldn't. Then they wanted me to join the brown car. I said I would rather face the knife than join a car. . . . When I was about to be released, the Lieutenant [one of the gang leaders] told me that this time around I got a pass because I [had certain friends]. He said if I ever came back [to the CYA], if I didn't join a gang, I wouldn't get a pass—I wouldn't make it.[34]

Seasoned wards may "test" a new ward by spitting on his pillow, stealing personal belongings, or demanding cigarettes. If the new ward doesn't appropriately challenge his testers, he is likely to become a regular victim of harassment and violence. A former ward describes witnessing the "orientation" of a new ward:

> This guy says to the new guy, "Got a smoke?" and the new guy says "Yeah."
> "Gimme one."
> "I only have enough to last me . . ." and WHAM the guy gets knocked out. From that point on, every day people'd walk by him, push him, shove him, whatever. Then one day he gets told that his laundry is ready for him in the back room. He goes back there, and nine guys are hiding, waiting for him. . . .[35]

According to a comprehensive report on life within the CYA, such "rat-packing" is common for wards without allies.[36] Interviews with staff and wards repeatedly highlight a frightening reality: thousands of young men and women are living their adolescence in an environment in which their physical and emotional safety is threatened on a daily basis.

Reentry: From Detention to Independence

Barriers to Successful Reentry

Although each individual faces unique barriers, common challenges face all youthful offenders reentering their communities. The following barriers, detailed below, have been identified by researchers and were repeatedly cited in interviews with parole agents, service providers, researchers, and former wards:

- Lack of educational options
- Lack of housing options
- Limited skills and education
- Gang affiliations and attendant racial tensions
- Institutional identity
- Substance abuse problems
- Mental health problems
- Lack of community supports and role models

• Legislative barriers that limit access to education, cash assistance, and public housing

Although daunting, these barriers are not intractable. As detailed later in this article, effective programs throughout the country have demonstrated that answers to these challenges do exist.

Limited Skills and Education. Although the average age for first commitments in 2001 was 17, wards consistently demonstrate reading scores ranging from 8th to 9th grade levels, and math scores ranging from 7th to 8th grade levels. Educational deficiencies emerge as one of the most salient challenges facing CYA parolees. Test score data from standardized exams administered in 2001 quantify the depth of these educational limitations.[37] These educational scores demonstrate the consequences of current state policies that allocate more money to corrections than to education.[38] Even without a criminal history, expecting a group of students in which only 11.5 percent pass the California High School exit exam to function and excel in the conventional economy seems naïve at

Table 4   Average Percentile Performance of Students by Subject by Grade Level 2001

Grade Level	Reading	Mathematics	Language	Science
Grade 9	13%	19%	16%	20%
Grade 10	10%	16%	8%	17%
Grade 11	11%	16%	13%	17%

Table 5   Percentage of Students Scoring at or above the 50th Percentile Based on National Norms

Grade Level	Reading		Mathematics		Language		Science	
	CEA	State-wide	CEA	State-wide	CEA	State-wide	CEA	State-wide
Grade 9	10%	35%	7%	51%	11%	53%	9%	41%
Grade 10	8%	34%	3%	45%	5%	42%	9%	46%
Grade 11	8%	37%	4%	46%	10%	*	8%	42%

*Data not available
CEA: California Education Authority (CYA School System)

Table 6   California High School Exit Exam May 2001 Results Percentage of CYA Students Passing

English-Language Arts	Mathematics	Average % Passing
17%	6%	11.5%

best. After two years of isolation in a correctional facility, youth are released into a work world in which employers expect a level of functional literacy for most entry-level jobs. Many wards also have limited English skills when they enter the CYA, and do not receive bilingual services within the institution to prepare them for sustainable employment.

Poor educational outcomes are compounded by a lack of job skills and poor work histories. Budget cuts since the late 1990s have reduced vocational program options within institutions.[39] Combined with a criminal record, attaining sustainable employment presents a huge barrier to self-sufficiency.

Lack of Educational Options. Given the poor educational outcomes of most CYA wards, access to post-release education is especially important. However, many parolees are unable to return to the same schools that they attended before incarceration due to the following factors:

- Public safety risks: Youth may feel threatened by former gang rivals and/or family members affected by the youth's criminal history;
- Age: The average age of CYA parolees upon release is 21, which excludes them from the state's responsibility to provide a public education;[40]
- Community opposition: Even for those students under 18 years of age, youth may encounter resistance to enrollment from teachers, school administrators, and parents of other students;
- Administrative hurdles: The process of transferring students' credits and transcripts is frequently not completed before release, thereby preventing a student from immediate enrollment. This delay creates a disruption in an educational history already defined by inconsistency. Teachers and administrators at the local school may be reluctant to expedite a process that will only ensure that a student with a criminal record can attend school.

Lack of Housing Options. CYA parole agents cited the lack of quality housing options as one of the greatest barriers to successful reentry. The majority of CYA youth return to live with their families in the same communities from which they were committed. However, for wards for which family placement is not a viable option, there are limited alternatives. There are few residential transitional and treatment beds available for ex-offenders. The inadequate supply forces many parole agents to settle for any available residential placement, regardless of the quality of care provided.

Gang Affiliations and Attendant Racial Tensions. The vast majority of wards are affiliated with gangs upon commitment to the CYA. Incarceration in secure facilities strengthens and solidifies gang relationships. For example, at N.A. Chaderjian in Stockton, most wards live in double-bunked cells, and are housed according to gang affiliation. Gang altercations are frequent and the entrenched gang culture makes individual relationships among rival gang members exceptionally difficult.[41]

Institutional Identity. After being labeled and treated as a delinquent and housed with hundreds of other youth with a criminal background, many offenders simply learn to be better criminals. The institutional policies, constant structure, and external discipline do not prepare wards for an independent life that requires internal discipline and motivation. This institutional identity also manifests itself in unrealistic and inflated expectations upon release; many wards are unprepared for the daily challenges of independent living, and do not recognize the substantial difficulties inherent in the transition process. Combined with the culture of violence within CYA institutions and camps, we can expect that institutional experiences, rather than rehabilitating, will only magnify the anger and criminal potential of this population.

Substance Abuse Problems. Although only a small portion of wards is committed for drug-related offenses, many report substance abuse problems that require treatment services. According to a 2000 CYA study, 74 percent of male wards and 68 percent of female wards have substance abuse problems.[42]

Mental Health Problems. The CYA population reflects the increased recognition of mental health needs within the criminal justice system nationwide. Estimates of mental health disorders within the national population of incarcerated youth range between 50 to 75 percent.[43] Within the CYA, rates of mental illness are very high: according to a preliminary report issued by the CYA in 2000, 45 percent of male wards and 65 percent of female wards had mental health problems.[44]

Lack of Community Supports and Role Models. The individual characteristics of CYA wards cannot be disentangled from their communities of origin. Many youthful offenders were raised in conditions of poverty, inadequate social supports, and family dysfunction and/or abuse. Most will return to the same conditions. Consequently, wards' ability to rehabilitate is highly dependent on their access to a continuum of care services that support them at each stage of the transition process from institution to home.

Legislative Barriers. Despite having served their time, many ex-offenders continue to serve a life sentence in the form of reduced educational and social service supports. Due to a number of legislative barriers, including the five discussed below, this population faces additional challenges in meeting their basic needs.

The last decade was marked by a rise in punitive legislation targeting correctional education programs. Motivated by the perception that prison had become too easy, two regulations were introduced in the 1990s that solidified barriers to accessing higher education:

- Students incarcerated in state or federal prisons are ineligible for federal Pell grants, which are used for secondary education.[45]
- Anyone with a drug conviction is prohibited from receiving federal financial aid to enroll in post-secondary institutions.[46]

A higher education is not an immediate consideration for most wards and parolees, given the low educational level of most CYA youth. However, although this restriction does not directly affect most of the CYA population, this punitive legislation undermines the rehabilitative potential of institutional education, and flies in the face of the well-documented benefits of institutional higher education programs.[47]

The 1996 Welfare Reform Act specifies that offenders with state or federal felony offense records involving the use or sale of drugs are subject to a lifetime ban on receiving cash assistance (TANF) and food stamps.[48] Although states have the discretion to opt out of this ban or to enforce a partial ban (on one form of assistance but not the other), California has chosen to deny benefits entirely to this population.[49] Although only a small portion of wards are committed for drug offenses, this elimination of transitional income support for certain offenders reflects a legislative commitment to continue the "war on drugs," despite the proven ineffectiveness of these policies.[50] Wards who rely on Supplemental Security Income (SSI) may be denied access to this social support if they violate a condition of their parole.[51] SSI is a federally administered income and health insurance program for qualified aged, blind, and disabled individuals. Although we do not have data on the number of wards who rely on SSI, when one considers the high rates of mental illness within the CYA population, as well as the high proportion of parole violators, it is evident that this legislation places at risk the health and safety of many young people with disabilities.

Most states prohibit ex-offenders with felony convictions from certain types of employment, such as childcare, education, and nursing. This legal barrier does not account for the many employers who do not hire ex-offenders due to stigma, fear, and bias.

Under the 1996 "One Strike" Initiative, local Public Housing Authorities were given the discretion to restrict access to public housing for people with drug convictions.[52] Depending on the policies of their local Housing Authority, CYA parolees may not be able to move in with their families who live in public housing.

Upon release, Youth Authority parolees are disqualified from voting in the state of California until successful completion of their parole process.[53] This prohibition further marginalizes and isolates voting-age parolees from mainstream society.

Additional Challenges to Providing Effective Transition Services[54]

- Supervision and enforcement take precedence over intervention and treatment at all stages of CYA institutionalization and parole.
- Transition planning does not begin until 30–60 days before a ward's Parole Consideration Date.
- Institutional and field parole staff receive inadequate professional development and specialized transition training; CYA staff with specialized caseloads (i.e., related to mental health and substance abuse issues and sex offenders) receive no special training.
- A significant lack of communication, coordination, and commitment exists among agencies that serve CYA youth; there is little collaboration between CYA and service agencies with appropriate expertise, such as the California Department of Mental Health.
- CYA leadership discourages collaboration and input from outside agencies.
- Transferring wards' educational records between institutional and community schools is often delayed.

The Current State of Reentry and Aftercare

Institutional education and service programs provide the first step in a ward's preparation for an independent life in the community upon release. The following section examines the structure of institutional transition programs currently operating in the CYA.

Educational Services

Education has been identified as one of the most effective methods for reducing recidivism.[55] Unfortunately, most juvenile offenders over the age of 15 do not return to school or do not graduate from high school after release from a correctional setting.[56] According to a preliminary CYA study in 1997, parolees with either a high school diploma, a GED, or a high school proficiency certificate were four times more likely to succeed on parole than those who did not attain this educational level.[57] CYA wards that participated in a post-secondary college program available at certain institutions had a significantly lower recidivism rate than the general population—80 percent of participants did not return to prison after release.[58] Another study demonstrates that prisoners who received a degree while serving time had a recidivism rate four times lower than that of the general population (15 percent compared to 60 percent).[59]

With the majority of wards of high school age or older, access to education is critical to their future success. In 1997, in response to documented problems within the CYA educational system, the California

Education Authority (CEA) was created to ensure the accreditation and development of quality standards within CYA high schools. The "No Diploma, No Parole" policy, implemented in 1998, reflects a further attempt on the part of the CYA to codify and enforce educational standards.[60] However, the policy has fizzled within institutions due to resource and staffing restraints and administrative lockdowns that prevent consistent enforcement of this policy.[61] Therefore, many wards continue to be released without a high school diploma or GED.

For most wards, the educational experience within the institution represents another disjointed step in an educational history largely defined by interruption and fragmentation. Although the majority of wards are between seventeen and twenty years of age (73.2 percent as of December 31, 2001), their skill levels resemble those of students in grades 4–8.[62] Prior to their commitment to the CYA, many have attended multiple county court schools, where repeated relocations create disruptions and wards frequently fail to complete a subject. At the CYA, an open enrollment policy necessitates the weekly entrance and exit of students, creating ongoing interruptions in the subject material and compelling teachers to teach in blocks. Although class size is limited to eighteen students, student skill levels within a single classroom may range from illiteracy to college-level proficiency. Administrative lockdowns compound irregular school attendance, perpetuate the gaps in students' knowledge and skills, and contribute to student frustration and reduced motivation.[63]

Special Education and Bilingual Services. The Youth Authority has been criticized for failing to provide legally mandated special education and bilingual services to wards. In 1998, the U.S. Department of Education, Office of Civil Rights determined that the CYA has failed to comply with the provision of required services to the estimated 26 percent of the wards who are English Learner students. An October 2001 review of the status of the Voluntary Resolution Plan designed to address these concerns found "continued deficiencies which they considered to be of a major and serious concern which if not corrected will lead to formal enforcement proceedings."[64] According to a CYA process report of the sex offender treatment program, "services for Spanish-speaking wards are limited. The absence of bilingual staff limits the services provided by program staff to monolingual sex offenders."[65]

The CYA has also been cited for failing to respond appropriately to calls for special education programs for students with disabilities. An audit conducted by the Inspector General indicated that only between 38 percent and 77 percent of wards at the Nelles facility were receiving adequate special education services.[66] In a recent lawsuit, the Prison Law Office indicated that deaf wards are not provided with the appropriate interpretive services necessary to successfully complete their Board-ordered programs, and then they are penalized for this failure.[67]

Despite the proven importance of education and repeated criticism about the quality of education services provided in the CYA, the California State budget for fiscal year 2002 included a reduction of $2.6 million for education services (Prop 98).[68] This spending reduction produced only fleeting savings: at an estimated cost of $1.7 million for each rehabilitation failure, these cost savings would be fully negated if only two individuals reoffended. As of 2006 the money for education has yet to be returned to the budget.

Transition Coordinator Program. The Transition Coordinator Program provides a valuable service to CYA wards in need of additional educational support. Through intensive counseling and specialized transition services targeting wards at high risk of low educational outcomes, transition coordinators assist students in achieving their educational and career goals and preparing for successful parole. These educators fill in a gap in educational programming; according to a recent Director's Report, "Parole agents and youth counselors . . . have neither the time nor the expertise to fashion an intervention strategy for a student's formal education program and plans for continued learning upon release."[69]

This program reflects a promising step toward creating a continuum of educational services. However, the staffing level of the transition coordinator program fails to meet wards' transitional needs. In response to a large regular and drop-in caseload, interviews with transition coordinators and other educational staff highlight the need for more Coordinator positions at each institution. Individual staff capabilities simply cannot compensate for daunting caseloads and insufficient resources.

Special Programs

Parole consideration depends on a ward's completion of an individualized series of programs and services mandated by the Youth Offender Parole Board (YOPB). Services include substance abuse counseling; individual counseling; and resource groups on topics such as anger management, parenting, and gang awareness.

Assignment to Special Programs. Consistent waiting lists at all special programs indicate the unmet service needs of many wards (see table 7). Wards' placement in special counseling programs is ultimately determined by the Youth Offender Parole Board, frequently driven by criminological management rather than medical necessity.

> Many of the assignments [to special programs] are made by fiat rather than by medical planning, and the recommendations come from entities not responsive to clinical input, education or feedback. . . . Clinical staff are subject to the enthusiasms of administrators and YOPB board members who have no training in mental health.[70]

Table 7   Institutional Programs

Program Type	# of Beds	Treatment Time	Wait List
Intensive Treatment Program (mental health)	273	19 months	5–10 wards
Specialized Counseling Program (mental health)	246	1 year	190 wards
Substance Abuse	1,300	8 months	Not available
Sex Offender	229	19 months	Not available

Note: These are estimates based on 2001 data (Steiner et al., 2001, 45).

Institutional programs primarily utilize group approaches to treatment and service provision. Steiner et al. determined that regardless of the intended focus of institutional treatment programs, "almost all rely on group therapy, the content of which may not vary much from program to program."[71] Numerous studies demonstrate that the group approach (such as the one employed by the CYA) is ultimately counterproductive in attempting to rehabilitate young offenders:

> [Y]outh who participated heavily in the group activities not only had higher recidivism than those who took part in more individualized and family treatments, but they also had higher recidivism than control group youth receiving no intervention. . . . The evidence suggests that many or most of these [delinquent] youth would be better served in programs that minimize rather than mandate interaction among delinquent peers.[72]

According to Stanford researchers assessing the mental health system at the CYA, the current number of authorized positions is insufficient to meet wards' mental health needs.[73] Intervention programs are further hindered by a lack of specialized staff training, staffing shortages, and insufficient resources dedicated to treatment services.

Institutional Staffing for Special Programs. Youth correctional counselors and parole agents comprise the primary staff support for special programs. Staff training is limited primarily to standard correctional policy and operations, with any program-specific training provided only as time and resources allow. An evaluation of the Karl Holton Drug and Alcohol Treatment Facility (DATF) determined that 69 percent of youth correctional counselors did not believe that they had adequate training to effectively perform their counseling duties.[74] Interviews with institutional staff members (conducted by Dan Macallair) yielded a consistent remark: staff members are trained to be prison guards, not social workers. Thus, despite the critical and difficult responsibilities of institutional staff, these employees are not adequately trained. Unfortunately, even parole agents' good intentions and personal commitment cannot fully mitigate the effects of inadequate preparation and training.

The following section outlines the treatment and intervention programs available to wards.

Mental Health.   Within the CYA, rates of mental illness are very high. "Many [wards] . . . are not treated or evaluated [for placement in mental health programs] because they have not called attention to their mental health problems through their behavior."[75] The CYA reports that in 2000, 45 percent of male wards and 65 percent of female wards had mental health problems. However, it is common for only the most extreme cases to be assigned to the specialized mental health programs due to an inadequate evaluation process and limited resources. According to a Treatment Needs Assessment report conducted by the Youth Authority, "due to limitations on available program resources, only the most seriously disturbed wards are referred for [psychological] evaluations."[76] Similarly, only the most serious cases ultimately receive the necessary treatment. According to CYA staff at N.A. Chaderjian, for example, the wards on the mental health unit have such extreme needs that "they should really be hospitalized" and the majority of wards should be receiving mental health treatment but are not.[77]

Substance Abuse.   We noted earlier that 74 percent of male wards and 68 percent of female wards have substance abuse problems that require treatment.[78] Substance abuse treatment is essential in reducing reoffense among juveniles. The presence of nine substance abuse treatment programs, however, does little to address these issues due to limited services provision and the lack of specialized training for staff members who operate these programs. Despite their identification as a substance abuse treatment program, facilities such as the Karl Holton Drug and Alcohol Treatment Facility in Stockton are staffed primarily by youth correctional counselors and parole agents who receive the bulk of their CYA training in custody and security, and very limited training in counseling. Treatment staff working in specialized living units have the same qualifications and training as staff in the regular living units that do not provide special services: in 1999, over 50 percent of treatment staff had a 2-year college degree or less.[79]

The conflicting custodial and counseling responsibilities of institutional staff severely hinder their capacity to dedicate sufficient time to their counseling and service responsibilities. The difficulty in effectively balancing these roles was identified in formal evaluations and through staff interviews as one of the greatest barriers to ensuring adequate service delivery.[80]

Sex Offender Program.   The CYA operates two formal sex offender programs, one in Northern California and one in Southern California.

The Youth Offender Parole Board maintains responsibility for sending wards to formal sex offender programs. As with the other intervention and treatment programs, the assessment process frequently identifies only certain wards for treatment; wards with histories of sex offenses but committed for another offense do not receive the benefits of these residential programs. The CYA is legally mandated to provide treatment to sex offenders, so that appropriate services are not necessarily provided to wards with the most severe needs.[81] Wards not assigned to one of the formal programs may receive "informal" treatment services comprised primarily of specialized resource groups and counseling sessions. Despite reports of in-house training efforts for professional program staff, CYA research staff identified the lack of required training as a significant limitation to program efficacy.[82] "It is important to note that there is no departmentally-mandated, sex offender-specific training requirement for professional and line staff working directly with program wards at [the formalized Continuum of Care Sex Offender Program]."[83]

Parole Services

The parole phase of reentry represents a vital period in the successful reintegration process of juvenile offenders, a time in which "the supposedly beneficial cumulative effects of the institutional experience should be transferred to community settings, reinforced, monitored, and assessed."[84] Upon release, most CYA parolees return to their families in the communities from which they were first committed. They face a number of structural and emotional barriers that frequently undermine any skills, motivation, and good intentions present at the time of release. The first three to six months after release is a critical period in the reentry process, and the extent of supports and services accessed during this transition phase may determine the future outcomes of parolees.

The supervision and support of CYA parolees is the primary responsibility of sixteen parole offices throughout the state. Parole agents play multiple roles, including law enforcement agent, job developer, referral specialist, and community liaison. Unfortunately, the quality of parole services is largely dependent on the skills and initiative of the individual parole agent. Parole services are highly fragmented and suffer from the lack of an organizational vision.

Research demonstrates that effective aftercare programs should incorporate both supervision and support services:

> When the response is predominantly, or exclusively, a matter of offender surveillance and social control (e.g. drug and alcohol testing, electronic monitoring, frequent curfew checks, strict revocation policies) and the treatment and service-related components are lacking or inadequate . . . neither a reduction in recidivism nor an improvement in social, cognitive, and behavioral functioning is likely to occur.[85]

Significantly, the CYA continues to emphasize social control over treatment. While the stages of parole supervision are progressively less restrictive, the emphasis remains one of control and law enforcement. As with institutional program staff, parole agents receive very limited training in service provision. Although CYA parole agents are expected to conduct supervision and intervention services, large caseload sizes, inadequate training, and geographic limitations frequently translate into an emphasis on surveillance over treatment in practice.[86] Parole offices are isolated physically and philosophically from the communities they serve. For example, the Oakland parole office, which serves a wide geographic area including Alameda, Contra Costa, and San Francisco counties, is located in a remote area close to the Oakland Airport, making access by public transportation difficult. This isolation severely hinders agents' capacity to meet parolees' needs and to provide appropriate services.

Agents are responsible for facilitating a reentry process that involves state, county, and local governmental agencies as well as community-based organizations. Navigating other governmental and local service agencies requires a commitment to interagency collaboration that is discouraged by current CYA policies:[87]

> Parole agents are not likely to have contact with the social workers or teachers or Probation officers who knew their parolees and their families over a period of years. Similarly, County Probation Departments, and judges and other human service workers are not likely to ever see or have a conversation with a Youth Authority Parole Agent.[88]

Parole agents and their clients could benefit tremendously from better collaboration and coordination among local agencies. CYA parole is guided by a leadership philosophy that CYA staff are best equipped to work with their offenders due to their correctional histories with them. We argue that a comprehensive approach, involving local, state, and county agencies and community-based organizations, provides a more effective intervention strategy.

A small proportion of wards are released after serving the maximum sentence, thereby entering their communities without any parole supervision. This small population would benefit from community support and case management services.

The capacity to provide reentry services depends primarily on resources. For example, out-of-home placement slots are funded primarily through the transition funds that are available to a particular parole office. The budget for 2002–2003 (May revision) included a $5 million reduction in the Parole Services and Community Corrections Program.[89] The implications of these cuts were far-reaching—proposed cuts included the elimination of the following parolee services:

- Two residential intensive drug treatment programs for parolees
- Transitional residential programs

- Furlough program for INS wards
- Electronic monitoring
- Job development and employment contracts
- Volunteers in Parole mentoring program

According to this budget, these cuts occur only in "non-critical parolee services, which will not affect parolee oversight or public safety."[90] We argue that eliminating these parole programs has a direct impact on public safety—by eliminating transitional placements, employment opportunities, and valuable mentoring relationships, these budget reductions remove the very programs most likely to reduce recidivism among parolees, leaving hundreds of youth without constructive transitional alternatives.

Principles of a Model Reentry Program: A Continuum of Care

Criminal justice experts have identified a continuum of care service model provided in a community-based setting as the most effective way to ensure a smooth transition into the community. The multiple service needs and histories of violent behavior among CYA wards necessitate a system of care that addresses the factors leading to criminal activities. Current systems emphasizing supervision and law enforcement rather than reintegration and support fail to attend to these issues. We recommend incorporating a wraparound strategy that provides a continuum of services to parolees and their families.

> Wraparound is not a service but a comprehensive intervention strategy. [It] is a definable planning process that results in a unique set of natural supports and community services that are designed to achieve a positive set of outcomes. Wraparound is a youth- and family-focused intervention strategy that uses flexible, non-categorical funding and is coordinated across . . . the mental health, juvenile justice, child welfare, and educational systems. The intervention strategy is appropriate across the continuum.[91]

These principles inform the following recommendations for reforming and improving the CYA reentry process.

A. *Implement the case management continuum of care model employed by the State of Missouri Division of Youth Services.*

> "Missouri's approach should be a model for the nation. Its success offers definitive proof that states can protect the public, rehabilitate youth, and safeguard taxpayers far better if they abandon incarceration as the core of their juvenile corrections systems."
> —Richard A. Mendel[92]

This recommendation involves systems change and requires the commitment and support of the CYA director and other government leaders. This approach provides consistency and support to youth throughout their custody and parole. The Missouri Department of Youth Services (DYS) employs a regional service delivery system with a continuum of care provided within each region. The DYS was identified by the American Youth Policy Forum as one of the "Guiding Lights" in juvenile justice reform, providing effective services at lower costs.[93]

Key elements of the DYS model include: case management, small-scale residential correctional centers, and parole/aftercare.

Each youth works with a single case manager throughout his or her tenure at DYS. The case manager conducts a comprehensive risk and needs assessment of each youthful offender and develops, monitors, and refines an individualized service plan to address both public safety and service concerns.

In contrast to the large training schools employed by the CYA, Missouri juvenile offenders are placed in one of a number of small-scale residential placements ranging from secure care facilities to group homes. This arrangement helps to prevent the cycle of intimidation and violence exacerbated by the large-scale, dormitory-style living conditions at the CYA.

Upon release from a correctional center, youth continue to work with the same case manager to find an appropriate placement and day treatment services. "Alternative Living" environments provide transitional services to help in the adjustment to independent living and employment. Youth are also supported and monitored through an Intensive Case Management Monitoring System, in which college students serve as "trackers" to provide mentoring and guidance to the youth and their families. Day treatment services include alternative education, counseling, life skills, and community service opportunities.

Researchers have identified this type of individualized service as a superior intervention method to group-based treatment.[94] In Missouri, reforms have resulted in lower recidivism and a less costly juvenile justice system: the DYS budget in fiscal year 2000 was $94 per day for each youth aged 10–17 years, one-third less than the juvenile correctional budgets of the eight surrounding states, and recidivism consistently hovers around 10 percent.[95]

B. Create a pilot program to utilize contract arrangements for institutional program services.

The current staffing structure, in which youth correctional counselors and parole agents provide the majority of human service and counseling opportunities to wards, forces staff to balance the conflicting responsibilities of surveillance and service provision. With the majority of training and work hours dedicated to custodial tasks, service provision remains a secondary and neglected component within the Youth Authority.

By hiring and/or contracting with qualified personnel hired solely to meet the service and education needs of the wards, the CYA can demonstrate its commitment to meeting wards' intense service needs without sacrificing its emphasis on security and public safety. During interviews, institutional staff identified this staffing structure, also referred to as counseling "out of post," as a promising, more cost-effective approach. Steiner et al. recommends contracting with other state agencies such as the Department of Mental Health to provide more effective psychiatric services.[96] A pilot program is recommended to enable an evaluation of the effectiveness of such an arrangement before creating department-wide policy changes.[97] Correctional staff at all facilities should receive additional training in effective counseling and service provision to address ongoing concerns about their capacity to provide the necessary support to wards.

C. Create additional community-based treatment and supervision slots for CYA wards.

Additional funding is needed for contracted services in the community, particularly in transitional residential and day treatment programs. Limited resources should be targeted at prevention and intervention programs with strong track records in preventing reoffense. Of course, even unlimited funding cannot alleviate the limited availability of treatment programs and other community resources in certain counties. However, the CYA can take the lead in collaborating with local governmental and community-based agencies to address these limitations. CYA parolees are frequently seen as "beyond hope"; this approach facilitates a greater community commitment to serving this population.

D. Transfer authority for determining length of stay and conditions of parole for CYA wards from the Youthful Offender Parole Board to the committing court.

> "The cities, counties and communities that are proving most successful in reducing juvenile crime rates are those that have focused comprehensively and engage key leaders from multiple sectors."
> —Richard A. Mendel[98]

California State Senator Richard Polanco has recommended the elimination of the Youthful Offender Parole Board and the realignment of responsibilities modeled after the process used for group home and probation camp placements. This proposal facilitates improved interagency collaboration and local control. Following are excerpts from Senator Polanco's proposal, which includes the following provisions:[99]

- Eliminates the YOPB;
- Empowers the juvenile court, with input from probation, prosecutors, the juvenile and his or her counsel, and victims, to set an initial parole consideration date and recommend treatment and programming at the time the minor is committed to CYA;
- Requires the CYA to notify the court if the recommended treatment programs are unavailable;

- Requires probation to monitor the ward's treatment and progress through visits every three months;
- Continues to use CYA parole agents for parole;
- Requires the juvenile court to monitor, through parole and probation, wards through parole until jurisdiction is terminated.

Benefits of this structure include:

- Enhanced local control. The local judge, with input from CYA, probation, local law enforcement, and other stakeholders, will decide when a ward is ready for release.
- Stronger link between CYA and the counties. Counties will have more input into what happens to their juveniles and the CYA will become a more responsive service provider.
- Increased CYA accountability. CYA will be held to higher standards because counties will have to pay for wards and will be responsible for wards when they are released back into their communities.
- Improved efficiency. The elimination of the YOPB removes a state body with too little knowledge of wards' histories and needs to play a valuable role in sentencing and parole.

E. Expand community corrections sanctions.

Placement in appropriate community sentencing programs provides an intermediate level of supervision in an ideal continuum of care. Community corrections methods, used successfully by model programs such as the Missouri Department of Youth Services, include the following.[100]

- Community Service: Mandatory work through which offenders give back to the community.
- Halfway Houses: Residential placements where offenders work and/or attend school and pay rent in the community while undergoing counseling and job training.
- Restitution: Offenders provide financial compensation to those victims and communities their actions have harmed.
- Drug Treatment: Residential or outpatient drug treatment is proven to reduce drug use and associated criminal behavior.
- Intensive Supervision: Authorities maintain a close watch on offenders (closer than in regular parole) to ensure that they meet their Board-ordered obligations.
- Fines: Assessed in proportion to people's ability to pay, fines provide a strong disincentive to criminal activity and help to find the court system and/or victims' funds.
- Electronic Monitoring: Helps maintain close surveillance for people ordered to home confinement, work programs, or drug counseling

F. Create educational alternatives.

To combat the low level of functional literacy among the CYA population, we recommend expanding educational options as one of the primary means for reducing recidivism and promoting self-sufficiency. Specifically, we recommend the following:

- Create a range of high school education options for parolees to ensure that both education and public safety goals are met.

- Create formal linkages with adult education programs and community colleges.

- Create an alliance with the local board of education to develop a seamless link between CYA schools and the community school and to prevent delays in school placement. For instance, the New Jersey Juvenile Justice Coalition (NJJJC) is working to build connections with the board of education in its efforts to have youth back in school within two days of release.[101]

- Establish alternative schooling options such as "schools within schools," in which students have access to smaller learning units and flexible instruction. Such programs have been identified as a promising method to reduce drug abuse and delinquency.[102]

- Establish and support alternative schools that provide education and support services to the entire family unit. Charter schools such as Los Angeles-based Save Our Future provide ex-offenders of all ages with the opportunity to attain a high school diploma while also receiving wraparound services.

- Rescind legislation barring access to Pell grants. Education provides the best opportunity for reducing recidivism. The average Pell grant in fiscal year 2001 was $2,057. One study indicated that the higher level of degree received was inversely related to the level of recidivism of offenders: individuals with an Associate's degree had recidivism rates of 13.7 percent, Bachelor's 5.6 percent, and Master's degree holders had 0 percent recidivism.[103]

G. Expand gender-specific services.

The need for gender-specific services has become more pressing as girls and young women are committed to the Youth Authority at increasing rates. Residential services for female offenders and parolees should be provided in a single-gender environment with staff experienced in providing services to this population. Female offenders have unique service needs that are best addressed through targeted programs that recognize the unique personal and criminal histories of this population. Traditional correctional practices fail to consider the long histories of emotional and physical abuse, sexual exploitation, and high poverty rates that characterize the female offender population. Services should be individualized, community-based, and family-focused.

H. Replicate model programs.

This is necessary in order to:

- Demonstrate that investments in quality reentry services provide cost-effective alternatives to parole by reducing recidivism at far lower costs than incarceration;

- Assist officials in exploring effective approaches for juvenile offenders that could enhance existing programs for individuals released from the California Youth Authority;

- Identify programs that officials might consider for adaptation to address existing gaps in California's current continuum of services;

- Demonstrate to community leaders, especially those affiliated with grassroots organizations, religious institutions, and other non-profit agencies, the role and efficacy of community-based programs for offenders in their home communities.

Conclusions and Areas for Future Research

Several areas of research were beyond the scope of this article but deserve closer attention:

- Greater attention should be paid to the specific needs of girls and young women in the Youth Authority. Female offenders remain an understudied population; the increasing proportion of girls committed to the CYA facility in Ventura increases the urgency of the need for gender-based services and intervention programs that address the root causes of their criminal behavior.[104]

- Due to the documented evidence about the relationship between foster care placement and juvenile delinquency, additional research on the outcomes of youth who lived in out-of-home placements before commitment to the CYA would be beneficial.

- The CYA should create a better tracking system for youth and young adults released from the CYA. Data collection should include a full recidivism measure, as well as educational, employment, and health outcomes. The National Institute of Justice study provides a potential template for data collection.[105]

The sobering facts about the outcomes for youth and young adults released from the Youth Authority demonstrate the ineffectiveness of the current "get tough" policies employed in the state of California and present an opportunity for reform. When youthful offenders leave the CYA, the barriers they face far outweigh the opportunities for a successful reintegration into the community. Indeed, the odds are against them: low education, high unemployment, and a greater than 50 percent chance that they'll reoffend. The emphasis on surveillance and protection to the exclusion of education and treatment has had serious detrimental consequences for individual offenders, their families, and the communities to which they return. This article highlights the disjointed approach to reentry and the need for increased collaboration among state, local, and nonprofit organizations. A comprehensive approach to reentry must also address the limited opportunities that face many of these individuals:

> [Paroled offenders] are struggling with the same stresses of poverty, the same limited opportunities, and same class and racial tensions as shape the lives of all youths, delinquent or not, who live in disadvantaged communities. Ultimately these issues must be confronted if we are to expect youthful offenders to establish meaningful lives in the community.[106]

During the course of interviews conducted for this article, many individuals identified the need and widespread support for improved reentry services for CYA youth and young adults. However, without state leadership, the future outlook for this population remains grim. We hope that this article will result in a formal commitment to reentry and aftercare as an integral component in a continuum of juvenile justice services.

Notes

[1] Josi, D. A. and D. Sechrest (1999). "A Pragmatic Approach to Parole Aftercare: Evaluation of a Community Reintegration Program for High-Risk Youthful Offenders," *Justice Quarterly* 16 (March).

[2] The Division of Juvenile Justice houses almost 6,000 of the state's most serious youthful offenders, ages 12–25. Over 50 percent were committed for violent offenses, and 38 percent have two or more prior commitments (Department of Youth Authority, 2001).

[3] Rivers, J. and T. Trotti (1989). "South Carolina Delinquent Males: A Follow-Up into Adult Corrections." Columbia: South Carolina Department of Youth Services, cited in Macallair, D. (1993). "Reaffirming Rehabilitation in Juvenile Justice." *Youth & Society* 25: 104–125.

[4] Jerry Harper, director, Department of Youth Authority at the time of the interview with the authors, 12 July 2002.

[5] Langan, P. and D. Levin (2002). "Recidivism of Prisoners Released in 1994." Washington, DC: Bureau of Justice Statistics, June.

[6] Linster, R., P. K. Lattimore, J. M. MacDonald, and C. A. Visher (nd). "Frequency of Arrest of the Young, Chronic, Serious Offender Using Two Male Cohorts Paroled by the California Youth Authority, 1981–1982 and 1986–1987." Washington, DC: National Institute of Justice Data Resources Program.

[7] U.S. Department of Justice (nd). *The Young Offender Initiative Errata Sheet.* Washington, DC: U.S. Department of Health & Human Services, and U.S. Department of Labor.

[8] Peter Hart Associates, Inc. (2002). "Changing Public Attitudes toward the Criminal Justice System: Summary of Findings." New York: The Open Society Institute. (February).

[9] Department of Youth Authority (2001). "Characteristics of First Commitments to the Youth Authority 1990 through 2001: A Comparison of First Commitment Characteristics 1990–2001." Sacramento: State of California Department of the Youth Authority Administrative Services Branch Research Division.

[10] Linster et al., "Frequency of Arrest of the Young, Chronic, Serious Offender."

[11] U.S. Department of Justice, *The Young Offender Initiative Errata Sheet.*

[12] Department of Youth Authority (1980). "Institutional Violence Reduction Project: The Impact of Changes in Living Unit Size and Staffing: California Youth Authority Final Report." January; Lerner, S. (1982). *The CYA Report: Conditions of Life at the California*

Youth Authority. Bolinas, CA: Commonweal Research Institute; Lerner, S. (1986). *The CYA Report Part Two Bodily Harm: The Pattern of Fear and Violence at the California Youth Authority.* Bolinas, CA: Commonweal Research Institute.

[13] Department of Youth Authority, "Characteristics of First Commitments to the Youth Authority 1990 through 2001."

[14] Todis, B. (2001). "Overcoming the Odds: Qualitative Examination of Resilience among Formerly Incarcerated Adolescents," *Exceptional Children*, 119–139.

[15] Ibid.

[16] Snyder, H. M. and M. Sickmund (1999). "Juvenile Offenders and Victims: 1999 National Report." Pittsburgh, PA: National Center of Juvenile Justice, Office of Juvenile Justice and Delinquency Prevention.

[17] Melton, G. (1997). "Why Don't the Knuckleheads Use Common Sense?" *Innovative Approaches for Difficult-to-Treat Populations.* Washington, DC: American Psychiatric Press, p. 354, quoted in Mendel, R. A. (2000). "Less Hype More Help: Reducing Juvenile Crime, What Works—and What Doesn't." Washington, DC: American Youth Policy Forum.

[18] Linster et al., "Frequency of Arrest of the Young, Chronic, Serious Offender."

[19] Department of Youth Authority, "Characteristics of First Commitments to the Youth Authority 1990 through 2001."

[20] Department of Youth Authority, "Characteristics of First Commitments to the Youth Authority 1990 through 2001"; Department of Youth Authority (2001). "Characteristics of CYA Population December 2001." Sacramento: State of California Department of the Youth Authority Administrative Services Branch Research Division; Department of Youth Authority (2001). "Characteristics of the Youth Authority's Institution Population (CYA and CDC Cases) June 30 Each Year, 1992–2001." Sacramento: State of California Department of the Youth Authority Administrative Services Branch Research Division.

[21] Department of Youth Authority (2003). "A Comparison of the Youth Authority's Institutional and Parole Populations June 30 Each Year, 1993–2002" Sacramento: State of California; Department of Youth Authority, "Characteristics of CYA Population December 2001."

[22] Department of Youth Authority, "Characteristics of the Youth Authority's Institution Population (CYA and CDC Cases)."

[23] Roche, T., V. Schiraldi, J. Ziedenberg, and L. Berman (2002). "Returning Adult Offenders in DC: A Road Map to Neighborhood Based Reentry: A Technical Assistance Report to the District of Columbia Criminal Justice Coordinating Council," *Center on Juvenile and Criminal Justice* (April), p. 17.

[24] Department of Youth Authority, "A Comparison of the Youth Authority's Institutional and Parole Populations"; Department of Youth Authority, "Characteristics of the Youth Authority's Institution Population (CYA and CDC Cases)."

[25] Department of Youth Authority, "Characteristics of the Youth Authority's Institution Population (CYA and CDC Cases)."

[26] Department of Youth Authority, "Characteristics of First Commitments to the Youth Authority 1990 through 2001."

[27] Ibid.

[28] Steiner, H., K. Humphreys, and A. Redlich (2001). "The Assessment of the Mental Health System of the California Youth Authority: Report to Governor Gray Davis" (December 31).

[29] Class Action No. CIV. S-01-0675 DFL-PAN-P.

[30] Former CYA ward, personal interview by author, 9 August 2002.

[31] Former CYA ward.

[32] Lerner, *The CYA Report Part Two Bodily Harm.*

[33] Former CYA ward.

[34] Former CYA ward.

[35] Former CYA ward.

[36] Lerner, *The CYA Report Part Two Bodily Harm.*

[37] Department of Youth Authority, "Characteristics of CYA Population December 2001"; Department of Youth Authority, "Comparison of Average Percentile Performance of Students by Subject by Grade Level for all CEA Students for 1998, 1999, 2000 and 2001" and "Percentage of Students Scoring at or Above the 50th Percentile Based on National Norms." *Standardized Testing and Reporting (STAR) Program 2001 Results.* Sacramento, CA; Department of Youth Authority, "Number and Percentage of Students Tested and Passing by School." *California High School Exit Exam May, 2001 Results.* Sacramento, CA.

[38] Connolly, K., D. Macallair, L. McDermid, and V. Schiraldi (1996). *From Classrooms to Cellblocks: How Prison Building Affects Higher Education and African American Enrollment in California.* San Francisco: Center on Juvenile and Criminal Justice.

[39] CYA staff, personal interviews, June–August 2002.

[40] Each person between the ages of 6 and 18 years (with certain exceptions) is subject to compulsory full-time education according to Ca. Code § 48200.

[41] CYA staff, personal interview and tour, 26 June 2002.

[42] Department of Youth Authority, "Characteristics of CYA Population December 2001."

[43] Coalition for Juvenile Justice (2000). *Annual Report 2000.* San Francisco: Author.

[44] Department of Youth Authority, "Characteristics of CYA Population December 2001."

[45] Higher Education Act of 1965, Title IV, Part A, Subpart 1, as amended.

[46] 20 U.S.C. 1091(r) (1) as cited in Allard (2002).

[47] Center on Crime, Communities & Culture (1997). "Education as Crime Prevention: Providing Education to Prisoners," *Research Brief.* New York: Center on Crime, Communities and Culture (September).

[48] Personal Responsibility and Work Opportunity Reconciliation Act of 1996, Pub. L No. 104-193 s. 15(a)

[49] Allard, P. (2002). "Life Sentences: Denying Welfare Benefits to Women Convicted of Drug Offenses," *The Sentencing Project,* February.

[50] Schiraldi, V. and B. Holman (2000). "Poor Prescription: The Costs of Imprisoning Drug Offenders in the United States." *Center on Juvenile and Criminal Justice* (June).

[51] Code of Federal Regulations § 416.1339(a)

[52] Pub L. No. 104-20

[53] Cal. Const., Art. II, § 4.

[54] CYA staff.

[55] Center on Crime, Communities & Culture, "Education as Crime Prevention."

[56] Ibid.

[57] Department of the Youth Authority (1999). "'No Diploma, No Parole' Diploma Policy Formalizes Education Commitment." *CYA Today Special Edition.* September.

[58] Department of the Youth Authority (1999). "In Addition to High School Diploma, Many CYA Students Earn Degrees." *CYA Today Special Edition.* September.

[59] Center on Crime, Communities & Culture, "Education as Crime Prevention."

[60] In some cases, completing these educational requirements may be unrealistic, due to short sentences and/or the youth's current educational status. Policy enforcement takes these factors into account.

[61] CYA staff.

[62] California Department of Youth Authority, "Characteristics of CYA Population December 2001."

[63] CYA staff.

[64] Senate Committee on Budget and Fiscal Review Subcommittee Number 4. 17 May 2002, p. 7.

[65] California Department of Youth Authority (2000). "CCSOP: Continuum of Care Sex Offender Program An Implementation and Process Report." August, p. 71.

[66] Ibid.

[67] Class Action No. CIV. S-01-0675 DFL-PAN-P.

[68] Senate Committee on Budget and Fiscal Review.

[69] Department of Youth Authority (2002). "Transition Coordinator Director's Report." March 13, p. 1.

[70] Steiner et al., "The Assessment of the Mental Health System of the California Youth Authority," p. 44.

[71] Ibid, p. 45.

[72] Mendel, "Less Hype More Help," p. 15.

[73] Steiner et al., "The Assessment of the Mental Health System of the California Youth Authority."

[74] Department of Youth Authority, "In Addition to High School Diploma, Many CYA Students Earn Degrees."

[75] Department of the Youth Authority (2000). "CYA Mental Health and Substance Abuse Treatment Needs Assessment: Description and Preliminary Findings." August.

[76] Ibid.

[77] CYA staff.

[78] Department of Youth Authority, "Characteristics of CYA Population December 2001."

[79] Department of Youth Authority (1999). "The Karl Holton Youth Correctional Drug and Alcohol Treatment Facility: An Implementation and Process Evaluation of the First Two Years." January.

[80] CYA staff; see also Steiner et al., 2001.

[81] Steiner et al., 2001.

[82] Department of Youth Authority, "CYA Mental Health and Substance Abuse Treatment Needs Assessment."

[83] Department of Youth Authority (2000). "CCSOP: Continuum of Care Sex Offender Program An Implementation and Process Report" (August).

[84] Office of Juvenile Justice and Delinquency Prevention (OJJDP) (1994). "Intensive Aftercare for High Risk Juveniles: Policies and Procedures: Program Summary." Washington, DC: U.S. Department of Justice.

[85] Ibid, p. 3.

[86] Parolee supervision progresses from periods of intense supervision to the case management phase, in which face to face contact may be reduced to once every two months. Parole agents' caseloads vary according to the intensity of supervision they are providing. The reentry period lasts for thirty days after release, and requires smaller caseloads. During the maintenance or case management period, caseloads may climb to fifty parolees or more per agent.

[87] CYA staff.

[88] Richardson, N. M. (2001). "Out of Sight Out of Mind. Central San Joaquin Valley Delinquents and the California Youth Authority." (September 4), p. 65.

[89] State of California, *California Governor's Budget 2002–03 May Revision.*

[90] Ibid, p. 67.

[91] Maryland Juvenile Justice Coalition (nd). "Principles of a Model Juvenile Justice System," p. 11.

[92] Mendel, R. A. (2001). "Less Cost, More Safety: Guiding Lights for Reform in Juvenile Justice." Washington, DC: American Youth Policy Forum.

[93] Ibid.

[94] Mendel, "Less Cost, More Safety."

[95] American Youth Policy Forum (2001). "Background Fact Sheets for Less Hype, More Help: Reducing Juvenile Crime, What Works and What Doesn't." *American Youth Policy Forum* (June 6).

[96] Steiner et al., "The Assessment of the Mental Health System of the California Youth Authority."

[97] Previous attempts at providing contracted services at the CYA have had mixed results. In FY 1994/95, Karl Holton DATF contracted a community-based substance abuse treatment provider but terminated the contract due to "unsatisfactory delivery of services." California Youth Authority, "The Karl Holton Youth Correctional Drug and Alcohol Treatment Facility," pp. 21–22.

[98] Mendel, "Less Cost, More Safety," p. 27.

[99] Polanco, R. (2002). "Juvenile Commitments to the California Youth Authority: A Proposal for Local Control & Improved Accountability." Sacramento: Department of Youth Authority.

[100] Bumby, K., L. Gramblin, and R. Kniest (2001). *Division of Youth Services Annual Report Fiscal Year 2001*. Jefferson City: Missouri Department of Social Services; Roche et al., "Returning Adult Offenders in DC."

[101] Steve Adams, telephone interview with author, 9 July 2002.

[102] Travis, J. (1998). "Preventing Crime: What Works, What Doesn't, What's Promising." *Research in Brief*. Washington, DC: National Institute of Justice (July).

[103] Center on Crime, Communities & Culture, "Education as Crime Prevention."

[104] Richie, B. E. (2000). "Exploring the Link Between Violence against Women and Women's Involvement in Illegal Activity." *Research on Women and Girls in the Justice System: Plenary Papers of the 1999 Conference on Criminal Justice Research and Evaluation— Enhancing Policy and Practice Through Research, Volume 3*. National Institute of Justice NCJ 180972. (September).

[105] Linster et al., "Frequency of Arrest of the Young, Chronic, Serious Offender."

[106] Josi and Sechrest, "A Pragmatic Approach to Parole Aftercare."

5

Still the "Best Place to Conquer Girls"[1]
Girls and the Juvenile Justice System

Meda Chesney-Lind and Katherine Irwin

Thirty years have now passed since the passage of the landmark Juvenile Justice and Delinquency Prevention Act (JJDPA of 1974) that focused national attention on the treatment of status offenders (a category that has historically included offenses that were traditionally female like runaway). In addition, over a decade has passed since the 1992 reauthorization of this same act; a reauthorization that specifically called for more equitable treatment of girls in the juvenile justice system. For both these reasons, it might well be time to take stock of progress made. Is the juvenile justice system now dispensing justice to girls or is it still haunted by its history of differential and unequal treatment?

A Century of Girls' Justice

Legislation

In 1974, when the original JJDPA was passed, reformers concerned about judicial abuse of the status offense category by juvenile courts were applying considerable pressure on Congress. Interestingly, although generally concerned about the legal treatment of status offenders, reformers were fairly silent on the status of girls in the system. Based largely on broad constitutional concerns about institutionalization for non-criminal statuses (like mental illness and vagrancy) common during the era, this federal legislation required that states receiving federal delinquency prevention money begin to divert and deinstitutionalize their status offenders. Despite erratic enforcement of this provision and

This chapter originally appeared in A. V. Merlo and J. M. Pollock (Eds.). *Women, Law and Social Control* (2nd Ed.). Boston: Allyn & Bacon, 2005. It is reprinted here with permission of the authors.

considerable resistance from juvenile court judges, it initially appeared that girls were the clear beneficiaries of the reform. Incarceration of young women in training schools and detention centers across the country fell dramatically in the decades since the JJDPA of 1974, in distinct contrast to patterns found early in the century.

Through the first half of the last century, the juvenile justice system incarcerated increasing numbers of girls. Girls' share of the population in juvenile correctional facilities (both public and private) increased from 1880 (when girls were 19 percent of the population) to 1923 (when girls were 28 percent). By 1950, girls had climbed to 34 percent of the total population of youth in custody and in 1960 they were still 27 percent of those in correctional facilities. By 1980, the impact of the JJDPA was clear, and girls had dropped to only 19 percent of those in any type of correctional facility.[2] However, while the impact of de-institutionalization was gendered in ways that arguably benefited girls, at the time Congress passed the act programs for girls in general (and female delinquents, in particular) were an extremely low priority. For example, a report completed in 1975 by the Law Enforcement Assistance Administration revealed that only 5 percent of federally funded juvenile delinquency projects were specifically directed at girls and that only 6 percent of all local monies for juvenile justice were spent on girls.[3] This was the case despite the fact that girls were, at the time of the passage of the JJDPA of 1974, a clear majority of those in institutions for status offenses. One study in Delaware done at the time the law was passed found that first-time female status offenders were more harshly sanctioned (as measured by institutionalization) than males charged with felonies; for repeat status offenders, the pattern was even starker: female status offenders were six times more likely than male status offenders to be institutionalized.[4]

In the ensuing years, the predictable happened as girls with a history of family dysfunction, physical and sexual abuse, and running away returned to the sometime violent and predatory streets (since virtually no programs targeted them and their needs), often to be victimized. The public, often led by juvenile court judges, pointed to this pattern and clamored for a return to the time honored means of protecting female status offenders—incarceration.[5]

Crucial ground was lost during the Reagan years, including the passage of legislation on "missing and exploited youth" as well as changes to the JJDPA, which permitted the incarceration of status offenders in violation of a "valid court order."[6] Years later, it would be revealed that the national hysteria about missing and abducted children was, essentially, a moral panic fueled by extensive media coverage of a few high profile and highly unusual child abductions. The vast majority of "missing" or "abducted" children, it turned out, were actually children caught in custody battles after contentious divorces or runaway youth. However, the laws passed during that period did erode the gains of the de-institutionalization movement by enhancing the abilities of law enforcement and others to track and hold missing children and publish their pictures so as to "re-unite" them with their parents.[7]

The tide turned briefly in girls' favor when the 1992 Reauthorization of the JJDPA was passed. This reauthorization was noteworthy precisely because it provided a forum for practitioners, activists, and scholars, all of whom voiced concerns about the deplorable options for and treatment of girls.[8]

A hearing held during the reauthorization of the act provided an important focus on the issues of gender bias that had long haunted the courts' treatment of and programs for girls, and at that hearing, perhaps for the first time, academics and practitioners who had worked with girls in the juvenile justice system had an opportunity to be heard. As a result of this historic hearing, when the Reauthorization was passed, the legislation funded states to begin their own needs assessments for girls in their systems. Specifically, the 1992 Reauthorization of the JJDPA required that each state should: (1) assess existing programs for delinquent girls and determine the needs for additional programming, (2) develop a plan for providing gender-specific services to girls, and (3) provide assurance that all youth were treated equitably, regardless of their sex, race, family income, and mental, physical, and emotional abilities. Through the "Challenge E" section of this act, over 25 states across the U.S. applied for and received funding to address these goals.[9]

The popular "challenge grant" activity created and supported initiatives that had already begun in certain states and rapidly spread to others. While there was optimism, however, that the passage of these new requirements would give birth to a new national focus on girls, the results have been somewhat uneven to date. As an example, the JJDPA required states receiving federal money "to analyze current needs and services for girls and to present a plan for meeting girls' needs" in their State Plans. Yet, a review of plans completed in 2002 by the Children's Defense Fund (CDF) and Girls Inc. concluded that

> many states had not taken significant steps toward implementing this framework. An overview of current state approaches finds that (1) a significant percentage of states acknowledge the need for gender-specific services; and (2) the majority of current state plans are lacking and inappropriate pertaining to gender issues.[10]

Beyond this, federal efforts to fund grants on girls' issues (both research and practitioner oriented) were initially issued by the Clinton administration and subsequently cancelled by the Bush administration on the heels of the September 11th attacks.[11] A scaled back version of the initiative was issued by the Bush administration in 2003.

Research and Girls in the System

A federal focus on girls' issues and programs is clearly long over due. One of the chief concerns raised at the time of the 1992 legislation was the general lack of information, research, and theories available about the causes and correlates of girls' offending that, in turn, left girls with a set of programs and interventions that were, at best, sorely lacking and, at worst, damaging and counterproductive. Commenting on the state of the field at the time the states were beginning their work, Reitsma-Street and Offord argued that there existed "a collection of policies and services for female offenders . . . propelled, as well as legitimated, by truncated theories and incorrect assumptions."[12] Where some programs were based on incomplete theories, others were just plain inappropriate. For example, some services did nothing more than reinforce derogatory and limiting gender stereotypes.[13] Even more problematic than enacting policies based on faulty information and archaic assumptions, a common practice was to fit girls into programs designed for boys. The philosophy was that if it worked for boys then it might work for girls too. More often than not, these programs, especially the sports activities, were considerably limited compared to what boys received.[14] Marian Daniel, the visionary practitioner who started Maryland's female only probation services unit, put it more bluntly: "For years people have assumed that all you have to do to make a program designed for boys work for girls is to paint the walls pink and take out the urinals."[15]

Indeed, emerging research has consistently found that girls confront different risk factors or challenges than boys. Summarizing U.S. and Canadian research, Corrado, Odgers, and Cohen argued that delinquent girls have high rates of physical and sexual victimization, drug addiction, poor academic achievement, and family conflict and abuse.[16] In addition, studies conducted of runaway youth reveal high rates of sexual and physical abuse among girls, often higher rates than what is found among runaway boys. In a Toronto runaway shelter study, for example, 73 percent of girls and 38 percent of boys reported a history of sexual abuse. Sexual victimization among girls predicted higher rates of drug abuse, petty theft, and prostitution. Interestingly, the same correlation was not found among boys.[17] A Seattle study of 372 homeless and runaway youth pointed to a similar pattern. In this study, 30 percent of girls and 15 percent of boys reported sexual victimization. In addition, girls were significantly more likely than boys to report being victimized in their homes and on the street after running away.[18]

The same trends seem to exist for institutionalized girls. In a Florida study of detained girls and boys, Dembo, Williams, and Schmeidler found that girls were more likely to have abuse histories than boys.[19] In addition, in an expanded study of 2,104 youth in a Florida assessment center, Dembo et al. argued that girls' trajectory towards problem behaviors was different than boys'. Where boys' law violations reflected their involvement in a delinquent lifestyle, girls' acting out related "to an abusive and traumatizing home life."[20] Similar findings came out of a California Youth Authority (CYA) study in which boys were likely to witness violence and girls were much more likely to be direct victims.[21]

Taken together, this research suggests that girls confront a separate pathway into the juvenile justice system, one that is marked by high rates of victimization and family turmoil. Therefore, girls seem to have unique needs that should be addressed with gender specific programs. Increased attention to girls' experiences and the more precise map of their trajectory into delinquency is one of the positive developments in the last decade and suggests that there is a firm foundation upon which to build a better system for girls. Despite this promising picture, a closer look at girls' status in the juvenile justice system suggests that the work has only just begun. Regardless of the increased information available about girls and the greater attention given to girls' needs, several national juvenile justice trends in the past decade have made meeting the needs of the 1992 Reauthorization Act extremely difficult. In the next sections, we will outline some of these trends and link them to larger social changes and argue how changes in girls' arrest and detention rates complicate the effort to provide girls with equitable treatment.

Girls' Arrest Trends

Policing "Violence" and Sexuality.   Since the mid-nineties, girls' and boys' arrest trends have diverged, with boys' arrests peaking in 1993 and girls' arrests continuing to climb. According to FBI reports, between 1993 and 2002 girls' arrests increased 6.4 percent, while arrests of boys actually decreased by 16.4 percent. From 2002 to 2006, girls' arrests declined 2.8 percent while arrests of boys declined 3.1 percent. As a result of these divergent patterns, girls now account for a growing share of those entering the juvenile justice system; in 1991 girls made up 23 percent of all juvenile arrestees, in 2002 they made up 28.8 percent, and in 2006 the percentage was 29.2.[22]

What makes this surge most noteworthy is that girls are increasingly being arrested for violent offenses, not traditional status offenses. Between 1991 and 2002, arrests of girls for serious violent offenses increased by 42.7 percent and arrests for girls' "other assaults" has increased by 120 percent. Increases in girls' arrest rates for a number of violent offenses outpaced boys' arrest rates between 1980 and 2000. For example, girls' arrests for aggravated assault, simple assault, and weapons law violations increased by 121 percent, 257 percent, and 134 percent (respectively). Boys' arrests also increased in these categories, but by much less (28 percent, 109 percent, and 20 percent).[23] From 2002 to 2006 aggravated assault declined slightly for both boys and girls. Other assaults increased 11 percent for girls and 2 percent for boys. Weapons violations increased 20 percent for girls and 32 percent for boys. Generally, dramatic percentage increases in girls' arrests should be reviewed with some care, since in the past, some dramatic increases in female participation in "non-traditional offenses" were actually the product of very small base numbers (particularly in the case of murder and forcible rape). However, in the case of girls' participation in the offenses mentioned here (particularly in the case of simple assault), the base numbers involved are relatively substantial, suggesting something significant is occurring. Because girls' and boys' arrest rates have not fluctuated together, Snyder argued that gender-specific factors were most likely at work during the last two decades.[24]

These trends created new challenges and pressures for the juvenile justice system already under criticism for its handling of girls' issues. Historically, girls were most likely to be arrested for status offenses, as noted earlier. In fact, research had long criticized the double standards within the juvenile justice system that seemed to target boys' index offenses through criminal charges and girls' immorality through status offense charges—a pattern that the JJDPA of 1974 seemed to indirectly address.[25] Three decades later, we have seen significant shifts in girls' arrests with girls more likely to be arrested and enter the juvenile justice system for traditionally "masculine" violations.

One of the first responses to these increases was to offer explanations, the quickest and simplest being that girls were changing. They were becoming increasingly like boys and, thus, were being arrested for violations that were historically viewed as boys' domain. This became an extremely popular explanation and touched off a frenzy of media attention on the topic of girls' violent emancipation.[26] Reports of gun toting and drug dealing girl gangsters became center stage of media reports for a short time—that is, until researchers started to investigate these arrest trends more carefully.

Upon closer examination, the surge in girls' violence reported in FBI arrest statistics seemed to be caused by something very different than changes in girls' violent behavior. The first indication that something more complex was occurring came when several self-report data sources failed to corroborate this "surge" in girls' arrests for violence. In fact, self-report studies often found that girls' were becoming less violent throughout the 1990s. In the Centers for Disease Control and Prevention's biennial Youth Risk Behavior Survey, girls self-reported involvement in physical fights decreased. In 1991, 34.2 percent of girls reported being in a fight versus 23.9 percent of girls in 2001. Boys' self-reported violence during the same time also decreased, but more slightly—from 50.2 percent to 43.1 percent.[27] A meta-analysis of data collected from 1991 to 1997 revealed that while both male and female violence rates declined, girls' rates declined more dramatically.[28] Girls' decreased rates of self-reported violence were also found in other studies. For example, a matched sample of "high risk" youth surveyed in the 1997 National Youth Survey and the 1989 Denver Youth Survey demonstrated significant decreases in girls' involvement in felony and minor assaults.[29]

It was becoming increasingly clear that, although girls were coming into contact with the juvenile justice system at a faster rate than boys for violent offenses, they were, in fact, not behaving more violently. What was changing was the policing of girls' behaviors, particularly the behaviors of girls of color, by official agencies (like police, school officials, and probation officers) in ways that track the new focus in the nineties on youth violence.

To understand how these policing practices emerged, it is important to examine the origins of the movement to get tough on juvenile violence. From 1983 to 1994, the United States experienced a tripling of homicide-victimization rates for black males between the ages of 13 and 17,[30] an approximately 70 percent increase in youth arrest rates for violent offenses, and a nearly 300 percent growth in youth homicide arrest rates.[31] These statistics led some to call the increased youth violence an "epidemic." Criminologists explained that the epidemic was caused by a combination of the introduction of new crack markets to inner-cities, increased distribution of guns among juveniles, and the involvement of gangs in the crack and underground gun markets (all far more relevant to boys' but not girls' violence).[32] The epidemic and its hypothesized causes ushered in an era of "get tough" anti-youth violence strategies including expelling students for everything from wearing gang attire to bringing weapons to school, installing gun detectors and hiring security guards in schools, conducting random searches of students' lockers, and creating anonymous hotlines for students to report potential violence and threats to authorities.

By 1995, the U.S. violence epidemic waned significantly. Attention on the subject of youth violence, however, did not abate. The collection of sensationalized school shootings, again virtually all male, with the most notorious being the Columbine High School massacre, riveted popular attention. By the late 1990s in the U.S., violence prevention legislation and programming also shifted, and in the early 2000s, anti-bullying programs, which promised to improve school climates and increase students' and teachers' feelings of safety, became a favorite violence prevention strategy among U.S. school districts.[33] In fact, by March 2004, 34 U.S. states had introduced anti-bullying legislation, most of which required schools districts to adopt anti-bullying policies.[34] This suggests that the initiative to combat the youth violence epidemic of the 1980s and early 1990s translated into an effort to do something about bullying by the early 2000s.

Many school policies maintained the "get tough" flavor of anti-gang and anti-gun practices from the late 80s and early 90s. Instead of placing security guards and gun detectors in hallways, schools employed hall monitors equipped with note pads and pens to report incidents of physical altercations or the use of threatening language. As a result, school officials, community members, and police were becoming increasingly sensitive to the violence problem as it played out in the everyday world of schoolyards, hallways, and other adolescent "hangouts."

It is important to note that anti-violence policies and practices, which had their origins in boys' violence, fell particularly heavily upon all girls and adolescents of color. Examining the specific practices initiated in the get tough on juvenile crime spirit not only reveals the mechanisms driving the girls' arrest trends from the 1990s to the early 2000s, but it helps identify an overarching process through which the juvenile justice system disproportionately arrests and detains girls of color—often for crimes of "violence."

Exactly how the tough policies of the last decade have impacted on patterns of girls' arrest is a bit complex but important to understand. There are actually three related forces likely at work: "relabeling" (sometimes called "bootstrapping") of girls' status offense behavior, "rediscovery of girls' violence," and "upcriming" of minor forms of youth violence (including girls' physical aggression).[35] Let's take each in turn.

Relabeling

Relabeling of behaviors that were once categorized as status offenses (non-criminal offenses like "runaway" and "person in need of supervision") into violent offenses cannot be ruled out in explanations of arrest rate shifts, nor can changes in police practices with reference to domestic violence.

The recent focus on mandatory arrest as a policy for domestic violence cases has had a very real, and one would hope, unintended consequence: a dramatic increase in the numbers of girls and women arrested for this form of "assault." A California study, for example, found that the female share of domestic violence arrests increased from 6 percent in 1988 to 16.5 percent in 1998. African American girls and women had arrest rates roughly three times that of white girls and women in 1998: 149.6 per 100,000 compared to 46.4.[36]

Such an impression is supported by case file reviews of girls' cases. Acoca's study of nearly 1,000 girls' files from four California counties found that while a "high percentage" of these girls were charged with "person offenses," a majority of these involved assault. Further, "a close reading of the case files of girls charged with assault revealed that most of these charges were the result of nonserious, mutual combat situations with parents." Acoca details cases that she regards as typical, including: "father lunged at her while she was calling the police about a domestic dispute. She (girl) hit him." Finally, she reports that some cases were quite trivial in nature including a girl arrested "for throwing cookies at her mother."[37] In another study, a girl reported that she was arrested for "assault" for throwing a Barbie doll at her mother.[38] In a number of these instances, the possibility that the child, not the parent, is actually a victim cannot be completely ignored, particularly when girls and defense attorneys keep reporting such a pattern. Marlee Ford, an attorney working with the Bronx Defenders Office, commented, "Some girls have been abused all their lives. . . . Finally, they get to an age where they can hit back. And they get locked up."[39]

Rediscovery and Upcriming

Girls have always been more violent than their stereotype as weak and passive "good girls" would suggest. A review of the self-report data reviewed earlier indicates that girls do get into fights and they even occasionally carry weapons; as an example, in 2001, about a quarter of girls reported that they were in a physical fight, and about one in twenty carried a weapon.[40] Until recently, girls' aggression, even their physical aggression, was trivialized rather than criminalized. Law enforcement, parents, social workers, and teachers were once more concerned with controlling girls' sexuality than they were with their violence, but recent research, which we will review below, suggests that may be changing. So, in part, the contemporary focus on girls' violence is actually a "rediscovery" of female violence that has always existed, although at much lower rates than boys' violence.

A related phenomenon, "upcriming," is likely also involved in the increases in girls' arrests. Upcriming refers to policies (like "zero tolerance policies") that increase the severity of criminal penalties associated with particular offenses. It has long been known that arrests of youth for minor or "other" assaults can range from schoolyard scuffles to relatively serious, but not life threatening, assaults.[41] Currie adds to this the fact that these "simple assaults without injury" are often "attempted," "threatened," or "not completed."[42] A few decades ago, schoolyard fights and other instances of bullying were largely ignored or handled informally by schools and parents. But at a time when official concern about youth violence is almost unparalleled and "zero tolerance" policies proliferate, school principals are increasingly likely to call police onto their campuses. It should come as no surprise that youthful arrests in this area are up as a consequence—with both race and gender implications. Specifically, while African American children represent only 42 percent of the public school enrollment, they constitute 61 percent of the children charged with a disciplinary code violation. And these violations have serious consequences; according to a U.S. Department of Education's report, 25 percent of all African American students, nationally, were suspended at least once over a four-year period.[43]

These trends in girls' arrest for violent offenses should not let us lose sight of the fact that large numbers of girls were also being arrested and referred to court for traditional female offenses, like runaway (in 2001 girls' runaway arrests exceeded those of boys'—the only offense category where this was true) and larceny theft (the bulk of which for girls was shoplifting). These two offense categories account for a third (33.2 percent) of female juvenile arrests but far less (16.4 percent) of boys' arrests.[44] In 2006, the two categories totaled 28 percent of all arrests of girls and 14 percent of all arrests of boys. These simultaneous trends—arrest of girls for historically male and historically female offenses—have also further complicated the efforts to craft gender specific or responsive ways to address girls' needs. Essentially, the juvenile justice system is being pressured to respond to the violent behavior of youth, including girls, while it still also faces all the complexities presented by more traditional girl offenders, who have always been the recipients of what Ruth Wells described as "throwaway services for throwaway girls."[45] And, as we've already suggested, the two groups often share more in common with each other than conventional wisdom might predict.

Juvenile Justice in the New Millennium

The Protective/Punitive System

Interestingly, at the same time that the juvenile justice system was becoming increasingly punitive and intolerant of juvenile violence—evidenced in the zero tolerance policies and practices in response to the youth violence epidemic and the spate of school shootings—there was another, contradictory trend, a return to an emphasis on protecting girls that justified the court's earliest involvement with female youth during the child saving era.

Despite the emphasis in the original JJDPA of 1974 to divert status offenders—a group that, as stated previously, is dominated by girls—from formal processing (e.g. referral to courts), between 1990 and 1999, the number of delinquency cases coming into juvenile courts involving girls increased by 59 percent (from 250,000 to 398,600) compared to a 19 percent increase for males (from 1,066,900 to 1,274,500). Looking at specific offense types, the report observed: "The growth in cases involving females outpaced the growth in cases involving males in all offense categories. Simple assault cases increased more than any other person offense for both genders (238 percent for females and 152 percent for males)."[46]

The increasing referral of girls to formal court processing may, in fact, be an ironic outcome of the 1990s research on girls' needs in the juvenile justice system. For example, by the mid-1990s research agendas had made it clear that girls confronted an entirely different set of circumstances in and out of the system. The overwhelming presence of victimization at home or on the streets gave a clear indication that young female offenders had different histories and service needs than boys.

A particularly poignant example of the balance between punitive and protective policies over girls characterizing this era was the 1995 Washington State "Becca's Bill" implemented in response to the murder of Rebecca Headman, a 13-year-old chronic runaway. After a series of runaway incidents and repeated calls to the police by her parents, Rebecca was murdered while on the streets. Under Becca's Bill, apprehended runaways could be detained in a crisis residential center for up to 7 days. Between 1994 and 1997, youth detention rates increased by 835 percent in Washington State and, by 1997, girls made up 60 percent of the detained population. According to Sherman, while there was Becca's Bill designed to save youths, mostly girls, from the streets in Washington by placing them in detention, there were no long-term community-based programs for runaway girls. In addition, as we will explain later, detention centers were certainly not universally safe havens for girls.[47]

The reliance on detention rather than treatment in the community, according to Corrado et al., was a trend in Canada as well. Looking at delinquency data and sentencing practices leading up to girls' detentions, Corrado et al. found that "the sentencing recommendations made by youth justice personnel are primarily based on the desire to protect female youth from high-risk environments and street-entrenched lifestyles."[48] Furthermore, they argue that reliance on detention came partly because of the:

> . . . inability of community-based programs to protect certain female youth, the difficulties these programs have in getting young female offenders to participate in rehabilitation programs when they are not incarcerated, and the presence of some, albeit usually inadequate, treatment resources in custodial institutions.[49]

The balance between punitive and protective juvenile justice practices affects girls in another way. At the same time that detention and arrest were being used to protect girls from the dangers of the streets, many jurisdictions were cracking down on youths' probation and court order violations. Although designed to get tough on repeat index offenders, sentencing youth to detention for probation and court order violations, in practice, did not distinguish between status and index offenses. Therefore, girls were placed in a precarious position under this practice. Status offending girls could be swept into detention through policies designed to protect them from the dangers of the streets, and, in the end, could be charged as criminal offenders through contempt of court and probation violations. In fact, as a study by the American Bar Association (ABA) and National Bar Association (NBA) found, this happened frequently in the 1990s. According to this study, girls in the U.S. juvenile justice system between 1991 and 1999 were more likely than boys to not only be detained, but to return to detention after being released. This was in large part through contempt of court, probation, and parole violations.[50]

There was an inherent irony in the protective-punitive confluence that underlies the arrest and, as we shall see, detention rates of girls during the 1990s and early 2000s. On one hand, although practitioners are becoming increasingly aware of girls' needs, specifically to address their extensive abuse histories, there are consistent reports of inadequate community-based programs to meet girls' needs. Therefore, in some jurisdictions, detaining girls has become the only "program" available. On the other hand, we also find a system that has become increasingly intolerant and punitive of certain offenses, such as violent crimes and contempt of court and probation and parole violations. This sets up a troubling trajectory towards incarceration for girls and one in which they were likely to find themselves either ignored and pushed aside when outside of the system, or set up for failure and certain punishment when they did become involved in the juvenile justice system.

Girls' Detention Trends

One indicator of the increasingly punitive nature of the juvenile justice system in the years after the 1992 Reauthorization Act was the rising detention rates among girls. Between 1989 and 1998, girls' detentions rose by 56 percent compared to a 20 percent expansion seen in boys' detentions, and the "large increase was tied to the growth in the number of delinquency cases involving females charged with person offenses (157 percent)."[51]

In addition to a distinctly gendered pattern in these increases, there also seemed to be clear race-based differences. For example, a study conducted by the ABA and NBA revealed that nearly half of girls in secure detention in the U.S. were African American. This is particularly interesting given that white girls made up a clear majority (65 percent) of the at-risk population.[52]

More worrisome is the fact that, despite the hype about violent girls, it was relatively minor offenses that actually *kept* girls in detention. Nearly half (40.5 percent) of all the girls in detention in the United States in 2001 were being held for either a status offense or a "technical violation" of the conditions of their probation, compared to only 25.3 percent of the boys. Girls being detained for "violent" offenses were far more likely than boys to be held on "other person" offenses (as opposed to more serious, part one violent offenses like aggravated assault, robbery, and murder). More than half of the girls but only a third of the boys in detention were held for these minor forms of violence. The percentages were essentially the same in 2003.[53]

Another troubling gender and race-based pattern in the use of detention was the reliance on private facilities since the early 1980s. The use of private facilities has a particular importance for girls, as they tend to make up a larger proportion of the institutionalized population in private vs. public facilities. Also interesting to note is the fact that 45 percent of the girls in private settings were detained for status offenses in 1997.

This is compared to 11 percent of boys who were detained in private facilities for status offenses.[54]

The use of private facilities presents some new and unique problems to the creation of equity in the juvenile justice system. Some have argued that the increasing trend to rely on private facilities has, in essence, created a bifurcated, or "two-track," juvenile justice system: one for white girls and another for girls of color. In 1997 whites made up 33 percent of the public detention population and 45 percent of individuals held in private facilities.[55] This disparity might be explained by looking at how girls' cases are handled. In her study of one Los Angeles district from 1992–1993, Miller discovered that white girls were significantly more likely to be recommended for placement in treatment facilities than Latinas and African American girls. In fact 75 percent of white girls received treatment recommendations compared to only 34 percent of Latinas and 30 percent of African American girls who received similar recommendations. Looking closely at probation officers' written reports, Miller found a surprising trend where white girls' offenses were more likely to be described as resulting from abandonment and low self-esteem and non-white girls' offenses were attributed to lifestyle choices.[56]

This trend has been corroborated in other studies. Robinson's examination of girls in a social welfare and a juvenile justice sample in Massachusetts revealed that 74 percent of girls in the welfare sample were white and 53 percent of girls in the juvenile justice sample were black. Although white girls seemed to be more likely to come into contact with the welfare rather than the juvenile justice system, Robinson found remarkably similar histories within both populations, especially with regards to their high rates of sexual victimization. One difference was that white girls tended to be charged with status offenses and non-white girls received criminal charges.[57]

Another disturbing trend, present in the earlier data on the offenses for which girls were detained, might be described as the "re-detention" of girls. Essentially once girls were released on probation in the 1990s, they were more likely than boys to return to detention—usually for a technical violation of the conditions of their probation. A study by the ABA and NBA not only found that girls were more likely than boys to be detained, but that they were more likely

> to be sent back to detention after release. Although girls' rates of recidivism are lower than those of boys, the use of contempt proceedings and probation and parole violations make it more likely that, without committing a new crime, girls will return to detention.[58]

Thus, in reviewing the data on detention practices, particularly the role played by minor aggressive offenses and technical violations, which are essentially proxies for status offenses, one can see the way in which the juvenile justice system has essentially married the protectionist logic to the new punitive emphasis in ways that distinctly disadvantage girls, particularly girls of color. And, while those in the system may argue that they are forced to detain girls "for their own protection," a review of the conditions in these facilities as well as the services provided suggests that they are anything but protective.

Girls' Experiences in Detention

There is considerable evidence to suggest that, like their experiences outside of institutions, girls' confront vastly different environments and obstacles than boys face while being detained. This trend has continued despite the fact that over half of all states have committed themselves to improving conditions for girls in the juvenile justice system, assessing girls' unique needs, and designing better programs for them. One enduring trend is that there continues to be a lack of programs for girls. In 1998, for example, Ohio judges reported that there were few sentencing options for girls. Two-thirds of judges surveyed disagreed with the statement that "there are an adequate number of treatment programs for girls" while less than one third of judges disagreed with this statement regarding services for boys.[59] In a San Francisco study, Schaffner, Shorter, Shick, and Frappier concluded that girls were "out of sight, out of mind" and that girls tended to linger in detention centers longer than boys. In fact, 60 percent of girls were detained for more than seven days, while only 6 percent of boys were detained for that long.[60]

Another concern noted by researchers examining the girls held in detention in Philadelphia was the "misdiagnosis of mental health issues."[61] As the Female Detention Project found, 81 percent of the girls studied had reported experiencing a trauma of some sort (sexual abuse, physical abuse, witnessing violence, and abandonment). The girls were diagnosed with "Oppositional Defiant Disorder" instead of "Post-Traumatic Stress Disorder" despite the fact that, according to the researchers, "many of the girls reported symptoms that are characteristics of Post-Traumatic Stress Disorder, but not ODD." Significantly, while ODD is "characterized by a persistent pattern of negativistic, hostile, disobedient and defiant—but not violent—behavior" most of these girls were detained for assaults, many school related. As a consequence of misdiagnosis, the girls were not getting the specific kind of treatment that they needed, many had used alcohol and other drugs, been hospitalized for psychiatric reasons, and about half had attempted suicide.[62]

There is also some evidence that girls are more vulnerable than boys to experiencing sexual abuse while being detained. In their study of 200 girls in California juvenile justice halls, Acoca and Dedel found several examples of abuse, including "consistent use by staff of foul and demeaning language, inappropriate touching, pushing and hitting, isolation, and deprivation of clean clothing." In addition, girls underwent strip searches while being supervised by male staff.[63]

Lack of female staff seems to place girls in vulnerable positions while being detained. In addition to increasing the chances that female wards will be abused by male staff, the lack of female staff also limits the programs and activities available for girls. Staff shortages in the Miami-Dade County Juvenile Detention Center for girls, for example, resulted in decreased outdoor recreation for girls. Ledermen and Brown reported that girls sometimes went as long as two weeks without outdoor recreation and were sometimes "locked down" due to shortage of staff. On some days, staff shortages resulted in girls' inability to attend school.[64]

Why do girls languish in detention? The answers are not too hard to find, unfortunately, once one begins to review the literature on probation officers' (and other court officials') attitudes toward female delinquents. Research has consistently revealed that despite their less serious offense profile, girls in the juvenile justice system are regarded as "more difficult" to work with.[65] A recent study of probation files in Arizona revealed stark gender and cultural stereotypes that worked against girls. Specifically, the authors found that "common images found in girls' probation files included girls fabricating reports of abuse, acting promiscuously, whining too much and attempting to manipulate the court system." Girls were universally seen as "harder to work with," "had too many issues," and were "too needy."[66] Even when girls were abused, they were somehow partially responsible for the abuse in the eyes of probation officers:

> They feel like they're the victim. They try from, "Mom kicked me out" to "Mom's boyfriend molested me" or "My brother was sexually assaulting me." They'll find all kinds of excuses to justify their actions. Because they feel if I say I was victimized at home that justifies me being out on the streets.[67]

Gender and Training Schools— Girls' Victimization Continues

Girls were 13 percent of youth "committed" to residential placements in 2001, up from 11.8 percent in 1997. That period actually saw an 8.8 percent increase in girls' commitments compared to a 1.5 percent decrease in boys' commitments. Girls are also being committed for different and less serious offenses than boys. In 2001, for example, roughly a third of girls (31.8 percent) were committed for either status offenses or technical violations, compared to only 14.2 percent of boys. In 2003, the percentage for boys remained the same; the percentage for girls declined slightly to 29.6. Over half (54 percent) the girls committed for a "person" offense were committed for non-index violent crimes (meaning simple assault); only 27.6 percent of boys doing time for violent offenses were committed for these less serious assaults. In 2003, the percentage for girls was 59.6, and the percentage for boys was 28.7.[68]

Exactly how this works can be seen in a recent study of 444 incarcerated youth in Ohio.[69] These researchers found that girls were just as likely as boys to be incarcerated for violent offenses and that approximately half of the youths incarcerated reported being charged with violent offenses. On the surface, this suggests that incarcerated Ohio girls were just as violent as boys. Upon closer examination, however, researchers discovered glaring gender differences in the severity of violent offenses, and, as Belknap et al. reported, focus group data with incarcerated girls revealed consistent accounts of girls being incarcerated for minor infractions, and, in some cases, for defending themselves. As a case in point, one girl revealed during a focus group interview that she was incarcerated for bringing a weapon to school. After being taunted and threatened by a boy at school and receiving no protection from school authorities, she hid a knife in her sock. While school authorities did not intervene in the boy's harassment, they did enforce the zero tolerance for weapons policy against the girl.[70]

Conditions in girls' residential facilities, like those found in detention centers, also suggest that while court officials often talk of protecting girls, the environments in training schools, if anything, fail to deliver on that promise. In fact, several recent scandals suggest that like their adult counterparts (women's prisons), juvenile prisons are often unsafe for girls in ways that are uniquely gendered. Take a recent investigation of conditions in the Hawaii Youth Correctional Facility in the summer of 2003 by the American Civil Liberties Union (ACLU). According to the ACLU report, there were no female guards on duty at night in the girls' ward, one reported case of rape of a girl by a male guard, and several reports of girls exchanging sex for cigarettes. The report also noted that male guards made sexual comments to female wards, talked about their breasts, and discussed raping them. While wards noted that rape comments decreased after the rape incident, White wrote that "wards expressed concern that the night shift is comprised entirely of male guards and they feel vulnerable after the rape because male guards could enter their cells at any time." The ACLU report also discovered that wards reported being watched by male guards while they changed clothes and used the toilet. Male guards were also present when girls took showers. And, like their counterparts in detention, girls had not received outdoor recreation for a week due to lack of supervising staff and girls were told that the situation may last for up to a month.[71] While critics of the ACLU report commented that the wards made up stories and severely exaggerated tales of abuse, in April of 2004, the guard implicated in the rape charge pleaded guilty to three counts of sexual assault and one count of "terroristic threatening of a female ward."[72] Although comprising a plea bargain, the legal rape case uncovered details indicating that the sexual abuse was more severe and alarming than wards originally reported to the ACLU.

Other scandals have surfaced at girls' institutions, and all of these incidents suggest that while authorities often use institutionalization as a means of "protecting" girls from the dangers of the streets and in their homes, many of the institutions that house girls perpetuate the gendered victimization that pervades girls' lives outside of these institutions.[73]

Girls and Juvenile Justice: What Does the Future Hold?

The recently reauthorized Juvenile Justice and Delinquency Prevention Act of 2002 supports the continued focus on girls. Specifically, the act requires states, again, to create "a plan for providing needed gender-specific services for the prevention and treatment of juvenile delinquency" and denotes a category of funding for "programs that focus on the needs of young girls at risk of delinquency or status offenses."[74] Perhaps this time, as more girls enter the various juvenile justice systems, the states will take more seriously the unique needs of girls.

Recent reports from a number of national organizations such as the American Bar Association, the National Bar Association, and the Child Welfare League have, once again, focused critical attention on the unmet needs of girls in the juvenile justice system.[75] Beyond the continued claim that girls lack adequate gender-specific programming, there is also the undeniable fact that the girls in the juvenile justice system need considerable advocacy. As this chapter has indicated, girls are currently caught between multiple trends in the juvenile justice system—trends that confront them with new and more severe levels of disadvantage than they experienced in the 1970s and 1980s. In the arena of contemporary justice trends, girls, especially girls of color, are bearing the brunt of "tough on crime" policies specifically in the form of mandatory arrest and zero tolerance initiatives towards youth violence. For example, where boys' arrest rates for violence peaked in 1994 (and has been declining since), girls' violence arrest rates have continued to climb since the early 1980s. In several twists and contortions of policies, laws, and initiatives meant to protect girls from victimization, we find that tough on violence responses have been deployed in ways that actually harm girls.

While the punitive turn in criminal justice has lashed out against girls in new ways, girls in the juvenile justice system continue to face the system's historic impulse to use correctional facilities to "protect" them. However traditional this protective pattern maybe, it also confronts girls with a new set of challenges as legal initiatives like Washington State's Becca's Bill exemplifies. Instead of unabashedly sweeping up female status offenders into the system for their protection, as was a common practice critiqued by the 1992 and 2002 JJDPA acts, legal initiatives like Becca's Bill turn status violators into criminal offenders. It seems that the juvenile court judges' desire to regain the ability to detain youth charged with status offenses has withstood the efforts of critics and reformers.[76]

Ultimately, the juvenile justice system's unfortunate return to its historic (and problematic) pattern of "protecting" girls, coupled with a simultaneous "get tough" trend permeating the entire criminal justice system, has had very negative consequences for girls, particularly girls of color. We find that girls are systematically being reclassified from status offenders "in need of protection and supervision" into criminals deserving strict control and harsh punishment.

What are the prospects for gender-specific programming, assuming that we could get it right? It has also been three decades since the second wave of feminism presumably rekindled a national focus on women's rights, yet girls and women remain a very low priority when it comes to public as well as private funding.

Youth services all too often translate into "boys' services" as can be seen in a 1993 study of the San Francisco Chapter of the National Organization for Women. The study found that only 8.7 percent of the programs funded by the major city organization funding children and youth programs "specifically addressed the needs of girls."[77] Not surprisingly, then, a 1995 study of youth participation in San Francisco after school or summer sports programs found only 26 percent of the participants were girls.[78] Likewise, problems exist with delinquency programming; in a list of "potentially promising programs" identified by the Office of Juvenile Justice and Delinquency Prevention, there were 24 programs cited specifically for boys and only two for girls. One program for incarcerated teen fathers had no counterpart for incarcerated teen mothers.[79] And things are apparently no better in the area of private funding. A 2003 study conducted by the Washington Women's Foundation reviewed 12,000 grants given by DC-area foundations in 2002 and 2003, and determined that only 7 percent of a total of $441 million went to programs serving girls or women.[80] Clearly, the sexism that has long haunted public policy relating to programming for girls haunts the world of private funding as well. In short, the prospects are about as dim as they were three decades ago in the area of programmatic funding.[81]

It is not clear, though, that the girls in the juvenile justice system cannot wait another generation for things to change. As their numbers increase daily in the detention centers and training schools, and as the scandals in those facilities become more common, it is long past time to pay attention to girls. Imagine how different the juvenile justice system would look if we, as a nation, decided to take girls' sexual and physical victimization seriously and arrested the perpetrators rather than criminalizing girls' survival strategies and jailing them for daring to escape.

Notes

[1] This phrase is taken from an inmate file by Rafter, N. H. (1990). *Partial Justice: Women, Prisons and Social Control*. New Brunswick, NJ: Transaction Books, in her review of the establishment of New York's Albion Reformatory.

[2] Calahan, M. (1986). *Historical Corrections Statistics in the United States, 1850–1984*. Washington, DC: Bureau of Justice Statistics.

[3] Female Offender Resource Center (1977). *Little Sisters and the Law*. Washington, DC: American Bar Association, p. 34.

[4] Datesman, S. and Scarpitti, F. (1977). "Unequal Protection for Males and Females in the Juvenile Court." In T. N. Ferdinand (Ed.), *Juvenile Delinquency: Little Brother Grows Up* (p. 70). Newbury Park, CA: Sage.

[5] Chesney-Lind, M. and Shelden, R. (2004). *Girls, Delinquency and Juvenile Justice* (3rd Ed.). Belmont, CA: Thompson-Wadsworth for a detailed review of this history.

[6] Ibid, p. 177.

[7] Joe-Laidler, K. A. and Chesney-Lind, M. (1996). "Running Away from Home: Rhetoric and Reality in Troublesome Behavior." *Journal of Contemporary Criminal Justice* 12 (2).

[8] See Chesney-Lind and Shelden, *Girls, Delinquency and Juvenile Justice* for details of these hearings.

[9] Belknap, J., Dunn, M., and Holsinger, K. (1997). *Moving Toward Juvenile Justice and Youth— Serving Systems that Address the Distinct Experience of the Adolescent Female*. Gender Specific Work Group Report to the Governor. Columbus, OH: Office of Criminal Justice Services, February.

[10] Children's Defense Fund and Girls Incorporated (2002). *Overview of Gender Provisions in State Juvenile Justice Plans*. Washington, DC: Children's Defense Fund and Girls Incorporated, August, p. 3.

[11] Ray, D. (2002). Letter to Glenda MacMullin, American Bar Association. Re: National Girl's Institute, March 20.

[12] Reitsma-Street, M. and Offord, D. R. (1991). "Girl Delinquents and Their Sisters: A Challenge for Practice." *Canadian Social Work Review* 8: 12.

[13] Gelsethorpe, L. (1989). *Sexism and the Female Offender*. Aldershot, England: Gower Publishing; Kempf-Leonard, K. and Sample, L. L. (2000). "Disparity Based on Sex: Is Gender-Specific Treatment Warranted?" *Justice Quarterly* 17: 89–128. Smart, C. (1976). *Women, Crime and Criminology: A Feminist Critique*. London: Routledge and Kegan Paul.

[14] Kersten, J. (1989). "The Institutional Control of Girls and Boys." In M. Cain (Ed.), *Growing Up Good: Policing the Behavior of Girls in Europe* (pp. 129–144). London: Sage. Mann, C. R. (1984). *Female Crime and Delinquency*. Tuscaloosa: University of Alabama Press.

[15] Chesney-Lind, M. (2000). "What to Do about Girls?" In M. McMahon (Ed.), *Assessment to Assistance: Programs for Women in Community Corrections*. Lanham, MD: American Correctional Association.

[16] Corrado, R., Odgers, C., and Cohen, I. M. (2000). "The Incarceration of Female Young Offenders: Protection for Whom?" *Canadian Journal of Criminology* 2: 189–207.

[17] McCormack, A., Janus, M. D., and Burgess, A. W. (1986). "Runaway Youths and Sexual Victimization: Gender Differences in an Adolescent Runaway Population." *Child Abuse and Neglect* 10: 387–395.

[18] Tyler, K. A., Hoyt, D. R., Whitbeck, L. B., and Cauce, A. M. (2001). "The Impact of Childhood Sexual Abuse or Later Sexual Victimization among Runaway Youth." *Journal of Research on Adolescence* 11: 151–176.

[19] Dembo, R., Williams, L., and Schmeidler, J. (1993). "Gender Differences in Mental Health Service Needs among Youths Entering a Juvenile Detention Center." *Journal of Prison and Jail Health* 12: 73–101.

[20] Dembo, R., Sue, S. C., Borden, P., and Manning, D. (1995). "Gender Differences in Service Needs among Youths Entering a Juvenile Assessment Center: A Replication Study." Paper presented at the Annual Meeting of the Society of Social Problems. Washington, DC, p. 21.

[21] Cauffman, E., Feldman, S. S., Waterman, J., and Steiner, H. (1998). "Posttraumatic Stress Disorder among Female Juvenile Offenders." *Journal of the American Academy of Child and Adolescent Psychiatry* 31: 1209–1216.

[22] Federal Bureau of Investigation (2003). *Crime in the U.S. 2002.* Washington, DC: U.S. Government Printing Office.

[23] Ibid, p. 239; Federal Bureau of Investigation (2001). *Crime in the U.S. 2000.* Washington, DC: U.S. Government Printing Office, p. 221.

[24] Snyder, H. N. (2001). *Juvenile Offenders and Victims National.* Washington, DC: U.S. Department of Justice, Office of Justice Programs, Office of Juvenile Justice and Delinquency Prevention, p. 5.

[25] See Chesney-Lind and Shelden, *Girls, Delinquency and Juvenile Justice.*

[26] For a review, see Chesney-Lind, M. (1999). "Media Misogyny: Demonizing 'Violent' Girls and Women." In J. Ferrel and N. Websdale (Eds.), *Making Trouble: Cultural Representations of Crime, Deviance, and Control.* New York: Aldine.

[27] Brener, N. D., Simon, T. R., Krug, E. G., and Lowry, R. (1999). "Recent Trends in Violence-Related Behaviors among High School Students in the United States." *Journal of the American Medical Association* 282: 330–446; Centers for Disease Control and Prevention (1992–2002). *Youth Risk Behavior Surveillance—United States, 1991–2001.* CDC Surveillance Summaries. U.S. Department of Health and Human Services. Atlanta: Centers for Disease Control.

[28] Brener et al., "Recent Trends," p. 444.

[29] Huizinga, D. (1997). *Over-time Changes in Delinquency and Drug Use: The 1970's to the 1990's.* Unpublished report. Washington, DC: Office of Juvenile Justice and Delinquency Prevention.

[30] Cook, P. J. and Laub, J. H. (1998). "The Unprecedented Epidemic in Youth Violence." In M. Tonry and M. H. Moore (Eds.), *Youth Violence. Crime and Justice: A Review of Research.* Chicago: The University of Chicago Press.

[31] Snyder, H. N. and Sickmund, M. (1999). *Juvenile Offenders and Victims: 1999 National Report* (NCJ 178257). Washington, DC: U.S. Department of Justice, Office of Justice Programs, Office of Juvenile Justice and Delinquency Prevention.

[32] Blumstein, A. (1995). "Youth Violence, Guns, and the Illicit-Drug Industry." *The Journal of Criminal Law & Criminology* 86: 10–34; Blumstein, A. and Cork, D. (1996). "Linking Gun Availability to Gun Violence." *Law and Contemporary Problems* 59: 5–24; Blumstein, A. and Wallman, J. (2000). *The Crime Drop in America.* Cambridge: Cambridge University Press.

[33] Olweus, D., Limber, S., and Mihalic, S. (2002). *Blueprints for Violence Prevention: Bulling Prevention Program.* Denver: Center for the Study and Prevention of Violence, Institute of Behavioral Science, University of Colorado at Boulder.

[34] Madigan, E. (2004). "Bullying by School Kids Gets Lawmakers' Attention." [Online] June 19, 2004, http://www.stateline.org/stateline/.

[35] For a full discussion of these issues see Chesney-Lind, M. and Belknap, J. (2003). "Trends in Delinquent Girls' Aggression and Violent Behavior: A Review of the Evidence." In M. Putallaz and P. Bierman (Eds.), *Aggression, Antisocial Behavior and Violence among Girls: A Developmental Perspective.* New York: Guilford Press.

[36] Bureau of Criminal Information and Analysis (1999). *Report on Arrests for Domestic Violence in California, 1998.* Sacramento: State of California, Criminal Justice Statistics Center.

[37] Acoca, L. (1999). "Investing in Girls: A 21st Century Challenge." *Juvenile Justice* 6: 7–8.

[38] Belknap, J., Winter, E., and Cady, B. (2001). *Assessing the Needs of Committed Delinquent and Pre-Adjudicated Girls in Colorado: A Focus Group Study.* Denver: A Report to the Colorado Division of Youth Corrections.

[39] Russ, H. (2004). "The War on Catfights." *City Limits,* February, p. 20.

[40] Centers for Disease Control and Prevention, *Youth Risk Behavior Surveillance.*

[41] Steffensmeier, D. J. and Steffensmeier, R. H. (1980). "Trends in Female Delinquency: An Examination of Arrest, Juvenile Court, Self-Report, and Field Data." *Criminology* 18: 62–85.

[42] Currie, E. (1998). *Crime and Punishment in America.* New York: Metropolitan Books.

[43] Harvard Civil Rights Project (2000). *Opportunities Suspended: The Devastating Consequences of Zero Tolerance and School Discipline.* Report from A National Summit on Zero Tolerance. Washington, DC, June 15–16, p. vi.

[44] Federal Bureau of Investigation, *Crime in the U.S. 2000*, p. 239.

[45] Wells, R. (1994). "America's Delinquent Daughters Have Nowhere to Turn for Help." *Corrections Compendium* 19: 4–6.

[46] Stahl, A. (2006, November). "Delinquency Cases in Juvenile Courts, 2002." *OJJDP Fact Sheet #2.* Washington, DC: U.S. Department of Justice, p. 1. [Online] http://www.ncjrs.gov/pdffiles1/ojjdp/fs200602.pdf.

[47] Sherman, F. (2000). "What's in a Name? Runaway Girls Pose Challenges for the Justice System." *Women, Girls and Criminal Justice* 1: 19–20.

[48] Corrado et al. "The Incarceration of Female Young Offenders: Protection for Whom?" p. 193.

[49] Ibid.

[50] American Bar Association and the National Bar Association (2001). *Justice by Gender: The Lack of Appropriate Prevention, Diversion and Treatment Alternatives for Girls in the Justice System.* [Online] http://www.njdc.info/pdf/justicebygenderweb.pdf.

[51] Harms, P. (2002). "Detention in Delinquency Cases, 1989–1998." *OJJDP Fact Sheet #1.* Washington, DC: U.S. Department of Justice, January, p. 1.

[52] American Bar Association and the National Bar Association, *Justice by Gender*, p. 20.

[53] Sickmund, M., Sladky, T. J., and Kang, W. (2004). *Census of Juveniles in Residential Placement Databook.* Washington, DC: U.S. Department of Justice. [Online] http://www.ojjdp.ncjrs.org/ojstatbb/cjrp/asp/selection.asp.

[54] Snyder and Sickmund, *Juvenile Offenders and Victims: 1999 National Report.*

[55] Ibid.

[56] Miller, J. (1994). "Race, Gender and Juvenile Justice: An Examination of Disposition Decision-Making for Delinquent Girls." In M. D. Schwartz & D. Milovanovic (Eds.), *The Intersection of Race, Gender and Class in Criminology.* New York: Garland Press.

[57] Robinson, R. (1990). Violations of Girlhood: A Qualitative Study of Female Delinquents and Children in Need of Services in Massachusetts. Unpublished doctoral dissertation, Brandeis University.

[58] American Bar Association and the National Bar Association, *Justice by Gender*, p. 20.

[59] Holsinger, K., Belknap, J., and Sutherland, J. L. (1999). *Assessing the Gender Specific Program and Service Needs for Adolescent Females in the Juvenile Justice System.* Columbus, OH: A Report to the Office of Criminal Justice Services.

[60] Schaffner, L., Shorter, A. D., Shick, S., and Frappier, N. S. (1996). *Out of Sight, Out of Mind: The Plight of Girls in the San Francisco Juvenile Justice System.* San Francisco: Center for Juvenile and Criminal Justice, p. 1.

[61] Ambrose, A. M., Simpkins, S., and Levick, M. (2000). *Improving the Conditions for Girls in the Juvenile Justice System: The Female Detention Project.* Washington, DC: American Bar Association, p. 1.

[62] Ibid, p. 2.

[63] Acoca, L. and Dedel, K. (1998). *No Place to Hide: Understanding and Meeting the Needs of Girls in the California Juvenile Justice System.* San Francisco: National Council on Crime and Delinquency, p. 6.

[64] Lederman, C. S. and Brown, E. N. (2000). "Entangled in the Shadows: Girls in the Juvenile Justice System." *Buffalo Law Review* 48: 909–925.

[65] Baines, M. and Alder, C. (1996). "Are Girls More Difficult to Work With? Youth Workers' Perspectives in Juvenile Justice and Related Areas." *Crime & Delinquency* 42: 467–485; Belknap et al., *Assessing the Needs of Committed Delinquent and Pre-Adjudicated Girls in Colorado.*

[66] Gaarder, E., Zatz, M. S., and Rodriguez, N. (2004). "Criers, Liars and Manipulators: Probation Officers' Views of Girls." *Justice Quarterly* 21: 14.

[67] Ibid, p. 16.

[68] Sickmund et al., *Census of Juveniles in Residential Placement Database.*

[69] Holsinger et al., *Assessing the Gender Specific Program and Service Needs for Adolescent Females in the Juvenile Justice System*.

[70] Belknap et al., *Assessing the Needs of Committed Delinquent and Pre-Adjudicated Girls in Colorado*.

[71] White, B. (2003). "American Civil Liberties Union Report on the Hawaii Youth Correctional Facility," June 3–July 23. [Online] http://www.acluhawaii.org/pages/news/030826youthcorrection.html, p. 16.

[72] Dingeman, R. (2004). "Ex-guard Guilty in Sex Assault." *Honolulu Advertiser*. April 30. [Online] http://the.honoluluadvertiser.com/article/2004/apr/30/in/in14a.html.

[73] See Chesney-Lind and Shelden, *Girls, Delinquency and Juvenile Justice*.

[74] Sharp, C. and Simon, J. (2004). *Girls and the Juvenile Justice System: The Need for More Gender Responsive Services*. Washington, DC: Child Welfare League.

[75] Ibid; American Bar Association and the National Bar Association, *Justice by Gender*.

[76] Chesney-Lind, M. and Pasko, L. (2004). *The Female Offender: Girls, Women and Crime* (2nd Ed.). Thousand Oaks, CA: Sage.

[77] Siegal, N. (1995). "Where the Girls Are." *San Francisco Bay Guardian*, October 4, pp. 19–20.

[78] Ibid.

[79] Girls Incorporated (1996). *Prevention and Parity: Girls in Juvenile Justice*. Indianapolis: Girls Incorporated National Resource Center.

[80] Viner, E. personal communication with Chesney-Lind, October 21, 2003.

[81] A more detailed discussion of programs for girls is found in chapter 10 of this book.

PART II

Prospects

6

Thinking Out of the Box
The Need to Do Something Different

Randall G. Shelden

Many, if not most, traditional approaches to the prevention and treatment of delinquency have not fared well. After more than 30 years of studying and teaching about the subject of crime and delinquency, I am convinced that some very fundamental changes need to be made in the way we live and think before we see any significant decrease in these problems. Adults persistently refer to the "problem of delinquency" with value-laden questions such as "What's wrong with kids these days?" The implication is that youths in trouble need to change their attitudes, their behaviors, their lifestyles, their methods of thinking, etc. Rarely does anyone think outside the box to propose radical changes in the system or society.

What is invariably included in this line of thinking is the use of labels to describe these youth (and adult offenders too). The labels change with the times. As Jerome Miller has noted, we began with "possessed" youths in the seventeenth century, moved to the "rabble" or "dangerous classes" in the eighteenth and late nineteenth centuries, revised the labels to "moral imbeciles" and "constitutional psychopathic inferiors" of the early twentieth century, followed by the "psychopath" of the 1940s and the "sociopath" of the 1950s, and finally to "compulsive delinquent," the "learning disabled," the "unsocialized aggressive" (or even the "socialized aggressive"), and finally the "bored" delinquent. "With the growth of professionalism," continues Miller, "the number of labels has multiplied exponentially."[1]

Miller cautions that the labeling process allows us to "bolster the maintenance of the existing order against threats which might arise from its own internal contradictions." The labels reassure us "that the fault

Portions of this chapter are taken from Randall G. Shelden, *Delinquency and Juvenile Justice in American Society*. Long Grove, IL: Waveland Press, 2006. Reprinted here with permission of Waveland Press.

lies in the warped offender and takes everyone else off the hook. More-over, it enables the professional diagnostician to enter the scene or with-draw at will, wearing success like a halo and placing failure around the neck of the client like a noose."[2] More importantly, we continue to believe that harsh punishment works, especially the kind of punishment that includes some form of incarceration, so that the offender is placed out of sight and, not coincidentally, out of mind.

As noted in article 1, we have succumbed to the "edifice complex." We love to build structures—a new courthouse, a new prison, a new cor-rectional center, a new police station, etc.).[3] Perhaps it is because politi-cians can point to a permanent structure as proof that they have done something about crime; or perhaps it is because the construction and operation of edifices are profitable and are staples of the huge "crime control industry."[4]

I believe we need to change our focus and look beyond blaming "troubled youth" or "criminals" for the problem of crime. It is time that those of us among the more privileged sectors of society consider that we are just as much a part of the problem—perhaps more so.

Reclaiming Youth at Risk: An Alternative Way of Framing the Problem

A perspective borrowed from Native American culture offers hope. In *Reclaiming Youth at Risk*, Larry Brendtro, Martin Brokenleg, and Steve Van Bockern outline a promising approach that challenges prevailing perspec-tives.[5] The authors define "reclaiming" as "to recover and redeem, to restore value to something that has been devalued." Recovering and restor-ing requires "reclaiming environments" marked by the following features:

- belonging to a supportive community, instead of being controlled by a depersonalized bureaucracy;
- meeting a person's needs for "mastery," instead of "enduring inflexible systems designed for the convenience of adults";
- involving young people in determining their own future, while at the same time recognizing the need to control harmful behavior;
- expecting young people to be givers, rather than merely recipients dependent on adults.[6]

Brendtro, Brokenleg, and Van Bockern observe that many youths grow up in environments that produce discouragement. The seeds of this discouragement are sown in the "four worlds of childhood"—family, friends, school, and productive work. When parents are stressed, schools are impersonal, and communities disorganized, the basic needs of chil-dren are not met. As a result, they become estranged. The authors refer to the "ecological hazards" confronting youth: (1) destructive relationships (causing feelings of rejection, the inability to trust, and of being unloved); (2) climates of futility (resulting in feelings of inadequacy and fear of failure); (3) learned irresponsibility ("as seen in the youth whose sense of powerlessness may be masked by indifference or defiant rebelliousness"); and (4) loss of purpose ("as portrayed by a generation of self-centered youth, desperately searching for meaning in a world of confusing values").[7]

In the section the book entitled "Climates of Futility," the authors discuss the expectations that people have about the possibilities of working with difficult youth. They challenge the pervasive negative attitudes and pessimism. The authors note that some of the early pioneers who worked with difficult youth "strongly challenged the indifference and pessimism of their times. They were incurable optimists who could always find cause for hope in the face of the most difficult problems." They cite as an example a Swiss educator who "created a castle school for outcast street urchins to demonstrate his revolutionary thesis that 'precious hidden faculties' could be found beneath an appearance of ignorance."[8] Today, however, pessimism is common in our approaches to "difficult youth."

Brendtro, Brokenleg, and Van Bockern discuss four key concepts contributing to the negativity in school climates today. The first is *negative expectations,* which "breed futility in both students and staff." In contrast, the high expectations of Jaime Escalante (the high school math teacher portrayed by James Edward Olmos in the film *Stand and Deliver*) encouraged and motivated his students in East Los Angeles to excel.

The second concept is that of *punitiveness.* Horace Mann, an important nineteenth-century educator, said that teachers need to respond to their most difficult students similarly to a doctor solving the challenge of a difficult case. "To become angry and punish such a child is as illogical as if a surgeon were to attack the limb he is treating."[9]

The third key concept is that of *boredom.* Jane Addams often described disadvantaged youth in Chicago as those who lack adventure in their lives.[10] Today, many kids are bored and need some sense of adventure (which they often get through gangs and other deviant activities).

The fourth concept, and an important one, is *irresponsibility.* Once again the authors quote Horace Mann, who said that education is an "apprenticeship in responsibility." If, however, education becomes only a routine of standardized tests rather than an adventure in expanding one's horizons, there will be little opportunity to set personal goals and to take responsibility for achieving them.[11]

Brendtro, Brokenleg, and Van Bockern discuss the role of "professional pessimism" in creating a negative environment. They include the following quotation from Floyd Starr, who founded a nonprofit home and residential school for delinquent and neglected boys in 1913, to demonstrate how attitudes have changed.

> We believe there is no such thing as a bad boy, that badness is not a
> normal condition but the result of misdirected energy. We believe
> that every boy will be good if given an opportunity in an environment
> of love and activity.

In contrast to Floyd's optimism, the authors quote a popular professional text on troubled children: "They are abusive, destructive, unpre-
dictable, irresponsible, bossy, quarrelsome, irritable, jealous, defiant—
anything but pleasant to be with. Naturally adults choose not to spend
time with this kind of child unless they have to."[12] The authors note:

> An examination of the history of childhood in Western society shows
> that negative attitudes toward difficult youth are deeply imbedded in
> the cultural milieu. Pioneers such as Jane Addams and Floyd Starr
> were not so much products of that culture as antagonists to it. Even
> today, the predominant patterns of thinking are pessimistic rather
> than optimistic. This way of thinking fixates on deviance to the
> exclusion of normality, illness to the exclusion of health.[13]

Brendtro, Brokenleg, and Van Bockern continue making the case for a
change in *our own attitudes and values toward youth*. Negative thinking leads
to negative feelings and actions. Our thoughts guide our feelings, which
in turn provide motivations and directions to our behavior. If we think
hate, we tend to feel hate and in turn act in hateful ways. We become
what we think and feel.

Negative labels assigned to a child lead to negative perceptions of the
child *as a person*. We need to learn to reject the behavior, while accepting
the child. The most successful youth workers are those "who can reframe
cognitions to foster the positive feelings and actions essential to the
helping process."[14] Paraphrasing German poet and educator Goethe, the
authors suggest that we must look beyond the negative behavior to find a
"germ of virtue" within the child. A liability can become an asset if we,
for instance, redefine "stubbornness" as "persistence."[15]

Today, however, collective attitudes toward difficult youth are
demeaning. For instance, one former head of the Office of Juvenile Justice and Delinquency Prevention declared that the mission of his office
and the nation was to hold "predators" accountable; the incendiary rhetoric seemed to be a blanket condemnation of all difficult youth. In stark
contrast, August Aichhorn (a pioneer in working with youth in Austria)
emphasized in 1925 that "wayward youth" (very different rhetoric from
frightening images of remorseless youths preying on the innocent)
needed guidance and direction.[16]

Brendtro, Brokenleg, and Van Bockern lament what they call the "tyr-
anny of obedience."

> The saga of discipline in Western civilization is a litany of futile
> attempts to compel the young person to obedient behavior. The con-
> sistent strategy has been to control all deviations by punishing or

excluding those who violate the rules. For centuries schools have used elaborate codes of regulations to attempt to instill compliant behavior. However, students have been highly resourceful in circumventing these rigid rules.[17]

These codes send the message that: "This you can do; this you cannot do; and if you do what you shouldn't, this is the price you pay."[18]

European conquerors were amazed that obedience was not part of the Native-American culture, often concluding that the lack of the trait represented a defect.

> The ethnocentric European was imprisoned in a cultural history where the fundamental "bond of society" had always been obedience: vassals obeyed lords, priests obeyed superiors, subjects obeyed kings, slaves obeyed masters, women obeyed men, and children obeyed everybody.[19]

In the Native American culture, "one man is as much a master as another, and since all men are made of the same clay, there should be no distinction or superiority among them."[20]

Brendtro, Brokenleg, and Van Bockern firmly believe that teaching obedience is wrong, for it does not teach responsibility. They discuss Rousseau's belief that children should be given "well-regulated freedom" to learn from experience and natural consequences.[21] They will then learn to be self-sufficient at an early age. Noting that obedience training is closely intertwined with the notion that children should follow rules, the authors state: "If rules are imposed by external sanctions, children will follow them as long as policed. When out of the range of surveillance, anything goes."[22] This reminds me of freeway drivers. Many will go as fast as they can, unless a police car is on the freeway, whereupon they will slow down. But when the police car gets off the freeway, the cars speed up again.

Reclaiming Youth at Risk offers a valuable new perspective. It represents an invaluable first step before considering solutions to the problems of delinquency—engaging in different ways of thinking. The comments of a deputy sheriff in Los Angeles, who heads a program that deals with gangs and related issues, also illustrates this kind of thinking: "To change the culture we have to change *our* culture." Law enforcement has to realize these kids have potential. Maybe if we can change the way we talk to them we can help them realize dreams they don't even know they have."[23]

Radical Nonintervention: Resurrecting an Old Perspective

Edwin Schur offered an excellent application of the "labeling" perspective to delinquency.[24] His approach was quite novel in 1973, and he considered a number of unchallenged assumptions about the problem of delinquency from a new perspective. His approach is perhaps even more relevant in today's atmosphere of "get tough" approaches to delinquency, especially "zero tolerance" policies.

Zero tolerance is one of the new mantras for the tough-on-crime stance. Schools have instituted policies that have had astounding consequences. At one school, the possession of a Nuprin tablet was deemed a violation of school drug policy. At another school, two six-year-old children were suspended for three days for pointing their fingers at other children and saying "bang, bang." Some high-school baseball players at one school were suspended for possessing "dangerous weapons" on school grounds—they had baseball bats in their cars. Zero-tolerance policies have contributed to "net widening." More and more minor offenses (or no offenses at all) are being processed formally by the police and the juvenile court. For example, ordinary fights at school or at home now constitute "assault."[25]

The *labeling* perspective does not address in any direct way the causes of criminal/deviant behavior; rather, it focuses on three interrelated processes: (1) how and why certain behaviors are defined as criminal/delinquent or deviant; (2) the response to crime or deviance on the part of authorities (e.g., the official processing of cases within the adult or juvenile justice system); and (3) the effects of such definitions and official reactions on the person or persons so labeled (e.g., how official responses to groups of youths may cause them to come closer together and begin to call themselves a gang).[26] One of the key components of the labeling perspective is that very often the nature of the official response to delinquency may actually make matters worse. Therefore, Schur argued for a more "hands off" approach that would avoid unnecessary labeling. Schur's radical nonintervention approach begins with the premise that we should "leave kids alone wherever possible."[27]

Schur noted that the traditional response to disenchantment with delinquency policies that had failed was to assume that the system merely needed improvement, which usually meant calls for more facilities or elaborate cost-benefit and systems analyses.[28] The result has been a larger system with much of the growth fueled by the net-widening effect of the "war on drugs." On any given day, more than 6 million people are somewhere within the criminal justice system, with perhaps another million or so in the juvenile justice system. The growth of the system has not diminished public fears; the fear of crime appears to be higher than ever.[29] Obviously something different is needed, and Schur's five suggestions are as relevant today as when he proposed them.[30]

1. *"There is a need for a thorough reassessment of the dominant ways of thinking about youth 'problems'."* Schur maintained that many, if not most, behaviors in which youth engage (including many labeled as "delinquent") are embedded in our social and cultural system and

that youthful misconduct is inevitable in any form of social order. We pay a huge price for criminalizing routine misbehaviors.

2. "Some of the most valuable policies for dealing with delinquency are not necessarily those designated as delinquency policies." Schur quotes a passage from *Struggle for Justice:* "To the extent, then, that equal justice is correlated with equality of status, influence, and economic power, the construction of a just system of criminal justice in an unjust society is a contradiction in terms."[31] It is necessary to go beyond the usual focus on isolation and punishment of individual offenders and to consider the inequality that exists in society.

3. *"We must take young people more seriously if we are to eradicate injustice to juveniles."* Schur noted that many young people lack a sound attachment to conventional society. The lack of respect noted by Schur is even more pronounced today. Society alternates between fearing the behaviors of youth and admiring young people. We often embrace diversity yet punish differences.

4. "The juvenile justice system should concern itself less with the problems of so-called 'delinquents' and more with dispensing justice." Schur was talking specifically about narrowing the jurisdiction of the juvenile court by reducing or eliminating court attention to status offenses. The intervening years have exacerbated the problem rather than ameliorating it. While some status offenders have been diverted from the juvenile justice system, other juveniles have been snared by net widening in the form of "bootstrapping," whereby a second status offense is labeled a "violation of a court order" (e.g., probation violation) or even "contempt of court." This has been especially the case for girls.[32]

5. *"As juvenile justice moves in new directions, a variety of approaches will continue to be useful."* Schur specifically suggested prevention programs that have a collective or community focus and promoted voluntary, noninstitutional programs that use "indigenous personnel." The Detention Diversion Advocacy Project (DDAP), the subject of article 8, is one such approach.

An Assessment of Schur's Ideas

As already indicated, much of what Schur articulated 30 years ago remains relevant in today's society, as does the labeling approach itself. While people may disagree on some of his points, the central thrust remains as true as ever, namely that the juvenile justice system extends far too broadly into the lives of children and adolescents.[33]

Mike Males forcefully makes the point that many criminologists and public policy makers blame kids for most ills of society while ignoring the damage done by adults.[34] Both James Alan Fox and John DiIulio predicted in 1995 that the United States would experience a rise in the teenage population that would result in a spike in the number of "adolescent super-predators."[35] Contrary to such dire predictions, the number of juvenile arrests for violent crimes dropped from 106,190 in 1995 to 56,467 in 2006.[36] In Los Angeles during the 1990s, two-thirds of the murder suspects were under 25, but in 2002 less than half were.[37] The same was true in the city of Oakland. Males chastises both James Q. Wilson and James Alan Fox for erroneously claiming that more young people means more crime. As Males correctly points out, in the years and in the states where there were a higher percentage of young males in the population, there were fewer violent crimes. Perhaps we would be more correct to stress the importance of greater intervention by the adult courts into the lives of "adult superpredators" instead of extending the reach of the juvenile court.

The overreach of the juvenile justice system is evident in the statistics on the number of cases handled by juvenile courts. From 1995 to 2004, the number of violent crime index cases decreased 42% and the number of property crime index cases decreased 35%. During the same time period, public order offenses increased 41%, and drug law violations increased 19%. Looking at individual components, the net widening effect is stark. Juvenile courts handled 70% more obstruction of justice cases (47% of all the public order offenses) and 23% more simple assault cases (70% of all person offenses).[38] The proportion of referrals to the juvenile court that are relatively petty acts is staggering. Why criminalize "normal" adolescent behavior like disturbing the peace and some minor fighting? (One may reasonably ask, "Whose peace is being disturbed?")

One of the important questions posed by the labeling perspective is: why are certain acts labeled "criminal" or "delinquent" while others are not? Another pertinent question is: how do we account for differential rates of arrest, referral to court, detention, adjudication, and commitment based on race and class? These are not merely academic questions; the lives of real people are impacted by "get tough" policies. We continue to criminalize normal adolescent behavior or behavior that should be dealt with outside of the formal juvenile justice system. Status offenses such as truancy and "incorrigibility" are primary examples. Criminalizing truancy has always seemed counterproductive. Why take formal police action because a kid is not going to school? Certainly, kids should stay in school—an education is a prerequisite for a decent life. Why use the immense power of the state to make kids stay in school? Likewise, kids should obey the reasonable demands of their parents, but they also should be left alone to figure things out for themselves. The state should intervene in private family matters only when direct physical or other obvious harms are being committed. How many times have we heard stories or read research reports on runaways who have experienced incredible abuse or discovered that many kids referred to juvenile court as "incorrigible" have been abused?[39]

If diversion is to work effectively, it is of paramount importance that *youths be diverted from the system itself*, rather than being caught in a "net widening" process. True diversion eases overcrowding. If detention centers (or any other type of correctional center) are plagued by chronic overcrowding, possible solutions include: (1) increase the space available (e.g., add rooms to the current structure or build a new one) or (2) remove a certain percentage of youths from the correctional system and divert them to a true alternative program (see article 8 for an example).

A New Paradigm: Restorative Justice

An emerging idea that has great potential is *restorative justice*. Space does not permit a thorough analysis of this interesting concept. However, this section briefly introduces the idea and touches on its potential. Seeking alternatives to a punitive response to crime, restorative justice emphasizes the needs of the victims, the offender, and the community. The restorative justice movement began in Canada with a case of two teenagers who went on a vandalism spree. The case was handled via a direct meeting between the victims and the two teenagers. The movement has proliferated throughout the world in an effort to seek peaceful and nonpunitive solutions.[40]

The central thrust of restorative justice is to try and ease the pain and suffering of all victims of crime and all forms of human rights abuses. The usual response to crime—especially violent crime—is the desire to seek retribution ("just deserts," or "an eye for an eye") against offenders. This response, however, is counterproductive. In fact, it goes against virtually every religious tenet. As Gandhi and Martin Luther King taught and practiced, the only way to end violence is *not* to reciprocate in kind. To end the cycle, someone needs to stop the violence. In his acceptance speech for the Nobel Peace Prize in 1964, King advised: "The choice today is not between violence and nonviolence. It is either nonviolence or nonexistence."[41]

Restorative justice embraces the idea that the only way to rid oneself of hurt and anger is through forgiveness. English poet Alexander Pope (1688–1744) penned the phrase "To err is human, to forgive divine."[42] Unfortunately, forgiveness seems out of step in our current political/economic system. Forgiveness would be more in line with an economic/political system "that sees acknowledgment of a harm done, and apology for it, and forgiveness offered in return, as processes that are personally healing for all involved and simultaneously restorative of community."[43]

The underlying aim of the restorative justice process is to cease further objectification of those who have been involved in the violent act—the victim, the offender, the families connected to these two individuals, and the community at large. Restorative justice encourages all of the individuals involved to engage in a healing process through traditional mediation and conflict resolution techniques in order to "help those affected by the harm dissolve their fears, and hates, and resentments and thereby recover a sense of their former selves." This process enables the person who has been harmed

> to achieve a greater sense of inner healing and closure for any trau-matic loss of trust, self-worth, and freedom . . . [while] the harmed person might also achieve a modicum of reparation for his or her losses as well as be able to reduce his or her fears of being harmed.[44]

Proponents of restorative justice know full well what a difficult sell this is within a capitalist society. As Dennis Sullivan and Larry Tifft observe, the change needed "transforms all of our conceptions of politi-cal economy—that is, how we view power and money, and how we assess human worth."[45] Embracing principles of restorative justice allows us to move beyond power and control to more healing resolutions.

Intervention Typologies

One of the most comprehensive overviews of delinquency preven-tion programs is provided by Joy Dryfoos.[46] She addresses four interre-lated problems: delinquency, teen pregnancy, drug abuse, and school failure. Her review of the research found that most prevention programs fall into one of three broad categories: (1) early childhood and family interventions, (2) school-based interventions, and (3) community-based and/or multicomponent interventions.[47] Programs that fall within the early childhood and family intervention category include two major types: (1) preschool/Head Start programs and (2) parent training/sup-port programs. Programs found within the school-based intervention category include three main types: (1) curricula, (2) organization of school (teacher training, team approach to problem solving, and alterna-tive schools), and (3) special services (counseling and mentoring pro-grams, health services, and volunteer work). Community-based interventions include three main types: (1) school–community collabo-ration programs, (2) community education, and (3) multicomponent comprehensive programs.

Dryfoos's review also distinguishes among programs that have been proven to be successful, those that have the potential for success but have not been evaluated systematically, and those for which evaluations have shown negative results. For the prevention of delinquency, some successful models include: the Perry Preschool program (a Head Start program in Ypsilanti, Michigan); the Syracuse Family Development Pro-gram; parent training programs (for example, the Oregon Social Learning Center in Eugene); school-based interventions, such as social skills train-ing programs and law-related education; several types of programs that focus on the organization of the school (including classroom-management programs that attempt to enhance bonding between the students and the teachers), alternative schools, cooperative learning arrangements (for example, Positive Action Through Holistic Education, or PATHE, in Charleston, South Carolina); and, finally, various community-based programs, such as the use of juvenile court volunteers (for example, Denver Partners) and runaway and homeless youth shelters (for example, the Neon Street Clinic in Chicago).[48]

Dryfoos also provides profiles of several successful programs that address the problem of substance abuse.[49] These include such school-based programs as life skills training programs, student assistance programs, Growing Healthy (developed by the American Lung Association), and the use of school-based clinics (for example, Adolescent Resources Corporation in Kansas City). She cites several community-based interventions, such as The Door in New York City and the Midwestern Prevention Project in Kansas City.

Components of Successful Programs

Research on the subject of community intervention has covered a wide variety of programs dealing with an equally wide variety of problems, ranging from drug abuse and delinquency to teen pregnancy and school failure. What are the ingredients of programs that have had some success? Do these successful programs have certain features that set them apart from others?

Successful delinquency treatment and prevention programs have several key ingredients. Mathea Falco and Ronald Huff both suggest that communities need to be aware of drug and/or gang problems and must avoid denial of problems.[50] Second, programs should target medium- to high-risk youths with intensive, multifaceted approaches that focus especially on the development of social skills (for example, conflict resolution) and address the attitudes, values, and beliefs that reinforce antisocial behaviors. Third, programs should offer alternatives to gang involvement (recreational programs, school events, jobs, and so on). Programs should provide explicit reinforcement and modeling of alternatives to pro-criminal styles of thinking, feeling, and acting. Fourth, community programs with a special focus on families and schools should be available to promote cooperation and interaction between these two institutions. Fifth, the staff should be well-trained, skilled individuals who have developed empathy and an understanding of a youth's subculture that does not patronize or discredit his/her beliefs. Sixth, link the program with the world of work by assisting youths in developing job skills. Seventh, the goals of the program should be specific and culminate in some kind of award (for example, a diploma). Eighth, realize that relapse is normal (whether we are dealing with drug or alcohol abuse or any pattern of negative, antisocial behavior) and that treatment is a continual process rather than a single episode; relapse-prevention techniques should always be employed to prepare for community adaptation. Lisbeth Schorr concludes:

> In short, the programs that succeed in helping the children and families . . . are intensive, comprehensive, and flexible. . . . Their climate is created by skilled, committed professionals who establish respectful and trusting relationships and respond to the individual needs of those they serve.[51]

The Effectiveness of Diversion.   Diversion began as an attempt to keep young offenders out of juvenile court. "If they were processed, the goal was to divert them out of the system as quickly as possible."[52] The basis for diversion is the belief that courts may inadvertently stigmatize some youths for relatively petty acts that could best be handled outside the court system or ignored entirely. Diversion programs are designed, in part, to deal with the problem of overcrowded juvenile courts and correctional institutions (including detention), so that greater attention can be devoted to more serious offenders.

Sociologist Richard Lundman examined several evaluations of diversion programs, including the Sacramento County Diversion Program (around 1,500 youths), several other California programs (around 2,500 youths), and the National Evaluation of Diversion Programs in four states (about 2,500 youths).[53] The programs included boys and girls. With few exceptions, the experimental groups (that is, children receiving the special treatment included within the diversion programs) did not differ significantly from the control groups in terms of recidivism. But it was also found that the recidivism rates for status offenders were almost identical for those diverted and those not diverted. Thus, diversion of status offenders at least does no greater harm. Because girls are far more likely to commit status offenses and minor crimes, perhaps diversion is especially suitable for them.

The National Evaluation of Diversion Programs covered four locations (Kansas City, Memphis, Florida's Orange County, and New York City). Youths were randomly selected to one of three comparison groups: (1) release with no services; (2) release with diversion services; or (3) further penetration into the juvenile justice system. The evaluation was done at two intervals: 6 months after diversion and again 6 months later. The results showed that there were no differences in recidivism rates among the three groups after both 6 months and 12 months. Significantly, doing nothing—no services, no further penetration into the system—was just as effective as providing services or further punishment!

Lundman also reviewed Youth Enhancement Services (YES) in Pennsylvania, which was funded in the early 1990s. The main attention of this program was on the overrepresentation of minorities in secure state facilities (75% of those incarcerated were minorities, even though they represented only 12% of the total youth population). The evaluation design was "quasi-experimental" in that participation in one of several types of services was voluntary for the juvenile offenders. Out of a total of 191 who were referred for this program, 83 (43.5%) chose not to participate (they were the designated "control group"). The remaining youths who volunteered were split into two groups: one that spent less than 30 hours in the various services provided during the course of one year and another group that spent at least 30 hours in such services.[54] The main goal of the program was to improve school performances and to reduce recidivism rates, especially for minority youth. A variety of existing community services was used, provided by such organizations as Girls Inc., Boys Clubs, and Camp Curtain YMCA.

The results showed little overall improvement in school performance among each of the three groups. However, the results showed that the control group had the highest arrest rate after two years (50.6%), while the "low attendance" group had a recidivism rate of 41.3% and the "high attendance" group had the lowest recidivism rate (25.8%). The program also did an effective job of keeping minority youths away from further trouble. The study suggested that the more youths participate in the services offered, the greater the chance they will succeed.

The primary treatment modes of most diversion programs are individual counseling, casework, and work experience, despite the fact that these types of treatments have had little success in other settings. They have not been effective in diversion programs, either. Rigorous evaluations of diversion programs consistently turn up mixed results.[55] The results for girls in diversion programs are even more problematic.[56] Christine Alder notes that girls constitute 40% of the participants in diversion programs but only about 25% of offense cases in the courts. Moreover, girls are referred for less serious offenses or, in some instances, no offense at all—being referred for personal problems, family difficulties, or school problems.[57] Alder also uncovered indications that girls with no prior offense records were far more likely than boys to be referred to diversion programs even though many of the boys had previous arrests. These findings suggest that many girls currently in diversion programs would have been released in times past. At a minimum, these programs may be unnecessarily monitoring girls who have not committed crimes but are simply having problems with their parents or their schools.

One study found that diversion programs did not yield significant differences between groups assigned to regular probation and groups assigned to special programs, such as day care treatment and group counseling.[58] Similarly, Mark Lipsey reported that enhanced probation or parole services had extremely modest effects on recidivism (3%). Only slightly more effective were release programs (5%), reduced caseloads (4%), and probation with restitution (4%).[59] Dennis Romig concluded that regular probation is just as successful as all the more expensive programs—if not more so. He declared that probation programs should have

the following ingredients: indigenous probation aides who are empa-
thetic and who set individualized and specific treatment goals for youth,
involvement of family, aides to monitor school attendance, active use of
the community, and a variety of treatment approaches.[60]

Broad-Based National Strategies[61]

Addressing the delinquency problem will require a national strategy;
the problem is not just local in nature. Elliot Currie suggests five general
categories for a national strategy to address the general problem of crime.

1. *Early educational interventions.* Programs such as Head Start are based
   on the assumption that delinquency is related to poor school performance and dropping out, which in turn are related to a lack of
   preparedness for school, especially among lower-class minorities.[62]

2. *Expanded health and mental health services.* Evidence suggests that the
   most violent youths suffer from childhood traumas of the central
   nervous system and exhibit multiple psychotic symptoms. Pre-
   and postnatal care could help prevent some of these traumas.[63]

3. *Family support programs.* Many violent youths have experienced
   severe physical, emotional, and/or sexual abuse. Abused children
   are far more likely than nonabused children to become abusers
   themselves.[64]

4. *Reentry programs.* Helping offenders after they have broken the law
   rather than merely warehousing them would alleviate the problem
   of recidivism. Currie notes that an ingredient found in virtually all
   successful rehabilitation programs is improving skills—work
   skills, reading and verbal skills, problem-solving skills, and so on.

5. *Drug and alcohol abuse treatment programs.* The war on drugs targets
   the manufacturing and distribution (the supply side) of drugs and
   arrests users rather than focusing on the demand side of drugs
   and how to treat addictions and abuse.

On a more general level, Currie suggests that we as a society need to
reduce racial inequality, poverty, and inadequate services. Perhaps most
importantly, we need to prepare the next generation better for the labor
market of the future. With this in mind, Currie outlines four general goals
for the decades ahead: (1) reduction of inequality and social impoverishment, (2) an active labor market policy that aims at upgrading job skills,
(3) a national family policy (for example, a family leave bill), and (4) promoting economic and social stability of local communities (the frequent
moving of capital and employment opportunities has forced many families
to relocate in order to seek better jobs, weakening the development of networks that could provide support). Finally, he notes the need for a national
research agenda to study the effectiveness of policies to find what works.

Sociologist Mark Colvin has also written about the need for national strategies.[65] He focuses on the concept of social reproduction, which refers to the process engaged in by institutions (primarily families and schools) to socialize children and prepare them for productive roles in society. His main thesis is that these institutions have largely failed to give growing numbers of young people social bonds to legitimate avenues to adulthood. The result is that many are becoming marginal to the country's economic institutions. The failure to invest in human development and human capital has resulted in some disadvantaged youths turning to crime and increasing expenditures for welfare and prisons. There is a need for a "national comprehensive program aimed at spurring economic growth, human development, and grass-roots, democratic participation in the major institutions affecting our lives and those of our children."[66]

Colvin argues that neither conservative deterrence approaches nor liberal approaches to rehabilitation have been very effective, mainly because they are reactive policies. Some prevention programs do not work because of a lack of funding, or a failure to address the larger problems in society, or because they often appear to target specific groups (for example, high-risk poor children) at the expense of middle-class taxpayers.

A comprehensive approach must aim at broader economic and human-development programs that affect large segments of the population (for example, the social security system versus welfare for the poor). The country must do what other industrialized nations do and consider seriously the need to develop human capital for the continued overall well-being of society. The U.S. system is so privatized that public or social needs are often undermined by private investment decisions.

We need to redirect our focus away from the question of "what to do about crime" to "what to do about our declining infrastructure and competitiveness in the world economy." Further, there is a need to establish an educational-industrial complex to replace the already declining military-industrial complex.[67] Education is the key. However, as Colvin notes, education must become more than what the term has traditionally meant—namely, formalized public schooling leading to a diploma. He says that education "must include families, schools, workplaces and communities." The educational-industrial complex must "reduce the marginalization of young people."

Colvin offers eight specific proposals.[68]

1. *Short-Term Emergency Measures.* Programs such as Civilian Employment Training Act (CETA), income subsidies for poor families, and other war-on-poverty programs would reduce immediate problems such as joblessness and human suffering. Colvin stresses the importance of implementing comprehensive programs that affect a broad spectrum of people.

2. *Nationwide Parent-Effectiveness Programs.* These types of programs should be required for all high-school seniors as well as

offered in adult education classes. Parent-effectiveness counseling programs for new parents should also be available.[69]

3. *Universal Head Start Preschool Programs.* Certified preschool programs should include free day care programs. These have proven to be very effective in preventing delinquency.

4. *Expanded and Enhanced Public Education.* (1) Increase teachers' salaries; (2) change certification to open up the profession to non-education majors so specialists (especially in math and science) can teach (the time and expense of taking methods courses can discourage otherwise qualified people from entering the teaching profession); (3) increase the school year to 230 days (from the 180-day average) to compete with Germany and Japan (which average 240 days per year); (4) focus especially on problem-solving skills; (5) offer nontraditional courses such as "outward bound" and apprenticeships; (6) use peer counseling and student tutoring; (7) eliminate tracking; (8) award stipends for attending school and bonuses for good grades to eliminate the need for students to work (this would also open up many unskilled jobs for unemployed adults); (9) establish nonviolent conflict resolution programs; and (10) get students more active in school policies to help prepare them for participating in democracy as adults.

5. *National Service Program.* After graduating from high school, a youth should have the opportunity to complete two years of national service and be given educational and vocational stipends for the work. National service could encompass a wide variety of public works projects—health care, nursing, environmental cleanup, day care services, care for the elderly, and so on. Young people would have the opportunity to participate in the improvement of their community, and the community could take advantage of youthful energy to help rebuild communities.

6. *Enhancement of Workplace Environments.* Young people must have hope that they are headed for a good-quality job. There should be labor laws that emphasize workplace democracy and create noncoercive work environments. This helps to attract and reward creative individuals who are needed to compete in a global economy.

7. *Programs for Economic Growth and Expanded Production.* Investments need to be aimed toward what is good for the general public rather than toward profit for the wealthy. Investment in research and industrial techniques should be encouraged.

8. *Progressive Income Tax System.* The current tax system is regressive and does not distribute income and wealth downward, thus contributing to poverty and inequality.[70]

Margaret Phillips suggests a theory-based intervention that combines the role of environmental (especially socioeconomic) factors with individual responsibility and powerlessness.[71] Her thesis is that the stress associated with poverty and feelings of powerlessness (which are correlated) results in the tendency to be present-oriented (that is, the inability to plan for the future because of a belief that one's life is out of control). This is part of the irresponsibility typically associated with crime and delinquency. "Empowerment is a prerequisite for taking responsibility, and the most basic kind of empowerment is economic, the ability to support oneself and a family."[72]

Phillips cites an almost perfect laboratory test of her theory. In the mid-1980s, the Hormel Meatpacking Company in Austin, Minnesota, broke a strike by hiring workers from outside the town. With many local workers left jobless, the rate of crime rose noticeably. There was a ripple effect common among plant closures: crime in general—especially domestic violence—increases, along with suicides, stress-related illnesses, and drug and alcohol abuse. There is a corresponding decrease in citizen participation in civic activities, which decreases the amount of informal social control. Phillips notes that there is abundant evidence that poverty and economic dislocation play an important role in crime, as well as in a lack of self-control.[73]

This would logically lead us to consider full employment as a solution to the crime problem, such as the Works Progress Administration (WPA) in the 1930s. If there is such a thing as a criminal personality type, then such a person would tend to be present-oriented and irresponsible. This kind of person sees him or herself as having little or no control over the future and is therefore extremely tied to the present. This theme can be seen, at least implicitly, in the techniques of neutralization noted by Sykes and Matza.[74] Many delinquents see themselves as effects, rather than as active doers. This leads to irresponsibility, which in turn leads to what Matza called "drift," a condition that places one at risk of becoming a delinquent.[75]

Phillips then turns to an area seemingly unrelated (and usually considered off-limits) to sociologists. Some medical evidence links poverty and the lack of security to fatalism and various physiological effects. Quoting studies by an epidemiologist[76] and a biologist,[77] she notes that there is a connection between the symptoms of stress and the lack of control over one's fate. Stress is associated with a lack of nurturing, not knowing what tomorrow will bring, seeing people suffering and dying on a regular basis, being subjected to criminal victimization, and so on. These stressors are especially pronounced in a society of scarcity (which includes many inner-city ghettos). A person's psychological defenses become limited, and one is unable to develop a sense of autonomy and the inner psychological strength to cope. When scarcity exists, a normal psychological defense mechanism is to view one's own situation as uncontrollable and oneself as helpless. This, in turn, leads to attempts to control others (via various sorts of crime, especially violence). It is easy to understand why delinquents from these kinds of backgrounds would be so present-oriented. The stress produced by poverty, discrimination, and oppression points to political and economic solutions.

Another outcome of the stress associated with poverty is a decrease in trust. There is a tendency to view others as potential enemies. A longitudinal study by Emmy Werner and Ruth Smith reinforces these ideas. High-risk children who led fairly stable lives came from families with at least two years between children; they had bonded closely with someone in the family. Good support networks helped them develop a belief that they had some control over their fate. In short, they had someone they could trust.[78]

Phillips focuses on some common causes of feelings of powerlessness (in addition to poverty itself and the corresponding lack of resources).

1. *Joblessness and Underemployment.* Jobs paying livable wages are necessary to avoid feelings of powerlessness.

2. *Population Size.* Small neighborhood units empower people (the "safety in numbers" idea).

3. *Alcohol and Drug Abuse.* To escape stress, people frequently turn to alcohol and/or drugs, which can lead to a lack of control. Addiction, in turn, creates irresponsibility and crime. There is a desperate need for more resources for both treatment and prevention.

4. *Low IQ.* The hard-core offenders, especially those in prison, have lower than average IQs. Resources for special education programs early in life would help.

5. *Child Abuse.* As noted earlier, families most at risk are those with low income and low educational levels. Family support programs offer one solution.

Phillips offers several interrelated proposals—beginning with programs that empower people and help them learn to help themselves and to be responsible. Prisons (including the popular boot camp programs) fail to do this. Some alternative sentencing programs may help (for example, victim-offender reconciliation, probation programs that require substance-abuse treatment, and so on).

On a national level, Phillips suggests that some of the following types of programs might well succeed:

1. *Full Employment.* Examples include WPA-type programs and "reindustrialization from below" (like the old Tennessee Valley Authority of the 1930s).

2. *Welfare Reform.* The inclusion of programs that would provide transitional publicly funded jobs.

3. *Health Care Insurance for All.*

4. *Low-Income Housing for the Homeless.*

In her conclusion Phillips states that the key to solving the problem is empowerment, which begins with having meaningful work at livable wages and developing tools that assist offenders in taking some control over their lives.

Other Pressing Matters

Addressing the Problem of Social Inequality

The extent of inequality in U.S. society has increased notably during the past two decades. The connection between social inequality (especially racial inequality) and delinquency has been noted by researchers time and time again during the past 100 or so years. This issue must be addressed if we intend to reduce crime and delinquency to acceptable levels.

Many of the problems facing the juvenile justice stem from the "war on drugs." A top priority should be ending the unjust "war" that has been declared on young people, the poor, and racial minorities.

Ending the War on Drugs

The "war on drugs" has had a devastating toll on American citizens, especially the poor and racial minorities. The negative consequences have been far-reaching: the exploding prison population (juveniles and adults), the targeting of racial minorities (and their disenfranchisement), and the enormous costs to taxpayers, with little or no impact on drug use. Before any meaningful changes can come about, the "war on drugs" should end or, at the very least, a "cease fire" should be declared until other options are studied and tried.

The drug war has helped create and perpetuate a "prison-industrial complex," which in turn is the result of an economic system driven by a "free market" philosophy that places profits above people. Profit is the motive, and people pursue profit by whatever means available. The behavior may be illegal, or it may be unethical, but those concerns are often overlooked in pursuit of gain. In a capitalist economic system, the production and distribution of "commodities" is the major goal. The law of supply and demand dictates that if a consumer wants a commodity, someone will take the risks to supply it. If the commodity has been labeled a "vice" and the criminal justice system attempts to limit access to it, the profits for supplying an illegal commodity increase. Demand does not decrease. This has been the case with all "vices"—from prostitution, to gambling, to alcohol, to drugs. Attempts to use the law to reduce either supply or demand have failed miserably—and have created unintended consequences. (Imagine what the consequences would be if gambling were suddenly prohibited in Nevada; the economy would be in chaos from the loss of revenues and loss of tourists.)

Making a product that is desired by the general public illegal opens the door to bribery, payoffs, and corruption to induce the police and the justice system to ignore the illegal behavior. It also creates the potential to make a great deal of money legitimately in the criminal justice system. As a result of fighting the drug war, the "criminal justice industrial complex" (of which the prison is one part) has become a booming business. The federal drug budget for 2008 was $13 billion.[79] Fighting the drug war is big business.

The fact is, we do not seem to be winning this "war." That is, we are not winning in the usual sense of the word: the drug problem is not getting any better, people are finding it easier and easier to obtain drugs, street prices of illegal drugs have dropped considerably, while hardly a dent has been made in the amount of drugs coming into the country. But in another sense many are, in fact, "winning"—if we define "winning" as making huge profits, the expansion of drug war bureaucracies, etc. Aside from the jobs created and the money made actually "fighting" the war (e.g., lucrative contracts to build prisons, providing police cars and various technology to fight crime, drug testing, etc.), there is plenty of money to be made on the supply side. Part of the problem is that drugs are a huge business enterprise.[80]

In other words, the "war on drugs" is too profitable to end. Too many people and too many government agencies and corporations are reaping profits from this war. In spite of the obvious obstacles that may lie in the way of ending this war, it is in the best interests of average citizens to change the current approach to drug use.

What are the available options? Do we legalize all drugs? Do we legalize them with some regulations and restrictions (e.g., minors prohibited from using)? Do we legalize only some drugs (e.g., marijuana)? Do we "decriminalize" some or all drugs by limiting the penalties? Do we involve the criminal justice system in only indirect ways, such as having "drug courts" (more about these below) or "drug treatment" sentences instead of jail or prison (as stipulated in a recent California referendum, known as Proposition 36)?

As we noted in the discussion of various "zero tolerance" policies, there has been a growing tendency to *overcriminalize* human problems. We should explore alternative ways to deal with day-to-day human problems, especially among kids at school. We have responded to the rare instances of extreme bloodshed (Columbine, for instance) by acting as if those behaviors were widespread. The fear generated by the extreme cases has let to policies that have turned many schools into little more than "day prisons" with police officers patrolling the hallways. They may be formally called "human resource officers" but they are still cops—with the power to arrest and collect information on youths believed to be "high risk" candidates for similar behavior. Similarly, fears about the dangers of drug use have fueled policies that overcriminalize certain behaviors and overpopulate prisons.

Since legalizing all drugs is politically unfeasible in the foreseeable future, a more modest recommendation would be to legalize marijuana, with some restrictions for youth (as we do with alcohol). Almost four in ten (39.1%) drug arrests are for marijuana, and 82.5% are for possession.[81] Even this modest proposal will receive considerable resistance, especially from those in charge of enforcing the drug laws and those profiting from the prison industrial complex. One common argument is that such a policy implies that we condone the use of marijuana. One response is that we condone the use of alcohol and, until recently, we condoned the use of tobacco (we can discourage use of marijuana—and other drugs as well—by using the methods that were so successful in reducing the demand for tobacco). Further, since there is no evidence that marijuana use leads to any serious problems (with some exceptions, to be sure)—and no one dies from it—why criminalize it?

Second, for those addicted to drugs, there should be treatment options.[82] It is clear that providing treatment instead of jail or prison is much more cost-effective. One study noted that every dollar spent on drug treatment results in an overall $3 social benefit (less crime, more employment, etc.). One illustration is the Treatment Alternatives to Street Crime (TASC) project. Instead of going to jail or prison, an offender is placed under community-based supervision in some drug treatment program.[83]

Soliciting Community Participation

Intervention strategies can help with drug treatment, offer alternatives to gang membership, and alleviate other delinquency problems. These strategies mobilize community members (for example, parents and concerned citizens), schools (for example, teachers), social service agencies (for example, mental health agencies), and other community elements (for example, churches) to participate in activities that focus on the family, supervision, and creating opportunities. On a more macro (national) level, policy makers and administrators must make decisions that provide leadership that places prevention before reaction. Policies must be adopted and administered that provide some degree of hope for at-risk youths.[84] A concerted national program—less political and more humanistic—is needed to correct the injustices that plague our inner cities.

Delinquency is not strictly a law enforcement or a criminal justice problem. Rather, it is a problem that needs to be addressed at both the community and societal levels. As Scott Cummings and Daniel Monti note, economic issues are paramount because "the prevalence of gangs in nearly every American city is related to the same recessionary and industrial changes transforming urban and public policy."[85] Indeed, there is little doubt that unemployment and underemployment are the residuals after industry has abandoned a community. Many of our cities have suffered from the loss of industry, which has impacted minorities more than any other group. As the industries depart, middle-class workers move from the cities, leaving behind those who cannot afford to follow the job markets. As poverty begins to encompass whole neighborhoods, urban blight and decay occur, providing a fertile breeding ground for the underclass youths to form gangs in answer to their despair, both economic and personal.

Further complicating the economic scenario is gentrification. The poor are displaced as the middle class and wealthy return to the inner city and begin to restore and rehabilitate property. As the real estate values increase, the poor are driven farther from the core of public services designed in large part to accommodate them. The lack of resources to compete for the improved properties causes despair and frustration for the young people in these families. It is no wonder that these same youths resort to the sale and distribution of illegal drugs as a response.

Within the past decade, the prevalence of guns in the hands of children, the apparent randomness of gang violence and drive-by shootings, the disproportionate racial minority role in homicides, and media depictions of callous youths' gratuitous violence have inflamed public fear. Politicians have exploited these fears and decried a coming generation of "brutally remorseless" superpredators."[86] Young people were demonized to muster support for policies under which youths can be transferred to criminal court and incarcerated. Some analysts predicted a demographic "time bomb" of youth crime,[87] but that contention was refuted by subsequent research.[88] Unfortunately, the fears generated remained and continue to affect policy.

Most programs are devised based on useful principles; drug courts, discussed in the next section, are one example. All programs, however, need to be evaluated to determine if they are meeting the needs of people who need help. Strategizing beyond routine ways of handling problems is a good beginning but constant vigilance is necessary to make sure that net widening does not creep in and that parties do not use the new developments for private gain rather than the public good.

Drug Courts

Drug courts originated in Dade County, Florida, in 1989. Both the criminal justice system and the public health system began to realize that drug abuse and the crimes associated with it would not go away simply by arresting people.[89] The main goals of drug courts are:

> to reduce drug use and associated criminal behavior by engaging and retaining drug-involved offenders in programmatic and treatment services; to concentrate expertise about drug cases into a single courtroom; to address other defendant needs through clinical assessment and effective case management; and to free judicial, prosecutorial and public defense resources for adjudicating non-drug cases.

Drug courts typically take the following actions: identification of defendants in need of drug treatment, referrals to treatment as soon as possible after appearing in court, and continual court supervision of community-based treatment. They also include regularly scheduled court hearings to monitor treatment program progress, plus mandatory drug testing. While the judge is a key player in the program, most drug courts try to function as a

> team in which prosecutors, defense attorneys and counselors work together to help offenders overcome their drug problems and resolve other issues relating to work, finances and family. Defendants who complete the drug court program either have their charges dismissed (in a diversion or pre-sentence model) or their probation sentences reduced (in a post-sentence model).[90]

Juvenile drug courts began in the mid-1990s; by November 2003, there were 294 such courts in 46 states and the District of Columbia with plans for another 112. Although a few have been evaluated, there remains at least one unresolved issue, namely "whether the juvenile justice system really needs juvenile drug courts." The approach used in adult drug courts (based on "therapeutic jurisprudence"[91]) is not a new concept in the juvenile justice system. It is based (at least in theory) on a "treatment" orientation. Jeffrey Butts and John Roman note that few juveniles have drug problems anywhere near as severe as the typical adult drug court participant. They note that the "typical youth referred to a juvenile drug court is 15 or 16 years old and has been drinking alcohol and smoking marijuana for a few years at most." Moreover, most teens

> are not likely to respond well to a program designed to intervene in an adult-style downward spiral of addiction and dependence. Drug-involved youth usually need improved relationships, exciting recreational opportunities, job preparedness, and perhaps family counseling to support them in making positive choices. In short, drug-involved youth are much like youth in general.

Although Butts and Roman question whether such programs are needed, they also explain why introducing juvenile drug courts may be necessary.

> Why then does the juvenile justice system need a "new" court model to handle drug-involved youthful offenders? Perhaps because juvenile courts have strayed too far from their historic problem-solving mission to mimic the "just deserts" orientation of criminal courts. The drug court process may be an important change in style and procedure for today's juvenile courts, albeit one that returns them to their traditional mission. Maybe the introduction of juvenile drug courts allows local juvenile justice systems to acquire treatment resources they otherwise would not be able to access. Juvenile drug courts may be valued not because they offer a new or innovative court process for juvenile offenders but because they enable local officials to leverage new resources for responding to teen drug use.[92]

Evaluations of adult drug court programs have generally found that they save money (at least in the short term) from the reduction in arrests, jail, and prison time, and the reduction of criminal behavior. Recidivism rates tend to be reduced both while the offender is in the program and after release. Drug use also decreases, as expected.[93] Examples of juvenile drug courts that have had positive results include the Santa Clara County (California) Juvenile Drug Treatment Court and the Kalamazoo County (Michigan) Juvenile Drug Treatment Court Program.[94] During five years of operation, almost 70% of the participants in the Kalamazoo program have had no new adjudications. A program in Erie, Pennsylvania also showed positive results, but the soundness of the data has been questioned.[95] Other evaluations that report positive results include a juvenile drug court diversion program in Delaware, a program called "Teamchild" in Seattle, and a program in Kentucky.[96]

A Final Word

Saul Alinsky, the twentieth-century social reformer, offered a highly informative parable for those who need a perspective to guide their efforts in seeking change. Imagine a large river with a high waterfall. At the bottom of this waterfall hundreds of people are working frantically to rescue those who have fallen into the river. One individual looks up and sees a seemingly never-ending stream of people cascading down the waterfall, and he begins to run upstream. One of his fellow rescuers hollers "Where are you going? There are so many people that need help here." The man replied, "I'm going upstream to find out why so many people are falling into the river."

Now imagine the scene at the bottom of the waterfall represents the juvenile justice system responding to crimes that have been committed and dealing with both victims and offenders. If you look more closely, you will discover that there are many people at the bottom of the stream working in relatively new buildings with all sorts of modern technology; they are paid well for their efforts and have excellent benefits. The money keeps flowing into this area, with all sorts of businesses lined up to provide services. Looking upstream, you find a very different scene. There are few people, the buildings are not as modern, and there is little new technology. The people aren't paid as well as those downstream; their benefits are not as good, and the turnover is quite high. Businesses aren't lining up to assist; budgets are insufficient; and workers constantly seek funds. More women work upstream. Their work is not as valued as the work men do (men are in charge downstream).

Some people choose to respond to problems related to crime and delinquency by working downstream. Good people are needed at all points of the process. As for me, I picture myself as the one checking upstream and asking "why?" You can choose your position. The most important consideration is to be able to say, "I tried." A lot of work lies ahead.

Notes

[1] Miller, J. (1998). *Last One Over the Wall* (2nd ed.). Columbus: Ohio State University Press, p. 234.

[2] Ibid.

[3] Shelden, R. G. (2006). *Delinquency and Juvenile Justice in American Society.* Long Grove, IL: Waveland Press, chapter 1.

[4] Shelden, R. G. and W. B. Brown (2000). "The Crime Control Industry and the Control of the Surplus Population." *Critical Criminology* 8 (Autumn).

[5] Brendtro, L. K., M. Brokenleg, and S. Van Bockern (2002). *Reclaiming Youth at Risk: Our Hope for the Future* (Revised Edition). Bloomington, IN: National Education Service.

[6] Ibid., p 4.

[7] Ibid., p. 8.

[8] Ibid., pp. 15–16.

[9] Ibid., pp. 16–17. Horace Mann (1796–1859) was "a famous American educator, born in Franklin, Massachusetts, and educated at Brown University and the Litchfield (Connecticut) Law. From 1827 to 1833 he was a representative in the Massachusetts state legislature and from 1833 to 1837 a state senator. During this period Mann was instrumental in the enactment of laws prohibiting the sale of alcoholic beverages and lottery tickets, establishing state hospitals for the insane, and creating a state board of education, the first in the United States. In 1837 Mann was appointed secretary to the board of education. [Online] http://encarta.msn.com/encyclopedia_761573402/Mann_Horace.html

[10] Jane Addams was one of the leaders of the "child saving movement." Her views on this subject are covered in her book *The Spirit of Youth and the City Streets* (1916). New York: Macmillan.

[11] Brendtro, Brokenleg, and Van Bockern, *Reclaiming Youth at Risk*, p. 17.

[12] Ibid., p. 18.

[13] Ibid., pp. 18–19.

[14] Ibid., p. 23.

[15] Ibid., p. 24.

[16] Ibid.

[17] Ibid., p. 30.

[18] Ibid., p. 31.

[19] Ibid., p. 32.

[20] Ibid., p. 31.

[21] Ibid., p. 32.

[22] Ibid., p. 33.

[23] Klein, G. (2004). "Gang Tackling." *Los Angeles Times*, November 25. The program is called "A Better L.A."

[24] Schur, E. (1973). *Radical Non-Intervention: Rethinking the Delinquency Problem.* Englewood Cliffs, NJ: Prentice Hall.

[25] Shelden, R. G. (2000). "Stop the War on Kids." *Las Vegas City Life*, May 10; *Los Angeles Times* (2003). "Zero Tolerance, Zero Sense." May 7 (editorial).

[26] Schur, E. (1971). *Labeling Deviant Behavior.* New York: Harper & Row. Other sources for the labeling perspective are: Becker, H. S. (1963). *Outsiders: Studies in the Sociology of Deviance.* New York: Free Press; Quinney, R. (1970). *The Social Reality of Crime.* Boston: Little, Brown; Lemert, E. 1951. *Social Pathology.* New York: McGraw-Hill. A more detailed summary is found in Shelden, *Delinquency and Juvenile Justice in American Society*, chapter 7.

[27] Schur, *Radical Non-Intervention*, p. 155.

[28] Ibid., p. 117.

[29] Shelden, R., W. Brown, K Miller, and R. Fritzler (2008). *Crime and Criminal Justice in American Society.* Long Grove, IL: Waveland Press.

[30] Schur, *Radical Non-Intervention*, pp. 166–170.

[31] American Friends Service Committee (1971) *Struggle for Justice.* New York: Hill and Wang, p. 16.

[32] Chesney-Lind, M. and R. G. Shelden (2004). *Girls, Delinquency and Juvenile Justice* (3rd ed.). Belmont, CA: Wadsworth.

[33] Note that there are differences between Schur's ideas and those of the authors of *Reclaiming Youth at Risk*. Schur's approach was designed to change society's punitive approach toward minor deviant behaviors, while reclaiming is aimed at hard-to-reach kids from extremely disadvantaged backgrounds.

[34] Males, M. (1999). *Framing Youth: Ten Myths about the Coming Generation*. Monroe, ME: Common Courage Press and (1996). *The Scapegoat Generation: America's War on Adolescents*. Monroe, ME: Common Courage Press.

[35] Bennett, W. J., J. J. DiIulio, Jr., and J. P. Walters (1996). *Body Count*. New York: Simon and Schuster. (This book has a number of misleading statements, most without supporting evidence.) References to comments by James Alan Fox about the "growing youth menace" are found in: Elikann, P. (1999). *Superpredators: The Demonization of Our Children by the Law*. Reading, MA: Perseus. See also Fox, J. A. (November 1997). *Trends in Juvenile Violence, 1996*. Washington, DC: U.S. Bureau of Statistics. Males also critiques the views of James Q. Wilson, best represented in *Thinking about Crime*. New York: Vintage Books, 1975.

[36] Federal Bureau of Investigation, *Crime in the United States, 1995*, table 32; *Crime in the United States, 2006*, table 32. [Online] http://www.fbi.gov/ucr/ucr.htm

[37] Males, M. (2002). "Forget the Youth Menace: Crime, It Turns Out, is a Grown-Up Business." *Los Angeles Times*, December 15.

[38] Stahl, A L., C. Puzzanchera, S. Livsey, A. Sladky, T. A. Finnegan, N. Tierney, and H. N. Snyder. 2007. *Juvenile Court Statistics 2003–2004*. Pittsburgh, PA: National Center for Juvenile Justice, p. 7. [Online] http://www.ojjdp.ncjrs.gov/publications/PubAbstract.asp?pubi=240291

[39] Chesney-Lind and Shelden, *Girls, Delinquency and Juvenile Justice*.

[40] Bonita, J., S. Wallace-Capretta, J. Rooney, and K. Mcanoy (2002). "An Outcome Evaluation of a Restorative Justice Alternative to Incarceration." *Contemporary Justice Review* 5: 319–338.

[41] Seldes, G. (ed.) (1996). *The Great Thoughts*. New York: Ballantine Books, p. 253.

[42] Ibid., p. 376.

[43] Sullivan, D. and L. Tifft (2000). *Restorative Justice as a Transformative Process*. Voorheesville, NY: Mutual Aid Press, p. 6.

[44] Ibid., p. 9.

[45] Ibid., p. 34.

[46] Dryfoos, J. (1990). *Adolescents at Risk*. New York: Oxford University Press.

[47] Ibid., p. 116.

[48] Ibid., pp. 132–144.

[49] Ibid., pp. 155–164.

[50] Falco, M. (1992). *The Making of a Drug-Free America*. New York: Times Books; Huff, C. R. (1990)."Denial, Overreaction, and Misidentification: A Postscript on Public Policy." In C. R. Huff (ed.), *Gangs in America*. Newbury Park, CA: Sage.

[51] Schorr, L. (1989). *Within Our Reach: Breaking the Cycle of Disadvantage*. New York: Anchor, p. 259.

[52] Shelden, *Delinquency and Juvenile Justice in American Society*, p. 332.

[53] Lundman, R. (2001). *Prevention and Control of Juvenile Delinquency* (3rd ed.). New York: Oxford University Press, pp. 125–148.

[54] Ibid., p. 142.

[55] Gibbons, D. and G. Blake (1976). "Evaluating the Impact of Juvenile Diversion Programs." *Crime and Delinquency* 22: 411–420; Decker, S. H. (1985). "A Systematic Analysis of Diversion: Net Widening and Beyond." *Journal of Criminal Justice* 13: 207–216.

[56] Decker, "A Systematic Analysis of Diversion"; Blomberg, T. (1978). "Diversion from Juvenile Court: A Review of the Evidence." In F. Faust and P. Brantingham (eds.), *Juvenile Justice Philosophy* (2nd ed.). St. Paul: West; Klein, M. (1980). "Deinstitutionalization and Diversion of Juvenile Offenders: A Litany of Impediments." In N. Morris and M. Tonry (eds.), *Crime and Justice: An Annual Review of Research, vol. 1*. Chicago: University of Chicago Press.

57 Alder, C. (1984). "Gender Bias in Juvenile Diversion." *Crime and Delinquency* 30, pp. 402–404.

58 Romig, D. (1978). *Justice for Our Children: An Examination of Juvenile Delinquent Rehabilitation Programs.* Lexington, MA: Lexington Books, pp. 129–132.

59 Lipsey, M. (1992). "Juvenile Delinquency Treatment: A Meta-analytic Inquiry in the Variability of Effects." In T. D. Cook et al. (eds.), *Meta-Analysis for Explanation: A Casebook.* New York: Russell Sage.

60 Romig, *Justice for Our Children*, pp. 133–137.

61 The following section is based on chapter 8 in Shelden, R. G., S. Tracy, and W. B. Brown (2004). *Youth Gangs in American Society* (3rd ed.). Belmont, CA: Wadsworth.

62 Currie, E. (1989). "Confronting Crime: Looking Toward the Twenty-First Century." *Justice Quarterly* 6:5–25.

63 Dryfoos, *Adolescents at Risk.*

64 Austin, J. and J. Irwin (2001). *It's About Time: America's Imprisonment Binge* (3rd ed.). Belmont, CA: Wadsworth; Irwin. J. (2005). *The Warehouse Prison: Disposal of the New Dangerous Class.* Los Angeles: Roxbury Press; Johnson, R. (2002). *Hard Time: Understanding and Reforming the Prison* (3rd ed.). Belmont, CA: Wadsworth; Welch, M. (2005). *The Ironies of Imprisonment.* Thousand Oaks, CA: Sage.

65 Colvin, M. (1991). "Crime and Social Reproduction: A Response to the Call for 'Outrageous' Proposals." *Crime and Delinquency* 37: 436–448.

66 Ibid., p. 437.

67 Ibid., pp. 439–440.

68 Ibid.

69 Patterson, G. R., P. Chamberlain, and J. B. Reid (1982). "A Comparative Evaluation of a Parent-Training Program." *Behavior Therapy* 13:636–650.

70 See especially: Zepezauer, M. and A. Naiman (1996). *Take the Rich Off Welfare.* Emeryville, CA: Odonian Press; Albeda, R., N. Folbre, and the Center for Popular Economics (1996). *The War on the Poor.* New York: The New Press; Derber, C. (1998). *Corporation Nation.* New York: St. Martin's Press; Ehrenreich, B. (2001). *Nickel and Dimed: On (Not) Getting By in America.* New York: Henry Holt and Co.; Perrucci, R. and E. Wysong (2003). *The New Class Society,* 2nd ed. New York: Roman and Littlefield; Phillips, K. (2002). *Wealth and Democracy.* New York: Broadway Books; Collins, C., B. Leondar-Wright, and H. Sklar (1999). *Shifting Fortunes: The Perils of the Growing American Wealth Gap.* Boston: United for a Fair Economy; Heintz, J., N. Folbre and the Center for Popular Economics (2000). *The Ultimate Field Guide to the U. S. Economy.* New York: The New Press.

71 Phillips, M. B. (1991). "A Hedgehog Proposal." *Crime and Delinquency* 37:555–574.

72 Ibid., pp. 558–559.

73 Ibid., p. 558.

74 Sykes, G. and D. Matza (1957). "Techniques of Neutralization." *American Journal of Sociology* 22:664–670.

75 Matza, D. (1964). *Delinquency and Drift.* New York: Wiley.

76 Sagan, L. A. (1989). *The Health of Nations.* New York: Basic Books.

77 Sapolsky, R. M. (1988). "Lessons of the Serengeti: Why Some of Us Are More Susceptible to Stress." *The Sciences* May/June: 38–42.

78 Werner, E. E. and R. S. Smith (1982). *Vulnerable, but Invincible: A Longitudinal Study of Resilient Children and Youth.* New York: McGraw-Hill, p. 563.

79 White House (February 2007). *Drug Control Strategy: FY 2008 Budget Summary,* p. 1. [Online] http://www.whitehousedrugpolicy.gov/publications/policy/08budget/exec_summ.pdf

80 Space does not permit exploring this topic in detail. See the following Web site: www.drugsense.org.

81 Federal Bureau of Investigation. (2007) *Crime in the United States, 2006. Arrests for Drub Abuse Violations: Percent Distribution.* [Online] http://www.fbi.gov/ucr/cius2006/arrests/index.html

82 Documented in both Inciardi, J. (2002). *The War on Drugs III.* Boston: Allyn & Bacon, chapter 10 and pp. 305–308; and Walker, S. (2001). *Sense and Nonsense about Crime and Drugs* (6th edition). Belmont, CA: Wadsworth, 2006, chapter 13.

[83] Inciardi, *The War on Drugs III*, pp. 306–307.

[84] Shelden et al., *Youth Gangs*, chapter 8.

[85] Cummings, S. and D. J. Monti (eds.) (1993). *Gangs: The Origins and Impact of Contemporary Youth Gangs in the United States.* Albany: SUNY Press, p. 310.

[86] Bennett, DiIulio, and Walters, *Body Count*, p. 27.

[87] Fox, J. (1996). *Trends in Juvenile Violence: A Report for the U.S. Attorney General on Current and Future Rates of Juvenile Offending.* Washington, DC: U.S. Department of Justice. For a critique of the rhetoric and policy changes, see Zimring, F. (1998). *American Youth Violence.* New York: Oxford University Press, p. 208.

[88] Elikann, P. (1999). *Superpredators: The Demonization of Our Children.* Reading, MA: Perseus Books; Males, M. (1999). *Framing Youth: Ten Myths about the Next Generation.* Monroe, ME: Common Courage Press.

[89] Belenko, S. (1998). "Research on Drug Courts: A Critical Review." *National Drug Court Institute Review* 1 (June).

[90] Ibid.

[91] Rottman, D. and P. Casey (1999). "Therapeutic Jurisprudence and the Emergence of Problem-Solving Courts." *National Institute of Justice Journal* (July).

[92] Butts, J. and J. Roman (2004). *Juvenile Drug Courts and Teen Substance Abuse.* Washington, DC: The Urban Institute. Quotes are taken from preface. [Online] http://www.urbaninstitute.org/pubs/JuvenileDrugCourts/preface.html

[93] Belenko, "Research on Drug Courts."

[94] Hartmann, D. J. and G. M. Rhineberger (2003). "Evaluation of the Kalamazoo County Juvenile Drug Treatment Court Program." Kalamazoo, MI: Kercher Center for Social Research, Western Michigan University. The Santa Clara program is cited in Belenko "Research on Drug Courts."

[95] Shafer, D. (December 7, 2004). "Drug Courts in Ohio." Paper presented before the faculty of the Department of Criminal Justice, University of Nevada–Las Vegas.

[96] Delaware Statistical Analysis Center (1999). *Evaluation of the Delaware Juvenile Drug Court Diversion Program.* Wilmington, DE: Delaware Criminal Justice Council; Ezell, M. (1996). *Teamchild: Evaluation of the First Year.* Seattle: Teamchild; Minor, K. I., J. B. Wells, I. R. Soderstrom, R. Bingham, & D. Williamson (1999). "Sentence Completion and Recidivism among Juveniles Referred to Teen Court." *Crime and Delinquency*, 45: 467–480. These evaluations are cited by the Juvenile Justice Evaluation Center: [Online] http://www.jrsa.org/jjec/programs/courts/

7

Restructuring Juvenile Corrections in California

Sele Nadel-Hayes and Daniel Macallair

The focus of this report is on identifying a system of correctional services that will replace the existing eight Division of Juvenile Justice institutions. In 2005 Governor Schwarzenegger began the largest administrative restructuring of the correctional system of California in 30 years. The California Department of Corrections and Rehabilitation, Department of Corrections, and Division of Juvenile Justice were consolidated into one large department. The purpose was to streamline management functions and establish a system of centralized control where sweeping reforms could be better coordinated and monitored.

Reorganizing the Juvenile Justice System

This article will present research findings showing how structural changes require closing structurally outdated large correctional institutions in favor of smaller county or regionally based facilities. The article will examine the significant budgetary, legal, and political constraints to implementing this new system. In California, the process of allocating funds is a time-intensive process of political negotiation that is often far removed from objective policy analysis. Despite the governor's promises of broad systemic reform, no new resources are being offered in this year's budget for youth corrections. As a result reform efforts will need to be carried out with little or no additional state funds.[1]

Second, as a result of a comprehensive lawsuit filed against the state for inhumane conditions within its youth correctional facilities, reforms will be strongly influenced by judicial mandates.

These mandates set timelines under which specific changes must be implemented. The mandates support many of the complaints that led to

Written especially for *Juvenile Justice in America: Problems and Prospects*.

the development of a new vision for juvenile corrections in California, and create an institutional minimum standard of care for and treatment of wards in the system. Finally, in a system affecting such diverse populations, it is often the case that some stakeholders' concerns are not addressed in the evaluation processes. The historical situation of juvenile corrections has allowed some groups more access to these processes than others and to the political capital necessary to further their agendas for the governance of the system. This article represents the contributions and opinions of many stakeholder groups not often heard in such proceedings, holding the level of influence of each constant.

The ability of decision makers to construct a replacement juvenile justice system relies on the ability of all stakeholders to communicate their needs strategically. Because some stakeholders have had significant influence over decision makers to guide the governance of the juvenile corrections system, this research has been conducted to supplement this influence with perspectives from populations not traditionally incorporated into the analysis. This will lead to a system more accountable to the general public and better able to meet the needs of the populations it seeks to serve. The primary goal of this article is to identify key elements of stakeholder visions and evaluate their feasibility within system constraints. Drawing upon stakeholder interviews and publications, these elements will represent a composite overview of the expectations for a new system of providing services to the juvenile population. The secondary goal of this article is to organize critical information about structural models from other jurisdictions and the baseline requirements of stakeholders to determine how the replacement system will function. As other states and regions have approached juvenile corrections from within different contexts, it is critical that elements of successful systems be translated into practices appropriate for California and lessons from other jurisdictions are reflected in the California system's design.

The scope of this article is limited to an analysis of how specific practices would function in California's context. It has been demonstrated that the state of juvenile corrections in California is unique in its design, oversight, evaluation, and impact. As such, successful practices in jurisdictions with vastly different populations, legal constraints, and political priorities may not be as successful here. This analysis allows all stakeholders to move toward choosing a system of care that appropriately serves the needs of California, beyond the extensive problems that have plagued the existing juvenile corrections system for decades and create the context for reform. In addition, this article will reflect the policy priorities of the larger juvenile justice reform community, not those who do not wish to see changes in the system, though their impact on the decision-making process will be addressed in the feasibility analysis.

Methodology

This research is grounded in four main sources of information: academic, practitioner, and advocate publications; comprehensive and strategic stakeholder interviews; Governor Arnold Schwarzenegger's 2005–06 California budget proposal and commentary from advocates; and legal documents from the California court system and other states' general laws. The resulting analysis is the construction of a model system of services to replace the existing DJJ system based on the priorities, concerns, and smart practices culled from the research process.

Literature Review

In the review of relevant literature, there exists the opportunity to identify smart practices from case programs, practitioners, and other experts. The literature reflects three general models for service provision for juveniles in the corrections system. Case studies of programs that represent a system of county-level care, programs that represent a privatized system of care, and programs that represent possibilities for reform within the existing institutional structure have been analyzed for possible inclusion in the California replacement model.

Stakeholder Interviews

The purpose of including stakeholder interviews is twofold. First, stakeholders provide critical input in developing system goals and evaluation criteria to ensure they reflect a broad span of perspectives. Because stakeholders represent a wide range of practitioners, they are uniquely capable of providing insight into the practical possibility of different models' functioning in California. In addition, the collective input of stakeholders allows for the construction of a baseline minimum standard of care against which proposed systems may be measured. As individuals identify key elements of a successful juvenile corrections system, these requirements will be combined to create a minimum standard that will satisfy as many stakeholders as possible. This will also allow competing priorities to be reflected in the final recommendations.

Budget Analysis

A critical initiator in the efforts to reform the existing California juvenile justice system is the substantial budgetary inefficiency caused by the high cost per ward without demonstrable reform outcomes and with such a failure of the rehabilitative and care goals of the system. The budget analysis section will provide an overview of the distribution of youth corrections funds in California as it functions presently in order to demonstrate the current funding priorities within the juvenile corrections system. In addition it will provide a starting point for the cost-benefit analysis of restructuring the system. Second, the budget analysis section will provide an overview of how the different proposals will allow for different allocations of the corrections budget and generate revenue from alternative funding streams.

Legal Analysis

The existing juvenile corrections system functions under the larger Youth and Adult Correctional Agency and within local, state, and federal laws.[2] This agency is currently undergoing a process or reorganization initiated by the office of the Governor. As the reorganization process continues, the laws and mandates governing the DJJ will shift and change. However, the inclusion of an overview of the legal constraints associated with the housing and care of juvenile wards is critical to the selection of an appropriate replacement structure. The legal analysis section will incorporate these changes into the design of the new structure, as well as the numerous reforms in response to the consent decree stipulation handed down as a result of *Farrell v. Allen*.

Present State of the DJJ

The effects of media, community, and governmental scrutiny of the DJJ system have resulted in significant attention to the problems with the existing system. While this article is not designed to encompass a detailed description of the myriad problems and system failures, it is important to situate the system within the larger context of juvenile justice reform in California. When the ward population reached its peak of 10,114 wards in June 1996, a flurry of academic and governmental evaluations and audits of the system were conducted. The goal of many of these studies was to better understand the population, services, and outcomes of the DJJ system. More recently, these studies have shifted to analytical reports on how the system should be serving the incarcerated population and the broader community affected by a youth population engaged in illegal and criminal behavior. The authors of these reports range in expertise and influence and many of the reports represent research performed by service providers and advocates with direct relationships to youth—those at risk of arrest or incarceration, those incarcerated at the point of service, and those being served post-release. Despite its clear relevance to system reform and restructuring because of its unique connection to the wards, this information has only begun to be utilized by decision makers. At present, large strides have been made by decision makers to incorporate input from these stakeholders into reform efforts, though significant disparities remain with respect to foundational priorities for the entire juvenile justice system.

Internal and Independent Audits and Evaluations

The Office of the Inspector General's Accountability Audit report outlines 241 recommendations for reform of the day-to-day operations of the existing DJJ facilities and programs based on four years of evaluation.[3] The OIG reviewed audits of the DJJ and documentation of its progress in implementing previous recommendations as well as the report issued by the Corrections Independent Review Panel in 1994. It also conducted site visits and reviewed ward and facility files, logs, and records at each of the eight DJJ institutions. Each of the recommendations from previous audits and generated from new information was classified according to the progress of the department in implementing them as fully, substantially, partially, or not implemented.

The most egregious unmet recommendations from previous audits were with respect to the Special Management Programs (SMPs) that allowed wards to be held on lockdown for 23 hours daily with 1 hour of recreation for longer than the temporary duration for which these programs were intended. At N.A. Chaderjian, 39 wards were on lockdown for over 30 days and three for over 200 days. At H.G. Stark, 103 wards are held in confinement for the sole reason that there are not enough teachers to provide each ward with mandated educational services. In fact, all of the studied institutions are failing to provide the mandated four hours daily of educational instruction on a consistent basis. An average of eighteen classes are cancelled daily at Ventura Correctional Facility due to teacher absences. At the Southern Reception Center, 78 percent of wards had cumulative subject scores below the 25th national percentile rate in 2004. The institutions are also failing to meet institutional mandates for assessment and treatment. At the Southern Reception Center, 85 percent of wards were not assessed within the 45-day required time period.

The DJJ is currently undergoing significant administrative reform. Governor Schwarzenegger's reorganization plan has instituted several reforms to the governance of all aspects of California corrections, including the DJJ institutions. The primary focus of the current reorganization is on improved management of the existing facilities and systems with the assumption that the persistent problems with the system will see solutions with these changes.[4] Toward this end, the plan imposes significant changes to consolidate the top level of administration and management to create one entity responsible for the Department of Corrections of which the DJJ is a part, the elevation of rehabilitation and treatment services, and the creation of proactive functions and responsibilities such as planning and research, risk management, and community partnerships.[5]

The new structure places existing institutions under the Department of Corrections and Rehabilitation. The Division of Juvenile Corrections is charged with efficiently operating and managing youth facilities and rehabilitating youthful offenders. Generally, the division will provide for the secure custody of wards, while providing the environment for carrying out its statutory mission of providing training, treatment, and rehabilitative services designed to protect public safety by returning wards to society better equipped to lead law-abiding lives.[6] Though this reorganization will have some impact on the efficiency of DJJ management and operations, it is not clear that it will have significant impact on the improvement of conditions of facilities, the ability of wards to better meet educational and treatment goals, and reduce costs and recidivism. In fact, existing leadership has identified these goals as primarily policy and budgetary goals not within the scope of the reorganization plan. As such, additional reform measures must be implemented in order to meet these goals.[7]

The Little Hoover Commission's hearings on DJJ reform have generated focused comments from expert practitioners on the goals and objectives of California's juvenile justice system as a whole. For the most part, these experts have expressed the importance of maintaining clear administrative distinction between DJJ and the larger Department of Corrections, to meet the long-term need for a state-level agency to coordinate juvenile justice policy, and institutionalized inspections and evaluations of facilities and programs by outside agencies. Specifically, experts have identified the critical need for elevated emphasis on rehabilitation in the DJJ to match the custodial responsibilities of the institution and to create and uphold a strategic plan for evaluating each institution's progress in meeting its responsibilities and institute sanctions when those responsibilities are not met.[8] These solutions come in response to the demonstrated failure of the DJJ to provide health, education, and re-entry programs even at the basic level mandated by California and federal laws and to create and sustain partnerships with local agencies capable of providing services and oversight. Perhaps most critically, experts have identified several means of funding these basic services employed by other states and municipalities that have been underutilized in California, if utilized at all.[9]

The General Corrections Review of the DJJ was conducted by Barry Krisberg and the National Council on Crime and Delinquency, an independent and well respected criminal justice research agency, for the purposes of this report. The review was completed at the request of the California Attorney General (AG), the DJJ (YA), and the Prison Law Office (PLO). The report provides findings and recommendations based on a three-year assessment of the entire DJJ system within the areas of Ward Classification, Access to Lawyers and Ward's Rights, Use of Force and Ward Safety, Restricted Programs including Special Management Programs and Temporary Detention, and Access to Religious Services. Krisberg reviewed current DJJ policies, training materials, statistical data, and interviews with wards and staff at the N.A. Chaderjian Youth Correctional Facility, the Herman G. Stark Youth Correctional Facility, the Fred C. Nelles Youth Correctional Facility, the Preston Youth Correctional Facility, the El Paso De Robles Youth Correctional Facility, and the Ventura Youth Correctional Facility.

Krisberg's key findings were that the DJJ invests a substantial amount of staff time and resources collecting detailed information about its wards, but these data are not organized into an effective system to guide either security or custody needs; that there is not an effective system to ensure that these data are incorporated in day-to-day custody, treatment, and training decisions; that facilities are unsafe and possess serious physical design issues that made security a difficult problem; that ward-on-ward abuse and excessive use of force by staff are common in all facilities studied; that wards are being held in restrictive programs for significantly longer periods than the temporary intent of the system; that the wards rarely, if ever, file grievances about being denied access to lawyers or legal reading materials and are rarely visited by attorneys; that the existing Ward Grievance System (WGS) is underutilized and therefore ineffective; and that access to religious services constitutes approximately 13 percent of ward complaint letters.[10]

DJJ Programs and Population

The DJJ has six areas of focus in its effort to meet the needs of juvenile corrections in California: Prevention and Early Intervention Advocacy, Transitioning Offenders to the Community, Handling of Violent Offenders, Restorative Justice, Public Safety, and Correctional Education.[11] At a time when the existing system and structure of services for wards in the DJJ is serving the fewest number of wards in the past fifteen years and has been highly criticized for its inadequate scope of services and its high recidivism rate, there exists an opportunity to evaluate the effectiveness of programs in meeting these goals. While different facilities have diverse ward populations and vary with respect to the services provided at the institutions, these six focus areas are theoretically applied to all institutions. Because the existing structure of DJJ facilities are large warehouse-style prison design, the scope of services is limited to those that can be administered most efficiently to the most wards.

Programs Overview. Three levels of programming—Basic Core Programs, Specialized Ward Programs, and Supplemental Ward Programs—comprise the treatment arm of the DJJ's joint charge to provide custodial and treatment services to California's juvenile offenders. Basic Core Programs are educational programs separated into three components—academic, career/vocational, and character education. These skills are theoretically transferable to post-release opportunities and wards have access to a variety of academic achievement programs such as remedial reading, writing, and mathematics, obtaining a high school diploma or GED, and college-level coursework toward an Associate degree.

Specialized Ward Programs consist of programs that are for individuals whose treatment needs exceed Basic Core Programs. These programs range from formal drug and alcohol abuse treatment and medical/psychiatric-intensive treatment to programs designed for specific ward populations like younger boys, females, and sex offenders. This level of programming also includes post-release skills-training programs, such as the Planned Re-Entry Program (PREP), work experience programs, and public service camps.

Supplemental Ward Programs focus on other aspects of treatment and development not met by the other levels of programming. These include relationship-building programs, as met by the Foster Grandparent Program and Volunteer Services; knowledge-building, as met by parenting programs and classes and the Free Venture program giving wards access to partnerships with businesses; and repeat-offender prevention, such as speaker bureaus where wards speak to local schools and organizations and victim services programs.

Statistics on Wards. The Office of the Inspector General's report held a central concern—that the DJJ had employed sophisticated data collection practices for wards entering the system in the reception centers, but failed to utilize this data for analytical purposes, to improve their system of care, or to evaluate their services.[12] Due to this failure, in-depth information about the ward population on a system-wide level is limited. Some facilities generate internal reports on incidents and other population management information, but this information is not available to the public. The population information necessary to determine how the system may be restructured to better serve the population is twofold. First, information about the home county or region of each ward will allow for accurate assessment of local facilities required to provide services and programs. Second, information about the offenses that led to the wards' DJJ incarceration will allow for accurate projection of the types of services and programs required by the wards. At present, this data is not consistently available, though it is collected in the reception centers. The most recent report on this information is from 2003 and was published by the Office of the Attorney General.[13]

The state's system of youth correctional institutions is comprised of eight facilities located throughout California that currently house approximately 3,300 wards. An additional 200 youth offenders are being housed in the general population of the adult Department of Corrections and 3,991 youth are being tracked as a condition of parole. Of the 3,314 wards in DJJ facilities, 3,164 or 95 percent are male. All 150 female juvenile offenders are housed in the Ventura Correctional Facility. Wards have an average length of stay of 22.4 months, though the range for length of stay is between 2 months and 6 years. Between July 2004 and February 2005, the average daily parole caseload was 4,040 of which 2,781 or 68 percent were placed on violation within this same period. This failure rate does not include former wards who re-offend beyond the duration of parole.

In 2003, 73 percent of 1,009 new placements in the DJJ were between 15 and 17 years of age, 3.9 percent were between 10 and 14 years of age, and 22 percent were age 18 or older. As shown in figure 1 below, the racial and ethnic composition of these 1,009 wards was 3.2

Figure I   Racial and Ethnic Composition of New DJJ Placements in 2003

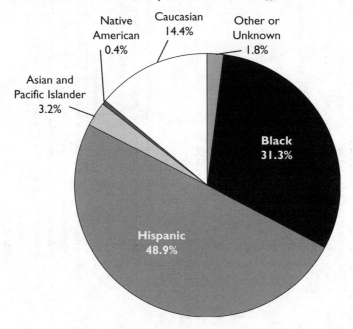

percent Asian and Pacific Islander, 31.3 percent Black, 48.9 percent Hispanic, 0.4 percent Native American, 14.4 percent Caucasian, and 1.8 percent Other or unknown.

Transition Plan

In determining the best system of care to replace the current structure of institutions, the goals for short-term and long-term outcomes must be considered. Table 1 shows goals identified by four main stakeholder groups—youth, advocates, and service providers; CDCR administrators; judges; and the general population of California, specifically identified as citizens and taxpayers, though non-citizens and non-taxpayers living in California may also share these goals.

Short-Term Goals

Short-term goals represent stakeholder and institutional requirements for the treatment of wards and the services offered by the system, primarily on a day-to-day basis. These goals have been identified because the current system lacks the oversight necessary to presume all wards are treated with the same standard of care. While some wards may experience an appropriate balance of rehabilitative and custodial services, audits and evaluations show the dearth of these services in all eight DJJ facilities.

Table I Stakeholder Goals

Stakeholder Group	Treatment and Care Goals	Desired Outcomes
Youth, Advocates, and Service Providers	• Wards are treated in facilities close to their homes. • Wards are housed in small facilities with a maximum of forty wards. • Wards are supervised by guards and specialists trained in youth care. • Wards are provided with basic necessary human services. • Wards have access to educational services. • Wards have access to mental health treatment services. • Wards have access to substance abuse treatment programs. • Wards have access to their personal files and an active voice in court proceedings.	• Change the values that have led to criminal activities to values that promote acceptable citizenship and pursuit of life-long learning. • Stabilized funding for juvenile services. • Reduced population in juvenile corrections institutions statewide. • Reduced violence in correctional institutions. • Enhanced re-entry programming. • Network of community-based alternatives to detention and incarceration.
State Corrections Administrators	• Prepare youthful offenders for release and success on parole. • Reduce levels of violence in lockups. • Employees are trained in de-escalating confrontations. • Procedures in place to monitor suicidal wards. • Classification of wards by offense.	• Transparency • Accountability • Uniformity • Offenders should leave the juvenile justice system more capable of productive participation in conventional society than when they entered. • Elevation of rehabilitation and treatment services to equal partnership with custodial functions. • Enhanced service delivery and reduced recidivism.
Judges	• Change youth behavior to prevent future offenses. • Residential treatment programs. • Place youths in the least restrictive environment "consistent with public safety."	• Reduce the incidence and severity of delinquent and criminal behavior. • Every effort is made by offenders to restore losses suffered by victims. • Wards develop self-esteem and strive for a more positive lifestyle. • Rehabilitate young people while they can still be changed.
Citizens and Taxpayers of California	• Low cost service delivery.	• Transparency • Accountability • Safe and secure community

Facilities.   Many advocates have emphasized the importance of the physical plant of treatment and care services. Drawing from successful models, housing wards in facilities near their home communities allows wards to work closely with family, school, and potential employers giving them access to localized networks from which they may draw support after release from the system. The ability to make connections to extra-institutional resources while serving their term of incarceration will allow for a continuum of care less disrupted than the existing system. Because the existing "warehouse-style" design of DJJ facilities breeds violence and ward abuse, housing wards in small facilities or small clusters within large facilities is highly preferred.[14] These structures allow wards to benefit from intensive case management and more personal relationships between guards and wards. The regulations for DJJ mandate a ward to guard ratio of 9 to 1, though many facilities are operating with ratios of up to 50 wards per guard.[15] Beyond the actual number of guards and staff responsible for custodial and rehabilitative services, advocates have emphasized the importance of special training and evaluations of guards to ensure they meet the standards of care for working with youth populations.

Facility administrators have expressed changes to the system of care that will promote less violence in the facilities to increase the safety of wards and personnel. In addition to sharing the youth and advocate goals that lead to improved relationships between wards and personnel, administrators believe that better classification and physical segregation of wards will lead to reductions in violence as wards with more "hardcore" offenses held separately from wards convicted of less-violent or non-violent offenses will allow personnel to specialize their custodial duties.[16] Because administrators are ultimately accountable to California taxpayers, they have the shared goal of housing and providing services to wards at the lowest efficient monetary cost.

Judicial representatives from juvenile courts throughout California have expressed concern with the safety of wards within the existing facilities. Many judges prefer residential treatment facilities that emphasize treatment, rather than strictly custodial functions. Some judges have sought to place wards in the least physically restrictive facilities that meet the particular requirements that maintain a level of public safety for the California population from the particular threats of youth wards. More specifically, judges have sought to identify a minimum level of security that will serve to protect the public from offenders based on the nature of his or her offense.

Services.   Youth within different levels of the juvenile justice system and former DJJ wards have identified three key areas in which the existing system has failed—services that provide basic human needs, educational services, and medical and other health services. Wards are granted rights to basic necessary care while wards of the system. These are mandated by the California Welfare and Institutions Code and include access to religious services of their choosing, adequate food and clothing, and a minimum level of recreation opportunities and physical activity.[17]

With respect to educational services, youth and advocates require basic academic and vocational education in a school district model that adheres to the same educational standards as public school districts. Though the existing Educational Services Agency is charged with meeting this standard, the structure of the system does not provide incentives to educational service providers and wards suffer significantly as a result. Not only are wards denied basic educational services as the minimum of four hours daily due to absentee teachers and administrative lockdowns, they are not given access to services that will allow them to excel outside of the system post-release, such as GED preparation or employability programs.

In terms of health services, wards should have access to medical care and information about the medications they are prescribed, specifically with respect to the effects of medications and alternatives to psychotropic drugs.[18] In addition, many wards require specialized treatment that will support and facilitate their transition to noncriminal behavior after their release. For example, specialized counseling, sex offender treatment, and other special behavior treatment should be provided in correctional treatment centers and intermediate care facilities.

In constructing reform measures and system evaluations, CDCR and DJJ administrators have set a baseline standard for service provision that services must prepare the wards for release and success on parole. This, combined with cost-minimizing goals for the overall system, does not allow for specific goals for service provision beyond this general requirement. In response to in-depth evaluations of the existing system, administrators have demonstrated a preference for improved systems of confinement rather than therapeutic services in their willingness to bring new programs to the existing facilities.[19]

Judges have demonstrated a preference for services that change youth behavior to prevent a future offense. This emphasis on reduced recidivism has been actualized in a myriad of innovative sentences for youth offenders, both within DJJ facilities and in the larger community. Many judges have adopted principles of restorative justice, a term that represents the process of identifying the harm the offender has caused to the victim and the broader community and charges the offender with tasks and responsibilities that are designed specifically to restore that deficit. These sentences range from intensive treatment services to personal apologies to proactive community service.

Monitoring and Oversight.   While many youth and advocate stakeholders identified critical changes to the system of setting policies for personnel contact with wards and enacting more stringent enforcement of guard conduct policies, the key stakeholders concerned with monitoring and oversight are the CDCR and DJJ administrators. While there have been many studies and reports on the opportunities for improved administration in the juvenile justice system, the key components of these stakeholders' goals for treatment and care of wards consist of better conflict management and problem-solving training for personnel and better monitoring of the needs of at-risk wards, such as those displaying suicidal tendencies or susceptible to attack by other wards.

Long-Term Goals

Long-term goals represent stakeholder and institutional priorities for the future of youth corrections, and for the post-release lives of California youth. The very existence of a separate corrections system for juvenile offenders demonstrates the understanding of youth as a population in need of different treatment from adult offenders. A central tenet of this need is the belief that youth are capable of reforming their behavior and not becoming repeat offenders in the juvenile or adult corrections system.

Many of the desired outcomes articulated by stakeholders reflect this overarching belief. In fact, it serves as a point of unity among stakeholders and helps to create a foundation for identifying new systems that meet stakeholder goals. In particular, many stakeholders have emphasized the need to change the values and circumstances that have led to criminal activities to values and opportunities that promote acceptable citizenship and pursuit of life-long learning. Youths should leave the juvenile justice system more capable of productive participation in conventional society than when they entered.

Legal Constraints

The selection of a new model of providing care to the existing ward population is constrained by the existing pathways to custody and treatment and new developments handed down as a result of litigation by families of current and former wards of the DJJ.

Pathways to Custody and Treatment.   As shown in figure 2, there are five options for how and where youth are served in the juvenile corrections system. This is decided primarily based on the type of offense the youth has committed and the outcomes of trials and hearings. When a juvenile is arrested by the police, he or she either receives a citation with a date to attend a court hearing or is taken to juvenile hall to meet with a probation officer. At the meeting with the probation officer, the youth may be further detained in juvenile hall, be mandated to receive informal probation, or his or her case may be closed. After further detention in juvenile hall, there is a detention hearing where it is decided whether the youth should be released until trial or further detained in juvenile hall. At the pre-trial hearing, there are four possible outcomes: charges may be dropped, charges may be reduced, charges may remain the same, or

Figure 2   Pathways in the Juvenile Justice System

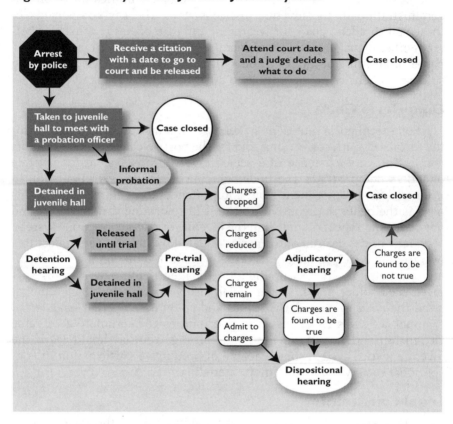

the youth may admit to the charges. If the charges are dropped, the case is closed. If the charges are reduced or remain the same, the youth attends an adjudicatory hearing where the charges are found to be true or not true. If the charges are found to be not true, the case is closed. If the charges are found to be true or if the youth admits to the charges in the pre-trial hearing, he or she must attend a dispositional hearing where it is determined which of five options the youth will be sentenced.[20]

Probation.   The youth is released to a parent or guardian with a list of strict rules from the court that must be followed. These rules range from mandates for school attendance, counseling services, house arrest, or association with specifically identified others. If the youth does not adhere to the rules, re-arrest can result.

Treatment Program.   The youth is sentenced to mandatory completion of a treatment program designed to provide specific rehabilitation for the problem that resulted in the arrest. These programs are typically for drugs, alcohol, violent behavior, and anger and range from residential to day treatment programs. The presiding judge may mandate a specific treatment program, particularly if the youth exhibits behavior for which no treatment programs exist within the geographical or financial reach of the youth or his family.

Out of Home Placement.   The youth is removed from the home of his or her parent or guardian and placed in a facility administered by social workers or counselors. Often these facilities house small numbers of other youth and may be in one's local community or in a different city or town. These facilities are also often administered privately, by non-profit and for-profit organizations, or by municipalities and have varying extents of security to serve a range of youth.

Camp or Ranch.   The youth is placed in a smaller secure or staff-secure training school run by the county's probation department. Presently, twenty counties operate such facilities, which are designed to house youth convicted of serious crimes or several prior cases as a last placement option before being sentenced to the DJJ.

Division of Juvenile Justice.   The youth is sentenced to one of the eight high security institutions operated by the DJJ after being convicted of a serious crime or as a last resort for lesser offenses. Wards of the DJJ are supposed to be under the age of eighteen unless they will finish their sentence before their twenty-first birthday in order to ensure youth convicted as adults receive the appropriate educational and treatment services.

Conditions of Treatment.   In November 2004, the Superior Court of California in Alameda County issued a consent decree in the case of Margaret Farrell v. Walter Allen, the director of the DJJ (*Farrell v. Allen*). The purpose of the consent decree was to mandate corrective action on the part of the DJJ in creating and implementing remedial plans to reduce violence and the need for the use of force within the DJJ, for the treatment and management of wards on suicide watch and those with psychiatric needs, for the hiring of a medical director, to evaluate special management programs and reduce the length of stay for wards in special management programs, and to hire an expert in the field of programmatic access for wards with disabilities.[21]

Based on recommendations from several expert reports released in early 2004, the court required the DJJ to address deficiencies in six areas: general corrections, mental health, medical care, education, sex offender treatment, and wards with disabilities. The consent decree also constructed a standard of monitoring compliance that allowed for the evaluation of the DJJ's implementation by a Special Master charged with determining whether a facility is in substantial compliance in an area.

Following the agreement of the consent decree, the court issued a consent decree stipulation to further mandate compliance of the conditions of treatment. First, the stipulation set dates by which the DJJ must submit interim and remedial plans for the six areas and re-titled the "General Corrections" area "Ward Safety and Welfare" to further emphasize therapeutic rehabilitation over custodial responsibilities. The stipulation also mandated four remedial steps: to end the lockdown model employed at N.A. Chaderjian Youth Correctional Facility and Herman G. Stark Youth Correctional Facility and institute an open programming model and later extend this model to all other institutions; to implement a ward incentive plan to encourage positive program through positive reinforcement; to ensure wards on the Special Management Programs are provided access to educational, treatment, and other services outside their cells on a daily basis; and to submit a programmatic description of the rehabilitative model chosen for the DJJ.

The court mandated the rehabilitative model meet ten guidelines.[22] These guidelines, along with stakeholder goals and priorities, inform the evaluation of the models outlined in the section on state-level programs.

Table 2   Transition Plan Principles

1. Programs must provide habilitation and rehabilitation and success in the community.
2. Youth must be placed in the facility closest to their homes and treatment services must be designed to include families, except where neither practical nor consistent with treatment goals.
3. Youth must be assigned to facilities and programs based on age, risk, and needs assessments.
4. Facilities and programs should maximize youth/staff interaction with adequate supervision and intervention.
5. Facilities and living units should provide a safe and supportive environment that promotes rehabilitative goals.
6. The DJJ must emphasize positive reinforcement rather than punitive disciplinary measures.
7. Lockup may be used only as a temporary intervention in emergencies or as a last resort.
8. All staff that supervise wards must be qualified to provide rehabilitative and treatment services and must be provided with the training and support they need to succeed in their jobs.
9. Programs should be based on evidence and best practices, and will be evaluated for effectiveness.
10. Transition planning for successful reintegration must be provided to wards prior to release to the community.

Budget

The transformation of the DJJ is constrained by the governor's corrections budget allocation for the overall system. Once the budget for the DJJ is approved, other resources may be identified as particularly appropriate for supplementing this allocation. The proposed budget is charged with all expenses associated with administration and operation of the DJJ's eight institutions and sixteen statewide offices serving parolees.

As a result of the numerous changes to California's juvenile justice system, two practices and circumstances have important impacts on the budget—a significant decrease in the size of the ward population and the disbursement of funds to counties to provide custodial, treatment, and supervision services to specific ward populations.

The governor's current budget proposal for DJJ is $400.2 million, a reduction of $8.1 million from the previous year's allocation. This allocation will allow for 3,860 positions in the agency and will be charged with serving the 3,330 wards projected to be housed in DJJ facilities by June 30, 2006, serving the 3,450 parolees projected by the same date, and providing local assistance to counties charged with parolee and other localized services.[23] Table 3 below outlines the five key areas that comprise these expenditures: Institutions and Camps, Parole Services and Community Corrections, Education Services, DJJ Board, and Administration.

Table 3   Budget Expenditure Areas

	Expenditure in thousands
Institutions and Camps	$310,525
Parole Services and Community Corrections	41,209
Education Services	44,522
DJJ Board	3,251
Administration	31,040
Distributed Administration	−30,347
Total	$400,200

In the most recently completed fiscal year, the ward per capita cost was $71,700, which included a wide range of custodial and treatment services (see figure 3 below).

County-Level Services

Presently, most counties operate facilities and programs designed to serve youth whose offenses do not warrant placement in the DJJ. While many large counties are able to offer a wide range of custody and treatment services, smaller counties often face challenges in meeting the needs of their juvenile population alone. These systems have been in place for many years, and serve to divert nearly all arrested youth from being placed in the DJJ. In 2003, 221,875 youth were arrested in California and only 1,008 or 0.4 percent were placed under wardship at the DJJ.[24] The others were released to probation departments, received counseling and were released, or were turned over to their parents or guard-

Figure 3   Ward Per Capita Cost for Fiscal Year 2004–05

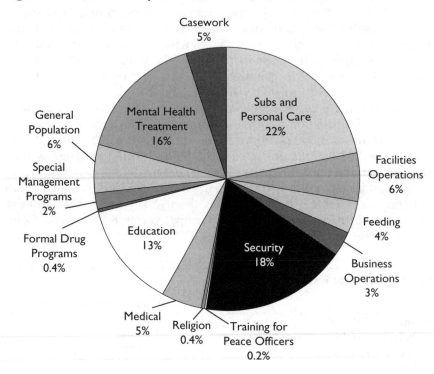

ians. Counties that have been particularly successful in diverting youth from the DJJ employ a range of intervention options.

In addition to housing youth in juvenile halls or in-home detention programs, twenty-eight counties operate ranches and camps designed as a "last chance" option for youth with repeat non-violent offenses or for whom probation has been deemed particularly promising for rehabilitation. Ranches and camps have varying rates of success.

Santa Cruz County, California.[25]   Santa Cruz County's juvenile corrections services are located within the Probation Department. It is guided by four values: family preservation, interagency collaboration and coordinated service delivery system, family involvement, and cultural competence. The continuum of services consists of early intervention, intake and detention, and supervision and special programs.

The early intervention programs are the Santa Cruz City Juvenile Diversion Program and the Watsonville City Juvenile Diversion Program. In Santa Cruz, the program is located at the Santa Cruz Police Department (SCPD) and is staffed by a county probation officer. The probation officer meets with the young person and his or her guardian upon arrest to determine how the intervention will be handled with the goal of diverting the young person from entering the formal probation and criminal justice system. In Watsonville, a non-profit student assistance agency called Pajaro Valley Prevention and Student Assistance has developed a program to serve students within the school district. Here, a probation officer screens all juvenile arrest reports and citations and meets with all first offenders in person to determine the need for counseling and intervention services.

If a young person is arrested for anything beyond a first offense, an intake probation officer investigates the offender to decide whether he or she can be released prior to or detained until a court hearing. The intake probation officer has the option to use community service hours, counseling, essays, Peer Court, Neighborhood Accountability Boards, educational classes, diversion through the police department, or referral to the district attorney in serious cases. After intake, youth have three options for custody: juvenile hall, home supervision and electronic monitoring, or the Youth Community Restoration Program (Y-CORP). If a youth is detained by the court in juvenile hall beyond ten days, a needs assessment determines whether he or she requires mental health counseling, substance abuse counseling, anger management groups, a victim awareness program, life skills program, job development programs, or a pre-placement program. Home supervision and electronic monitoring are mandated by the court to allow youth to remain in their homes under the supervision of probation aides. Youth have restricted options for leaving their homes (generally for school, work, authorized treatment programs, or other approved appointments) and remain in these programs between citation and the conclusion of dispositional hearings. Y-CORP is an alternative to commitment days in juvenile hall where youth work on community restorative projects such as stream clearance and erosion control. Each day of work is performed in lieu of one day in juvenile hall. Y-CORP is also conducting a job training and mentoring project with local businesses to provide subsidized employment to youth instead of placement in juvenile hall.

Supervision and special programs are programs that contribute to reductions in juvenile crime in the county. These programs include a juvenile community court, increased police presence in some communities, regional general supervision, gang intervention, intensive supervision for high-risk offenders, placement prevention programs, out of home placements, and a juvenile job placement program.

These programs are often funded by joint sources, including matching grants and staff support from individual cities, mental health agencies, the federal government, and the state. The overall budget for juvenile probation services is approximately $5.3 million.

The probation department sought to reform its detention practices in four ways: reduced population in juvenile hall, reduced recidivism, reduced length of stay, and reduced Latino population of detainees.

Between 1997 and March 2005, the juvenile hall population fell from 61 to 18 wards and has reduced its average length of detention to 10 days, which is significantly less than the 27-day statewide average. Ninety-five percent of youth placed in home detention programs completed their programs without re-offending and ninety-eight percent of youth in the electronic monitoring program completed all scheduled meetings and court dates. The average daily Latino population in juvenile hall decreased 49 percent between 1998 and 2003.[26]

Santa Clara County, California.[27]   Santa Clara County provides juvenile corrections services primarily within the juvenile detention division and the juvenile probation division of the county's probation department. The Juvenile Detention Division operates the juvenile hall and several programs designed to divert some juvenile offenders from secure custody. The Juvenile Probation Division operates five programs: early intervention, supervision, treatment, rehabilitation, and record-sealing.

The Juvenile Detention Division is designed to serve youth in juvenile halls on a temporary basis, preferring to provide services to assist youth with their social reintegration back into the community and address their social, physical, behavioral, psychological, and emotional needs. Before a young person is admitted to juvenile hall, a probation officer conducts a screening to determine whether he or she may be better served by release to a responsible adult or community release program. Many of the on-site programs are targeted to extremely specialized segments of the population and wards are placed in programs based on needs assessment. The assessment is conducted for youth held in juvenile hall for over 72 hours and is conducted with a multi-agency approach where youth are evaluated for educational, substance abuse, mental health, referral, case management, and transition planning needs. The juvenile hall also houses some offenders who are being detained for a specific period of time due to court order. These youth have access to the same assessment and services as those being housed for transitional purposes prior to an adjudicatory or dispositional hearing.

On-site programs include substance abuse treatment and education, mental health treatment and counseling, planned parenthood, religious services and counseling, gang intervention, victim awareness, anger management, Girl Scouts, career planning, maintenance and community service work programs, Foster Grandparent Program, support network for battered women, outreach programs, cultural diversity programs, and literacy programs and are operated in part by community-based organizations.

Two detention alternatives operated by this division are the electronic monitoring program, where youth may be monitored remotely and participate in probation group counselor supervision instead of being housed in juvenile hall and weekend maintenance and community service work programs for youth with minimal charges or offenses.

The Juvenile Probation Division operates programs that serve youth who are arrested but whose cases are not sent to the county's district attorney for prosecution. Within its five service areas, the division operates multiple specialized programs and three levels of custodial services. Table 4 below shows these programs by service area.

Table 4   Services and Programs of the Juvenile Probation Division

Service Area	Program
Early Intervention	Restorative Justice Program
	Victim Services
	Traffic Court
	Truancy Abatement and Burglary Suppression
	Screening Intake Services
Supervision Services	Probation Supervision
	Alternative Placement Academy
	First Offender Close Up Services (FOCUS)
	Gang Violence Suppression
	Court Support
	Foster Care
Treatment Services	Substance Abuse Services
	Mental Health Services
	Domestic Violence and Family Violence Services
	Youth Education Advocate Services (for special education)
Rehabilitation Services	Juvenile Rehabilitation Facilities
	Ranch Adjustment and Orientation Programs
	Community-based Aftercare
Record-Sealing Services	Record-sealing application and procedural support

---

In 2003, the juvenile hall had an average daily population of 242 wards (2003 annual report). The department also served 412 youth in probation-related services, programs, and facilities. The total budget for Probation Services in 2003 was $95.4 million, which also provided for 927 FTE positions. For 2005, the budget proposes $95.7 million for 778 FTE positions and reduced service provision.

The department is subject to performance-based budgeting by the County administration. As such, the department has identified five outcome measurements on which budgetary decisions are based: successful completion of probation, no new offenses, payment of victim restitution, completion of community service, and successful enrollment in school, training, or employment. Table 5 below shows that for the period between 2003 and 2004, the department had succeeded in ensuring their services contribute to positive trends in almost all of these outcome areas.

Table 5   Outcomes of Juvenile Probation Department

Outcome	2003	2004	Change
Rate of successful completion of probation	89%	96%	Increase 7%
Rate of payment of restitution to victims	77%	79%	Increase 2%
Rate of completion of community service work	87%	93%	Increase 6%
Rate of successful enrollment in school, training, or employment	96%	87%	Decrease 9%
Rate of clients with new sustained petitions (recidivism)	38%	35%	Decrease 3%

State-Level Programs

Model state-level facilities operate under stringent state-mandated guidelines but represent a wide range of facility structures. Missouri and Utah have gained attention as model systems because they continually evaluate their programmatic offerings and for their ability to meet goals of treatment and confinement. Both states emphasize the importance of therapeutic rehabilitation and focus on ensuring youth who are released from their systems have a plan to deter them from the possibility of re-entry. Wards' needs are assessed and treated in small regional facilities and incorporate the resources unique to that area that are beneficial to the ward's rehabilitation—their families, business and professional networks, and others. Finally, services are located within Human Services divisions on the state level, completely separate from adult corrections, recognizing the importance of the potential for juvenile offenders to be habilitated and rehabilitated differently than adults.

State of Utah.   The mission of the Utah Division of Juvenile Justice Services is to provide comprehensive services for at-risk youth within the framework of the Balanced and Restorative Justice Model (BARJ). Accountability, competency development, and community safety are the goals and philosophical foundations of the model.

The Utah BARJ has twelve guiding principles:

• Protect the community by providing the most appropriate setting for the youthful offender.

• Provide secure, humane, and therapeutic confinement to a youth who has demonstrated that he/she presents a danger to the community.

• Hold youth accountable for delinquent behavior in a manner consistent with public safety through a system of graduated sanctions, rehabilitative measures, and victim restoration programs.

• Provide a continuum of diverse early intervention, community-based, and secure correctional programs.

- Promote a functional relationship between a youth and his/her family and/or assist the youth in developing the skills for alternative or independent living.
- When it is in the best interest of the youth and community, provide placements in close proximity to the youth's family and community.
- Promote ongoing research, evaluation, and monitoring of division programs to determine their effectiveness.
- Strengthen rehabilitative opportunities by expanding linkages to human service programs and community resources.
- Provide assistance to the juvenile court in developing and implementing appropriate offender dispositions.
- Provide for efficient and effective correctional programs within the framework of professional correctional standards, legislative intent, and available resources.
- Promote continuing staff professionalism through the provision of educational and training opportunities.
- Provide programs to increase public awareness and participation in Juvenile Justice Services.

The care of Utah's delinquent youths is primarily provided by Juvenile Court Probation, the Division of Child and Family Services, and the Division of Juvenile Justice Services. The Division of Child and Family Services has day care and residential services for dependent and neglected children. In addition, the Division of Child and Family Services provides services to youths under the age of 12 who have been found to be delinquent and youths over the age of 12 who are less seriously delinquent. Probation provides day treatment programs and supervision to youthful offenders. This population largely includes youths who are still in the homes of their parents or are in the custody of the Division of Child and Family Services. The Division of Juvenile Justice Services provides care for delinquent youths who require removal from home. It is a division of the Department of Human Services and the Board of Juvenile Justice Services that is responsible for approving policy. The division's director provides statewide policy leadership and administrative oversight. The division was reorganized during FY 2001 to increase its efficiency and provide better services to delinquent youths and the community. The reorganization led to a change from three regional offices with a coordinating central office to four programmatic offices: Early Intervention Services, Community Programs, Correctional Facilities, and Rural Programs.

The division's residential programs range from community-based programs to secure care. In addition, Juvenile Justice Services administers Utah's receiving centers, youth service programs, locked detention, detention diversion programs, and residential work programs, providing graduated responses to youths in proportion to the severity of their behavior and according to their needs for treatment. The continuum has evolved change in response to a variety of factors including resource availability, innovations in treatment and programming, community values, and changing demographics. In addition, initiatives of the Utah State Legislature and juvenile justice partners have sought to enhance the continuum and have changed the manner in which programming is applied.

Utah's Serious Youth Offender law, enacted by the 1995 legislature, was designed to move some youths beyond the Juvenile Justice System and to provide more severe sanctions for the most serious juvenile offenders and to remove them from costly juvenile programs that appeared to be having little impact. To qualify as a serious youth offender, a youth must be at least 16 years of age at the time of an offense and meet one of three offense criteria. Youths who are at least 16 and meet either of the first two criteria are charged directly in the adult court system. Juveniles who are charged with one of the 10 serious felony offenses are initially given a hearing in Juvenile Court. If the state meets its burden to establish probable cause to believe that the juvenile committed one of the specified crimes, the Juvenile Court binds the juvenile over to the adult court system. Transfer can be avoided if the juvenile meets all three of the following criteria: (1) the minor has not previously been adjudicated delinquent for a felony offense involving the use of a dangerous weapon; (2) the offense was committed with one or more other persons and the youth appears to have a lesser degree of culpability than the confederates; and (3) the minor's offense was not committed in a violent, aggressive, or premeditated manner.

During 2004, Utah's population of 10–17 year old youths numbered 310,053, a slight increase above the number in 2003 (309,475). Beginning

---

Table 6   Criteria for Qualification as a Serious Youth Offender

Criteria

1. Youth is charged with murder or aggravated murder.
2. Youth is charged with a felony-type offense after having been committed to a secure facility.
3. Youth is charged with at least one of 10 serious felony offenses.
   a. Aggravated arson
   b. Aggravated assault
   c. Aggravated kidnapping
   d. Aggravated burglary
   e. Aggravated robbery
   f. Aggravated sexual assault
   g. Discharge of a firearm from a vehicle
   h. Attempted aggravated murder
   i. Attempted murder
   j. Felony-type offense involving the use of a dangerous weapon

in 2004, the age group is expected to grow steadily and reach 341,000 by 2010. The majority of these youth (75 percent) live in four urban counties of Weber, Davis, Salt Lake, and Utah. Another 9.5 percent of all youths live in three of the state's fastest-growing counties, Cache, Washington, and Iron. Based on an analysis of individuals who turned 18 during the 2003 calendar year, nearly 38 percent of Utah's youths will have some contact with the juvenile justice system by age 18. Nearly 3 percent will be found by the Juvenile Court to be victims of dependency, neglect, or abuse. Over 29 percent will be charged with at least one offense and referred to the Juvenile Court. In a substantial number of cases, involvement with the court will lead to in-home supervision by Juvenile Court probation or transfer of custody from parents to the Division of Juvenile Justice Services or the Division of Child and Family Services.[28]

Table 7   Population and Costs for Programs

Program	Population, 2004 (includes duplicates)	Daily Cost per Ward
Receiving Centers	7,848 referrals	Varies
Work Programs	289	$150.21
Detention	6,378	$140.91
Multi-use Facilities	22.6 youths per night (non-secure facilities)	Varies
Case Management	2,311	$10.15
Observation and Assessment	732	$198.72
Community Programs	1,836	Non-residential: $13–$121 per hour Residential: $55–$232 per day
Secure Facilities	402	$185.84

State of Missouri.[29]   The mission of the Division of Youth Services is to enable youth to fulfill their needs in a responsible manner within the context of and with respect for the needs of the family and the community. DYS programs are established to provide the mandated services enumerated in Chapter 219.016 in the Revised Statutes of the State of Missouri. These services include assessment, care and treatment, and education of all youth committed to its care and custody by the juvenile courts and to those youth committed by the courts of general jurisdiction through dual sentencing provision. The division's primary goal is to provide a menu of residential and community services in numerous locations statewide to prevent re-offense.

The constitution of Missouri established the State Board of Training Schools in 1945, mandating for the first time the "rehabilitation and guidance of juvenile offenders." Through this mandate, the training schools were considered to be educational rather than penal institutions. In 1974, the Division of Youth Services was created and located within the Department of Social Services.

The system's creation was based on one key principle: the importance of serving youth in close proximity to their homes in the least restrictive environment as possible utilizing a decentralized management approach. Currently, the division operates 33 residential programs and 11 day treatment programs located in numerous communities statewide. Through the agency's case management system, youth are assessed and placed in the level of care most appropriate to meet their individual needs of treatment and education. All services provided to youth and their families are identified through each youth's Individual Treatment Plan.

Missouri's approach to treating and educating the youth committed to DYS is unlike that found in other states. Within the residential programs operated by DYS, efforts are made to replicate a home-like setting where youth are held accountable for their actions while learning socialization skills. This approach is believed to better prepare youth to return to their homes and communities as positive and productive members of the community. While in the community, an array of community-based services including alternative education and tracking are utilized to provide community supervision and to continue treatment and education services. The youth's service coordinator manages all services and supervision of youth.

DYS was recognized in the report "Less Cost, More Safety: Guiding Lights for Reform in Juvenile Justice" sponsored by the American Youth Policy Forum, a Washington, D.C.-based youth advocacy group.[30] Missouri's juvenile justice programming was praised for its holistic, child-centered, therapeutic approach to the rehabilitation of juveniles within the greater context of community safety at costs well below those of most states.

Recommendations

The new system of juvenile corrections must utilize county-level services and the services of non-profit and other private sector agencies to serve the current wards. Counties will be charged with serving current DJJ wards that have been placed there for all non-violent offenses. The state will contract with local non-profit agencies and for-profit service providers to serve violent offenders and repeat offenders sentenced for all kinds of crimes. The following recommendations are necessary steps in building this new statewide system of juvenile services.

Data Analysis and Reporting Must Reflect Quality Data Collection

Findings in the OIG and LCCD reports show that the DJJ has reached a high level of excellence in collecting information with respect to wards' background, circumstances of offense, educational achievement, and special needs requirements. However, this data often lies unused because the system has no formal processes of data analysis or reporting beyond exclusively custodial functions, such as the monthly population movement summaries. In addition, as the systems available to treat wards extend beyond the state level, these systems of data analysis and reporting must be implemented in order to ensure appropriate ward placement and treatment, budget allocation, and program evaluation.

Counties Are Able to Serve Wards Appropriately

Across California, county-operated juvenile halls are able to provide specialized services, including basic necessities and other training programs in small facilities with substantially better rates of success. In addition to the case studies of Santa Cruz and Santa Clara counties, the ability of probation departments to successfully operate juvenile corrections programs and facilities rests a great deal on their ability to draw upon local community resources that provide youth with long-term opportunities that prevent them from returning to criminal activity.

The local service provision model that has proven successful in other states is particularly appropriate for California counties based on four key findings. First, county governments are already responsible for provision of local services that the juvenile offender population requires, specifically with respect to employment, health, education, and economic development. They have the infrastructure to build partnerships between agencies to support the existing probation departments to serve youth holistically. Many counties also have research and evaluation measures in place to satisfy funding relationships with the state and allow for a smooth transition to employing these methods in juvenile corrections.

Second, many counties have existing systems that are successfully serving youths and could be expanded with additional resources. These systems include facilities, staff, administrators, and community networks that limit the need to build new facilities and train new personnel. Most importantly, this network structure allows for easy integration of state mandates for custody and treatment to ensure the jurisdictions perform within the guidelines of the state's plans for corrections and public safety.

Third, county-level service provision provides a critical balance between state-level uniformity and local-level accountability and transparency. While the current DJJ structure allows for significant departures from standards of custody and treatment because its governance is distanced from daily operations, county-level services promote transparency and accountability because local communities are actively engaged in the process of rehabilitating youth. This, combined with the recommended system of program and service evaluation by the state, will allow the system to be held to immediate and more general standards of excellence.

Finally, in order for counties to successfully take on the responsibility of housing and treating former wards of the DJJ, they will require significant funding opportunities to expand the continuum of interventions and services. Some of this funding may be transferred from the current DJJ budget on the state level. In addition, counties are uniquely positioned to leverage these funds with other state and foundation dollars to increase the impact of their work. The transfer of funds is a key element to transferring responsibility for care—many counties will require significant increases to their juvenile services budgets, as the youth population they are required to serve will increase substantially. Resources for expanding county services will require a permanent state funding stream that reallocates state resources from DJJ to county-administered programs.

In order to achieve this transition as seamlessly as possible, there are three policy areas that require implementation: a formula and system of disbursement for transferring funds to counties from the state, an agency or task force responsible for providing technical support to county probation departments, and a comprehensive system of oversight and management on the state level.

As discussed earlier, the state has existing methods in place for transferring funds to counties to provide critical services. Some counties have received grants and other funds from the state to increase care for juvenile populations in the probation system and in foster care. The same process of applying for and disbursing funds to counties may be applied to the improved systems of custody and treatment. The formula for determining how much counties should receive per ward may be constructed conservatively or to reflect the shifting priorities of juvenile corrections in California. For the conservative formula, the state may calculate the percentage of the $71,700 annual cost of housing a ward in the DJJ that is for custodial and service provisions and the percentage that is for management and oversight funds. Using the percentages from FY 2004, this would be a transfer of $63,670 to the counties, and the state would retain $8,030 per ward per year for management. Most counties currently spend between $140 and $180 per ward per day, which represents a savings in some cases.

Second, the state may use some or all of the funds currently being used for management and oversight to provide technical support to counties whose existing systems of custody and treatment require significant reform in order to better house wards being transferred from the DJJ. Many counties in California use the DJJ to house wards because they are not equipped to serve youth offenders. These counties may also be provided with smart practices from other counties and opportunities to share resources with other counties in order to take advantage of potential partnerships that may prove beneficial in the new process of housing youth. Because the recommended structure does not transfer custodial and treatment responsibilities for wards with violent offenses or persistent repeat offenders, many of the high-cost infrastructural expenses will not be required of counties without existing secure facilities in place. Finally, the state may utilize the opportunity created by the governor's CDCR reorganization to tailor the system of management and oversight to the practice of supporting counties to use their resources efficiently to meet statewide goals for custody, treatment, and public safety.

Private Sector Agencies Serve Youth Efficiently

There are two main ways in which contracting with non-public agencies may best meet the system's goals for custody and treatment. First, non-profit agencies are currently serving individuals in programs that address the root causes of their interaction with the justice system and they are doing so efficiently. Because existing funding sources are limited, these agencies operate extremely streamlined programs that are specialized for different youth populations out of necessity. On the local level, they have been created to respond to problems and conditions unique to the communities they serve. As such, these agencies represent a key population whose skills are not being utilized by the state to rehabilitate the juvenile populations. Many of these agencies, however, have relationships with county service agencies in place. With respect to for-profit corrections agencies, the state may utilize an RFP process to engage agencies in the competition necessary to find the point of equilibrium where prices are low and service quality is high. These agencies may be utilized to provide the most secure custodial services, as they may be in the best position to utilize economies of scale to serve youth.

The primary challenge associated with contracting these services with non-public agencies is that significant oversight and regulations will be required in order to ensure the standards of care employed by these agencies are correlated with the principles of serving youth. This may be costly or unwieldy to implement, but are critical to the overall success of the system. In addition, the state must utilize its recommended system of data analysis to determine which youth cannot be served in juvenile halls and what the root causes are of the circumstances that require more secure custody. Then, for-profit agencies may be targeted for service provision that specialize in those needs. Because contracts may be constructed to be renegotiated in the short-term, it is possible to specifically match agencies with the needs of wards.

Conclusion

This article has provided key recommendations for a successful transition from the existing youth corrections system to one that is more capable of meeting the goals for custody and treatment of juvenile offenders for improved public safety. In the present climate of reforming the system, there exists an opportune moment to demonstrate the state's commitment to true therapeutic rehabilitation of youth in the corrections system.

Notes

1 Schwarzenegger, A. (2004). *Governor's Budget Summary 2005–06: Corrections and Law Enforcement*. Sacramento, CA.

2 Youth and Adult Correctional Agency (2004). *2005 Budget*. Sacramento, CA.

3 Cate, M. (2005). Testimony at the Little Hoover Commission Hearings. Sacramento, CA; California Office of the Inspector General (2005). *Accountability Audit: Review of Audits of the California Youth Authority 2000–2003*. [Online] http://www.oig.ca.gov/pdf/AccountabilityAudit-DJJ.pdf.

4 Schwarzenegger, A. (2005). *A Government for the People for a Change* (Governor's Reorganization Plan 2: Reforming California's Youth and Adult Corrections). [Online] http://cpr.ca.gov/pdf/GRP2.pdf

5 Ibid.

6 Ibid.

7 Hickman, R. (2005). Testimony at the Little Hoover Commission Hearings. Sacramento, CA.

8 Burrell, S. (2005). Testimony at the Little Hoover Commission Hearings. Sacramento, CA.

9 Steinhart, D. (2005). Testimony at the Little Hoover Commission Hearings. Sacramento, CA.

10 Krisberg, B. (2003). *General Corrections Review of the Division of Juvenile Justice*. National Center on Crime and Delinquency, Oakland, CA.

11 California Youth Authority (2005). *February 2005 Population Movement Summary*. Sacramento, CA.

12 Cate, Testimony at the Little Hoover Commission Hearings.

13 Lockyer, W. (2003). *Juvenile Justice in California*. Sacramento, CA.

14 Books Not Bars (2004). *Transforming the California Youth Authority*. San Francisco, CA.

15 Cate, Testimony at the Little Hoover Commission Hearings.

16 Hickman, Testimony at the Little Hoover Commission Hearings.

17 Center on Juvenile and Criminal Justice. *Reforming the Juvenile Justice System*. [Online] January 23, 2005, http://www.cjcj.org/jjic/reforming.php

18 Ibid.

19 Cate, Testimony at the Little Hoover Commission Hearings.

20 The Data Center (2003). *California Criminal Justice Research Guide*. Oakland, CA.

21 Sabraw, Judge Ronald M. (2004) *Farrell v. Allen Consent Decree*. Oakland, CA.

22 Sabraw, Judge Ronald M. (2005) *Farrell v. Allen Consent Decree Stipulation*. Oakland, CA.

23 Schwarzenegger, *A Government for the People for a Change*.

24 Lockyer, *Juvenile Justice in California*.

25 County of Santa Cruz (2004). *Fiscal Year 2005 Probation and Juvenile Hall Budget*. Santa Cruz, CA.

26 Rhoades, J. P. (2004). *Juvenile Detention Reform in Santa Cruz County*. Annie E. Casey Foundation Pathways Series. Baltimore, MD.

27 Santa Clara County Probation Department (2003). *Annual Report*. San Jose, CA

28 Utah Division of Juvenile Justice Services (2004). *2004 Annual Report*. Salt Lake City, UT.

29 Missouri Department of Social Services, Division of Youth Services (2004). *Programs and Services*. Jefferson City, MO.

30 Mendel, R. A. (2000). "Less Hype More Help: Reducing Juvenile Crime, What Works—and What Doesn't." Washington, DC: American Youth Policy Forum.

8

An Alternative to Detention
The Detention Diversion Advocacy Project

Randall G. Shelden

Juvenile delinquency continues to be viewed as a major social problem, fueled by media reports of increasing numbers of young people joining gangs and engaging in violence. The solutions offered by politicians and criminal justice officials, with few exceptions, are variations on conservative models of crime control, namely, "getting tough" on delinquents through greater use of incarceration and the certification of delinquents as adults.

One of the major consequences of this approach has been the overcrowding of virtually all the major correctional institutions in America, both at the adult and the juvenile level.[1] In addition, previous research has clearly demonstrated that the punitive approach to delinquency is, in the majority of cases, nonproductive and may actually create more problems.[2] One of these problems is the overrepresentation of minorities in detention and juvenile correctional centers.[3]

> It is clear that minority youth are more likely than others to come into contact with the juvenile justice system. Research suggests that this disparity is most pronounced at the beginning stages of involvement with the juvenile justice system. When racial/ethnic differences are found, they tend to accumulate as youth are processed through the system.[4]

A census of incarcerated juveniles in 2003 found that the rate of detention per 100,000 juveniles was 83, while the rate for detained blacks was 214. The total detention rate for person crimes was 26; the rate of blacks

This is a revision of a report originally published by OJJDP in 1999 (http://cjcj.org/pdf/ojjdp_ddap.pdf). The original study was conducted in 1997. The program discussed here has been extended to other cities and at least one additional evaluation has been completed, to be noted at the end of this article.

detained for those crimes was 73. The total property crime rate was 20 versus 49 for blacks, and the total rate of detention for drug offenses was 7 versus 17. The comparison for public order offenses was 9 versus 23; the total rate for technical violations was 19 versus 42 for blacks.[5]

There are now several alternatives to the use of secure facilities; most of these alternatives are classified as "diversion" programs. In many cases, however, the youths "diverted" into the programs might not have been formally processed under other circumstances. These programs are examples of "net widening" rather than true diversion.[6]

Diversion

Diversion programs attempt to draw youthful offenders away from the juvenile justice system. The basis for diverting youths is that courts may inadvertently stigmatize relatively petty behavior that would be better handled outside the court system or ignored entirely. Diversion programs are designed, in part, to deal with the problem of overcrowded juvenile courts and correctional institutions (including detention), so that greater attention can be devoted to more serious offenders.

The theoretical background for diversionary tactics is labeling theory, which evolved from the work of Frank Tannenbaum. In 1938, he wrote about the effects of segregating certain types of behavior and labeling them unacceptable or evil.[7] The act of labeling often stimulates precisely the behavior society is trying to control. Tannenbaum discussed what happens when the community defines an act as delinquent. The community characterizes the behavior one way, but youths frequently see the behavior differently. The label shifts from the act to the actor. Society and its institutions try to make everyone fit their conceptions of acceptable behavior, and youths increasingly find themselves defined in negative terms. If youths feel as though anything they do will be labeled "bad," they may start to accept the label and turn to a group that offers alternative values and attitudes.

Howard Becker observed that social groups create deviance by labeling acts as "deviant" and treating those so labeled as "outsiders."[8] Edwin Lemert believed that labeling leads to "secondary deviance."[9] If people break rules but see themselves as conformists, they commit primary deviance. In contrast, secondary deviance is the result of a label imposed publicly by others to the extent that it becomes part of an individual's identity. Thus, processing a youth through the juvenile justice system may actually create delinquency, while ignoring the behavior would allow it to be normalized or dealt with informally in the community.

One of the most immediate responses to the labeling perspective was the President's Commission on Law Enforcement and Administration of Justice report that called for the creation of "Youth Services Bureaus" to develop alternative programs for juvenile offenders in local communities.[10] Virtually every community, regardless of size, established such bureaus, which did divert some youths, especially status offenders and other nonserious delinquents, from the juvenile court.

Unfortunately, the Youth Services Bureau concept was far from clear and unambiguous. "The recommendation that community services be coordinated by the bureau assumed that there was a wealth of services to be coordinated when, in fact, the lack of such agencies and services had been an impediment to successful juvenile court work" in the first place.[11]

Conflicting expectations, findings, and conclusions emerged from the widespread, disjointed, and complicated social experiment. Many studies show that diversion programs successfully reduce subsequent deviance. However, other studies have found no impact, and some studies report that diversion programs are detrimental.[12]

Proponents of diversion programs cite numerous studies, such as the diversion project in Colorado that involved comparisons between an experimental group of diverted youths and a control group that was processed through the juvenile justice system. The diversion program administered individual, parental, and/or family counseling to the diversion cases, resulting in significantly lower recidivism rates.[13] Another program often cited, The Adolescent Diversion Project, showed that diversion need not be limited to status offenders or other minor offenses. The large-scale diversion project in Michigan included juveniles accused of criminal acts. Although most of the project's offenders admitted to criminal acts, each of the various diversion programs reported lower recidivism rates than normal court processing cases.[14]

The most successful diversion projects have been those that provide more intensive, comprehensive services.[15] Especially important is the use of experienced youth workers. For example, a project in St. Louis found that the most experienced youth workers were able to foster greater behavioral changes than were inexperienced workers.[16] An evaluation of diversion programs in Pennsylvania found that community-based alternatives do a much better job of preventing recidivism.[17] Similarly, a study in Colorado found that regardless of race, juveniles referred to various diversion programs had very low recidivism rates.[18] Several other recent studies confirm that diversion programs reduce recidivism.[19]

Opponents of diversionary projects, on the other hand, cite studies that show diversion projects to be unsuccessful.[20] In one analysis of a police diversion program, it was discovered that diversion aggravated rather than deterred recidivism.[21] Other researchers found that receiving service, regardless of whether the intervention was in a traditional juvenile justice setting or in an alternative program, resulted in an increase in perceptions of labeling and self-reported delinquency.[22]

Widening the Net or True Alternatives?

The establishment of youth bureaus in the 1960s was not a novel development. The process of diverting youth away from existing institutions has ebbed and flowed since the New York House of Refuge opened in 1824. Although the term "diversion" was not used, the House of Refuge was intended as a more humane alternative to adult institutions. In time, it became as repressive as its adult counterparts. Over the next century new institutions emerged to take its place. With each "new" institution or "alternative," the number of youths being processed in a formal manner increased.[23]

Diversion has created concern over such issues as recidivism, prejudice, discrimination, and civil rights violations. The issue of *net widening* has probably received the most attention. Ideally, a true diversion program (and the original concept behind diversion) seeks to take those who would ordinarily be processed within the juvenile justice system and place them into some alternative program. So, for instance, if normally you would have 1,000 youths processed within the system, a true diversion would be to take, say, 300 of these youths away from formal processing and treat them in an alternative setting. Net widening occurs if (using these same numbers) 300 youths who would not otherwise have been part of the 1,000 processed are assigned to alternative programs. Thus, instead of processing only 1,000 youths (300 in diversion programs and 700 within the juvenile justice system), the total becomes 1,300 (1,000 processed through the system while an additional 300 are assigned to other programs). In this example, the net widens to incorporate another 300 youths. Several studies have found that this is exactly what has occurred, at both the police and intake stages.[24]

Part of the net-widening problem stems from the fact that as many as half of all referrals come directly from schools, parents and welfare agencies, bypassing the police and juvenile court intake officers. Ironically, these are the people and local agencies that were supposed to serve youth in the first place, in lieu of legal processing.[25]

Two additional problems include certain constitutional issues and charges of differential treatment based on race. One of the biggest problems with diversion is that it can essentially be "disposition without adjudication." In other words, a youth may be assigned to a particular avenue of informal correction even though he or she has not been officially adjudicated as a "delinquent."[26] Researchers have found evidence of systematic differential treatment of blacks, with black females, for instance, being more likely to be incarcerated for status offenses, while their white counterparts were more likely to be diverted.[27] As noted in article 6, if diversion is to work effectively, it is of paramount importance that *youths are really diverted from the system itself*, rather than being ensnared in a net-widening process.

The Detention Diversion Advocacy Project (DDAP)

The Detention Diversion Advocacy Project (DDAP) is a program sponsored by the Center on Juvenile and Criminal Justice (CJCJ) in San Francisco, California. The program's major goal is to reduce the number of youth in court-ordered detention and to provide them with culturally relevant community-based services and supervision. Youths selected are those who are likely to be detained pending their adjudication. DDAP provides an intensive level of community-based monitoring and advocacy that is not presently available elsewhere.

Disposition case advocacy has been defined as "the efforts of lay persons or nonlegal experts acting on behalf of youthful offenders at disposition hearings."[28] It is based in part on the more general concept of case management, which seeks to achieve two major outcomes: (1) the coordination of services from a variety of organizations and (2) continuity of care.[29] The main focus of case management is to develop a network of human services that integrates the development of client skills and the involvement of multiple service providers.[30]

The program is designed to accomplish the following goals:

1. to provide multilevel interventions to divert youth from secure detention facilities;

2. to demonstrate that community-based interventions are an effective alternative to secure custody and that the needs of both the youths and the community can be met at a cost savings to the public; and

3. to reduce disproportionate minority incarceration.

Part of the impetus for the establishment of this program was the fact that the San Francisco juvenile detention system had been the focus of criticism for 40 years because of its overuse of detention and its failure to develop suitable alternatives. San Francisco had a detention rate that ranked third in the state.[31] In California, African-American youth were 4.4 times as likely to be sentenced to confinement than were white youth; Hispanic youth were 3.8 times more likely to be confined.[32] More than one-half of all the referrals (63%) were African-American youth, far in excess of their proportion in the general population. In 2003, there were 16,782 juveniles in custody in California—a rate of 392 per 100,000.[33] The detention rate was 128 per 100,000, and the commitment rate was 263 per 100,000. The custody rate for whites was 217 per 100,000; for blacks the rate was 1,246, and for Hispanics it was 448.[34] One of the major reasons for the high use of incarceration was the absence of intermediate options.

Racial disproportionality is a serious problem nationwide. African Americans represent 16% of the youth population, 28% of juvenile arrests, 37% of youth who are detained, 35% of the youth who are judicially waived to criminal court, and 58% of the youth admitted to state prisons.[35] (See figure 1 in article 2.)

In addition to the high levels of minority incarceration, youths in the juvenile justice system often reflect a plethora of high-risk elements. Risk factors include inadequate family support, school failure, negative peer associations, and insufficient community-based services. Because most adjudicated youths are released from secure detention without community follow-up or supervision, high-risk factors remain unaddressed.[36]

The overuse of detention is partly attributable to the failure of probation department staff to consider alternative options at the time a youth is taken into custody. The juvenile probation department in San Francisco consistently recommended detention in the majority of the cases; one study found a 77% detention rate.[37] As demonstrated in other jurisdictions, when community agencies are present to advocate for alternatives to detention, secure custody rates decline. A study by the Massachusetts Department of Youth Services found that advocacy on behalf of youth at detention hearings by community agencies leads to significant reductions in unnecessary detentions. When advocacy is combined with intensive case management, youths receive a wide range of quality services.[38]

In an attempt to relieve overcrowding in juvenile detention, the Spofford Detention Center Project in New York developed a case management system. Detention was viewed as an opportunity to identify the specific needs (e.g., medicine and education) of each detainee. A computer-based system was created to organize the information about each youth. The program expanded to include a volunteer aftercare program through which the youth and his or her family received assistance after the youth was released. Case management both reduced the time spent waiting for court hearings and used the time available to collect information useful in meeting the needs of youths, who were frequently from deprived neighborhoods. The program was recognized for excellence in the management of public facilities by organizations such as the Ford Foundation and the Kennedy School of Government at Harvard University.[39] The case management system is also used in The Key Program, Inc. in Boston, Massachusetts. Youth are *closely supervised,* meaning that they are monitored on a 24-hour basis and must conform to some very strict rules concerning work, school, counseling, victim restitution, etc.[40]

The Rand Corporation conducted a study that also supports case advocacy. The study compared two groups of randomly selected youths: a control group that probation officers had recommended for incarceration and an experimental group that received disposition reports written by case advocates. Of those who received case advocacy disposition reports, 72% were diverted from institutional care, compared to 49% of the control group. The Rand study found tremendous resistance from juvenile justice officials, particularly probation officers, to alternative dispositions—especially the alternatives recommended by case advocates. Probation staff apparently resented the intrusion into what was traditionally their "turf."[41]

The funding under the 1992–93 Children's Services Plan allowed for start-up costs and an initial collaboration of five San Francisco agencies: OMI Pilgrim Community Center, the Potrero Hill Neighborhood House, the Vietnamese Youth Development Center, Horizons Unlimited, and CJCJ. Other cooperating institutions included the Juvenile Probation Department, the Public Defender's Office, the San Francisco Education Services Corporation, the Log Cabin Ranch aftercare program, and the Omega Boys Club. Funding has been provided through several local sources, including the City of San Francisco. (A voter proposition provided that 1% of all city revenues should fund services for children.) This collaboration led to the establishment of DDAP to provide case advocacy and case management for youths who would otherwise be detained. CJCJ oversees the DDAP project.

As of the end of 1995, a total of 612 clients had been referred to DDAP, of which 77% were accepted (470). Of the remaining cases, a total of 358 were accepted by the court and placed within the DDAP program for supervision.

The DDAP program involves two primary components:

1. **Detention Advocacy:** This component involves identifying youth likely to be detained pending their adjudication. Once a potential client is identified, DDAP case managers present a release plan to the judge. The plan includes a list of appropriate community services that will be accessed on the youth's behalf. Additionally, the plan includes specified objectives as a means to evaluate the youth's progress while in the program. Emphasis is placed on maintaining the youth at home and if the home is not a viable option, the project staff will identify and secure a suitable alternative. If the plan is deemed acceptable by a judge, the youth is released to DDAP's supervision.

2. **Case Management:** The case management model provides frequent and consistent support and supervision to youth and their families. The purpose of case management is to link youths to community-based services and to closely monitor their progress. Case management services are "field oriented," requiring the case manager to have daily contact with the youth, his or her family, and significant others. Contact includes a minimum of three in-person meetings a week. Additional services are provided to the youth's family members, particularly parents and guardians, in areas such as securing employment, day care, drug treatment services, and income support.

Clients are primarily identified through referrals from the public defender's office, the probation department, community agencies, and parents. The selection is based on a risk assessment instrument developed by the National Council on Crime and Delinquency (NCCD). Those whose risk assessment scores indicate that they would ordinarily be detained because of their likelihood of engaging in subsequent criminal activity are targeted. Jerome Miller terms this the "deep-end" approach.[42] By focusing on *detained* youth, the project insures that it remains a true diversion alternative, rather than an example of "net widening." Youths are screened by DDAP staff to determine if they are likely to be detained and whether they present an acceptable risk to the community.[43]

Client screening involves gathering background information from probation reports, psychological evaluations, police reports, school reports, and other pertinent documents. The types of services needed are determined through interviews conducted with youths, family members, and adult professionals. After the evaluation of the potential client, DDAP staff presents a comprehensive community service plan at the detention hearing and requests that the judge release the youth to DDAP custody.

Because the project deals only with youths who are awaiting adjudication or final disposition, their appropriateness for the project is based on whether they can reside in the community under supervision without unreasonable risk and on their likelihood of attending their court hearings. This is similar in principle to what often occurs in the adult system when someone is released on bail pending court hearings (e.g., arraignments, trial).

The primary goal of the project is to design and implement individualized community service plans that address a wide range of personal and social needs. For example, the case manager may seek services that address specific linguistic or medical needs. The youth's participation as well as the quality and level of services provided is monitored by DDAP staff. The purpose of multiple collaborations is to insure that the project represents and addresses the needs of various San Francisco communities in the most culturally appropriate manner. DDAP has adopted a more unified approach to combat the deeply embedded reputation of San Francisco youth services as fragmented by ethnicity and race. DDAP has become a neutral site within the city; it is staffed by representatives from CJCJ and several other community-based service agencies mentioned earlier (e.g., Horizons Unlimited, Potrero Hill Neighborhood House, and the Vietnamese Youth Development Center).

More specific goals include: (1) insuring that a high proportion of clients are not rearrested while participating in the program; (2) achieving a high court reappearance rate; (3) reducing the population of the Youth Guidance Center; and (4) reducing the proportion of minority youths in detention. Currently, the Youth Guidance Center is the only place of detention in the city. It has a capacity of 137, but the daily population typically ranges from 140–150. The average length of stay is around 11–12 days.

Data and Sampling Procedures

In 1997 the author conducted an evaluation of this program.[44] The data from the two samples were from the files of the San Francisco Department of Juvenile Probation. Systematic random sampling techniques were used to select the control group and the DDAP group for comparison. Selected sociodemographic and legal variables were obtained for all youths who spent three or more days in detention during the calendar year 1994. Originally, only DDAP referrals during 1994 were to be used ($n = 189$), but additional names were drawn from referrals during the second half of 1993 in order to have a larger sample. A total of 271 from each group were eventually selected (total $n = 542$). Data included age, race, gender, prior referrals (including the charges), prior risk scores, prior placements, subsequent referrals (including the charges), subsequent placements, and subsequent petitions.

Additional information was obtained for the DDAP sample through intake forms that had been filled out for each client by a case worker (unfortunately, time did not permit collecting this information for the control group). The type of information available on the intake forms included neighborhood of residence, highest grade completed, number of times expelled or suspended, whether or not the youth was attending school, parents living with youth or not, drug usage, and several poverty indicators (e.g., living in public housing, receiving welfare assistance, etc.).

Key Concepts Defined

The *dependent variable* in the study was *recidivism*, which was operationally defined as a referral to the juvenile court on a new offense subsequent to the original referral to either DDAP or to the control group. Data were not available (because of either time or monetary restraints) on other possible measures of recidivism (e.g., "police contacts," arrests as an adult, etc.). Recidivism was subsequently subdivided into *serious recidivists* and *minor recidivists*. The former included those referred to court on felonies or other serious charges (e.g., robbery, murder, burglary, grand theft, or drugs), while the latter included misdemeanors (e.g., petty larceny, simple assault). Other measures of recidivism were also used, namely subsequent petitions and subsequent out-of-home placements.

One of the most important *independent variables* was the *nature of previous offenses* for those with prior referrals. This was operationalized as (1) *serious violent* (robbery, murder, assault with a deadly weapon, rape, etc.), (2) *serious other* (burglary, grand theft, drugs, etc.), (3) *minor offenses* (e.g., petty larceny, simple assault, disturbing the peace, etc.), and (4) *technical offenses* (violating a court order, etc.).

Another key independent variable was *risk scores*. These were divided into four major categories: (1) under 10, (2) 10–14, (3) 15–19, and (4) 20 or more. However, after discovering that some intake workers stopped adding up the points once a youth reached a score of 10 (so that an exact "10" could theoretically be a "15" or a "20" or more), it was decided to operationalize this variable as either *low risk* (under 10) or *high risk* (10 or higher). According to the risk assessment form, a score of 10 or more indicates that the youth is a "danger to himself or others," likely to "abscond," or is "without adequate adult supervision." Scores higher than 10 result in the youth remaining in detention.

A Sociodemographic Profile of the DDAP Group

The intake forms provided more detailed information about the youths handled by DDAP during 1994 (the first full year of operation, n = 189). This section summarizes that information for the 189 cases handled by the program. (As already noted, intake forms from 1993 were too incomplete to be included here.) The intake forms summarized several sociodemographic variables for each case.

The majority of the subjects were members of minority groups, with African Americans accounting for just over half (56.1%) of the sample (see table 1). Asians and Hispanics constituted almost 30 percent of the group (29.6%), while white youths were almost 13 percent of the group (12.7%). Most participants were male (82.5%), and they tended to come from one of four neighborhoods (some of these areas border each other and so they were combined to simplify the presentation): Potrero/Bayview Hunter, Excelsior/Visitacion, Mission, and the Haight District. The twin neighborhoods of Potrero Hills and Bayview Hunter were most common, constituting one-fourth of all DDAP clients.

Table 1   Sociodemographic Characteristics of the 1994 DDAP Cases (n = 189)

	%	N
Race		
White	12.7	24
African American	56.1	106
Hispanic	13.2	25
Asian	16.4	31
Other	1.6	3
Gender		
Male	82.5	156
Female	17.5	33
Neighborhood (n = 188)		
Potrero/Bayview Hunter	24.9	47
Excelsior/Visitacion	14.8	28
Mission	12.7	24
Haight	12.2	23
OMI	6.9	13
Tenderloin	5.8	11
Other	22.2	42

	%	N
Family (*n* = 188)		
Intact (both natural parents)	27.0	51
Mother only	46.0	87
Father only	8.5	16
Relative	13.2	25
Other	4.7	9
Living Arrangements (*n* = 188)		
With parent(s)	82.5	156
Relative	14.8	28
Other	2.1	4
Highest Grade (*n* = 178)		
8th or less	14.0	25
9th	30.3	54
10th	32.6	58
11th	13.5	24
12th	2.2	4
GED	7.3	13
Attending School (*n* = 181)		
Yes	53.6	97
Ever Expelled/Suspended (*n* = 187)		
Yes	24.1	45
Drug of Choice (*n* = 187)		
None	46.5	87
Marijuana	44.9	84
Other	8.6	16
Used Last 90 days (*n* = 187)		
Yes	46.0	86
Frequency of Use (*n* = 79)		
Daily	32.9	26
Once a week	19.0	15
Twice a week	43.0	34
Once a month or less often	5.1	4
Employed		
Yes	10.7	20
Poverty Indicator		
Yes	41.5	78

The most common family arrangement was living with mother only. School was problematic for these youths; only a slight majority (53.6%) was attending school at the time they entered DDAP, and about one-fourth had been either expelled or suspended at least once.

Over half of the clients had used drugs (53.5%), and almost half (46%) had used them at least once during the 90 days prior to DDAP referral. About one-third used drugs on a daily basis; marijuana was the most popular drug used. Most of the DDAP clients were not employed, and just over 40% were living in poverty.

Group Comparisons (DDAP Group versus Control Group)

As noted in table 2, there were several significant differences between the DDAP sample and the control group sample—and many of the differences are somewhat surprising. First, a greater percentage of the control group were younger (over one-fourth were 14 and under). Second, the control group had a higher percentage of females. This in itself would lead one to predict a lower recidivism rate, since females traditionally have a lower rate of criminal involvement than males. Third, the DDAP group was significantly more likely to have a risk score of 10 or higher that would traditionally predict a higher recidivism rate for the DDAP group, which was not the case. Fourth, the control group had a higher percentage of participants with three or more referrals. This seems to conflict with the lower overall risk scores of the control group, since presumably multiple referrals could indicate a strong probability of recidivism and "risk." Fifth, as far as the nature of the prior offenses, no significant differences were found between the two groups: each group was about equally likely to have prior serious offenses. Sixth, the DDAP group was more likely to have had prior placements.

Most of the differences might have led to a prediction of a slightly higher recidivism rate among the DDAP group (e.g., more males, higher risk scores, prior placements), yet the most significant finding of the evaluation study was that *the DDAP group had a much lower recidivism rate*. In fact, *the overall recidivism rate for the control group was almost double that for the DDAP group*. Moreover, there was quite a large difference for the

Table 2   General Comparisons between DDAP Sample and Control Group (*n* = 542)

	DDAP	Control	Significance
% 14 and Under	15.1	27.3	p. < .001
% Minorities	88.9	85.6	ns
% Female	15.9	22.9	p. < .05
% Risk Score (10 or more)	84.2	59.4	p. < .001
% with 3 or more priors	19.9	38.7	p. < .001
Nature of Prior Offenses			
% with prior serious violence	23.2	30.3	ns
% with prior serious other	28.4	23.6	ns
% with prior placements	27.3	15.5	p. < .001
Recidivism			
% serious recidivist	23.6	45.8	ns
% total recidivist	34.3	60.1	p. < .001
% 2 or more subsequent referrals	14.4	50.2	p. < .001
% with subsequent violence	9.2	24.7	p. < .001
% 2 or more subsequent petitions	5.2	21.5	p. < .001
% with subsequent placements	18.1	24.0	p. < .001

rate of *serious recidivism* (defined as subsequent referrals for major felonies). The control group was more than three times more likely to have had two or more subsequent referrals. Even more dramatically, the control group was *almost three times more likely to be referred for a violent crime*. Further, the control group was about *four times more likely to have two or more subsequent petitions* and slightly more likely to have subsequent placements. All of these relationships were statistically significant at the .001 level, except for gender differences and subsequent placements.[45]

The comparisons included a control for age. Older youth had a lower recidivism rate, which could be attributable to turning 18—thus additional crimes would be processed in the adult system rather than referred to juvenile court. Tables 3 and 4, however, show that the comparisons between the two groups remained essentially the same. Recidivism rates were still significantly higher for the control group.

Controlling for additional variables (see table 5), we still find that the DDAP clients fared significantly better. So, for instance, among those with high-risk scores (10 or higher), the overall recidivism rate for the DDAP clients was 33% compared to 58% for the control group. The highest recidivism rates for the DDAP group were found among those with three or more referrals (exactly 50%); but they were still significantly lower than the control group (70.5%).

Interestingly, those in the control group for whom the data would normally predict a low rate of recidivism (e.g., low-risk scores, no previous referrals, no prior placements, with minor previous offenses, and girls) uniformly had higher rates of recidivism than those in the DDAP group. Each category except for gender was statistically significant (for

Table 3   Group Comparisons for Referrals Age 14 and Under (*n* = 115)

	DDAP	Control	Significance
% Minorities	87.8	90.5	ns
% Female	26.8	31.1	ns
% Risk Score (10 or more)	83.3	47.3	p. < .01
% 3 or more prior referrals	9.8	35.1	p. < .001
Nature of Prior Offenses			
% with prior serious violence	22.0	21.6	ns
% with prior serious other	24.4	24.3	ns
% with prior placements	17.1	10.8	ns
Recidivism			
% serious recidivist	31.7	63.5	ns
% total recidivist	43.9	74.3	p. < .001
% with 2 or more subsequent referrals	17.1	63.5	p. < .001
% with subsequent violence	24.4	40.5	ns (p. < .09)
% with 2 or more subsequent petitions	2.4	32.4	p. < .001
% with subsequent placements	26.8	31.1	ns

girls, the difference between the DDAP group and the control group was substantial). In fact, in almost every case the recidivism rate for the control group was double that of the DDAP group. This finding lends support to the frequent charge that the juvenile justice system takes youths with a low potential for delinquency and makes matters worse.[46]

Table 4   Group Comparisons for Referrals Age 15 and older (n = 427)

	DDAP	Control	Significance
% Minorities	89.1	83.8	ns
% Female	13.9	19.8	ns
% Risk Score (10 or more)	87.0	64.0	p. < .01
% 3 or more prior referrals	21.7	40.1	p. < .001
Nature of Prior Offenses			
% with prior serious violence	23.5	33.5	ns
% with prior serious other	29.1	23.4	ns
% with prior placements	29.1	17.3	p. < .01
Recidivism			
% serious recidivist	22.2	39.1	ns
% total recidivist	32.6	54.8	p. < .001
% with 2 or more subsequent referrals	13.9	45.2	p. < .001
% with subsequent violence	6.5	18.8	p. < .001
% with 2 or more subsequent petitions	5.7	17.3	p. < .001
% with subsequent placements	16.5	21.3	ns

Table 5   Recidivism Rates for DDAP and Control Groups, by Selected Variables

	Recidivism Rates		
	DDAP	Control	Significance
High-Risk Scores (10 or more)	32.8%	58.4%	p. < .001
Low-Risk Scores (under 10)	31.4	62.7	p. < .02
With Three or More Prior Referrals	50.0	70.5	p. < .02
With No Prior Referrals	25.0	43.0	p. < .01
With Previous Placements	33.8	66.7	p. < .001
With No Prior Placements	34.5	58.8	p. < .001
With Serious Prior Offenses	42.1	70.5	p. < .001
With Serious Violent Prior Offenses	42.9	68.3	p. < .01
With Minor Prior Offenses	28.1	69.0	p. < .01
Blacks Only	38.5	66.4	p. < .001
Males Only	35.1	63.6	p. < .001
Girls Only	30.2	48.4	ns
15 and over	32.6	54.8	p. < .001
14 and under	43.9	74.3	p. < .001

Table 6 breaks down these rates more fully, comparing recidivism rates by risk scores for the two groups. As shown in this table, the rate for *serious recidivists* was consistently higher among the control group for most of the variables noted here. Thus, 44% of the "high-risk" control group youths were serious recidivists, compared to only 23% of the control group. More critical was that among "low-risk" groups, only 13% of the DDAP youths were serious recidivists *compared to almost half (49%) of the control group.* In other words, not only was the recidivism rate consistently higher among the control group but also the youths detained in the juvenile justice system who committed another offense were far more likely to return on a more serious charge, *even when they were considered to be "low risk"* (see also tables 2–4).

Table 6   Risk Scores and Recidivism Rates, DDAP versus Control Group

	DDAP	Control	Significance
Low Risk			
Recidivist	31%	63%	p. < .01
High Risk			
Recidivist	33%	58%	p. < .001
Low Risk			
Serious recidivist	13%	49%	
Minor recidivist	16	14	p. < .001
High Risk			
Serious recidivist	23%	44%	
Minor recidivist	11	15	p. < .001

Other Measures of "Recidivism"

Obviously the term "recidivism" can be defined in many different ways, as can the concept of "success." One possible measure is *subsequent petitions.* Actually, this could be considered a much better measure of success or failure because so many referrals are never petitioned to court for more formal hearings. One could conclude that the petitioned cases are the cases with the most evidence or are the most serious and that those not petitioned to court have little or no evidence or are not serious enough to warrant further court action.

As shown in table 7, the differences between the DDAP group and the control group remain significant when petitions are the measure. Whereas only about 24% of the DDAP group had at least one subsequent petition, almost half (47.8%) of the control group did. When considering age, those 14 and under had a significantly higher recidivism rate, as was the case for males, those with three or more prior referrals, and those

Table 7   Subsequent Petitions as a Measure of Recidivism

	Percent with One or More Subsequent Petitions	Significance
DDAP	23.6	
Control	47.8	p. < .001
14 and Under	45.2	
Over 14	33.1	p. < .05
White	40.6	ns
Black	35.8	ns
Other	33.5	ns
Male	37.8	ns
Female	26.7	p. < .05
High Risk (10 or more)	35.2	ns
Low Risk (under 10)	38.9	ns
Prior Referrals		
None	26.6	
One	29.4	
Two	42.2	
Three or more	49.1	p. < .001
Nature of priors		
Serious	43.2	
Minor	31.1	p. < 001
Prior Placements	35.7	
No Prior Placements	35.7	ns

with the most serious prior referrals. Race and prior placements did not correlate with subsequent petitions, nor did risk scores predict subsequent petitions.

Still another possible measure of recidivism was referral to court on a charge of violence (see table 8). Once again, group differences surfaced, but this time the differences were more dramatic. *The control group was almost three times more likely than the DDAP group to return to court on a charge of violence.* Also, note that there was a rather large difference when considering age, as more than one-third of those 14 and under had subsequent referrals for violence, compared to only 12% of the older youths. Note that the differences between white and black youth were negligible; both were significantly higher than other racial groups. Not surprisingly, the greater the number of prior referrals and the more serious the prior referrals, the greater was the likelihood of being returned on a charge of violence. One might speculate that keeping a youth within the juvenile justice system tends to create a strong likelihood of subsequent violence. More will be said about this in the next section.

Finally, as shown in table 9, subsequent out-of-home placements as a measure of recidivism were considered. While the differences between the DDAP and the control group youths were not statistically significant,

Table 8   Subsequent Violence as a Measure of Recidivism

	Percent with Subsequent Violence	Significance
DDAP	9.2	
Control	24.7	p. <.001
14 and Under	34.8	
Over 14	12.2	p. <.001
White	17.4	
Black	20.6	
Other	10.7	p. <.05
Male	18.1	
Female	12.4	ns
High Risk	14.1	
Low Risk	19.3	ns
Prior referrals		
None	13.0	
One	13.4	
Two	18.8	
Three or more	23.9	p <.05
Nature of priors		
Serious	20.6	
Minor	14.8	p <.05
Prior Placements	15.5	
No Prior Placements	17.4	ns

Table 9   Subsequent Placements as a Measure of Recidivism

	Percent with Subsequent Placements	Significance
DDAP	18.1	
Control	24.0	ns
14 and Under	29.6	
Over 14	18.7	p. <.05
White	24.6	
Black	22.6	
Other	16.9	ns
Male	21.5	
Female	19.0	ns
High Risk (10 or more)	22.8	
Low Risk (under 10)	15.9	ns
Prior Referrals		
None	13.0	
One	13.4	
Two	23.4	
Three or more	35.8	p. <.001
Nature of priors		
Serious	27.3	
Minor	18.0	ns
Prior Placements	29.3	
No Prior Placements	18.8	p. <.05

the control group nevertheless was slightly more likely to have subsequent placements. Subsequent placements were also more likely for younger youths and for youths with the most priors, the most serious priors, and those with prior placements.

Summary of the Findings

It seems obvious that the youths referred to DDAP were more successful than those not referred, at least in terms of the key measure of success—recidivism. The term *recidivism,* however, can have different meanings and can be measured in different ways. Given the available data, at least three popular measures can be used: a referral to court on a new offense (and this can be further broken down to a focus on violent offenses, as we have done here), a referral that results in an actual petition to go before a judge for possible adjudication, and a referral that results in some sort of out-of-home placement (e.g., group home, institution, etc.). By each of these three measures, the DDAP group is decidedly more successful.

To counter the possibility that we were comparing "apples and oranges," we looked at several kinds of data and concluded that the DDAP group was, overall, not significantly different from the control group. *In fact, on several measures the DDAP group had characteristics that would lead to the prediction that **their** recidivism rates would be higher.*

The data suggest that the risk scores themselves are relatively poor predictors of outcome, unless, as already noted, many of the assessment forms were not filled out properly. Since this is not known for sure, we have to base our conclusion on existing risk scores. However, the problem with the risk scores may be irrelevant anyway, because there is an even more important fact to consider. It cannot be denied that DDAP accepted many cases that conventional wisdom suggested were "dangerous" youth who posed a "threat to public safety" (whether this assessment is based on risk scores or some other criteria) and were successful. DDAP took youthful offenders who otherwise would sit in detention for several days or even weeks, intensely supervised them over an extended period of time, and placed them into community-based programs (that incidentally are not formally connected with the juvenile justice system), which enabled these youths to lead productive lives without trouble with the police. We don't know, of course, how many subsequently became adult offenders later in life; but by the same token, we don't know how many of the control group became adult offenders.

What reasons account for the apparent success of this program? From the data collected by the author in 1997 and information from previous research, several reasons seem of paramount importance.

First, the caseloads of the DDAP case workers are extremely low in comparison to the caseloads of most probation officers. The DDAP workers average about ten cases each. Regular probation officers in major urban areas have caseloads ranging from 50 to 150. Smaller caseloads typically result in more intensive supervision, and more intensive supervision means that the case worker is more likely to be aware of potential problems and pitfalls. Indeed, with small caseloads they can spend more "quality time" with their clients *in the field* (e.g., in their homes, on the street corners, at school), rather than on the phone or endless hours in an office doing paperwork and other bureaucratic chores.

Second, DDAP is a program that is "out of the mainstream" of the juvenile justice system. It is a true "alternative" rather than one of many bureaucratic extensions of the system. This means that normal bureaucratic restrictions do not generally apply. For instance, the qualifications for being a case worker with DDAP are not as strict as you might find within the juvenile justice system (e.g., age restrictions, educational requirements, arrest records, "street" experience, etc.). From casual observations of some of these case workers, this researcher was impressed with their dedication and passion to helping youth. Moreover, the backgrounds of these workers were similar to the backgrounds of some of their clients (e.g., similar race, neighborhood of origins, language, etc.).

Third, the DDAP premises are less formal, less intimidating, less harsh, and friendlier. There are no bars, no concrete buildings, no devices for screening for weapons as you enter the building, no cells for "lockdown," etc. Further, the DDAP workers are not "officers of the court" with powers of arrest and the usual accoutrements of such occupations (e.g., badges, guns).

There could also be a possible fourth explanation (albeit one for which we lack the data to draw a firm conclusion). As mentioned above, smaller caseloads allow DDAP case workers the luxury of being "on top of the case"—constant contact with the youth may make it more likely that DDAP case workers will be able to "nip in the bud" any potential problems. Another possibility is the possible effect on law enforcement officers. If an officer is aware that a youth is a participant in DDAP, he or she may contact the case worker rather than arresting the suspect. We have no way of knowing whether or not this occurs with any degree of regularity. If it does, it would be a positive sign. Youths from more privileged backgrounds are often treated this way by the police, if it is believed that someone in authority can "handle" the youth informally. Many youths have been saved from the stigma of formal juvenile processing by such intervention by significant adults in their lives.

Recommendations

Given the apparent success of DDAP, additional funding and an overall expansion of the program seems warranted. Specifically, it is highly recommended that more youths, especially those with high-risk scores should be included in diversion programs. It seems obvious that many so-called "dangerous" youth can be handled within their own community.[47]

The record-keeping procedures on the part of DDAP workers need to be improved. Specifically, more detailed information should be collected, including information about the kinds of programming in which each client participated. Too many intake forms, and other information contained in case files, were incomplete or missing completely (this was especially true for the 1993 cases).

This research should be considered only a beginning; funding for additional research is essential. Specifically, subsequent research should be conducted that would include in-depth interviews of program participants, family members, DDAP case workers, and heads of programs to which DDAP clients were referred. Larger samples from both DDAP and control groups should be drawn and studied. Also, sampled cases should be followed up to their adult years to find out how many became adult offenders. Future research should carefully examine *what accounts for the apparent success of DDAP.* To which types of programs were nonrecidivists referred? What did their case workers do? In short, what did DDAP do on behalf of young people that was beyond what is normally done for them?

A serious reassessment of the existing *risk assessment instrument* also seems warranted, with emphasis on the accuracy of the predictability of the risk assessment instrument itself. We must remember that initiating a referral to the court system is a serious step that can have far-reaching, often negative, consequences in the life of a youth, even if he or she isn't detained. A "risk assessment" instrument using a numerical scale, even if it is based on "scientific research," should not be passively accepted as the final decision. The assignment of a "risk score" (or any other "objective" numerical score) should not go unquestioned.

Finally, it is suggested that this program remain a "true alternative" to the formal juvenile justice system. To put it bluntly, we should never allow this program to become "bureaucratized," co-opted, or otherwise "taken over" by the existing juvenile justice system or any other existing bureaucracy. The best crime control is often done in the community, without the interference of any formal, bureaucratic system. Many good ideas have been corrupted by formalization and powerful interests.[48] The lives of our youth, our families, and our communities are at stake. The formal systems of social control have not proven themselves to be very successful.

Policy Implications

The findings reported here have very broad implications in terms of national and local policies. During the past couple of decades we have witnessed a resurgence of a conservative agenda toward crime and delinquency. The various "get tough" policies (e.g., mandatory sentencing, increasing waivers of juveniles to the adult system, the "war on drugs," the increase in executions) have had a negligible effect on the crime problem. Rather, the policies have filled prisons, jails, and juvenile institutions beyond their capacity. The policies have expanded an already huge "crime control industry" that has a vested interest in perpetuating the problem because it is profitable to do so.[49]

The primary reason why this is possible is that we as a society continue to insist that the problems of crime and delinquency (and related problems, such as drug and alcohol abuse) be handled primarily as legal rather than as social or medical problems.[50] Rarely do these approaches address any of the major root causes of crime, such as poverty, lack of educational opportunities, unemployment, racial inequality, etc. In fact, it can be argued that such policies have exacerbated these problems.[51] It is significant that when looking at the DDAP group alone, the one variable that is most strongly associated with recidivism is poverty. Hence, expanding programs like DDAP without simultaneously addressing issues like poverty and inequality will not be enough.

This last point is further underscored by the results of a study that focused on one of the areas with the highest concentration of DDAP clients, the Bayview area of San Francisco. The study found that the heaviest concentration of sales of crack cocaine was almost exclusively in the poorest housing projects of this community. Residents there have been on the margins of the economy since the 1960s. The study also found that this mostly African-American community "has been cut off from the city's economic life" as the prospects for good jobs declined steadily. The community itself has deteriorated to such an extent that the residents have little control. The rising rates of drug sales (especially crack) have occurred simultaneously with increases in unprotected sex and the concomitant rise in cases of sexually transmitted diseases, including AIDS. The authors concluded that these problems have been influenced by "long-term community economic conditions and opportunities." Community residents see their parents, neighbors, and themselves cut off from the surrounding communities with little hope for the future.[52]

As more and more offenses (or no offenses at all) are processed formally by the juvenile justice system, the net of social control widens. Crime policies rarely consider the actual *needs of children and their families*. It is essential to do so *prior* to contact with the juvenile justice system to avoid the labeling and stigma that attach once processing begins. As the DDAP evaluation showed, those who were diverted from the system fared much better than those processed through the system. Abundant research shows very clearly which programs are effective, and the most effective programs have little or no connection with the more established juvenile justice system.[53]

One of the main reasons for the success of such alternative programs is the fact that they tend to stress the *strengths* of at-risk youths rather than the weaknesses. The more effective programs focus on *building strengths* so as to add to the *resiliency* of youths.[54] The more traditional approaches tend to emphasize the negative aspects of youth and focus on faults and negative behaviors. Perhaps it is too easy to focus on the nega-tive. The media seems preoccupied with the negative side of life (witness the never-ending violent programming during the local news hour on television). Another factor distracting attention from possible workable solutions is that we as a society have a fixation on the "quick fix." One could say we suffer from an "Excedrin syndrome" as we continue to search for quick and easy solutions to very complex problems.

It is the opinion of this author that solutions will not come from entrenched bureaucracies. Large institutions too often lose sight of origi-nal goals (in this case reducing delinquency and crime) and instead focus primarily on the survival of the bureaucracy itself. The solutions will come from local communities and groups of activists with few formal ties to the established bureaucracies. It will take a lot of hard work on the part of dedicated people who have genuine compassion for our youth. And we can expect a great deal of resistance from the more established bureaucracies, in particular the juvenile justice system.

New Developments

Since this evaluation was completed DDAP has expanded into sev-eral new locations, notably in Baltimore, Washington, DC, and Philadel-phia. An evaluation was conducted on the program in Philadelphia, also showing positive results.[55] The most recent DDAP program in California started in 2002. *Pathways to Change* was part of a program called Safe Pas-sages, a collaborative effort among city and county officials, community-based organizations, and community members organized to create pro-gramming for Oakland youth.

The Pathways to Change case managers come from six partnering agencies, many of which have decades of experience providing services in Oakland. These partnerships include organizations based in different neighborhoods and specializing in issues ranging from individual and family counseling, job training, youth violence issues, and substance abuse treatment. Pathways to Change is now one of two initiatives for youth offenders in Oakland under a program known as the *Mentoring Cen-ter,* whose mission

> is to improve the quality and effectiveness of mentoring programs and to provide a direct service mentoring program model designed to transform the lives of the most highly at-risk youth. Founded in 1991, The Mentoring Center (TMC) was created to serve as a techni-cal assistance and training provider for Bay Area mentoring pro-grams. TMC has served more than 800 mentoring programs in its 12 years of operation in the Bay Area. As a result, TMC has worked with more than 25,000 youth and volunteer mentors. The Mentoring Cen-ter provides technical assistance and training to approximately 50–85 mentoring efforts, and direct mentor training to 1,700–2,500 volun-

teers and program staff annually. TMC's technical assistance and training services are tailored for organizations such as school districts, individual local schools (K–12), colleges and universities, juvenile detention facilities, faith-based organizations, community-based organizations, municipal/public institutions, and private businesses. As a direct service provider, TMC serves between 90–130 adjudicated and incarcerated youth between the ages of 13–25 annually through two intensive mentoring and intervention efforts: The Transition Program and the Positive Minds Group. In response to overwhelming requests to conduct our programs at other locations, TMC began the Positive Minds Group On-Location program, a condensed form of our services conducted at local schools and community centers. TMC also leads the City of Oakland's two initiatives that serve youth offenders, Pathways to Change and Project Choice. The Mentoring Center's Youth Services Division specializes in working with the most highly at-risk youth, those youth who are no longer simply at-risk but immersed in their risk behaviors.[56]

The following are among the specific services provided by TMC:

- Technical assistance and training to the boards, staff, and mentors of diverse youth mentoring programs;
- The Transformative Intervention Institute—an intensive three-day training for organizations serving youth offenders and highly at-risk youth;
- The Mentoring Institute for Trainers and Managers, a course offered at UC Berkeley;
- The development, field-testing, and evaluation of new mentoring models for underserved youth populations;
- Raising public awareness about mentoring and encouraging individuals to volunteer as mentors; and
- Conducting direct service programs for highly at-risk youth.

In San Francisco DDAP continues to operate, with one interesting new development. The CJCJ began a modified program based on the same principles but applied to post-adjudicated juvenile offenders. Thus, instead of finding alternatives to detention, they are seeking alternatives to institutionalization. This program is called New Options. This program has taken advantage of several sources of funding made available in California, such as California Systems of Care (SB 933), Medi-Cal (SB 163), and the Federal Title IV-E Waiver project.[57]

This project provides community-based case management for high-end offenders, with a designated placement expeditor from the public defender's office. The placement expeditor is an attorney within the public defender's office, who is assigned to identify youths committed to out-of-home placement that could potentially be diverted to community-based services. Identified youths are referred to CJCJ for an assessment and background investigation. If the youth is determined to be a good candidate for placement diversion, the CJCJ case worker develops a community-based case plan. The CJCJ case manager then notifies the public defender placement specialist and a "change in circumstance" hearing is requested (this is spelled out in the California Welfare and Institutions Code Section 778). During this hearing, the case is presented to the court, where the judge determines whether to release the youth to CJCJ's case management services or to continue the youth in out-of-home placement. In a growing number of cases, CJCJ is receiving referrals directly from judges.

CJCJ utilizes an intensive case management model in order to divert youths from out-of-home placement. CJCJ case managers provide service to youth and their families through direct intervention and by brokering services from community agencies. CJCJ's case management with high-risk youths consists of five elements: assessment, planning, referral, monitoring, and supervision.

Assessment: The case manager begins collecting information about the youth from the referral source and meets with the youth's parents and others who have information about the youth. The assessment provides the foundation for the case planning. The assessment of a youth and his/her family covers the following: (1) *current offense*; (2) *arrest/detention history*; (3) *out-of-home placement history*; (4) *family composition*; (5) *physical/mental health status*; (6) *educational/vocational history*; (7) *peer group*; (8) *social services involvement*; (9) *substance abuse issues*; (10) *housing situation*; (11) *employment experience/history*; (12) *interests/hobbies*.

Case Planning: After assessment, the individual case plan is developed in conjunction with the youth, court staff, probation personnel, family members, and community-based service providers. The planning process is used to identify the necessary interventions that will serve as alternatives to out-of-home placement. Planning is a systemic process of establishing goals and of developing activities and interventions. The CJCJ model of case planning allows for the creation of comprehensive service continuums tailored to the unique issues and needs of a youth and his/her family. Additionally, case managers can focus on strengths, assets, and resources of individual youth, their families, and their communities/neighborhoods. CJCJ case planning is important for the following reasons.

- The planning process gains the involvement and commitment of the youth, the family, social network members, and professionals.

- The plan identifies roles and activities, which help the case manager with follow-through and accountability.

- The plan serves as a guide for the case manager and is used to monitor completion of tasks, activities, responsibilities, and achievement of objectives.

- The goals, objectives, and activities of the plan provide a means of evaluating the plan's impact on the youth.

Referral: Once the assessment has been completed and a plan outlined, programs and services are identified. In addition to the specific service needs of the youth and their family, determining appropriate service referrals involves giving special consideration to the following: (1) *youth/family ethnicity*; (2) *cultural values, principles, and practices*; (3) *neighborhood/ community in which youth/family reside*; and (4) *youth/family desires, preferences, and priorities*. When appropriate services, activities, and providers have been located, the case manager works with the youth and his/her family to insure follow through. In most instances, a CJCJ case manager will attend all initial intake meetings with the service provider.

Monitoring: Once appropriate services are arranged, it is the responsibility of the CJCJ case manager to monitor the youth's progress. Case monitoring requires maintaining contact with providers to insure that services are meeting identified needs and that the youth is adjusting to the program's expectations. In the event that the youth fails to comply with program requirements, case managers will intervene and make the appropriate program adjustments, such as locating a more suitable service provider.

Intensive Supervision: Intensive supervision works to promote community adjustment by monitoring compliance and providing support to assist youth in overcoming adversities and patterns that lead to recidivism. Monitoring and intensive supervision are essential to an effective community-based diversion program for youthful offenders. Intensive supervision in CJCJ's case management works to: (1) *determine the extent to which the service plan is being implemented*; (2) *determine achievement of the case plan objectives*; (3) *determine service and support outcomes*; (4) *identify the emergence of new youth/family needs requiring changes in the service plan*; and (5) *provide consistent, close supervision to promote public safety and insure compliance*.

Monitoring and supervision often involve daily contacts during hours when youth are not participating in a program—usually between 7:00 PM to 12:00 AM on weekdays and all day on weekends. Case managers make daily curfew checks to monitor progress. Case managers conduct a minimum of three face-to-face contacts with the youth per week in the field (at school or at home). At least one face-to-face parental conference takes place with the youth's parent/guardian per week in the early stages of the program. Additional meetings with youth and/or family are conducted as individual plans dictate.

If a youth falters while in the program, supervision levels are adjusted upwards until the situation stabilizes and progress is demonstrated. Progress reports are submitted to the assigned probation officer monthly, in addition to weekly personal contact with the officer. If a youth commits a serious violation, he/she is immediately reported to the probation department. Every effort is made to stabilize the situation when difficulties arise, and termination is used only as a last resort and in consultation with the probation department. Case managers carry pagers and respond to crisis calls on a 24-hour basis. The typical caseload is ten clients per manager. Clients receive services until jurisdiction terminates or the terms and conditions of the probation order are amended.

This initial pilot phase of the program was very successful. Of the first 30 youths diverted from out-of-home placement and returned to the community under CJCJ case management services, only one was returned to the Youth Guidance Center (YGC) for subsequent placement. Youths in the program had an average foster care rate classification level of 12. Since the monthly county costs for a level 12 placement is $4,600, diversion saved San Francisco over $33,690 a month in foster care payments (an annual total of $404,280).

The following two case examples illustrate the benefits of the New Options program.

> Tiffany W. is a 15 year old who has a history of substance abuse and multiple placement failure. She absconded from her most recent out-of-home placement while on a weekend pass. She has numerous prior referrals to the Youth Guidance Center for offenses that include drug sales, robbery, and prostitution. Her first contact occurred at the age of 12. When she is not in the custody of the juvenile justice system she resides with her drug-addicted mother and two siblings in the Bayview/Hunters Point area. While confined in the YGC she was referred to CJCJ by the Public Defender's Office. Tiffany was released to CJCJ's intensive case management services with provisions that include wraparound family services such as substance abuse services plus counseling and family therapy for Tiffany and her mother. CJCJ's caseworker also assisted her mother to obtain a Section 8 voucher that allowed them to move to a three-bedroom home in the Ingleside District. Tiffany has been home with her mother for eight months. Their relationship has improved, and both have remained clean and sober. She has not reoffended and is scheduled to graduate with her high school class this year.
>
> Nicholas K. is a 16-year-old male with a long history of juvenile justice system involvement. When he was referred to CJCJ, he was on his fifth placement failure in four years. He is a special education student who functions at the fourth grade level, and he is currently taking psychiatric medications for ADHD. He was placed back home with his father and two siblings in a three-bedroom home in San Francisco's Western Addition district (his mother died two years ago). His CJCJ case manager was able to obtain an updated Individual Education Program that allowed Nicholas to be placed in a private school at the cost of $2,000 a month. He has been enrolled in the school for four months and is thriving. His CJCJ case manager also obtained family therapy, substance abuse, and anger management services and his progress and adjustment is monitored on a daily basis. He has been removed from out-of-home placement consideration. He has not re-offended, and he has remained clean and sober.

Social Justice and Economic Incentives

As discussed in article 2, the majority of people convicted of crimes come from a very few disadvantaged communities. Programs that target the problems of people who live in poverty-stricken areas and the behaviors that can lead to arrest and imprisonment can save states and communities millions of dollars. New York spends $42,000 per inmate annually.[58] If that money were spent to improve neighborhoods in Harlem, the Bronx, and Brooklyn, communities might not lose so many of their youth to delinquency and crime. "Framing the debate as one of economics rather than simply social justice can provide political cover for officials to try out innovative alternatives to traditional incarceration."[59]

Juvenile crime has dropped steadily in the last decade, yet the number of youths sent to juvenile prisons in some states has soared. In Illinois, the numbers increased from 1,800 in 1994 to 3,100 in 2004.[60] If local authorities evaluated and treated offenders, the community paid the costs, but if they sent the youths to the state juvenile prison system, the state paid. "Redeploy Illinois" was created in 2004 to help communities keep youths at home. In the four areas in which it was instituted, the program reduced admissions to juvenile prisons by 33% and taxpayers saved $2 million on an initial investment of $1.5 million. The program provides money to assess and treat mental illness, substance abuse, learning disabilities, and unstable living arrangements.

Ten years ago Deschutes, Oregon, asked the state if, in exchange for reducing the number of juveniles sent to state-run detention centers, it would give the county the money it had been spending to incarcerate the youths from Deschutes. The community received nearly $4 million over seven years and used it for the Community Youth Investment Program. Teens caught stealing cars or assaulting people were required to apologize to victims, pay restitution, and participate in service projects. In the seven years, the youth incarceration rate dropped 25% and arrests declined 28%. The state stopped funding the program in 2003, and Deschutes has been paying for the community-based justice initiative.[61]

This article discussed DDAP in depth and mentioned a number of promising alternatives to incarceration. These are by no means the only possibilities, but all of them begin with the premise that there are more effective approaches than punishing youths by confining them. If we can move beyond punitive responses, we have the opportunity to save communities and their most important resource—young people. The social justice inherent in that premise benefits everyone.

Notes

[1] Shelden, R. G. (2006). *Delinquency and Juvenile Justice in American Society*. Long Grove, IL: Waveland Press, chapter 12; Feldman, R. A., T. E. Caplinger, and J. S. Wodarski (1983). *The St. Louis Conundrum*. Englewood Cliffs, NJ: Prentice-Hall.

[2] Miller, J. (1998). *The Last One Over the Wall* (2nd ed.). Columbus: Ohio State University Press; see also article 3 by Males, Macallair, and Corcoran in this volume.

[3] Bortner, M. A. and L. M. Williams (1997). *Youth in Prison*. New York: Routledge; Feld, B. C. (1999). *Bad Kids: Race and the Transformation of the Juvenile Court*. Oxford: Oxford University Press; Pope, C. and W. Feyerherm (1995, second printing). *Minorities and the Juvenile Justice System: An Executive Summary*. [Online] http://www.ncjrs.gov/pdffiles/minor.pdf; Wordes, M., T. S. Bynum, and C. J. Corley (1994). "Locking Up Youth: The Impact of Race on Detention Decisions." *Journal of Research in Crime and Delinquency* 31: 149–165.

[4] Building Blocks for Youth (April 2000). *And Justice for Some*. [Online] http://www.buildingblocksforyouth.org/justiceforsome/jfs.html

[5] Sickmund, M., T. J. Sladky, and W. Kang (2005). Census of Juveniles in Residential Placement Databook. [Online] http://www.ojjdp.ncjrs.org/ojstatbb/cjrp/

[6] Frazier, C. E. and S. R. Lee (1992). "Reducing Juvenile Detention Rates or Expanding the Official Control Nets: An Evaluation of Legislative Reform Effort." *Crime and Delinquency* 38: 204–218; Macallair, D. (2001). *Widening the Net in Juvenile Justice and the Dangers of Prevention and Early Intervention*. San Francisco: Center on Juvenile and Criminal Justice. [Online] http://cjcj.org/pubs/net/netwid.html

[7] Tannenbaum, F. (1938). *Crime and the Community*. New York: Columbia University Press.

[8] Becker, H. S. (1963). *Outsiders*. New York: Free Press.

[9] Lemert, E. (1951). *Social Pathology*. New York: McGraw-Hill.

[10] President's Commission on Law Enforcement and Administration of Justice (1967). *Task Force Report: Juvenile Delinquency and Youth Crime*. Washington, DC: U.S. Government Printing Office.

[11] Gibbons, D. C. and M. D. Krohn (1991). *Delinquent Behavior* (5th edition). Englewood Cliffs, NJ: Prentice Hall, p. 313.

[12] Polk, K. (1995). "Juvenile Diversion: A Look at the Record." In P. M. Sharp and B. W. Hancock (eds.), *Juvenile Delinquency*. Englewood Cliffs, NJ: Prentice Hall.

[13] Pogebrin, M. R., E. D. Poole, and R. M. Regoli (1984). "Constructing and Implementing a Model Juvenile Diversion Program." *Youth and Society* 15: 305–324; see also Frazier, C. E. and J. K. Cochran (1986). "Official Intervention, Diversion from the Juvenile Justice System, and Dynamics of Human Services Work: Effects of a Reform Goal Based on Labeling Theory." *Crime and Delinquency* 32: 157–176; Gilbert, G. R. (1977). "Alternate Routes: A Diversion Project in the Juvenile Justice System." *Evaluation Quarterly* 1: 301–318.

[14] Davidson, W. S. II, R. Redner, R. Admur, and C. Mitchell (1990). *Alternative Treatments for Troubled Youth: The Case of Diversion from the Justice System*. New York: Plenum.

[15] Dryfoos, J. (1990). *Adolescents at Risk*. New York: Oxford University Press.

[16] Feldman, Caplinger, and Wodarski, *The St. Louis Conundrum*.

[17] Welsh, W. N., P. W. Harris, and P. H. Jenkins (1996). "Reducing Overrepresentation of Minorities in Juvenile Justice: Development of Community-Based Programs in Pennsylvania." *Crime and Delinquency* 42: 76–98.

[18] Woodburn, S. G. and K. English (2002). *Disproportionate Minority Analysis of Juvenile Diversion in Colorado*. Denver: Colorado Department of Public Safety. [Online] http://www.jrsa.org/pubs/juv-justice/reports/colorado-juvenile-diversion.pdf

[19] A review of these studies is found in McCord, J., C. Widom, and N. Crowell (eds.) (2001). *Juvenile Crime and Juvenile Justice*. Washington, DC: National Academy Press.

[20] Rojek, D. G. and M. L. Erickson (1982). "Reforming the Juvenile Justice System: The Diversion of Status Offenders." *Law and Society Review* 16: 241–264.

[21] Lincoln, S. B. (1976). "Juvenile Referral and Recidivism." In R. M. Carter and M. W. Klein (eds.), *Back on the Street: Diversion of Juvenile Offenders*. Englewood Cliffs, NJ: Prentice Hall.

[22] Elliott, D., D. Huizinga, and S. Ageton (1985). *Explaining Delinquency and Drug Use*. Beverly Hills, CA: Sage; Lincoln, "Juvenile Referral and Recidivism"; see also Lipsey, M. W. (1981). "Evaluation of a Juvenile Diversion Program: Using Multiple Lines of Evidence." *Evaluation Review* 5: 283–306.

23 See article 1 in this volume.
24 Rausch, S. and C. Logan (1983). "Diversion from Juvenile Court: Panacea or Pandora's Box." In J. Klugel (ed.), *Evaluating Juvenile Justice*. Beverly Hills, CA: Sage; Lundman, R. J. (1993). *Prevention and Control of Delinquency* (2nd ed.). New York: Oxford University Press; Macallair, *Widening the Net*.
25 Polk, "Juvenile Diversion," p. 372.
26 Bullington, B., J. Sprowls, D. Katkin, and M. Phillips (1978). "A Critique of Diversionary Juvenile Justice." *Crime and Delinquency* 24 (January): 59–71.
27 Bortner, M. A., M. L. Sunderland, and R. Winn (1985). "Race and the Impact of Juvenile Deinstitutionalization." *Crime and Delinquency* 31 (January): 35–46.
28 Macallair, D. (1994). "Disposition Case Advocacy in San Francisco's Juvenile Justice System: A New Approach to Deinstitutionalization." *Crime and Delinquency* 40: 84.
29 Moxley, R. (1989). *Case Management*. Beverly Hills, CA: Sage, p. 11.
30 Ibid., p. 21.
31 Steinhart, D. and P. Steele (1988). *San Francisco Detention Survey: Results and Recommendations*. San Francisco: National Council on Crime and Delinquency.
32 Males, M. and C. Macallair. (February 2000). *The Color of Justice: An Analysis of Juvenile Adult Court Transfers in California*. [Online] http://www.buildingblocksforyouth.org/colorofjustice/coj.html
33 Snyder, H. N. and M. Sickmund (2006). *Juvenile Offenders and Victims: 2006 National Report*. Washington, DC: U.S. Department of Justice, Office of Juvenile Justice and Delinquency Prevention, p. 201.
34 Ibid., p. 213.
35 National Council on Crime and Delinquency (January 2007). *And Justice for Some: Differential Treatment of Youth of Color in the Juvenile Justice System*, p. 3. [Online] http://www.nccd-crc.org/nccd/pubs/2007jan_justice_for_some.pdf
36 Dryfoos, *Adolescents at Risk*; see also article 4 by Byrnes, Macallair, and Shorter in this volume.
37 Steinhart and Steele, *San Francisco Detention Survey*; Macallair, "Disposition Case Advocacy in San Francisco's Juvenile Justice System."
38 Krisberg, B., J. Austin, K. Joe, and P. Steele (1988). *A Court that Works: The Impact of Juvenile Court Sanctions*. San Francisco: National Council on Crime and Delinquency; Austin, J., W. Elms, B. Krisberg, and P. Steele (1991). *Unlocking Juvenile Corrections: Evaluating the Massachusetts Department of Youth Services*. San Francisco: National Council on Crime and Delinquency.
39 Shelden, R. G. (September 1999). *Detention Diversion Advocacy: An Evaluation*, p. 3. [Online] http://www.ncjrs.gov/pdffiles1/ojjdp/171155.pdf; see also Krisberg, B. and J. F. Austin (1993). *Reinventing Juvenile Justice*, Beverly Hills, CA: Sage, pp. 178–181.
40 Krisberg and Austin, *Reinventing Juvenile Justice*, pp. 178–181.
41 Greenwood, P. W. and S. Turner (1991). *Implementing and Managing Innovative Correctional Programs: Lessons from OJJDP's Private Sector Initiative*. Santa Monica, CA: Rand Corporation, p. 92.
42 Miller, *The Last One Over the Wall*; Miller, J. (1996). *Search and Destroy: African-American Males and the Criminal Justice System*. New York: Cambridge University Press.
43 While the goals are to deal with "nonviolent" youth, this does not preclude the inclusion of some youth who may exhibit violent behavior. According to the original project proposal, several factors were considered to determine whether it would be in the interest of public safety to release the youth to the project: (1) the level of participation and role in the offense(s) charged, (2) the circumstances surrounding the alleged offense(s), (3) whether there is a pattern or history of violent behavior, and (4) the final disposition of previous referrals. As noted in this report, several youths (including many who were successful in this program) had violent incidents in their backgrounds.
44 Shelden, *Detention Diversion Advocacy*.
45 It should be noted that when considering the *entire* group of youths referred to the court during 1994, from which the sample was drawn, the overall recidivism rate was 58%,

remarkably close to the rate for the sample as a whole. Also, the overall rate of subsequent petitions was 50%.

[46] Schur, E. (1971). *Labeling Deviant Behavior*. New York: Harper and Row; Schwartz, I. (1989). *(In)justice for Juveniles*. Lexington, MA: Lexington Books.

[47] See, for example Miller, *The Last One Over the Wall*.

[48] Elias, R. (1993). *Victims Still: The Political Manipulation of Crime Victims*. Newbury Park, CA: Sage.

[49] Shelden, R. G. and W. B. Brown (2000). "The Crime Control Industry and the Management of the Surplus Population." *Critical Criminology* 8 (Autumn); Reiman, J. (2007). *The Rich Get Richer and the Poor Get Prison: Ideology, Crime, and Criminal Justice* (8th ed.). Boston: Allyn & Bacon; Austin, J. and J. Irwin (2001). *It's About Time: America's Imprisonment Binge* (3rd ed.). Belmont, CA: Wadsworth.

[50] Prothrow-Stith, D. (1991). *Deadly Consequences*. New York: Harper/Collins.

[51] Miller, J. G. (1996). *Search and Destroy*.

[52] Bowser, B. P., M. T. Fullilove, and R. E. Fullilove (1990). "African-American Youth and AIDS High Risk Behavior: The Social Context and Barriers to Prevention." *Youth and Society* 22: 54–67.

[53] For documentation see the following: Dryfoos, *Adolescents at Risk*; Chesney-Lind and Shelden, *Girls, Delinquency and Juvenile Justice*; Shelden, R. G., S. K. Tracy, and W. B. Brown (2004). *Youth Gangs in American Society* (3rd ed.). Belmont, CA: Wadsworth; Hawkins, J. D., R. F. Catalano, and J. Y. Miller (1992). "Risk and Protective Factors for Alcohol and Other Drug Problems in Adolescence and Early Adulthood: Implications for Substance Abuse Prevention." *Psychological Bulletin* 112: 64–105; Shelden, *Delinquency and Juvenile Justice in American Society*.

[54] Hawkins, Catalano, and Miller, "Risk and Protective Factors"; Hawkins, J. D. and J. G. Weis (1985). "The Social Development Model: An Integrated Approach to Delinquency Prevention." *Journal of Primary Prevention* 6: 73–79.

[55] Feldman, L. B. and C. E. Jubrin (2002). *Evaluation Findings: The Detention Diversion Advocacy Program Philadelphia, Pennsylvania*. Washington, DC: Center for Excellence in Municipal Management, George Washington University. http://cjcj.org/pdf/ddap_philly.pdf

[56] For more information see their Web site: http://www.mentor.org/program_services.html

[57] With a few minor editing changes, the following information is taken from the description provided on a special CJCJ Web site: http://cjcj.org/pdf/new_options.pdf

[58] Lee-St. John, J. (March 26, 2007). "A Road Map to Prevention." *Time* 169: 56.

[59] Ibid., p. 57; while ideally social justice would be sufficient incentive in and of itself, economics may ultimately be more persuasive.

[60] Editorial. (May 2, 2006). "Saving Money, Saving Kids." *Chicago Tribune*, p. 14.

[61] Lee-St. John, "A Road Map to Prevention," p. 57.

9

Alternatives to the Secure Detention and Confinement of Juvenile Offenders

James Austin, Kelly Dedel Johnson, and Ronald Weitzer

Court officials must balance the interests of public safety with the needs of youth when making decisions about which program to place a juvenile offender and which level of restriction is required. Juvenile offenders who commit serious and/or violent crime may require confinement to protect public safety and intensive supervision and intervention to become rehabilitated. On the other hand, many offenders can be effectively rehabilitated through community-based supervision and intervention.

Secure detention differs from secure confinement both in terms of the reasons a youth is being held and in the range and intensity of programs available to an offender in each setting. Secure detention refers to the holding of youth, upon arrest, in a juvenile detention facility (e.g., juvenile hall) for two main purposes: to ensure the youth appears for all court hearings and to protect the community from future offending. In contrast, secure confinement refers to youth who have been adjudicated delinquent and are committed to the custody of correctional facilities for periods generally ranging from a few months to several years. These confinement facilities have a much broader array of programs than detention facilities.

Status offenders do not require secure detention to ensure their compliance with court orders or to protect public safety. However, recent data indicate that one-third of all youth held in juvenile detention centers are detained for status offenses and technical violations of probation.[1]

This chapter originally appeared as a Juvenile Justice Bulletin published by the Office of Juvenile Justice and Delinquency Prevention (September 2005) under contract number OJP-2000-298-BF. It is reprinted here, with minor editing, by permission of James Austin. The original included several appendices that, due to space limitations, could not be included here. Interested readers can go to the following Web site to find these: http://www.ncjrs.gov/pdffiles1/ojjdp/208804.pdf

Detaining youth in facilities prior to adjudication should be an option of last resort only for serious, violent, and chronic offenders and for those who repeatedly fail to appear for scheduled court dates. Secure detention and confinement are almost never appropriate for status offenders and certain other small groups of offenders—those who are very young, vulnerable, first-time offenders; those charged with nonserious offenses; and those with active, involved parents or strong community-based support systems.

It is the large group of offenders who fall in the middle in terms of the seriousness of their crimes that prove challenging to the juvenile justice system. The public's heightened concern about crime and the increased emphasis on juvenile accountability in the past two decades may have further contributed to the juvenile justice system's reliance on secure detention and confinement for most juvenile offenders. Clearly, quality and accessible community-based alternatives must exist to enable the judicious use of expensive detention and confinement programs to meet the needs of both the juvenile offender and the community.

The Need for Alternatives to Secure Detention and Confinement

Alternatives to secure detention and confinement are needed for several reasons, two of which are described below:

- **Crowding.** Over the past 15 years, crowded detention and confinement facilities have become more common. Between 1990 and 1999, the number of delinquency cases involving detention increased by 11 percent, or 33,400 cases.[2] Over the same time period, the number of adjudicated cases resulting in out-of-home placement (e.g., training schools, camps, ranches, private treatment facilities, group homes) increased 24 percent, from 124,900 in 1990 to 155,200 in 1999.[3] As a result, approximately 39 percent of all juvenile detention and confinement facilities had more residents than available beds.[4] As the system becomes more crowded, detention staff must learn how to manage continuous admissions and releases and the general lack of stability in such a setting.

  Crowding can create dangerous situations in terms of facility management; it also is detrimental to the rehabilitation and treatment of the youth who are confined. In addition to the logistical problems inherent in crowded conditions (e.g., where youth will sleep, how they will be fed, how they will be educated), crowded conditions can also give rise to violence. Youth are more likely to have to be transported to the emergency room as a result of injuries sustained during interpersonal conflicts in crowded facilities.[5] Youth who are detained for long periods of time usually do not have the opportunity to participate in programming designed to further their educational development (e.g., obtaining a general equivalency diploma). In addition, treatment programs in detention facilities are not designed to address chronic problems (e.g., substance abuse, history of physical or sexual abuse) requiring sustained and intensive interventions. Instead, programming in detention facilities is generally designed to assist youth in adjusting to the correctional environment, ease the transition back to the community upon release, and identify problems needing long-term intervention. Thus, while the youth is in detention, long-term educational and mental health needs are often put on hold. Between 50 and 70 percent of incarcerated youth have a diagnosable mental illness and up to 19 percent may be suicidal, yet timely treatment is difficult to access in crowded facilities.[6] In the worst case scenario, crowded facilities lead to increased institutional violence, higher operational costs, and significant vulnerabilities to litigation to improve the conditions of confinement.

- **Unproven effectiveness of detention and confinement.** The time a youth spends in secure detention or confinement is not just time away from negative factors that may have influenced his or her behavior. Detaining or confining youth may also widen the gulf between the youth and positive influences such as family and school. Research on traditional confinement in large training schools (i.e., correctional units housing as many as 100 to 500 youth), where a large majority of confined youth are still held in the United States, has found high recidivism rates. As many as 50–70 percent of previously confined youth are rearrested within 1 or 2 years after release.[7] Some states have limited the size of these facilities, while others continue to operate 300- and 400-bed training schools. In either configuration, although the long-term nature of a youth's sentence affords a greater opportunity to provide necessary treatment, educational, vocational, and medical services, confinement in these facilities represents a significant separation from the communities to which all youth will return and therefore creates a substantial obstacle in terms of community reentry upon release.

Community-based programs are cost-effective solutions for a large number of delinquent youth. These alternatives to secure detention and confinement are intended to reduce crowding, cut the costs of operating juvenile detention centers, shield offenders from the stigma of institutionalization, help offenders avoid associating with youth who have more serious delinquent histories, and maintain positive ties between the juvenile and his or her family and community.

Between the 1960s and mid-1990s, significant research demonstrated that community-based programs (e.g., intensive supervision, group homes, day reporting centers, probation) were more effective than traditional correctional programs (e.g., training schools) in reducing recidivism and improving community adjustment.[8] Even studies with less favorable results showed that community-based programs produced outcomes similar to those of traditional training schools but at significantly reduced costs.[9]

Studies conducted on state and local levels also testify to the effectiveness of well-structured, properly implemented, community-based programs as alternatives to secure correctional environments. For example, Massachusetts relies less on holding youth than most other states, turning instead to a network of small, secure programs for serious offenders (generally fewer than 20 youth per facility), complemented by a full continuum of structured community-based programs for the majority of committed youth. These programs allow for a greater connection between the youth and his or her family, school, and other community-based support systems and have shown powerful effects in reducing subsequent involvement in delinquency.[10] States can reduce their reliance on secure detention and confinement, choosing instead to place youth in graduated sanctions programs that are responsive to the risks and needs of the delinquent youth.

Expanding the Use of Alternatives to Secure Detention and Confinement through Systems Change

Strategically matching youth with needed programming requires a cross-system commitment to the objective assessment, classification, and placement of youth. Assessment and classification tools designed for this purpose require buy-in from multiple stakeholders in various youth-serving agencies. New public-public and public-private partnerships need to focus on the common goal of expanding the use of alternatives to detaining or confining youth. Jurisdictions must forge new relationships with program providers and other state agencies to ensure the delivery of a comprehensive continuum of care and to fill gaps in service delivery. Further, integrating new methodologies (e.g., objective classification and risk assessment instruments) into juvenile justice decision-making processes will rely on key systems change strategies, especially in the use of data and scientific research to structure those decisions.

Four approaches are used to reduce the reliance on detention and secure confinement and to improve the overall conditions of confinement in secure facilities. These reform or systems change strategies can be categorized as:

- Special program initiatives—often funded by federal, state, or local governments or private foundations—that entice jurisdictions to implement new alternative programs.
- New legislation that requires changes in current agency practices.

- Administrative reforms, whereby an agency issues a new procedure designed to process youth in a manner that does not require additional funding or new legislation.

- Litigation that either local interest groups or the federal government initiate to confront gross violations of juvenile offenders' constitutional rights.

Each approach has its own relative strengths and weaknesses in initiating systemic changes that affect the number of youth held in secure facilities.

Special program initiatives are designed to test innovative approaches in a select number of highly motivated jurisdictions. Typically, the jurisdiction must be willing to craft a relatively small pilot program that delivers treatment services to youth who otherwise would be detained or placed in secure confinement. Absent the delivery of intensive treatment services, targeted youth will recidivate in increasing numbers. Jurisdictions implement special program initiatives most often for several reasons, the primary of which is they face little risk of failing on a large scale because the pilot efforts are relatively small. However, many structural problems that limit its ability to effect large-scale change are associated with this strategy. Usually, the amount of available funds is limited, which means that the number of youth who can be diverted from custody is small. Limited funding also means that high-quality and effective treatment services may not be delivered as promised. Further, when the special funds are exhausted, pilot programs are often discontinued. Even if the program proves to be successful, local conditions that provide incentives in one jurisdiction may not be present in others, making it difficult to simply export the model to other jurisdictions.

Legislative reforms are, by nature, more systemic in scope and are less dependent on the use of treatment services as a condition of reform. In this approach, the state legislature—based on a perceived need for change—enacts new laws requiring the juvenile court or juvenile correctional agencies to alter current practices. In recent years, many states have implemented laws requiring youth adjudicated for certain offenses to be held for a specific period of time or to be tried and sentenced as adults—policies that have resulted in the increased use of detention and confinement. However, legislative reforms can also be used to depopulate juvenile correctional facilities and, in certain key areas, legislative reforms could be quite powerful. For instance, many jurisdictions allow adults in pretrial detention to be released on bail. In addition, adults are, by statute, credited for time spent in pretrial detention. Juveniles generally are not afforded these same options or credits, nor do youth generally receive time off for good behavior, which would reduce the length of their confinement after they have been adjudicated and committed to the juvenile correctional system. Legislative reforms regarding these policies could be a powerful tool in effecting a significant change in the reliance on confinement for juvenile offenders.

Similarly, **administrative reforms** are rarely employed to effect reductions in confinement, but they could be extremely productive. Most states grant the juvenile correctional agency the authority to decide when to release youth from secure confinement. Internal policies and criteria based on agency priorities are developed to govern these decisions. The most attractive feature of administrative reforms, unlike the other approaches noted here, is that they do not necessarily require additional funding, staff, or other resources.

Through its Juvenile Detention Alternatives Initiative (JDAI), the Annie E. Casey Foundation has invested significant resources in developing new administrative practices and alternative programs to reduce the use of secure detention.[11]

Among the models developed were several administrative practices that have proved to be quite successful in large jurisdictions struggling with a burgeoning detention population.[12] Key reforms included establishing objective screening criteria and risk assessment instruments (like those described below) to limit the use of secure detention to high-risk cases; case processing reforms (e.g., new police referral procedures, 24-hour intake, reduction of attorney continuances, fast-tracking hearings, case expediters, increased automation) to speed case flow and to ensure that youth are not held in detention unnecessarily; and alternatives to secure detention to reduce facility overcrowding and to lower operating costs.

Litigation-based reforms are the most divisive and protracted means of achieving systems change. They often require both parties to invest in years of expensive investigation and negotiation to reach a settlement. Although consent decrees have been the vehicle for correcting conditions of confinement such as inadequate medical, mental health, and educational services, passage of the Prison Litigation Reform Act (PLRA) of 1995 (Pub. L. No. 104-134) has severely restricted this approach. The PLRA restricts litigation by prisoners and also curtails the involvement of federal courts in the operations of state correctional facilities. In some cases, however, litigation may be the only method to achieve systemic reforms.

This chapter discusses in detail the model of integrating administrative reforms and special program initiatives such as those undertaken by the Annie E. Casey Foundation's JDAI. In this model, an objective assessment of risk and a knowledge of programs that have been shown, through rigorous research, to be more effective than others in reducing recidivism and meeting the diverse needs among juvenile offenders should inform the choice among alternative programs. Specifically, two key companion approaches are required: (1) the development of objective, valid, and reliable tools to make placement decisions among these programs; and (2) the expansion of the existing range of program alternatives to ensure that evidence-based programs with varying levels of restrictiveness and types of services are available. Both approaches must coexist and be enhanced and sustained by ongoing training and development of new programs and public and private partnerships.

Objective Classification and Risk Assessment

Research has shown that approximately 54 percent of males and 73 percent of females arrested will have no further contact with the juvenile justice system.[13] Even without juvenile justice programming, most youth will have no further involvement in the system. The critical task is to target only those youth who need intervention services and to match them with the appropriate kinds and levels of programming they need, rather than to serve youth who are unlikely to commit another crime.

In general, "classification" refers to the process of determining the level of custody to which an offender should be assigned. "Risk assessment" refers to the process of determining an offender's risk of reoffending, receiving technical violations, failing to appear before the court, or other negative outcomes. Classification and risk assessment play a vital role in determining the number and type of youth best suited for either diversion or release from confinement. Diversion programs have been criticized at times for expanding the use of sanctions for more minor offenses rather than decreasing the overall number of youth in secure settings. Some critics have claimed that diversion programs are often unable to attract the large number of candidates needed to reduce the size and costs of the detained and confined population.[14]

To guard against these problems, states should consider both the attributes of good risk assessment and classification instruments and how they can be used at different decision points when developing alternatives to detention and confinement. Without objective classification and risk assessment procedures and policies that have been tested to ensure their reliability and validity, it is extremely difficult for even the best-intentioned program to succeed.

The key attributes of objective classification and risk assessment instruments are:

- They employ an objective scoring process.
- They use items that can be easily and reliably measured, meaning that the results are consistent both across staff and over time as they relate to individual staff members.
- They are statistically associated with future criminal behavior, so that the system can accurately identify offenders with different risk levels.

The type of risk one is trying to predict can range from risk of failure to appear to risk of rearrest, to risk of probation or parole failures on technical grounds, to risk of institutional misconduct, to risk of escape. Classifying confined youth according to their propensity to escape or to commit violent or other serious acts while incarcerated is desirable. However, because these events are quite rare, it is often difficult to develop a predictive instrument. Types of risk vary—so, too, the criteria used to assess risk should vary. Therefore, more than one risk assessment instrument should be used, although they may share many common features.

At times, the level of risk an offender presents becomes secondary to policy objectives and facility priorities. For example, an administrator might want to ensure that certain types of youth are not placed in a low-security setting regardless of their risk of escaping or committing violent crimes (e.g., sex offenders, high-profile inmates). In these situations, the classification system minimizes the potential for a highly publicized negative incident to harm the reputation of the facility and correctional agency.

Some states have yet to implement any form of objective classification system, some use an objective process at each decision point throughout the system, and some use objective classification instruments to guide certain decisions but not others. When thinking about which type of instrument to use, states should consider how different types of classification and risk assessment systems are appropriate for different decision points in the juvenile justice process (see figure 1). Key points include the initial detention decision, the decision to use dispositional alternatives (which may include commitment to a secure facility), initial classification, internal classification, and reclassification. At each decision point, an assessment instrument is needed to categorize offenders into the relevant categories, which depend on the objective at each point.

Research and evaluations have shown objective classification and risk assessment systems to be both reliable and valid. The systems ensure that detained and confined youth are assigned to the most appropriate program considering public safety and their needs while permitting them to maintain close relationships with their families and communities when possible. If a youth is assigned to a secure facility, classification and risk assessment procedures help those in authority decide where the youth will be housed, with whom, and to which programs or services he or she will be assigned. Finally, as the youth nears release, classification and risk assessment tools should help staff to determine when and how the youth will be returned to his or her family and community.

Classifying youth should not be arbitrary. To ensure that offenders are classified systematically according to risk level and program needs, specially designated classification staff must be given the authority to transfer and place youth. By understanding the attributes of the confined youth population and combining this knowledge with accurate population projections, juvenile correctional agencies can better estimate their future facility, staffing, and program needs, thereby structuring the facilities to meet the needs of confined youth. Figure 1 illustrates the major stages in the juvenile court process and the various dispositions typically available.

Figure 1   Risk Assessment and Classification at Various Decision Points

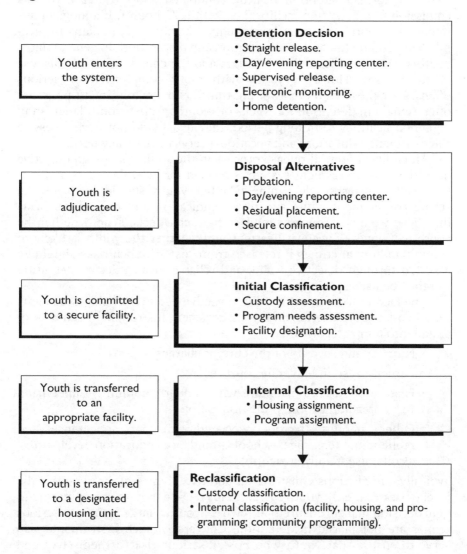

The Process

Detention Risk Assessment

After arrest, the first major decision is whether the youth should be detained. In most jurisdictions, the court makes this decision; in others, probation or detention agencies are authorized to determine whether

detention is warranted. The initial decision is often reviewed and final-
ized in a formal detention hearing conducted shortly after a youth's
admission to a detention facility (i.e., within 72 hours). If a judge determines that continued detention is required, the youth remains in juvenile hall pending his or her adjudication and disposition. In general, most
youth are detained for only a few days and the courts efficiently dispose
of their cases. However, youth with more complicated or serious
offenses, or those who are awaiting transfer to a commitment program,
often remain in detention for weeks or months. When youth languish in
detention facilities for a long period, they usually do not have access to
the treatment, education, and vocational services that they need.

Much like a pretrial release process in the adult system, an objective
detention risk assessment system is needed for juvenile courts and correctional agencies to determine whether youth should be placed in
secure confinement while awaiting adjudication and disposition hearings. The two major concerns in reaching such a decision are whether the
youth will appear for court hearings and whether the youth is likely to
commit additional crimes if released from custody. Such risks should be
assessed through objective, valid, and reliable means. Secure detention
can then be used sparingly.

The factors to be considered in objective detention risk assessments
(and in other classification and risk assessment instruments) can be separated into four categories:[15]

- Number and severity of the current charges.
- Earlier arrest and juvenile court records.
- History of success or failure while under community supervision
  (e.g., preadjudication, probation, parole).
- Other "stability" factors associated with court appearances and
  reoffending (e.g., age, school attendance, education level, drug/
  alcohol use, family structure).

Typically, jurisdictions construct an additive point scale to quantify the
level of risk that each youth reviewed for release or detention presents to
help decision makers ensure that low-risk youth charged with nonserious
crimes are not placed in detention. Conversely, such instruments also
serve to ensure that youth who pose a serious risk to themselves and
others are not readily released without proper supervision.

A number of jurisdictions use objective detention risk assessments to
reduce the number of youth detained prior to formal adjudication. Sacramento, CA; Multnomah County, OR; and Cook County, IL, implemented
risk assessment instruments as part of their involvement with the Annie
E. Casey Foundation's JDAI. Administrators in Cook County, IL, for example, combined the use of a validated risk assessment instrument with an
array of alternatives to detention for those youth who do not require
secure custody. Immediately upon a youth's arrest, on-call probation staff

completes an objective detention risk assessment before the initial detention decision. The assessment's numerical score produces a recommendation to either detain or release and, if release is recommended, the assessment outlines any special conditions that may be required.

These new programs and procedures ensured that law enforcement had additional options for dealing with delinquent youth. The implementation of this detention risk assessment system in the 1990s, which was part of the county's larger effort to reduce crowding in its detention facilities, resulted in the effective diversion of many youth who previously would have been detained.[16] The number of annual admissions to the Cook County detention center was reduced by approximately 1,100 cases between 1995 and 1997, with the rate of admission for detention referrals decreasing from 70 percent to approximately 45 percent.[17]

A similar effort is now underway in Georgia where a comprehensive detention risk assessment system has been implemented as part of a memorandum of agreement between the state and the U.S. Department of Justice (resulting from a Civil Rights of Institutionalized Persons Act investigation). Preliminary results indicate that the system has not had as much impact on the detention system's crowded conditions as originally hoped. In contrast to Cook County, which significantly decreased crowding after recalibrating some of the items and category weights,[18] Georgia has not, to date, experienced those same decreases due to lack of complete buy-in from all stakeholders. Whereas a pilot test of the instrument showed it to be both valid and reliable, the state's sporadic use of the instrument in all jurisdictions has limited its effectiveness.

Risk Assessment to Guide Court Dispositional Alternatives

The juvenile court has wide discretion over who shall be committed to confinement and, in certain cases, the length of that sentence. Unlike the structured guidelines that the adult system has adopted, few jurisdictions have attempted to develop a structured mechanism to guide juvenile placement decisions among an array of dispositional alternatives. This is not surprising because most states have retained an indeterminate sentencing structure without guidelines. Nonetheless, states should, at a minimum, examine regularly the level of disparity in sentencing that may occur within their juvenile courts and try to minimize any differences through training and legislative reform. Systems change efforts may be required to leverage the power of both laws and policies to ensure sentencing decisions are free from bias and inconsistency.

States that decide to develop placement guidelines for the juvenile court should base them on both policy considerations and empirical research. Using a consensus-building process, representatives from a cross-section of juvenile justice decision makers determine the items to be included, their relative weights, the severity ranking of current offenses, and which types of placement will be available to different types of offenders. Once validated, scores representing the risk to reoffend can be combined with a matrix identifying various placement options. Using such instruments, the court can suggest community-based alternatives for offenders with lower scores, while offenders with higher scores are considered for secure custody.

Wiebush and colleagues highlight the benefits of the matrix approach—most importantly, that the two dimensions of risk and proportionality are derived separately (the former, empirically, and the latter, from a consensus-based process).[19] This separation permits decision makers to make distinctions among youth who commit similar offenses but who differ in their risk to reoffend.

External/Custody Classification

If a youth is assigned to secure confinement, staff should apply a specific classification instrument to establish custody level, thereby determining the type of facility to which the youth should be assigned. Some youth may require long-term placement in a maximum security facility, while others may be better suited to a short-term program with fewer security restrictions. These decisions should be based on the seriousness of the youth's current offense, prior system involvement, history of escape, and other factors shown to be related to the risk posed to public safety. In the detention risk assessment process, youth are sometimes placed in restrictive settings regardless of their level of risk because agency policy or state law requires it. The custody classification system strives to place the youth in the least restrictive custody level required to ensure the safety of staff and other youth.

Custody classification has four essential components—initial screening, initial classification, reclassification, and program needs assessment:

- **Initial screening.** Trained intake staff should screen youth immediately after their assignment to secure confinement. The most common type of screening instrument is a checklist with questions regarding the youth's medical and mental health needs, substance abuse history, and other information that might indicate the need to place the youth in a special housing unit for further assessment and observation by medical, mental health, and classification staff. The major objective of this review is to ensure that youth with severe mental health, medical, and other management issues are identified so they can be separated from the general confinement population until a more careful assessment can be made.

  Initial screening is also important for detention facilities. As indicated earlier, the high volume of admissions and the relatively short length of stays reflect a detained population that is in constant flux. Because many youth only spend a few days in detention, often there is not enough time to secure all of the public records required for a rigorous classification assessment.

- **Initial classification.** Classification staff determine a youth's custody level using an initial classification form that includes standard risk factors for escape or institutional misconduct. Because many youth are experiencing their first admission to a custodial setting, initial classification places emphasis on the youth's current offense, prior juvenile record, success or failure on probation, and various measures of community stability (e.g., age, school attendance, family structure). If the youth has been confined previously, his or her earlier institutional conduct should also play an important role in the initial assessment.

- **Reclassification.** The reclassification form is used to reassess the youth's initial classification designation through a review of his or her conduct during the first 60 to 90 days in a facility. Consequently, it places more emphasis on institutional behavior and less on the youth's prior offenses and criminal history. Youth with the longest period of confinement will occupy the greatest proportion of a facility's bed capacity and are most likely to be reclassified on a regular basis. Because most youth will not become involved in serious misconduct, the reclassification process allows youth with positive behavior patterns to be placed in lower custody levels and thus will conserve expensive high-security bed space.

- **Program needs assessment.** The final component of a custody classification system requires that each youth's need for services and treatment be assessed in a more in-depth manner than during the initial screening.[20] The resulting data are used to assign a youth to a facility, housing unit, or program that provides the most appropriate and most needed services commensurate with the youth's custody level. For example, if a needs assessment reveals a youth's heavy involvement with alcohol and/or drugs, his or her placement in a residential substance abuse treatment housing wing or program would be appropriate. Staff with expertise in mental health, education, vocational training, and medical care should conduct the needs assessment process. In some systems, separate assessments are required to learn if the youth is eligible for special education services, has mental health disorders, or has other special needs that staff without specialized training may not have detected. Specialized assessments need to be reviewed and consolidated into a single comprehensive treatment plan under the direction of a caseworker or treatment committee.

Internal Classification

After the youth is assigned to a facility through external classification, internal classification should be used to determine where the youth will be housed and in which programs he or she will participate. The housing decision is critical, as many incidents that require staff to use force often stem from either an improper housing decision or lack of proper supervision. Most juvenile correctional facilities have self-contained housing units with one or more youth to a room and open areas in which large numbers of youth congregate to watch television, play card games, and engage in other recreational activities. It is in these environments that internal classification systems play a critical role. If implemented properly, the number of adverse incidents can be reduced.

In making internal classification decisions, a number of factors should be considered. For example, physical size, history of mental illness, medical condition, and gang involvement are reasons to either separate certain youth from one another or house them in specialized units. It may also be useful to create special housing units that reward youth for good institutional conduct.

Parole/Community Release and Reentry

The last critical decision point to be governed by objective classification is the decision to release a youth from custody. This decision has gained greater attention on a national level under the rubric of "reentry" or "offender transition." In some states (e.g., California, Illinois), a juvenile parole board makes the decision; in others, it is the judge's decision. Elsewhere, the juvenile correctional agency has broad discretion about whom to release and when. The agency's ranking of offense severity and risk of recidivism often governs this decision. The release decision is very similar to the detention risk assessment decision, as both are primarily concerned with risk to public safety.

A number of jurisdictions use the same instrument to determine the level of community supervision that probationers and parolees need, typically modeled after the Model Case Management System.[21] Using a set of eight items shown to have a statistical relationship to the likelihood of reoffending, the instrument distinguishes groups of offenders with different levels of risk, suggesting that different levels of community supervision are needed.

Common Attributes of Classification and Risk Assessment Systems

The foundation of systems change relies on data and accountability. Criminal justice data are used, for example, in estimating the need for specific services among the at-risk population, projecting the number of eligible participants for a new program or service, and identifying an intervention's effectiveness in reducing recidivism or attaining other long-term outcomes. Nowhere, however, is the need to rely on data more critical than in the development of objective classification and risk assessment instruments. Although common sense and professional experience may certainly guide the initial construction of the tools, the individual items and the weights used in scoring must be found to be statistically related to the targeted outcome (e.g., risk of failure to appear, risk to reoffend). Further, solid data and statistical relationships are at the heart of developing training modules to ensure the proper use of the instruments. Ensuring that two staff would classify a given youth in the same way and ensuring the integrity of override provisions are particularly critical.

Objective classification and risk assessment systems must allow for some level of discretion through the use of overrides. Any classification or risk assessment system will produce a substantial number of false positives (offenders who were predicted to recidivate but do not) and false negatives (offenders who were expected to succeed but do not). Consequently, staff must have the ability to alter, or override, the scored custody level based on their professional judgment and consideration of other factors that may not be related to risk. The danger is that overrides, if used excessively, can easily undermine consistent decision making. Conversely, if overrides are underused, staff may not be exercising the appropriate level of professional judgment, which also serves to misclassify youth.

The general standard is that 5 to 15 percent of the confined population should be classified based on an override and not the original classification score. Furthermore, override decisions should be balanced: half of the overrides should result in a lower custody or risk level and half should result in a higher custody or risk level.

Override factors should be separated into two types—discretionary and nondiscretionary. The former reflects a decision by the classification staff to depart from the scored custody level. For example, if a youth is scored as minimum custody but the staff believes that he or she poses a higher risk to the security of the facility's operations, the scored custody level can be overridden to medium custody. However, a supervisor must review and approve such overrides to ensure staff are using them in an appropriate manner.

Nondiscretionary overrides, as their name implies, are mandatory and must be used in certain situations. For example, the agency may have a policy that all youth tried as adults or who will be transferred to the adult correctional system after reaching age 18 will never be classified lower than medium custody. Similarly, a jurisdiction may have a policy that youth adjudicated for serious sex offenses may not be placed in minimum custody until they are within 60 days of their scheduled release dates.

Objective classification and risk assessment systems are important tools for ensuring that youth are placed in assignments that provide a level of supervision commensurate with the level of risk that the youth presents. Many youth can do well under community supervision or in community-based programs that avoid the negative consequences of secure custody (e.g., high program costs, separation from family and community). The key is selecting the youth who are appropriate for these alternative programs without jeopardizing public safety. Objective instruments, such as those described above, can provide a systematic method for placement in alternative programs and can guide the sensible use of expensive, secure-custody beds.

Special Program Initiatives

The second resource needed to decrease reliance on secure custody is an array of alternative programs that feature varying levels of supervision and types of services. In FY 2000, 16 states and territories used OJJDP funds to reduce their reliance on secure custody. Of these, seven states had done so from 1995 to 2000. Funded program activities included victim and offender mediation and rehabilitation, workshops, peer courts, electronic monitoring, and home detention. Unfortunately, very few of these programs have conducted rigorous evaluations to measure their effectiveness.

However, rigorous evaluation of a number of other programs that provide alternatives to secure custody have been shown to be effective. Because relatively few studies have been done on any one type of program, replication evaluations of comparable programs in different jurisdictions are clearly needed. In many cases, evaluation studies of a particular program type differ in the research methods and juvenile samples used, making it difficult to compare results across sites even within the same program category.[22] Finally, some programs have been evaluated soon after implementation. Such evaluations must be treated with caution because, typically, some time after initial implementation is needed for a program to become fully institutionalized and to produce consistent results. As Lipsey and Wilson noted, programs more than 2 years old tend to produce larger positive effects on their clientele than newer programs.[23]

Examples of Alternatives to Secure Detention

Several alternatives to secure detention are outlined here—from outright release to supervised release to residential programs.

Outright Release.   Few published studies have examined directly or indirectly the effectiveness of releasing youth to their families prior to adjudication. A study from Kentucky reported that when court personnel strictly adhered to criteria for detaining youth, the number of youth released to their families or nonsecure residential alternatives was substantially increased. The result was a slight increase in the number of failures to appear before the court but no increase in rearrests prior to final case disposition.[24]

Supervised Release. Youth judged too risky for outright release, either because they are unlikely to appear for adjudication or are likely to commit new offenses, can be placed on supervised release rather than in secure detention. Federal mandates to reduce the number of youth held in secure detention have fostered the development of various enhanced supervision programs aimed at youth considered too risky for traditional unsupervised release. The programs discussed below—home detention, electronic monitoring, intensive supervision, day and evening reporting centers, and skills training programs—provide more intensive supervision than ordinary probation, and many also provide services to help troubled youth and their families.

- **Home detention.** In contrast to outright release, home detention requires offenders to remain at home during specified time periods: (1) at all times, (2) at all times except when in school or working, or (3) at night (curfews). Additional conditions such as drug testing may also be imposed. Youth who violate these conditions risk being placed in secure detention. Home detention programs vary in the intensity of contact between supervisors and youth, but contacts are more frequent (often daily) than in the case of traditional probation. Many, but not all, home detention programs use paraprofessional outreach workers in lieu of probation officers to both mentor and supervise youth. Home detention provides considerable cost savings compared with secure and nonsecure placements.[25]

  Descriptive studies report high levels of success: most youth appear for adjudication and only a small proportion are returned to detention for new offenses. An evaluation of a program in Tuscaloosa County, AL, found that home detainees were no more likely to recidivate than a preadjudicatory group held in secure detention.[26] A study of seven different home detention programs, six of which provided counseling or other services in addition to supervision, found that most youth (71–89 percent) completed the programs without incident and appeared in court.[27] Between 8 percent and 25 percent of the youth were returned to secure detention, mostly for violations of their conditions of release but very few (2–5 percent) for committing new offenses. In Ohio, 91 percent of youth detained at home did not reoffend, appearing in court for adjudication. A San Diego program reported a 97 percent success rate for home detention clients.[28]

- **Electronic monitoring.** Electronic monitoring, often used in conjunction with home detention, monitors an offender's whereabouts via an electronic device attached to the wrist or ankle and by random phone calls to his or her residence. Electronic monitoring is intended to reduce the costs of supervision, reduce institu-

244 Part II: Prospects

tional populations, allow the offender to remain in school while under supervision, and enhance the potential for rehabilitation by keeping offenders at home and in close contact with family members. Few published evaluations of electronic monitoring exist, even though such monitoring is widely used for juveniles.[29] Some evidence does show that youth differ from adults in their response to electronic monitoring.[30] Vaughn reviewed eight electronic monitoring programs. Most were used as alternatives to prehearing detention, four were used to supplement probation, and three were used for offenders released early from an institution. Failure rates in the programs ranged from 4.5 percent to 30 percent; most of the failures resulted from technical violations rather than new offenses.[31] A study of youth detained at home in Lake County, IN, reported that those assigned to electronic monitoring had a higher program completion rate (90 percent versus 75 percent) and a lower recidivism rate (17 percent versus 26 percent) than youth who were not monitored electronically.[32]

- **Intensive supervision.** Many intensive supervision programs (ISPs) function primarily as alternatives to confinement for adjudicated offenders (to be discussed later). But ISPs can also serve as alternatives to secure detention for juvenile arrestees. One model program is San Francisco's Detention Diversion Advocacy Program (DDAP) [see article 8], an ISP that incorporates rehabilitative treatments tailored to offenders' special needs. Parents, the public defender's office, the probation department, and community agencies refer juveniles to DDAP. Among the referred youth, DDAP identifies those likely to be detained prior to adjudication, designs a release plan that includes a list of community services and specific objectives that DDAP will oversee, and presents this plan to the court. Offenders live at home or at a suitable alternative site in the community and meet with DDAP case managers a minimum of three times a week. Offenders' families are also provided with needed services.

An evaluation study that the Youth Guidance Center conducted in 1997 compared 271 DDAP clients with a random sample of 271 youth who spent at least 3 days in detention.[33] Using various measures of recidivism and controlling for age, risk score, number of prior referrals, number of previous out-of-home placements, nature of prior offenses, and race, the center found that the DDAP group was significantly less likely to recidivate than the detained group. The overall recidivism rate for the DDAP group was about half that for the detained group (34 percent versus 60 percent, respectively). Similarly large differences were found in recidivism involving violent crimes. DDAP success rates are even more striking because the DDAP group had a greater percentage of high-risk youth than the control group.

Shelden suggests a number of reasons for DDAP's success: small caseloads, caseworkers' freedom from bureaucratic restrictions of the juvenile justice system, the similar backgrounds of DDAP case-workers and clients, and an emphasis on rehabilitative services coupled with specific goals to track clients' progress. Any assess-ment of the program must consider that DDAP personnel select DDAP clients, raising the possibility of selection effects on the out-come. DDAP case managers may have selected clients who were most likely to succeed in the program. It is thus difficult to deter-mine how much of the program's remarkable success is due to the clients selected or to the program itself, but if the positive results were largely due to the program, this would appear to be a model worth replicating elsewhere.[34] (For more details on the program see article 8 in this reader.)

For additional information, contact:
Center on Juvenile and Criminal Justice
54 Dore Street
San Francisco, CA 94103
415-621-5661
415-621-5466 (fax)
or
1234 Massachusetts Avenue NW, Suite C1009
Washington, DC 20005
202-737-7270
202-737-7271 (fax)
cjcj@cjcj.org
www.cjcj.org

• **Day and evening reporting centers.** Day and evening reporting centers are nonresidential programs that require offenders to report daily activities to case managers. They are a mechanism for enhanced supervision of offenders but differ from ISPs because they provide services such as drug treatment, job training referrals, life skills services, and counseling. Little research exists on juvenile reporting centers.

One promising program model for juveniles is found in Cook County, IL, where minors charged with a probation violation or apprehended on a warrant participate 5 nights a week in county-funded evening reporting center programs. The goal of these programs is to prevent prehearing detention—the focus is exclusively on preventing delin-quent behavior and ensuring that youth appear in court. Evening reporting centers operate from 4 PM to 9 PM daily, and participants are involved with the program for between 5 and 21 days (generally, until their next court date). Youth participate in educational and vocational programs, counseling, recreational activities, and life development workshops (e.g., lectures on delinquency, local government, alcohol and drugs, and health issues; workshops on conflict resolution, employment, and parenting skills). Dinner is provided as an incentive for participation. Center staff work closely with home confinement officers and probation staff to transport youth to and from the program. Seven facilities currently handle about 25 youth each; the newest center targets families. The program evidenced a success rate of 92 percent from December 1995 to August 2001. Youth were determined to be successful if they were not rearrested while participating in the program. The average length of participation for successful youth was 21 calendar days. As of August 2001, Cook County's evening reporting centers have served 7,730 youth.

For additional information, contact:
Mark Morrissey, Deputy Chief Probation Officer
Juvenile Probation and Court Services
Circuit Court of Cook County
1100 South Hamilton Avenue
Chicago, IL 60612
312-433-6569
www.cookcountycourt.org/services

- **Skills training programs.** One example of a nonresidential skills training program is Fresh Start, Baltimore, MD. Fresh Start was established to provide hands-on training and education for juvenile delinquents in the Baltimore area. The primarily voluntary program targets youth ages 16–19 who are convicted of nonviolent crimes and who typically come from low-income, high-crime neighborhoods. The 40-week program is designed to help youth learn practical skills such as carpentry and boat repair and to integrate education and employment experience. Fresh Start has recently partnered with local colleges so that program graduates can attend college-level courses at a reduced cost. In 2000, Fresh Start added a Workforce Development Center to its array of program services. Each Fresh Start graduate is assigned to a job retention counselor who helps the youth navigate common workplace challenges. Approximately 90 males graduate from the program each year. Approximately 50 percent of those who enter the program complete all modules, and those who finish the first 8 weeks have an 80 percent completion rate. Fresh Start tracks its graduates for 3 years after program completion. Graduates from 1997 to 2000 had a rearrest rate of 19 percent and a reincarceration rate of 7 percent, well below the rearrest rate of 75 percent that other Maryland Department of Juvenile Justice programs reported.[35] About 66 percent of the graduates were employed, and 15 percent continued their education (figures provided by Fresh Start). Currently, another Fresh Start program is being established in Washington, DC. Seventy percent of the funding comes from a contract with the Maryland Department of Juvenile Justice, and the remainder comes from philanthropic and corporate donations.

For additional information, contact:
Greg Rapisarda
Fresh Start
Living Classrooms Foundation
802 South Caroline Street
Baltimore, MD 21231
410-685-0295
202-479-6710, ext. 240
410-752-8433 (fax)
www.livingclassrooms.org

Residential Programs. Not all youth can reasonably or safely be returned to their homes, but neither do they warrant secure detention. Residential programs for youth awaiting adjudication are less studied than at-home alternatives. Young and Pappenfort analyzed foster home programs, detention homes, and programs for runaways that serve as alternatives to secure detention. Youth in these programs had negligible rates of new offenses while awaiting adjudication and low rates (10 percent or less) of running away.[36] Many jurisdictions administer combinations of residential programs and various at-home alternatives. Lubow evaluated three JDAI programs that the Casey Foundation sponsored in Cook County, IL; Multnomah County, OR; and Sacramento County, CA. The programs combined home confinement, day or evening reporting centers, and temporary, nonsecure shelters. In all three sites, the alternative programs were implemented without sacrificing appearance-in-court rates or pretrial rearrest rates. In Cook County, for example, the failure-to-appear rate was reduced by 50 percent.[37] More recent data on the Cook County programs for youth served between January 1997 and August 2001 indicate the completion rate[38] for program participants was 93 percent for home confinement, 92 percent for evening reporting centers, 94 percent for electronic monitoring, and 96 percent for nonsecure shelters (figures provided by Cook County Circuit Court).

For additional information, contact:
Mark Morrissey, Deputy Chief Probation Officer
Juvenile Probation and Court Services
Circuit Court of Cook County
1100 South Hamilton Avenue
Chicago, IL 60612
312-433-6569
www.cookcountycourt.org/services

An example of a residential skills program that is not combined with an at-home alternative is the Gulf Coast Trades Center (GCTC), a private, nonprofit organization that has served troubled youth in the Houston, TX, area since 1971. GCTC serves youth ages 16–19 who are referred by the Texas Youth Commission or by a probation officer. The program provides education, job training, life skills planning, and aftercare programs. GCTC also runs the Youth Industry Program, which trains youth in carpentry skills, and the Raven School, which prepares students to take the General Educational Development test. Other youth are trained and permitted to work in the culinary arts, horticulture, automotive technology, desktop publishing, and secretarial positions. Recent evaluation results demonstrate that from September 1999 through August 2000, 84 percent of the participating youth completed the program and 70 percent were employed when they left the program. In addition, 1999–2000 graduates had a 16 percent rearrest rate, compared with a rearrest rate of approximately 54 percent among all youth released from the Texas Youth Commission in 1999.[39]

For additional information, contact:
Thomas Buzbee
Gulf Coast Trades Center
143 Forest Service Road, #233
New Waverly, TX 77358
936-344-6677
936-344-2386 (fax)
gctc@gctcw.org
www.gctcw.org

Examples of Alternatives to Secure Confinement

In the 1970s and 1980s, alternative programs for juveniles targeted status offenders and less serious delinquents. Since then, an increasing number of programs, including intensive supervision and home detention, serve more serious offenders along with status offenders and minor delinquents. Other programs, such as group homes, are specifically designed to accommodate the needs and risks of chronic or serious and violent offenders outside the walls of traditional correctional facilities.

Diversion.   Diversion takes place when law enforcement and court personnel exercise their discretion to keep individual youth from entering the court's jurisdiction. This has long been an integral, and largely unstudied, part of the juvenile justice system. Diversion programs began to appear in the 1970s in response to concerns regarding deteriorating conditions in crowded juvenile institutions, federal mandates and funding, and legal action by youth advocates. Diversion programs divert youth from traditional forms of secure detention and confinement into a variety of alternative treatments and modes of supervision. Generally, youth in diversion programs are not wholly removed from the jurisdiction of the juvenile court and its traditional sanctioning powers.

Empirical studies of diversion conducted in the 1970s yielded mixed results: some studies found that recidivism was reduced, others found no positive effects on recidivism, and still others yielded mixed results.[40] More recent studies of diversion have found significant effects in reducing recidivism.[41] More compelling evidence of the efficacy of diversion is found when a diversionary philosophy is embraced on a statewide basis. In 1974, Massachusetts closed its training schools and developed a range of alternative community-based programs and small-scale secure facilities. An initial analysis of statewide data did not indicate lower recidivism rates for community-based clients than for training school offenders, but in areas of Massachusetts where community-based programs were implemented properly, with a diversity of programs available, recidivism among the youth in community-based programs decreased.[42] A later study of the Massachusetts system found that recidivism rates in the state were better than or equal to those in other states studied.[43] Utah closely replicated the Massachusetts example and, after the first year, experienced a significant decline in recidivism among serious and chronic juvenile offenders.[44] The example of Massachusetts suggests that "what works" may not be any one particular alternative program but rather a variety of programs that can be drawn on to meet the different needs of a diverse population of juvenile offenders and their communities.

Intensive Supervision Programs.   ISPs are sometimes only nominally intensive. Some differ very little from traditional supervision, with intermittent contacts and surveillance. Some studies of ISPs find little difference in recidivism rates compared with either traditional probation or confinement,[45] while other studies report lower recidivism rates for program youth or recidivism rates comparable to youth released from confinement, often at a lower cost.[46]

Sontheimer and Goodstein found that intensive supervision and aftercare paid off for serious juvenile offenders in Pennsylvania in that they were less likely to reoffend than offenders who received traditional probation.[47] Studying a North Carolina project, Land and colleagues found that intensive supervision and aftercare reduced future offending more significantly among youth who committed less serious offenses—primarily status offenses (e.g., running away, truancy)—than did traditional supervision. In addition to concerns about the appropriateness of placing status offenders in an intensive supervision program, after 3½ years, researchers also found no long-term difference in subsequent delinquency between youth assigned to intensive supervision and those assigned to traditional supervision.[48] Whether an ISP is linked to appropriate rehabilitation services or is based simply on monitoring and control seems to influence an ISP's chances of success.[49]

Several demonstration ISPs exist, including those in Wayne County, MI, and Lucas County, OH. Barton and Butts conducted a 5-year evaluation of three home-based ISPs in Wayne County, comparing juveniles randomly assigned to the home-based programs with similar groups of youth committed to state institutions. Recidivism rates, measured using official charges and self-report data, were comparable for experimental and control group youth. The latter were more likely to be charged with serious offenses and less likely to be charged with status offenses than the former. The controls were also likely to reoffend more quickly after release than the youth assigned to an ISP.[50]

Wiebush conducted a similar study in Lucas County, OH. This ISP involved small caseloads, frequent contacts with offenders, mandatory community service, involvement in treatment services, and control measures such as random drug tests and curfews. Wiebush compared youth in an ISP with those paroled after release from a Department of Youth Services (DYS) facility. Both groups registered fairly high recidivism rates within 18 months of release—82 percent for the ISP youth and 83 percent for the DYS youth. No significant differences existed between the groups in rates for felony, misdemeanor, or status offense charges, but the ISP youth were significantly more likely to be charged with technical violations of probation/parole.[51]

An example of a successful intensive probation program that includes a wide range of services and programs for youth and their families is the Tarrant County Advocate Program-North (TCAP) in Texas. Started in November 1994, TCAP is funded by Tarrant County Juvenile Services. Approximately 50 youth at a time participate in the 4–6-month program, which serves an average of 210 youth per year. Most are male (95 percent) and Hispanic (49 percent) or white (47 percent), and approximately 80 percent are involved with gangs. TCAP uses paid mentors or advocates to link youth and their families with community-based services. These advocates contact the families three or four times per week, tailoring the program to fit individual family needs. Program activities include counseling, job training, subsidized youth employment, vocational training, anger management classes, tutoring, community service restitution projects, character development courses, and parent education classes. During 2002, TCAP served 527 youth and their families; 385 families completed the program. Of these youth, 96 percent were successfully maintained in the community or were diverted from out-of-home placement or commitment to the Texas Youth Commission.[52]

For additional information, contact:
Belinda Hampton, Director
Tarrant County Advocate Program-North
112 NW. 24th Street, Suite 118
Fort Worth, TX 76106
817-625-4185
817-625-4187 (fax)

Community-Based Treatment and Therapy. Multisystemic therapy (MST) has been introduced in at least 25 locations in the United States and Canada. As of 1998, more than $10 million has been spent researching its effectiveness. Designed to address multiple factors linked to juvenile antisocial and illegal behaviors, MST may be appropriate for youth with serious behavior disorders, including violent and chronic offenders who might otherwise be confined. MST youth remain at home and receive treatment focused on their interpersonal, peer, family, and school problems and needs. One goal is to promote parental supervision and authority. A review of research evaluating MST programs in a number of southern states showed decreased rates of recidivism among violent and chronic juvenile offenders.[53] Available literature suggests that MST is one of the most effective treatments.[54]

Studies of violent and chronic juvenile offenders find that MST programs register between 25 and 70 percent reductions in rates of rearrest and are also linked to decreases in youth's mental health problems and improvements in family functioning.[55] MST has been evaluated in multiple well-designed clinical trials. These studies, conducted in Memphis, TN, and South Carolina, show that MST participation can have significant positive effects on juvenile offenders' problem behavior (including conduct problems, anxiety withdrawal, immaturity, and socialized aggression), family relations, and self-reported offenses immediately after treatment. Fifty-nine weeks after referral, MST youth had slightly more than half as many new arrests than control group youth, spent an average of 73 fewer days incarcerated in juvenile justice facilities, and showed reductions in aggression with peers. After nearly 2½ years, MST youth were half as likely to be rearrested as control group youth.[56]

One promising MST program is the Family and Neighborhood Services (FANS) project in South Carolina. Operating out of a community mental health center, the project is based on the principle that multiple types of interventions (family, community, school, etc.) are needed for juvenile offenders. FANS assigned small caseloads to therapists who worked with juveniles and their families for an average of 4 months. Caseworkers had frequent, often daily, contact with these families. Juveniles in the program had substantial offense histories, averaging 3.5 arrests and 9.5 weeks of confinement prior to program entry. In evaluating FANS, Henggeler, Melton, and Smith compared program youth with control group youth who were on normal probation and had similar offense histories. More than a year after the project began, significant differences were found between the FANS and control groups in the following areas, among others: absence of rearrest (FANS: 58 percent; control: 38 percent) and subsequent confinement (FANS: 20 percent; control: 68 percent). In addition, FANS youth experienced increased family cohesion and reduced aggression with peers, and the FANS program was judged cost effective, at about a fifth the cost of institutional placement.[57]

MST is a model program of the OJJDP-funded Blueprints for Violence Prevention project.[58]

For additional information, contact:

Marshall E. Swenson
Manager of Program Development
MST Services
710 J. Dodds Boulevard
Mt. Pleasant, SC 29464
843-856-8226
843-856-8227
marshall.swenson@mstservices.com
www.mstservices.com
or
Scott Henggeler, Ph.D.
Family Services Research Center
Department of Psychiatry and Behavioral Sciences
Medical University of South Carolina
171 Ashley Avenue
Charleston, SC 29425
843-876-1800
843-876-1808 (fax)
henggesw@musc.edu

Residential Treatment.   Community residential centers provide 24-hour supervision of offenders, usually nonviolent offenders. Studies in the 1970s of group homes found that they either performed better or no worse than state institutions in reducing recidivism. However, Lipsey and Wilson's review of the literature found that teaching family homes (where a small number of delinquents live with supervising adults who focus on modifying behaviors) were effective in reducing recidivism. This type of program was one of only two interventions out of 83 studied shown to be consistently effective in reducing recidivism among institutionalized youth. Teaching family homes produced an approximately 30–35 percent reduction in recidivism rates (juveniles not receiving treatment had a recidivism rate of 50 percent).[59]

Treatment foster care (TFC) programs use adult mentors and non-delinquent peers to isolate delinquent youth from the negative influences of criminally involved peers. Youth receive treatment and intensive supervision at home, in school, and in the community. TFC also provides services to the youth's biological family with the ultimate goal of family reunification. TFC programs target youth with serious and chronic histories of delinquent behavior who are at risk of confinement. Evaluations have demonstrated that, compared with control group youth, TFC youth spent 60 percent fewer days in confinement over a 12-month period, ran away from the program three times less often (on average), and used drugs less often.[60]

Another model program is VisionQuest. Founded in 1973, Vision-Quest is a national program through which serious juvenile offenders spend several months in outdoor programs, such as wilderness camps, followed by 5 months in a residential home in the community. The group home component prepares youth for reintegration into their families and communities by formulating education goals, improving relationships with family members, and establishing plans for the future. As a multidimensional program, it is not possible to separate the effects of the outdoor program from the group home experience. Greenwood and Turner evaluated San Diego, CA's VisionQuest by comparing program youth with offenders who had been incarcerated in a county correctional institution.[61] Although the VisionQuest group contained more serious offenders than the control group, offenders in the former were less likely to be rearrested during the year after release (55 percent versus 71 percent). After controlling for differences in group characteristics, the VisionQuest group was about half as likely to reoffend as the previously incarcerated group.

For additional information, contact:
VisionQuest National, Ltd.
600 North Swan Road
P.O. Box 12906
Tucson, AZ 85732
520-881-3950
visionquest@vq.com
www.vq.com

Common Characteristics of Promising and Effective Program Initiatives

The existing body of research suggests that, overall, community-based alternatives to secure detention and long-term confinement of juvenile offenders tend to be at least as successful in reducing recidivism as traditional detention and confinement. The literature evaluating various alternatives is uneven and mixed, but some general conclusions can be drawn regarding programs that appear to produce positive results.

The most successful programs are based on interventions that are intensive (involving frequent contacts with offenders), sustained (involving continuous monitoring for a substantial period of time), holistic (covering several aspects of the juvenile's life), and linked to serious rehabilitative services.[62] Krisberg and Howell's survey of research concluded that "alternatives to secure confinement for serious and chronic juveniles are at least as effective in suppressing recidivism as incarceration, but are considerably less costly to operate." They identified nine studies of community-based alternatives to confinement that appear to demonstrate that such alternatives perform well in reducing recidivism. However, only three of these studies used randomized experimental designs.[63]

By contrast, programs that are unsuccessful in reducing recidivism include deterrence programs such as boot camps and "shock" probation programs (e.g., Scared Straight), and individual or group counseling sessions that lack clear plans to address offenders' problems.[64] MacKenzie found a preponderance of evidence showing that the boot camp and shock types of deterrence programs either did not affect subsequent offending or actually increased recidivism. Similarly, most wilderness programs for juveniles have not been shown to effectively reduce recidivism.[65]

Results are mixed for intensive supervision, home confinement, and community residential programs: their success depends on the inclusion of appropriate rehabilitative services. Structured rehabilitative treatments focused on specific skills and behaviors appear to have beneficial effects regardless of where they take place.

Lipsey's meta-analysis of 443 studies of juvenile programs (both inside correctional institutions and in community-based environments) found that treatment programs that were employment- or behavior-oriented and that provided multimodal treatment were the most successful. His analysis also indicated that rehabilitative treatments in community settings reduced recidivism more effectively than treatments in custodial institutions, though Lipsey notes that further research is needed to sort out possible confounding factors. Lipsey classified studies into several "treatment modality" categories and statistically evaluated their effectiveness in reducing recidivism. Following are the categories in order of effectiveness, with the estimated percentage of recidivism rates for treatment and control groups, respectively:[66]

- Employment (32/50).
- Multimodal (38/50).
- Behavioral (38/50).
- Skill oriented (40/50).
- Community residential (42/50).
- Release, probation/parole (45/50).
- Reduced caseload, probation/parole (46/50).
- Restitution, probation/parole (46/50).
- Individual counseling (46/50).
- Group counseling (47/50).
- Other enhancement, probation/parole (47/50).
- Family counseling (49/50).
- Vocational training (59/50).
- Deterrence programs (62/50).

Lipsey and Wilson conducted an updated 1998 meta-analysis of 117 programs targeting serious offenders but found no significant differences in the effectiveness of treatment programs based in the community and those operating within institutions. However, this does not undermine Lipsey's earlier finding regarding the possible benefits of community-based alternatives because he includes within the "institutional" category residential treatment centers, group homes, and camps in addition to more traditional correctional facilities.[67]

Among the interventions for noninstitutionalized serious offenders, interpersonal skills training, individual counseling, and behavioral programs have consistently shown strong positive effects in reducing recidivism. Multiple service programs and restitution ordered as the sole condition of parole/probation were less effective. Wilderness/challenge programs, early release from probation/parole, deterrence, and vocational programs were clearly ineffective. The effectiveness of academic programs, advocacy casework, and family counseling was unclear. Based on the 1998 analysis, recidivism figures for the most successful programs, compared with recidivism rates among the control group, were as follows:[68]

- Individual counseling (28/50).
- Interpersonal skills (29/50).
- Behavioral programs (30/50).
- Multiple services (36/50).
- Employment (39/50).

Some important caveats should be borne in mind when evaluating findings in the literature on alternatives to incarceration, particularly with regard to reported recidivism rates for traditional correctional versus alternative programs. Many of the alternative programs, such as intensive supervision and day reporting, may result in greater scrutiny of offenders and, hence, higher rates of reported recidivism. This might account for the lack of significant differences found in some studies between these programs and more traditional approaches. Higher or similar recidivism rates for youth in alternative programs compared with youth in traditional detention and confinement may be, at least in part, a "program effect" rather than a substantive program weakness. For example, because ISPs impose greater supervision and often more constraints than traditional forms of probation, participating offenders have a greater number of technical violations and thus return to correctional institutions. When combined with treatment programs and other services, however, evidence exists that recidivism is reduced.[69]

Another important issue is the extent to which program participants have been selected appropriately according to an objective assessment of risk and needs. As noted throughout this document, the way in which offenders are assessed and targeted has everything to do with the extent to which programs will produce quality outcomes and whether their cost effectiveness can be demonstrated. Unfortunately, not all alternative programs utilize quality risk assessment and classification systems, leaving them vulnerable to competing theories about the reasoning behind the outcomes produced. For example, if an ISP is determined to be effective in reducing recidivism but does not document the proper selection of program participants, it could be argued that the program simply accepted offenders who were not at high risk of reoffending to begin with. Thus, program integrity, and the quality and usefulness of outcome evaluations, depends on the certainty with which the program was delivered to its intended target population. The success of alternative programs rests on the careful selection of appropriate clients (via risk and needs assessment) and the delivery of sound programming that responds to the constellation of needs for services and supervision that individual youth present.

Conclusion

Despite recent decreases in juvenile crime, many jurisdictions continue to struggle with crowding in their detention and secure confinement facilities. In addition to the negative impact of crowding on the facility's ability to deliver quality programming and to maintain safety and security, it is quite clear that many youth do not require secure detention or confinement to ensure their appearance in court or to prevent future reoffending. To reduce their reliance on these types of programs, jurisdictions must develop and use objective assessment tools and make available a continuum of evidence-based programs.

Current literature offers insight into the types of programs shown to be most effective in deterring juvenile crime and in addressing the root causes of delinquency. Most of these do not feature secure custodial settings but instead work with youth in the communities in which they live, go to school, and work. Further, the use of objective classification and risk assessment instruments at various decision points in the juvenile justice system has been shown to lead to the appropriate alternative placement of juvenile offenders without compromising public safety. These reforms can be achieved by several methods. Whether through new program initiatives or legislation-, administrative-, or litigation-based reforms, each jurisdiction bears the responsibility for enhancing its programmatic alternatives to meet the needs of the youth it serves.

Notes

[1] Arthur, L. 2001. "Ten ways to reduce detention populations." *Juvenile and Family Court Journal* 52(1):29–36.

[2] Harms, P. 2003. *Detention in Delinquency Cases, 1990–1999*. Fact Sheet. Washington, DC: U.S. Department of Justice, Office of Justice Programs, Office of Juvenile Justice and Delinquency Prevention.

[3] Puzzanchera, C. 2003. *Juvenile Court Placement of Adjudicated Youth, 1990–1999*. Washington, DC: U.S. Department of Justice, Office of Justice Programs, Office of Juvenile Justice and Delinquency Prevention.

[4] Sickmund, M. 2002. *Juvenile Residential Facility Census, 2000: Selected Findings*. Washington, DC: U.S. Department of Justice, Office of Justice Programs, Office of Juvenile Justice and Delinquency Prevention.

[5] Ibid.

[6] Wasserman, G., Ko, S., and McReynolds, L. 2004. *Assessing the Mental Health Status of Youth in Juvenile Justice Settings*. Washington, DC: U.S. Department of Justice, Office of Justice Programs, Office of Juvenile Justice and Delinquency Prevention; Mears, D. 2001. "Critical challenges in addressing the mental health needs of juvenile offenders." *Justice Policy Journal* 1(1):41–61.

[7] Krisberg, B. 1997. *The Impact of the Juvenile Justice System on Serious, Violent and Chronic Juvenile Offenders*. San Francisco, CA: National Council on Crime and Delinquency; Winner, L., Lanza-Kaduce, L., Bishop, D., and Frazier, C. 1997. "The transfer of juveniles to criminal courts: Reexamining recidivism rates over the long term." *Crime and Delinquency* 43(4):548–563; Fagan, J. 1996. "The comparative advantage of juvenile versus criminal court sanctions on recidivism among adolescent felony offenders." *Law and Policy* 18(1 and 2):77–113; Wiebush, R., Baird, C., Krisberg, B., and Onek, D. 1995. "Risk assessment and classification for serious, violent, and chronic juvenile offenders." In J. Howell, B. Krisberg, D. Hawkins, and J. Wilson (Eds.). *A Sourcebook: Serious, Violent, and Chronic Juvenile Offenders*. Thousand Oaks, CA: Sage Publications.

[8] For a review of these studies see Howell, J. C. 1995. *Guide for Implementing the Comprehensive Strategy for Serious, Violent and Chronic Juvenile Offenders*. Washington, DC: U.S. Department of Justice, Office of Justice Programs, Office of Juvenile Justice and Delinquency Prevention.

[9] Ibid.

[10] Coates, R., Miller, A., and Ohlin, L. 1978. *Diversity in a Youth Correctional System*. Cambridge, MA: Ballinger; Krisberg, B., Austin, J., and Steele, P. 1989. *Unlocking Juvenile Corrections*. San Francisco, CA: National Council on Crime and Delinquency.

[11] Read the Foundation's *Pathways to Juvenile Detention Reform* for guidance on planning, executing, promoting, and sustaining juvenile detention reform (Annie E. Casey Foundation. 2000. *Pathways to Juvenile Detention Reform*. Baltimore, MD: Annie E. Casey Foundation).

[12] Ibid.

[13] Snyder, H., and Sickmund, M. 1999. *Juvenile Offenders and Victims: 1999 National Report*. Washington, DC: U.S. Department of Justice, Office of Justice Programs, Office of Juvenile Justice and Delinquency Prevention.

[14] Austin, J., and Krisberg, B. 1982. "Unmet promise of alternatives to incarceration." *Crime and Delinquency* 28(3):374–409; Austin, J. 2001. *Controlling Prison Population Growth Through Alternatives to Incarceration: Lessons Learned From BJA's Corrections Options Demonstration Program*. Washington, DC: U.S. Department of Justice, Office of Justice Programs, Bureau of Justice Assistance.

[15] These categories have been shown to have statistically significant relationships to recidivism among juvenile offenders. See, e.g., Hardyman, P. 1999. *Georgia Department of Juvenile Justice External Classification System Users Manual*. Washington, DC: The Institute on Crime, Justice and Corrections at The George Washington University; Johnson, K., Wagner, D., and Matthews, T. 2002. *Missouri Juvenile Risk Assessment Re-Validation Report*. Madison, WI: National Council on Crime and Delinquency.

[16] Lubow, B. 1999. "Successful strategies for reforming juvenile detention." *Federal Probation* 63(2):16–24.

[17] Stanfield, R. 2000. *Pathways to Juvenile Detention Reform Overview*. Baltimore, MD: Annie E. Casey Foundation.

[18] Ibid. Cook County changed the wording on some items and increased or decreased the number of points awarded for various items to ensure that scores on the instrument were statistically associated with risk.

[19] Wiebush, Baird, Krisberg, and Onek, "Risk assessment and classification for serious, violent, and chronic juvenile offenders."

[20] The needs assessment looks for issues requiring long-term treatment, whereas the initial screening typically looks for issues that would put the youth in immediate danger (e.g., suicidal behavior, medical conditions).

[21] Wiebush, Baird, Krisberg, and Onek, "Risk assessment and classification for serious, violent, and chronic juvenile offenders"; Baird, S. C., Sturrs, G., Connelly, H. 1984. *Classification of Juveniles in Corrections—A Model Systems Approach*. Washington, DC: U.S. Department of Justice, Office of Justice Programs, Office of Juvenile Justice and Delinquency Prevention.

[22] Lipsey, M., and Wilson, D. 1998. "Effective intervention for serious juvenile offenders." In R. Loeber and D. Farrington (Eds.). *Serious and Violent Juvenile Offenders*. Thousand Oaks, CA: Sage.

[23] Ibid.

[24] Kihm, R., and Block, J. 1982. "Response to a crisis: Reducing the juvenile detention rate in Louisville, Kentucky." *Juvenile and Family Court Journal* 33(1):37–44.

[25] Ball, R., Huff, C., and Lilly, J. 1988. *House Arrest and Correctional Policy: Doing Time at Home*. Beverly Hills, CA: Sage Publications.

[26] Smykla, J., and Selke, W. 1982. "Impact of home detention: A less restrictive alternative to the detention of juveniles." *Juvenile and Family Court Journal* 33(2):3–9.

[27] Young, T. M., and Pappenfort, D. M. 1979. *Use of Secure Detention for Juveniles and Alternatives to Its Use*. Report. Washington, DC: U.S. Department of Justice, Office of Justice Programs, National Institute of Justice.

[28] Ball, Huff, and Lilly, *House Arrest and Correctional Policy*.

[29] Cohn, A., Biondi, L., Flaim, L. C., Paskowski, M., and Cohn, S. 1997. "Evaluating electronic monitoring programs." *Alternatives to Incarceration* 3(1):16–24.

[30] Roy, S. 1997. "Five years of electronic monitoring of adults and juveniles in Lake County, Indiana." *Journal of Crime and Justice* 20(1):141–160.

[31] Vaughn, J. 1989. "A survey of juvenile electronic monitoring and home confinement programs." *Juvenile and Family Court Journal* 40(4):1–36

[32] Roy, S., and Brown, M. 1995. "Juvenile electronic monitoring program in Lake County, Indiana: An evaluation." In J. Smykla and W. Selke (Eds.). *Intermediate Sanctions: Sentencing in the 1990s*. Cincinnati, OH: Anderson Publishing.

[33] Shelden, R. G. 1999. *Detention Diversion Advocacy: An Evaluation*. Washington, DC: U.S. Department of Justice, Office of Justice Programs, Office of Juvenile Justice and Delinquency Prevention.

[34] Ibid.

[35] See PEPNet's Web site.

[36] Young and Pappenfort, *Use of Secure Detention for Juveniles and Alternatives to Its Use*.

[37] Lubow, "Successful strategies for reforming juvenile detention."

[38] Remaining free of arrest while in the program, not after release.

[39] Figures provided by GCTC and found on the Texas Youth Commission's Web site.

[40] Stanford, R. 1984. "Implementing the multigoal evaluation technique in diversion programs." In S. Decker (Ed.). *Juvenile Justice Policy: Analyzing Trends and Outcomes*. Beverly Hills, CA: Sage; Ezell, M. 1992. "Juvenile diversion: The ongoing search for alternatives." In I. Schwartz (Ed.). *Juvenile Justice and Public Policy*. New York: Lexington.

[41] Rojek, D. 1986. "Juvenile diversion and the potential of inappropriate treatment for offenders." *New England Journal on Criminal and Civil Confinement* 12(2):329–347; Davidson, W., Amdur, R. L., Mitchell, C. M., and Redner, R. 1990. *Alternative Treatments for Troubled Youth: The Case of Diversion from the Justice System*. New York: Plenum Press.

[42] Coates, Miller, and Ohlin, *Diversity in a Youth Correctional System*.

[43] Krisberg, Austin, and Steele, *Unlocking Juvenile Corrections*.

[44] Krisberg, B., and Howell, J. 1998. "The impact of the juvenile justice system and prospects for graduated sanctions in a comprehensive strategy." In R. Loeber and D. Farrington (Eds.). *Serious and Violent Juvenile Offenders*. Thousand Oaks, CA: Sage.

45 Greenwood, P., and Turner, S. 1993. "Evaluation of the Paint Creek Youth Center: A residential program for serious delinquents." *Criminology* 31(2):263–279; Murray, C., and Cox, L. 1979. *Beyond Probation*. Beverly Hills, CA: Sage.

46 Barton, W., and Butts, J. 1990. "Accommodating innovation in a juvenile court." *Criminal Justice Policy Review* 4(2):144–158; Fratto, J., and Hallstrom, D. 1978. "Conditional release and intensive supervision programs." *Juvenile and Family Court Journal* 29(4):29–35; Wiebush, "Juvenile intensive supervision: The impact on felony offenders diverted from institutional placement."

47 Sontheimer, H., and Goodstein, L. 1993. "Evaluation of juvenile intensive aftercare probation." *Justice Quarterly* 10(2):197–227.

48 Land, K., McCall, P., and Parker, K. 1994. "Logistic versus hazards regression analyses in evaluation research: An exposition and application to the North Carolina court counselors' Intensive Protective Supervision Project." *Evaluation Review* 18(4):411–437.

49 MacKenzie, D. 1997. "Criminal justice and crime prevention." In *Preventing Crime: What Works, What Doesn't, What's Promising*. Washington, DC: U.S. Department of Justice, Office of Justice Programs, National Institute of Justice.

50 Barton and Butts, "Accommodating innovation in a juvenile court."

51 Wiebush, "Juvenile intensive supervision: The impact on felony offenders diverted from institutional placement."

52 See Tarrant County's Web site.

53 Henggeler, S. 1997. *Treating Serious Anti-Social Behavior in Youth: The MST Approach*. Washington, DC: U.S. Department of Justice, Office of Justice Programs, Office of Juvenile Justice and Delinquency Prevention.

54 Lipsey and Wilson, "Effective intervention for serious juvenile offenders"; Krisberg and Howell, "The impact of the juvenile justice system and prospects for graduated sanctions in a comprehensive strategy"; Cullen, F., and Gendreau, P. 2000. "Assessing correctional rehabilitation: Policy, practice, and prospects." In J. Horney (Ed.). *Criminal Justice 2000*, vol. 3. Washington, DC: U.S. Department of Justice, Office of Justice Programs, National Institute of Justice, pp. 109–160.

55 Mihalic, S., Irwin, K., Elliott, D., Fagan, A., and Hansen, D. 2001. *Blueprints for Violence Prevention*. Washington, DC: U.S. Department of Justice, Office of Justice Programs, Office of Juvenile Justice and Delinquency Prevention.

56 Henggeler, S., Mihalic, S. F., Rone, L., Thomas, C., and Timmons-Mitchell, J. 1998. "Multisystemic therapy." In D. Elliot (Ed.). *Blueprints for Violence Prevention*. Boulder, CO: Center for the Study and Prevention of Violence, Institute of Behavioral Sciences, University of Colorado at Boulder; Kazdin, A., and Weisz, J. 1998. "Identifying and developing empirically supported child and adolescent treatments." *Journal of Consulting and Clinical Psychology* 66(1):19–36; Thornton, T. N., Craft, C. A., Dahlberg, L. L., Lynch, B. S., and Baer, K. 2000. *Best Practices of Youth Violence Prevention: A Sourcebook for Community Action*. Atlanta, GA: Centers for Disease Control and Prevention, National Center for Injury Prevention and Control.

57 Henggeler, S., Melton, G., and Smith, L. 1992. "Family preservation using multisystemic therapy: An effective alternative to incarcerating serious juvenile offenders." *Journal of Consulting and Clinical Psychology* 60(6):953–961.

58 See Mihalic et al., *Blueprints for Violence Prevention*.

59 Lipsey and Wilson, "Effective intervention for serious juvenile offenders."

60 Chamberlain, P., and Mihalic, S. 1998. *Blueprints for Violence Prevention. Book Eight: Multidimensional Treatment Foster Care*. Boulder, CO: Center for the Study and Prevention of Violence.

61 Greenwood, P., and Turner, S. 1987. *The VisionQuest Program: An Evaluation*. Santa Monica, CA: RAND. Although more recent data were unavailable at the time this chapter was written, a description of VisionQuest was included here because the program remains one of the most well-known and best regarded.

62 Dryfoos, J. 1990. *Adolescents at Risk: Prevalence and Prevention*. New York: Oxford University Press; MacKenzie, "Criminal justice and crime prevention."

[63] Krisberg and Howell, "The impact of the juvenile justice system and prospects for graduated sanctions in a comprehensive strategy," p. 360.

[64] Andrews, D., Zinger, I., Hoge, R., Bonta, J., Gendreau, P., and Cullen, F. 1990. "Does correctional treatment work? A clinically relevant and psychologically informed meta-analysis." *Criminology* 28(3):369–404; Dryfoos, *Adolescents at Risk*; Jensen, G., and Rojek, D. 1998. *Delinquency and Youth Crime* (3rd ed.). Long Grove, IL: Waveland Press; Lipsey, M. 1992. "Juvenile delinquency treatment: A meta-analytic inquiry into the variability of effects." In D. Rosenbaum (Ed.). *Community Crime Prevention: Does it Work?* New York: Russell Sage Foundation; Lipsey and Wilson, "Effective intervention for serious juvenile offenders"; MacKenzie, "Criminal justice and crime prevention."

[65] MacKenzie, "Criminal justice and crime prevention."

[66] Lipsey, "Juvenile delinquency treatment."

[67] Lipsey and Wilson, "Effective intervention for serious juvenile offenders."

[68] Ibid.

[69] Parent, D., Byrne, J., Tsarfaty, V., Valade, L., and Esselman, J. 1995. *Day Reporting Centers*. Washington, DC: U.S. Department of Justice, Office of Justice Programs, National Institute of Justice.

10

Innovative Programs for Girl Offenders

Meda Chesney-Lind

Girls on the economic and political margins, particularly those who find their way into the juvenile justice system, share many problems with their male counterparts. They are likely to be poor, to be from disrupted and violent families, and to have trouble in school. In addition, girls confront problems unique to their sex, notably sexual abuse, sexual assault, dating violence, depression, unplanned pregnancy, and adolescent motherhood. Both their experience of the problems they share with boys and the additional special problems that they face are conditioned by their gender, as well as by their class and race. Specifically, because families are the source of many of the serious problems that girls face, solutions must take into account that some girls may not be able to stay safely at home.[1]

Background

There is a tremendous shortage of information on programs that have been proven effective in work with girls. Indeed, many studies that have evaluated particular approaches do not deal with special gender issues, and frequently programs do not even serve girls. In addition, programs that have been carefully evaluated are often set in training schools (clearly not the ideal place to try any particular strategy). Finally, careful evaluation of most programs tends to show that even the most determined efforts to intervene and help often show very poor results. Of course, the last two points may well be related; programs set in closed institutional settings are clearly at a disadvantage and, as a consequence, tend to be less effective.[2] Readers might also want a more extensive con-

Portions of this chapter were taken from Meda Chesney-Lind and Randall G. Shelden, *Girls, Delinquency and Juvenile Justice* (3rd ed.), 2004, with permission from the publisher, Thomson/Wadsworth, Inc.

sideration of promising community-based programs for girls, but unfortunately these have been few and far between.

While we wish we could publish a list of programs that have been empirically documented to work with girls, that goal is still a bit beyond reach. However, the last decade of the twentieth century did show remarkable movement toward an understanding that gender-responsive and girl-focused programming is necessary. The Minnesota Women's Fund noted that the most frequent risk factors for girls and boys differ, and that for girls the list includes emotional stress, physical and sexual abuse, negative body image, disordered eating, suicide, and pregnancy. For boys the list included alcohol, polydrug use, accidental injury, and delinquency.[3] Though clearly not all girls at risk will end up in the juvenile justice system, this gendered examination of youth problems sets a standard for examination of delinquency prevention and intervention programs.

Alder points out that serving girls effectively will require different and innovative strategies because "young men tend to be more noticeable and noticed than young women."[4] When girls go out, they tend to move in smaller groups; there are greater proscriptions against girls "hanging out"; and they may be justly fearful of being on the streets at night. Finally, girls have many more domestic expectations than their boy counterparts, and these may keep them confined to their homes. Alder notes that this may be a particular issue for immigrant girls.

There is some encouraging news: girl-serving organizations (such as the YWCA and Girls Inc.) have begun to realize their responsibility for girls who are in the juvenile justice system. Recent reviews of promising programs for girls indicate that programs are emerging that specifically target the housing and employment needs of youth, while also providing them with the specific skills they will need to survive on their own.[5] These often include a built-in caseworker/service broker, as well as counseling components. Clearly, many girls will require specialized counseling to recover from the ravages of sexual and physical victimization, but the research cautions that approaches that rely simply on the provision of counseling services are not likely to succeed.

Programs must also be scrutinized to ensure that they are culturally specific as well as gender specific. As increasing numbers of girls of color are drawn into the juvenile justice system (and bootstrapped into correctional settings) while their white counterparts are deinstitutionalized, there is a need for programs to be rooted in specific cultures. Because it is clear that girls of color have different experiences of their gender, as well as different experiences with the dominant institutions in the society, programs to divert and deinstitutionalize must be shaped by the unique developmental issues confronting minority girls, as well as build on the specific cultural resources available in ethnic communities.[6]

This review also indicates, though, that innovative programs must receive the same sort of stable funding generally accorded their more traditional/institutional counterparts (which are generally far less innovative and flexible). A careful reading of the descriptions of novel programs reveals that many rely on federal funds or private foundation grants; the same reading reveals how pitifully few survive for any length of time. To survive and thrive, they must be able to count on stable funding. The recent pressure exerted by Congress on states to conduct an inventory of programs that are specifically focused on girls may begin to exert more pressure on those receiving federal funding to, in the words of Abigail Adams over two centuries ago, "remember the ladies."[7]

Programs must also be continually scrutinized to guarantee that they are serving as genuine alternatives to girls' incarceration, rather than simply functioning to extend the social control of girls. There is a tendency for programs serving girls to become more "security" oriented in response to girls' propensity to run away. Indeed, a component of successful programming for girls must be continuous monitoring of closed institutions. If nothing else can be learned from a careful reading of the rocky history of nearly two decades of efforts to decarcerate youth, it is an appreciation of how fraught these efforts are with difficulty and how easily their gains can be eroded.

Finally, much more work needs to be done to support the fundamental needs of girls on the margin. We must do a better job of recognizing that they need less "programming" and more support in order to live on their own, since many cannot or will not go back home again. Before we review some of the most promising programs for girls, we need to discuss some of the most persistent problems of designing and implementing such programs.

Shortchanging Girls: Patterns within Youth-Serving Programs

Because the majority of delinquency prevention programs are co-ed, the specific needs of girls are either shortchanged or simply ignored because of the population of boys who outnumber them. Programs that are single-sex within the juvenile justice system provide far more options for boys than for girls. In fact, a list of "potentially promising programs" identified by the Office of Juvenile Justice and Delinquency Prevention cites 24 programs specifically for boys in contrast to only 2 programs specifically for girls.[8] Ironically, one program geared for incarcerated teen fathers has no counterpart for incarcerated teen mothers.

Often programs tend to miss the "at-risk" years for girls. A comprehensive survey of 112 individual youth-oriented programs (for both delinquent and nondelinquent youth) showed that less than 8 percent provided services to girls between the ages of 9 and 15, the crucial determining years of adolescence and the years when self-esteem plummets.

Rather, services and programs tended to serve girls younger than the age of 9 and those between 14 and 21 years of age.[9]

Moreover, the few programs available for girls often tend to address single issues, such as teen pregnancy and mothering, although occasionally other problems like substance abuse or gang behavior are included. This pattern is largely a result of issue-specific funding initiatives, but it means that girls' often interconnected and overlapping problems get ignored. Similarly, programs tend to be more intervention oriented ("reactive") rather than preventive, concentrating more on girls who are already in trouble than on girls who are at risk of getting into trouble.[10]

Unfortunately, at-risk youth possess high degrees of overlap in services needed; thus, girls who are drug addicts may also have histories of being abused, suicidal tendencies, academic difficulties, and/or be in need of gainful employment. Patterns of multiple service needs are unfortunately increasing just as public funding to meet these needs has proportionately decreased. Ultimately, at-risk youth's multiple needs point to the necessity of more comprehensive programming than is available within any single program or system. Some research has suggested the need for inter-agency, inter-disciplinary collaborations to address these needs.[11]

The Ms. Foundation for Women found that most programs for girls typically respond to the outcome or symptoms of girls' distress, rather than addressing the underlying structural problems of inequality and poverty that affect so many girls. Also, few programs address the special problems that girls of color experience. Likewise, programs geared specifically to the needs of lesbian and bisexual girls and those with disabilities are virtually nonexistent. In general, programs do not provide services within a context that acknowledges the realities of sexism, racism, classism, and heterosexism as problematic forces in their lives. Thus, little is offered in the way of giving girls the information and support needed to fathom and combat these mechanisms of multiple marginality.[12]

Are Gender-Specific Programs Necessary?

Despite the mounting evidence that girls have rather severe problems, youth programs have in the main ignored the needs of girls (or assumed that programs crafted to meet the needs of boys will also work for girls); some would contend that the jury is still out on the need for gender-specific programming. Indeed, there appears to be a belief in some quarters that within the juvenile justice system, gender-specific programming is not necessary. In a General Accounting Office study, the results of a national survey of chief probation officers were reported (the chiefs are mostly males, we should note). The report noted that though these juvenile court officials felt that "insufficient facilities and services were available to status offenders," they also believed that status offenders do not need gender-specific services, "except for gynecological services and pre-natal care." They also reported that these same high-level court administrators did not feel that "any significant gender bias concerns" emerged in the treatment of female and male status offenders.[13]

This perspective on girls' delinquency, and lack of interest in the special needs of girls, is both ironic and yet consistent with the juvenile justice system's checkered past with reference to the treatment of girls. Although currently the court is embracing and valorizing equal treatment largely as a way to justify current practices and avoid change, early court history reveals just the reverse. Indeed, a careful reading of the situations of girl and women offenders reveals that whether we are in a legal and social environment that supports "equal treatment" or one that argues for "special treatment," girls and women tend to be losers.

Programming as if Girls Mattered: Getting Past Girls Watching Boys Play Sports

As we have already noted, programming for girls in the juvenile justice system needs to take into consideration their unique situations and their special problems. Traditional delinquency treatment approaches have been shaped mostly by commonsense assumptions about what youths—mostly boys—need. Sometimes girls will benefit from these assumptions, sometimes they will not. "For years people have assumed that all you have to do to make a program designed for boys work for girls is to paint the walls pink and take out the urinals."[14]

Lack of Validated Gender–Specific Programs: Programming and the "Forgotten Few"

A good snapshot of where we are nationally on girls' issues and programming can be seen from a brief overview of the activities of 23 states that successfully applied for challenge grant funds from the Office of Juvenile Justice and Delinquency Prevention. This review indicates that most states are in the very early stages of understanding the needs of girls in their systems. As a result, of the states where information was available (21), virtually all (95%) used some of these funds to gather data on the characteristics and needs of the girls in their systems. Slightly over a third (38%) funded a specific new program for girls or expanded an existing program that seemed successful. (We emphasize "seemed" to make the point that many a program is started because, from someone's perspective, it "feels" good or they have a "gut feeling" it will work; many continue, with no evidence of effectiveness, because it "seems to work.") About a quarter (28%) of the states held either a conference and/or undertook special training on girls' needs, and slightly under a quarter (23%) formed special committees. Finally, only ten percent of the states indicated that their committees were involved in the crafting of specific legislation and/or system policy changes.[15]

Among other needs that programs for girls should address are the following: dealing with the physical and sexual abuse in girls' lives (from parents, boyfriends, pimps, and others); the threat of HIV/AIDS; dealing with pregnancy and motherhood; drug and alcohol dependency; confronting family problems; vocational and career counseling; managing stress; and developing a sense of efficacy and empowerment. Many of these needs are universal and should be part of programs for all young people, but they are particularly important for young women.[16]

A good example of the synergy between understanding the dimensions of girls' problems and the crafting of evaluations of programs with this information in mind comes from the work of Sibylle Artz and Ted Riecken. Their review of the outcomes of thirteen individual antiviolence initiatives in Canadian schools shows the importance of focusing on gender and the desirability of establishing interventions that are gender specific. Moreover, their research reminds us that both girls and boys have a gender, and that both could benefit from attention to the specific ways that masculinity and femininity work in the lives of young people. Employing pre- and posttests of self-reported violence of both student and parent participants as well as school-based data on the same, the researchers quickly concluded that "one size does not fit all" in violence prevention.[17]

Specifically, the researchers found that "boys are far less likely than girls to participate in student groups that promote violence prevention" and that "boys are less likely than girls to adopt the anti-violence messages of their schools' violence prevention programs."[18] Girls, even those with a history of violence, were more likely to see violence as problematic and to change as a result of intervention (particularly interventions based on skills-based programs and positive reinforcement). General "consciousness raising" was found to be ineffective with both sexes. Finally, males tended to be reached only when men participate in violence prevention efforts and when fathers (not mothers) condemn bullying.[19]

Violence

Even though girls were being reached by the messages in the generic curriculum, the researchers noted that antiviolence curricula needed to be expanded to include sexual and domestic abuse because virtually no programs cover these issues. Other work by these researchers, based on in-depth interviews as well as self-report data, indicate that violent girls were much more likely than nonviolent girls to have histories of abuse and current experiences with abusive boyfriends. Girls' violence often tends to be a mimicking of the male violence in their lives (they come from homes with dominating and abusive fathers). Girls fight with other girls either to excite boys and get their attention, or they fight in order to be seen to be as good as boys.[20]

Finally, Artz concludes that the prevention of girls' violence means recognizing that "the two kinds of violence against women, male-to-female and female-to-female, have their origins in the same belief systems." That is, a system of sexual inequality that valorizes male violence as a means of exerting power and influence and has girls growing up "seeing themselves through the eyes of males."[21]

Running Away, Education, and Trauma

Another important issue unique to girls is that of running away. Any successful program for girls must address their needs for safe housing, and in some instances, legal emancipation. Economic support for these choices is also clearly desirable and available in some parts of Canada and Australia, but sadly unlikely given the current hostility in the United States to young women living independently.[22]

At-risk girls have severe emotional problems, and significant numbers may have educational disabilities.[23] Thus, programming for female adolescents should invariably address academic difficulties. The educational neglect of young minority women, particularly African Americans, must be addressed.[24] Likewise, any program that encourages girls to succeed in the traditionally male-dominated subjects of math and science is likely to bolster self-esteem, school performance, and even career prospects.[25]

Many at-risk girls have had histories of trauma, which set the stage for substantial problems with depression, self-image, and attempted suicide. One researcher stated the gender bias in our society very succinctly by noting that "no one will demand and obtain intervention for her because in our country it is more often slashed tires, not slashed wrists, that are noticed."[26] Indeed, automobiles (and their parts) often seem to be more valued than human beings, especially women. Programming for young women should address, without labeling them as pathological, histories of sexual and physical abuse. Girls' problems with substance abuse, which are substantial, should be informed by the understanding that often, for girls, polydrug use is a way of self-medicating.[27]

Peers and the Importance of Age

Negative peer influence is one of the major causative factors in delinquency. Most girls join negative peer groups or even gangs so that they feel like they "belong" and are accepted somewhere.[28] Indeed, almost half (45%) of girls in the juvenile justice system report feeling little or no love or acceptance while growing up.[29] Consequently, girls, particularly delinquent girls, need the positive influence and support of new peers and adult mentors that will encourage them to break or renegotiate bonds with people who have been harmful influences. Thus, ready access to a broad network of adult mentors and peer counselors who are sensitive to girls' issues and problems should be made available.

Girls seem to prize connectedness and relationships with other people more than boys do.[30] In this respect, a relational approach that emphasizes trust and relationship building with positive female role models would be highly beneficial. However, trust can only be developed when girls perceive their programs as being "safe" spaces where they do not have to fear condemnation. This entails creating an atmosphere that allows girls to express their thoughts and emotions freely and appropriately.

Similarly, program staff must be affirmative by acknowledging the worth of each girl despite her attitude or background. Girls' programs also need to create separate time and space for girls, apart from boys, so that issues related to sexism will not be overshadowed by boys' more disruptive behavior.

Programs for at-risk girls should ideally begin before adolescence, by age 9 or 10, and continue through the rest of adolescence. This is consistent with research that suggests that earlier preventive approaches are the most effective.[31] Likewise, programs, particularly those that are issue specific, need to provide transition and after-care services that support young women in maintaining the progress they have made.

Recreation: Beyond Girls Watching Boys Play Sports

Many at-risk girls may engage in delinquent behavior simply because there is little else to occupy their free time. Unfortunately, all too often these programs end up being "girls watching boys play sports." Structured recreation should consist of varied activities, including sports, leadership opportunities, programs and projects, arts and crafts, community service, ethnic and culturally oriented activities, dances, and social events. These provide a great way for girls to learn new skills, develop responsibility, increase self-esteem and self-confidence, befriend other girls, and, most importantly, have fun. Additionally, time and energy spent on rewarding activities dissuades girls from wanting to engage in delinquent or self-defeating behavior in the first place. Girls already embedded within the juvenile justice system frequently state that had they had opportunities to engage in meaningful, interesting activities, they probably would not have fallen into the system. In the words of one girl at the Hawaii Youth Correctional Facility, having "something to do, like a job or something" could have helped her to be delinquency-free. Likewise, another girl in the same facility stated that "if you're smart and strong enough and keep busy, you can stay out of trouble."[32]

Programs should invariably work to empower girls. This entails building on girls' innate strengths, skills, and creativity to develop their voices and their abilities to assert themselves. In this respect, girls need to be able to identify positively with themselves and each other. They also need the opportunity to aid in the design, implementation, and evaluation of programs that are geared for their benefit. Similarly, programs should continually reevaluate their effectiveness and remain flexible to change.

Quality programming for at-risk girls entails a commitment to positive youth development. To this end, young women, rather than being in need of "fixing," need to be "empowered" through effective prevention- and intervention-oriented approaches. This ultimately entails respecting female development processes and celebrating the uniqueness of girls and women.

In the remaining pages of this chapter we will provide brief summaries of some specific programs that have been established during the past couple of decades to address at-risk girls.

Programs for Girls

In the pages that follow we rely heavily on several sources that provide reviews of programs for girls, especially *Prevention and Parity: Girls in Juvenile Justice.*[33] Few of these programs have been subjected to rigorous evaluation, so as you read, judge elements of the programs against what we currently know about effective and ineffective strategies for working with troubled girls. The section concludes by suggesting some policy implications that emerge from the review.

Children of the Night

Children of the Night is a program begun in 1979 in southern California to aid young prostitutes, the majority of whom are girls who have run away from abusive homes. The current director, Lois Lee, started it while she was a graduate student in sociology at UCLA studying the relationships between prostitutes and their pimps in the Los Angeles area. Lee asked herself, "Why would a girl stand on a street corner and do something deplorable, then give all the money she earned to a pimp?" Soon she began to offer her apartment as a temporary shelter to the young males and females who wanted to escape the life.[34]

Children of the Night rely heavily on volunteers and obtain funding from a variety of sources, including individuals and foundations. The program consists of: (1) a twenty-four-hour hotline (1-800-551-1300) for those who want someone to talk to or to get off the streets and away from pimps; (2) a walk-in center in Hollywood that provides medical aid, clothing, crisis intervention, and referrals for housing, drug counseling, schools, jobs, and foster home placement, among other things; (3) free professional counseling by volunteer psychologists and psychiatrists; (4) an outreach component whose trained volunteers walk the streets distributing informational materials to potential clients and engaging in on-the-spot counseling; and (5) a "turn-in-a-pimp" component that entails cooperation among the youths, the agency, the police, and the court system (the aim here is to obtain court testimony against pimps to assist in the prosecution of individuals who otherwise might go free because of lack of evidence).

Since the program opened, more than 10,000 girls and boys (roughly 40 percent of the total have been males) have gone through the program, with an estimated 80 percent having been successful (i.e., not returned to the streets). Virtually all had experienced sexual and other forms of abuse within their families. Almost all were under eighteen, the majority under sixteen. About one-third were eligible for existing shelter programs because they had no place to live. Over half came because no other resources were available to them. The most positive feature of the program is its provision of direct, emergency services. Serving as a broker for services, as many programs do, may also be effective, but only if young people are able to access and use the services. The counseling component is clearly sensitive to the abuse backgrounds of the street youth, but is not an adequate substitute for educational and realistic employment programming.

Girls' Detention Advocacy Project

This program is modeled by the Detention Diversion Advocacy Project (DDAP), which is reviewed in article 8 of this book. The program is operated by a San Francisco organization called The Center for Young Women's Development, which was founded in 1993. The mission of this program is stated as follows:

> The Center for Young Women's Development strives to build a safe haven and possibilities for young women who have been in the juvenile justice system, incarcerated, homeless, or adversely affected by poverty. The goal of the Girls' Detention Advocacy Project is to support the women in juvenile detention and help them get out and stay out of the system.[35]

The staff use the center's own special curriculum called "Lift Us Up, Don't Lock Us Down." The program also provides self-advocacy training, leadership development, court accompaniment, mentorship, support groups, legal education, self-care methods, and life skills. As does the larger DDAP program, GDAP staff maintain contact with clients after they are released. Unfortunately there has yet to be an evaluation of this program.[36]

National Programs of Girls Inc.[37]

Girls Inc. recently published a summary of the existing "state of the art" as far as programs for girls are concerned. It begins with a look at its own national program, which sponsors affiliates and outreach programs at more than nine hundred program sites.

Girls Inc. sponsors three types of programs that are most significantly linked to those who are "at risk" of getting into trouble. These programs are offered "through a network of 1,000 sites nationwide and are facilitated by trained professional staff." Funding for the various programs comes from several major foundations, such as the Lilly Endowment, W. K. Kellogg Foundation, Nancy Reagan Foundation, David and Lucile Packard Foundation, Annie E. Casey Foundation, and the W. T. Grant Foundation. Among the programs are the following:

Friendly PEERsuasion. This program provides assistance to help young women avoid substance abuse "by providing accurate information, practicing refusal skills and developing healthy, fun ways to reduce stress and teaching what they have learned to younger children."

Operation SMART. This is a program that helps build skills and interests in science, math, and "relevant technologies" in order to "encourage young women to persist in these areas vital to everyday life and interesting, well-paying careers."

Preventing Adolescent Pregnancy. This program helps girls avoid early pregnancy through fostering communication skills, providing health education, and helping them plan for the future through four age-appropriate components known as "Growing Together," "Will Power/ Won't Power," "Taking Care of Business," and "Health Bridge." The first two of these components have been translated into Spanish. Girls who go through the program assume roles as "peersuaders" for younger girls.

Media Literacy. This unique program helps girls think critically about the power of the media and how manipulative it can be, and especially its effects on girls and women.

Discovery. This program partners girls with women leaders in their communities to develop and practice leadership and advocacy skills and construct community action projects. One of the principal strengths of the program is the opportunity for decision making, taking responsibility, and initiating projects in collaboration with experienced women.

Project Bold. This program helps girls develop strategies for self-defense (including physical techniques) and helps them seek out and talk with caring adults about the problem of violence.

Sporting Chance. Girls benefit if sports become an integral part of their lives. Early participation in sports teaches discipline and cooperation as well as competition. Sporting Chance encourages girls to learn sport skills; increase their coordination, endurance, and strength; to have fun; and to learn about the history of women in sports.

Economic Literacy. This is a program that gets to the heart of one of the most important issues facing any young person, but especially young women—namely, financial concerns. Included in this program (which starts as early as six years of age) are such basic problems as money management, investments, how money affects people both locally and globally, and how to develop skills to be financially self-sufficient.

Local Programs Sponsored by Girls Inc.

A program in Minneapolis known as The City, Inc. Community Intervention for Girls provides a comprehensive range of services, addressing such issues as substance abuse, employability, parenting, and urban poverty. Two specific programs within this grouping include *Kupona Ni'Uhuru* (which means "healing is freedom") and *Oshki Bug* (meaning "new leaf"), both based upon healing practices of African American and Native American cultures. These two cultures represent the majority of girls served by The City, Inc. Included within these programs are alternative schools for girls who cannot attend regular public schools and a group home for those who need more intensive attention.

A program in Baltimore known as the *Female Intervention Team* (FIT) supervises and provides various treatment services for adjudicated delinquent girls or those in need of services. The founder of this program, Marian Daniel, wanted to design a program to "make it look as if girls might want to come." They have an "infant and toddler" program to help young women learn good parenting skills. They also provide family counseling and tutoring, recreation activities, and close monitoring by FIT "case managers" who, by using the "case management approach," are able to provide more intensive services than do regular probation officers.

The *Harriet Tubman Residential Center* in Auburn, New York, is another program sponsored by Girls Inc. and one of the ones that responded to our questionnaire. The girls in this program have been adjudicated in juvenile court. What we find most interesting about this program is that it is research based. That is, the program description includes a review of the literature on the problem of female delinquency in addition to research on developmental theory. Therefore, this program focuses on women's issues and development and tries to offer services that relate to these issues. The program description includes four specific "outcome objectives": (1) self-management (this includes such things as personal hygiene and developing responsibility for one's own physical well-being); (2) relationship building (includes interacting with peers and parents, and developing an understanding of nonviolent methods of solving problems); (3) empowerment and self-direction (focusing on such issues as academics, vocational development, and independent living); and (4) future orientation (includes setting personal goals and a sense of future direction). The program takes into account the differences between the way boys and girls develop and how they view their surrounding world (e.g., boys tend to be "task oriented" whereas girls focus on "building relationships").

The *P.A.C.E. Center for Girls Inc.* (P.A.C.E. stands for Practical, Academic, Cultural, and Educational) is a program located in Jacksonville, Florida. This program is a "gender-sensitive, non-profit, non-residential, community-based program providing comprehensive education and therapeutic intervention services to troubled girls." The program focuses on at-risk girls between the ages of twelve and eighteen. Begun in 1985, it now has been replicated in several other locations, including Bradenton, Orlando, Miami, and Tallahassee.

Also included among the P.A.C.E. programs is the *Escambia Bay Marine Institute,* a nonresidential program for both male and female adjudicated offenders, especially those with problems at school. These youths have been unsuccessful in the more traditional school settings and they are placed in this program when they have been recommended for expulsion by the school board. The program offers "accelerated remedial education, vocational and employability skills training, and personal/group/family counseling in a motivating environment with a caring and skilled staff."[38]

The P.A.C.E. program takes a holistic approach and focuses on providing such services as life management skills, community service, counseling, and self-esteem building. It offers both day programs and after-care services. It provides a fully accredited high school program that works toward a high school diploma and also gives those who want it an opportunity to enroll in college-preparatory classes while developing career plans and building self-esteem. P.A.C.E. also has programs (e.g., through counseling and life management assistance) that address pregnancy and drug abuse, cultural awareness, and responsible health choices, and encourages involvement and volunteerism in the community (by requiring each girl in the program to participate in at least two different community service projects). P.A.C.E. also provides after-care and placement services.

The Department of Justice and OJJDP praised the P.A.C.E. program as a model program rated much higher than any other. P.A.C.E. is cited by the OJJDP publication *What Works: Promising Interventions in Juvenile Justice.*[39] The University of Florida does yearly evaluations, and thus far the outcomes have been very positive, showing a success rate of 78 percent.

A unique program is the *Marycrest Euphrasia Center,* located in Independence, Ohio. Funded by the Ohio Department of Youth Services, this is one of the few residential centers licensed for female offenders who are mothers and who can have their children live with them while they are in the program. Most are African American, ranging in age from thirteen to twenty-one, and have been convicted of a felony. *Marycrest* has been operating for 125 years; the *Euphrasia Center* is only two years old. It provides these young women with a curriculum that includes health services, individual and group counseling, family therapy, substance abuse therapy, parent effectiveness training, regular high school educational classes, job readiness and vocational training, and an on-site nursery. It has also developed an evaluation methodology to monitor the program.[40]

Another rather unusual program, one that targets a specific Asian American group called the *Hmong,* is known as *Peem Tsheej Nthais Hluas* (which translates as "Struggle for Success for Young Women"). Located in St. Paul, Minnesota, the program focuses on keeping families intact and helping girls (who are the first generation of their families to grow up in this country) live in two different cultures while giving them support for educational and vocational choices. More specifically, the program is an intervention program that was originally founded as a diversion to gang involvement. It has been expanded to include any *Hmong* girl either directly involved in the juvenile justice system or seriously at risk of becoming involved. Culturally based activities are part of the program, in addition to job referrals, employment training, and educational support. There is a day program and a drop-in center, both of which are highly visible in the community and easily accessible.[41] These are just a few of several promising programs that have developed in recent years. A complete summary of all these programs is well beyond the scope of this book. A partial listing of these and other programs can be found in the report of Girls Inc. and on its Web site.

Policy Implications and Future Directions

Programming for girls in the juvenile justice system is exceedingly challenging. First, effective delinquency intervention programs, even for boys, are very scarce. A careful reading of the literature reveals that there is no universal curative for male delinquency. To this rather bleak situation is added the female dimension: the forces that bring girls into the juvenile justice system present challenges and issues that service providers are only now acknowledging.

It is clear that if deinstitutionalization of youths is still a societal goal, then sound criticisms of the movement must be addressed. One major and often repeated concern is that youngsters released from detention centers and other institutional settings end up on the streets, where they become victims of a criminal subculture that knows only too well how to prey on their vulnerabilities. The failure of the deinstitutionalization movement to anticipate this problem can be attributed, in retrospect, to girls' invisibility within the juvenile justice system. Their low profile meant that programming for them never happened. The very limited number of dollars targeted for girls' programming during the 1970s demonstrates this very clearly. Upon release from facilities, the girls were simply referred to systems and service providers whose understanding of girls' lives, problems, and delinquency was minimal at best.

During that same decade, however, a few experiments in programming for girls were undertaken. Some, as this chapter has related, used traditional methods, though modified by the insights of feminism. Others, and particularly efforts in subsequent years, were and are more ambitious. Certain themes emerge from the small number of innovative programs. First, if counseling is to be included—and it should be part of a solid program for girls—it must be sensitive to issues such as sexual abuse, rape (including date rape), violence in teenage sexual relationships, and the special problems that girls face (particularly those who are parents) in housing and employment. Second, the program should go past counseling per se to the areas of skill building, particularly in the employment area. Third, the program should meet the needs of girls who cannot safely return to their families. In this regard, we should focus on the urgent need for teens to have access to medical, dental, educational, and housing resources. As a society, we have been reluctant to provide long-term, stable solutions to the problems of teens in conflict with their families. The consequence has been a paucity of effective services for an estimated 133,500 runaway and 59,200 throwaway youths, many of whom are girls.[42]

Some of the more recent programs reviewed here show even more promise, especially since they are becoming more culturally sensitive and aware of the special needs of girls. The new programs address some of the most pressing needs of young women in trouble and at risk, such as help with problems of physical and sexual abuse, drug involvement, the AIDS virus, pregnancy and parenting issues, and many more. The author is pleased to find such innovative programs have emerged in recent years and hopes that they will continue to spread.

Notes

[1] For more detail on these and related issues see Chesney-Lind, M., and R. G. Shelden (2004). *Girls, Delinquency and Juvenile Justice* (3rd ed.). Belmont, CA: Wadsworth.

[2] Lipsey, M. (1992). "Juvenile Delinquency Treatment: A Meta-analytic Inquiry in the Variability of Effects." In T. A. Cook et al. (eds.), *Meta-Analysis for Explanation: A Casebook*. New York: Russell Sage.

[3] Cited in Adolescent Female Subcommittee (1994). *Needs Assessment and Recommendations for Adolescent Females in Minnesota*. St. Paul: Minnesota Department of Corrections.

[4] Alder, C. (1995). "Delinquency Prevention with Young Women." Paper presented at the Delinquency Prevention Conference, Terrigal, New South Wales, p. 3.

[5] Schwartz, I. M., and F. Orlando (eds.) (1991). *Programming for Young Women in the Juvenile Justice System*. Ann Arbor, MI: Center for the Study of Youth Policy; Girls Inc. (1996). *Prevention and Parity: Girls in Juvenile Justice*. Indianapolis: Girls Inc. National Resource Center.

[6] Amaro, H. (1995). "Love, Sex, and Power: Considering Women's Realities in HIV Prevention." *American Psychologist* 50: 437–447; Amaro, H., and M. Agular (1994). "Programa Mama: Mom's Project: A Hispanic/Latino Family Approach to Substance Abuse Prevention." Rockville, MD: Center for Substance Abuse Prevention, Mental Health Services Administration; LaFromboise, T. D., and B. Howard-Pitney (1995). "Suicidal Behavior in American Indian Female Adolescents." In S. Canetto and D. Lester (eds.), *Woman and Suicidal Behavior*. New York: Springer; Orenstein, P. (1994). *Schoolgirls*. New York: Doubleday.

[7] Rossi, A. (1973). *The Feminist Papers: From Adams to Beauvoir*. New York: Columbia University Press, pp. 10–11.

[8] Girls Inc., *Prevention and Parity*.

[9] American Association for University Women (AAUW) (1992). *How Schools Are Shortchanging Girls*. Washington, DC: AAUW Educational Foundation.

[10] Ms. Foundation for Women, National Girls Initiative (1993). *Programmed Neglect, Not Seen, Not Heard: Report on Girls Programming in the United States*. New York: Ms. Foundation for Women.

[11] Arella, L. (1993). "Multiservice Adolescent Programs: Seeking Institutional Partnership Alternatives." *Journal of Youth and Adolescence* 22: 283–295.

[12] Ms. Foundation for Women, *Programmed Neglect, Not Seen, Not Heard*.

[13] Government Accounting Office (GAO) (1995). *Juvenile Justice: Minimal Gender Bias Occurring in Processing Non-Criminal Juveniles*. Washington, DC: Letter Report, pp. 3–4.

14 Marian Daniel, quoted in Girls Inc., *Prevention and Parity*, p. 34.

15 Chesney-Lind, M., D. Mayeda, N. Marker, V. Paramore, and S. Okamoto (1998). *Trends in Delinquency and Gang Membership: An Interim Report to the Hawaii State Legislature.* Honolulu: University of Hawaii at Manoa, Social Science Research Institute.

16 Schwartz and Orlando, *Programming for Young Women in the Juvenile Justice System.*

17 Artz, S., and T. Riecken (1997). "What, So What, Then What?: The Gender Gap in School-Based Violence and Its Implications for Child and Youth Care Practice." *Child and Youth Care Forum* 26 (4): 291–303.

18 Ibid, p. 296.

19 Ibid, p. 298.

20 Artz, S. (1998). *Sex, Power and the Violent School Girl.* Toronto: Trifolium Books.

21 Ibid, p. 204.

22 Alder, C. (1986). "Unemployed Women Have Got It Heaps Worse." *Australian and New Zealand Journal of Criminology* 19: 210–224.

23 Dryfoos, J. G. (1990). *Adolescents at Risk: Prevalence and Prevention.* New York: Oxford University Press; Hugo, K. E., and R. B. Rutherford, Jr. (1992). "Issues in Identifying Educational Disabilities Among Female Juvenile Offenders." *Journal of Correctional Education* 43: 124–127; Girls Inc., *Prevention and Parity*; Belknap, J., Dunn, M., and Holsinger, K. (1997). "Moving toward Juvenile Justice and Youth-Serving Systems that Address the Distinct Experience of the Adolescent Female." Cincinnati, OH: Gender Specific Services Work Group.

24 Arnold, R. (1995). "The Processes of Victimization and Criminalization of Black Women." In B. R. Price and N. Sokoloff (eds.), *The Criminal Justice System and Women.* New York: McGraw-Hill; Orenstein, *Schoolgirls.*

25 Sadker, M., and D. Sadker (1994). *Failing at Fairness.* New York: Scribner.

26 Wells, R. H. (1994). "America's Delinquent Daughters Have Nowhere to Turn for Help." *Corrections Compendium*, November, pp. 4–6.

27 Howell, N., and S. P. Davis (1992). "Special Problems of Female Offenders." *Corrections Compendium* 12: 1, 5–20.

28 Girls Inc., *Prevention and Parity.*

29 American Correctional Association (1990). *The Female Offender: What Does the Future Hold?* Washington, DC: American Correctional Association.

30 Gilligan, C. (1982). *In a Different Voice: Psychological Theory and Women's Development.* Cambridge: Harvard University Press.

31 Ms. Foundation for Women, *Programmed Neglect, Not Seen, Not Heard.*

32 Chesney-Lind et al., *Trends in Delinquency and Gang Membership*, p. 45.

33 Girls Inc., *Prevention and Parity.*

34 For additional information on Children of the Night, see its Web site: http://www.childrenofthenight.org/. The information about this program is taken from this Web site and from an interview by Randall Shelden in October 1988 with the director and founder of the program, Dr. Lois Lee.

35 Taken from the following Web site: http://www.reentrymediaoutreach.org/sp_education_cyw-gdap.htm

36 For additional information see their Web site: http://www.cywd.org/.

37 The following information is taken from the Web site Information Central for Girls Inc.: http://www.girlsinc.org/ic/page.php?id=1.2.5.

38 (www.escambia.k12.fl.us/alted.djj_programs.htm).

39 Office of Juvenile Justice and Delinquency Prevention (1994). *What Works: Promising Interventions in Juvenile Justice.* Washington, DC: Department of Justice. For an updated review see the following: Office of Juvenile Justice and Delinquency Prevention (1998). *Guiding Principles for Promising Female Programming.* http://ojjdp.ncjrs.org/pubs/principles/contents.html.

40 Girls Inc., *Prevention and Parity*, pp. 36–37.

41 Ibid, pp. 37–38.

42 Finkelhor, D., G. Hotaling, and A. Sedlak (1990). *Missing, Abducted, Runaway, and Throwaway Children in America: Executive Summary.* Washington, DC: U.S. Department of Justice, p. 4.